ECONOMIC AND SOCIAL
Made Simple

R. Knowles, M.A., and
J. Wareing, B.A., M.Sc.

Made Simple Books
W. H. ALLEN London
A Howard & Wyndham Company

Printed and bound in Great Britain
by Richard Clay (The Chaucer Press) Ltd
Bungay, Suffolk
for the publishers W. H. Allen & Company Ltd,
44 Hill Street, London W1X 8LB

ISBN 0 491 01567 4 casebound
ISBN 0 491 01577 1 paperbound

Foreword

The study of economic and social geography has changed considerably in recent years. The nature and distribution of human activity over the earth's surface remains the core of the subject matter, but new questions are being asked about this activity and new techniques are being developed to allow them to be answered. The subject is now more problem-orientated and the analysis and explanation of current problems have become much more important than simple description.

The purpose of this book is not to break new ground, but to review recent developments and bring together in one inexpensive volume work which is dispersed in many specialist textbooks. An attempt has been made to achieve a balance between oversimplification and over-elaboration, and to present essential concepts in a clear, concise manner. It is hoped that the interest of the reader will be sufficiently stimulated to investigate these concepts further, and the suggested further reading at the end of each chapter should provide guidance in this respect.

This book, together with its companion volume, *Physical Geography Made Simple*, should be of value to a variety of people. First, to those who are coming to academic geography for the first time, especially to those studying for GCE Advanced Level or ONC/OND examinations. It should also provide a concise introduction to first-year courses in further and higher education, including degree courses with a geography component, HNC/HND, and Certificate in Education courses. Technical jargon has been kept to a minimum and the book does not presuppose detailed background knowledge. It is hoped, therefore, that the layman will also find much of interest here. Secondly, it should be of value to geography teachers and others who wish to keep abreast of developments in the subject at a time of rapid change.

R. KNOWLES
J. WAREING

Table of Contents

PART THREE: ECONOMIC GEOGRAPHY

PART FOUR: SETTLEMENT GEOGRAPHY

PART FIVE: GEOGRAPHY AND PLANNING

PART ONE: THE STUDY OF ECONOMIC AND SOCIAL GEOGRAPHY

CHAPTER ONE

MAN AND ENVIRONMENT

Geography is currently going through an exciting period in its development as new problems are identified and new methods of analysis are formulated. It is not easy to say precisely what geography is about because geographers often hold different views of the subject, and these views change from time to time, but this is not surprising since geographers are interested in a very wide range of problems and rapid advances are being made in the subject, as they are in all branches of knowledge.

Because geography involves such a wide range of knowledge, the subject has been divided into two major areas of study. The first of these is **physical geography**, which is concerned with the physical environment of landforms, weather and climate, soils, and plants and animals (see *Physical Geography Made Simple*). The second is **human geography**, which is concerned with man's activities over the surface of the earth. In many ways this is a false distinction since the activities of man take place within the physical environment, and the physical environment is considerably affected by these activities, but the division is a useful one and in this book the physical environment will only be considered in relation to man.

Human geography can be studied in two principal ways. First, the earth's surface can be studied part by part. This is the approach of **regional geography**, which seeks to understand the unique character of an area as produced by the interaction of human activity and the physical environment. Secondly, human activity over the earth's surface can be studied part by part. This is the approach of **systematic geography**, which isolates particular elements such as agriculture, industry or transport, and seeks to understand their spatial patterns and the processes which have produced them.

The systematic approach is currently much more important, although regional geography was dominant until about 1950, and economic and social geography are the major areas of study in systematic human geography. These focus on different aspects of human activity but are very closely interlinked.

Social geography is concerned with man and how he lives: with the geography of population and settlement; with the forms and processes of social interaction in space; and with the cultural attitudes that produce landscapes and affect ways of life.

Economic geography is concerned with how man makes a living: how he utilises the resources of the earth, applies his technology to agriculture and industry and how he develops transport methods to rearrange space to his advantage by bringing sources of supply and demand closer together.

1

Current Approaches to Human Geography

Although it is not easy to say what geography is about, there are at present two major approaches to human geography which influence the questions that geographers ask and the methods that they employ. Geography is first concerned with the study of man's relationships with the environment in which he lives, and secondly with the study of how man uses and organises space. These can be considered as two systems, or structures within which all parts are related to each other to form a functioning whole.

In the study of man's relationships with the environment (which is used in this chapter to mean the physical environment), geographers are concerned with identifying and analysing the form and nature of the **ecological system** in which man interacts with the environment, being influenced by it and in turn modifying it.

In the study of man's use and organisation of space, geographers are concerned with identifying and analysing the form and nature of the **spatial system** in which man interacts with man through his economic, social and political activities.

Of course, these two systems are not independent of each other but operate on the one hand to divide the world into a number of distinctive divisions or regions, and on the other to link these regions together, especially through the resource processes discussed in Chapter Twenty-five.

Man and Environment

The idea of geography as the study of man's relationship with the environment has a long history and has led to a long-standing debate about the position of man in relation to nature: first, whether man is part of, or apart from, nature; secondly, about the extent to which man is affected by the environment.

From Classical times onwards, the idea that man is a product of the environment was dominant, and in the nineteenth century the work of Darwin in the biological sciences, which showed that life developed under the selective action of natural forces, seemed to confirm scientifically the position of man as a creature adapted to his environment. At the same time, work in the social sciences showed regularities in human behaviour—that marriage rates in England, for example, were affected by the price of corn—and the conclusion was reached that man was not free, but was ruled by natural and economic laws.

This resulted in many geographers focusing their study on the effects of the physical environment on man, in which man was seen as a passive creature moulded by natural forces, and the geographers' task as being the identification and formulation of the scientific laws which governed the relationship. This approach is known as **determinism** or environmentalism, and simple cause and effect laws—which can be stated as: 'if conditions *a* and *b* exist, then condition *c* will be the consequence'—were formulated to explain the distribution and activities of man. Thus, according to E. C. Semple, where 'hot moist equatorial climates encourage the growth of large forests which harbour abundant game and yield abundant fruits, they prolong the hunter stage of development and retard the advance to agriculture'.

However, determinism was criticised for two main reasons. First, it is clear that similar physical environments do not produce the same responses, and the Mediterranean civilisations of Greece and Rome did not develop in similar climatic conditions in Australia, South Africa, Chile or California. Also, man can respond in the same way to different environments; and there is a considerable similarity in European settlement in the varied environments of North America. Secondly, although environment influences man, man also influences the environment, and the cause–effect relationship of determinism is too simple to explain this.

As a result, the idea that man is controlled by nature was rejected and other geographers stressed the fact that man is free to choose. Nevertheless, this choice must be made within the limits set by nature, although these limits are wide enough to give man a lot of scope. This approach, in which the emphasis is firmly placed on man rather than nature, and in which man is seen as an active force rather than a passive being, is known as **possibilism**.

In reality, of course, the balance between man's freedom and nature's control varies from place to place and from time to time, and the extremes of possibilism and determinism must be replaced by a sliding scale in which man and nature act and react with each other in a very complex system.

Man's reaction to the environment and his action upon it can be considered as an **interaction model** or system, and one of the tasks of the geographer is to identify its major parts and to measure their relative importance. The three basic elements in this model, man, the environment and the relationships between them are examined next.

The Influence of Environment on Man

Most geographers take a possibilist rather than a determinist view today, although some introductory texts still adhere to the earlier approach. This is not to say that the role of the environment is unimportant, because it provides the setting within which man operates, presenting him with a range of opportunities and constraints. Nevertheless, it is not easy to measure the influence of environment on man because of the complexity of the relationships in the interaction model. An increasing number of people are living in the man-made environments of cities and their relationship with the natural environment is not direct, but even the dwellers of the built environment are dependent on the earth for food and raw materials.

The environmental factor which does affect all people directly is climate, and it has been suggested that it is the basic reason for man's racial differences of skin colour, size and shape. It is not clear how it affects human activity despite centuries of speculation about its effects on character and behaviour. Aristotle believed that peoples of cold climates were brave but deficient in thought while the peoples of warm climates were thoughtful but without spirit. The medieval Arab historian Ibn Khaldun compared the stolidity and lack of vivacity among peoples of cold climates with the passionate natures and ready abandonment to physical pleasures of peoples in warm zones. Both these writers, sharing views that have been held through history, saw the climatic zones between these extremes, usually the places in which they were writing, as producing more ideal human beings. This view, that there is some climatically ideal zone, has been developed more recently by Ellsworth Huntington and S. F. Markham. According to their theories, the climates of areas in moderately cool zones with frequent cyclonic activity and rapid changes of weather, such as Western Europe, New England and Japan, stimulate individuals to mental activity and nations to world leadership.

This sort of conclusion is very difficult to substantiate because climate is only one of many factors which affect human activity, but climate does affect behaviour. According to Raymond Chandler, when the Santa Ana blows in Los Angeles, this hot, dry, irritating wind causes 'meek little wives to feel the edge of the carving knife and study their husbands' necks'. There is clear statistical evidence of a correlation between crime, suicide and weather conditions, and certain types of climate are clearly beneficial for sufferers from particular diseases. Attempts have been made to measure the suitability of an environment for human activity, and comfort, discomfort and danger zones can be identified. These are shown in Fig. 1.1.

Of course, man can modify these effects by creating his own climates, and this has been done for a very long time. Man has used fire for more than half a million years and advanced societies are using very sophisticated central heating or air-conditioning systems, but these only operate indoors on a small scale and attempts to effect major modifications to the climate are very limited. Climate remains a potent influence on human activity.

Despite advances in technology, man is still ultimately dependent on the physical environment for all his material needs and desires. Of course, the nature of this dependence varies from society to society, from primitive societies where drought results in famine, to advanced societies where the connection with the environment is much more complicated, but the ultimate source of all food and raw materials remains the same for all groups. More than half the world's labour force is employed in the primary industries of farming, fishing, forestry and mining, upon which the physical environment is the dominant influence.

It is not only through the range and abundance of its natural resources that the environment affects man, but also through the fact that one of its most important characteristics is constant change. Three main types of change can be identified and they affect man in quite different ways, having both positive and negative effects on human activity.

The first of these is long-term regular change such as the silting of coasts and rivers. Silt plays an important role in maintaining the fertility of flood plains for agriculture, but also hastened the decline of the important medieval port of Bruges in Belgium and the Cinque Ports in southern England. The second, and probably the most important, is short-term regular change such as the rhythm of the seasons, which closely regulates agriculture, or the annual migrations of animals and fishes, which dominate the lives of hunters and fishermen. Sometimes these rhythms falter and unusual weather conditions may bring bumper harvests, but the change can just as easily be disastrous, and the failure of the monsoon often brings severe hardship in India. However, it is the third type—rapid unpredictable change, such as earthquakes, hurricanes, cyclones or floods—which affects man most spectacularly. Floods in the Mississippi valley and in Brisbane in 1974, and the evacuation of the island of Heimaey, off Iceland, following the volcanic eruptions of 1973, show how dramatically natural conditions can change and present serious hazards to man.

However, despite such setbacks, man has extended his dominion to almost all parts of the earth, and his history is one of an increasing ability to use the environment to his best advantage. This dominion can never be complete because of the powerful restraints imposed by nature, but geographers are increasingly turning their attention to the study of man's impact on the

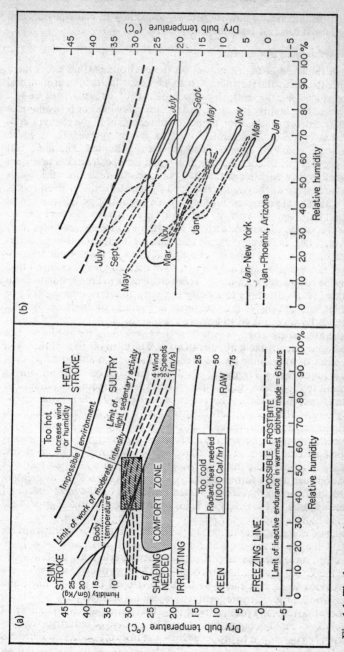

Fig. 1.1. The human relevance of climatic ranges (after V. Olgyay). (a) The comfort zone, surrounded by zones of discomfort and danger, within the range of climates experienced on the earth. (b) Note how the climates of New York and Phoenix fall outside the comfort zone in most of the six months plotted.

environment to understand how it operates, to identify its consequences and to suggest how it can best be managed.

Man's Impact on the Environment

Although the scale of man's impact on the environment has accelerated rapidly since the Industrial Revolution, man has been a factor in environmental change for at least 40,000 years, since the late stages of the Pleistocene ice age. Early man used fire, his first great tool, to drive animals while hunting, and since he had little control over this tool, the accidental effects of its use could be considerable. Later, fire was deliberately used to improve grasslands to which grazing animals could be attracted and more easily hunted. The impact of primitive peoples can be considerable, and when European settlers first went to the Americas they did not enter a totally untouched world, since the forests and grasslands were already much modified by human activity. Even today, primitive agricultural groups use fire in the system of shifting agriculture known as 'slash and burn' and few parts of the world have not been affected by man.

As a consequence of human activity since the Pleistocene, and especially since *c.* A.D. 1750, it is very difficult to define the term **natural environment** because so many parts of what is generally taken to be the natural environment, such as vegetation and animal life, have been so greatly changed that they might be considered man-made. These changes have been brought about as a result of man's attempts to modify the earth to increase its capacity to support him, and to satisfy his increasingly large range of needs and desires. Two methods have been used to achieve these ends.

First, the area of the **ecumene**, which is the Greek term for the 'inhabited earth', has been extended in a number of ways. The most obvious of these has been the series of migrations by which man has spread to almost all parts of the earth (Chapter Five). The most extensive of these has been the outpouring of Europeans to the almost empty lands of the Americas, southern Africa and Australasia since A.D. 1500. The ecumene has been further extended by technology. New areas of human occupancy have been created by drainage and land reclamation schemes such as the Delta Project in Holland or by large-scale irrigation schemes such as the Aswan Dam in Egypt. The margins of cultivation have been extended by the development of drought tolerant plants, the breeding of animals capable of thriving in hot climates and new methods of cultivation such as dry farming (Chapter Eleven). Technology, by creating a demand for minerals, has led to human settlement on the most hostile of environments such as the desert oil fields of the Sahara or the high-altitude tin mines in Bolivia, and even the sea floor is now being exploited.

Second, and more important, man has **intensified** his use of the environment to increase its productive capacity. In the field of agriculture new high-yielding crops have been developed such as the 'miracle rice', IR-8, responsible for the Green Revolution in south-east Asia, artificial fertilisers have been developed to sustain them, pesticides developed to protect them and machines produced to cultivate them. High-yielding animals have been bred, such as sheep that regularly produce twins, pigs that fatten quickly and cows that produce milk with a high butter-fat content. In the field of industry, new processes have been developed to produce large quantities of goods, new materials such as plastics have been created, and the size and range of the demand for raw materials has been greatly expanded.

For a very fortunate minority of the world's population living in the advanced economies, the consequences of all this activity have been a vast increase in the standard of living and the removal of most of life's risks and uncertainties. However, this has not been without its price, and some of the most serious problems that man faces arise from the increasing demands that he is placing on the environment. These demands, which are now placing a severe strain on some areas and some resources, are caused by the interaction of four main factors.

The first of these is **population growth**. The population of the world is not growing at a constant rate but, as can be seen from Table 1.1, it is growing exponentially, or at an accelerating rate (Chapter Eight).

Table 1.1.   World Population Growth

World population growth To present		World population growth Projected	
Time	Total	Time	Total
10,000 B.C.	5–10 million	1981	4,500 million
Time of Christ	250 million	1986	5,000 million
1650	500 million	1995	6,000 million
1820	1,000 million	2003	7,000 million
1930	2,000 million	2010	8,000 million
1960	3,000 million	2016	9,000 million
1975	4,000 million	2021	10,000 million

Source: After J. E. Spencer and W. L. Thomas.

The table shows that whereas it took two million years for world population to reach 1,000 million, this figure was doubled in just over a century, doubled again in only 45 years, and is expected to double again in only 35 years. The consequence of this is clear. More land and natural resources will be needed, more waste will be created and the impact on the environment will be immense. It has been calculated that the carrying capacity of the earth is 30,000 million people at a starvation level and that this figure will be achieved in 100 years unless population growth levels off.

The second factor, closely associated with the first, is the **rise in aspirations** which serves to multiply the impact of population growth. Standards of living are high and increasing in advanced economies, with a consequent high level of demand for resources. These standards are naturally the ones to which the developing countries aspire and so any process of development will increase the pressure on resources. It has been calculated that the birth of an American child has an impact on the environment which is forty times as great as the impact caused by the birth of an Indian child because of the difference in the amount of resources that each will consume in his lifetime. The environmental consequences of a rise in living standards in India are clear.

Thirdly, this impact is increased **by advances in technology**. A desire for increased standards of living can only come about if man is capable of achieving them, but this power has been given by technology. Technological change is exponential and man's power to change the environment is increasing rapidly. Technology affects the environment in two ways. First, the ability of man directly to cause environmental change is increased. The development of the steel plough in the nineteenth century enabled the mid-latitude grasslands to be cultivated for the first time because the new plough could cut through the tough prairie sod, while the development of steam-driven ships enabled all of the 100 or so species of whale to be hunted instead of just the five which were slow enough to be caught by oarsmen. Secondly, entirely new substances such as plastics, DDT and radioactive wastes have been introduced into nature. As technology has developed, the number of ways in which man affects the environment has increased and their effects have become more widespread.

The final and probably the most important factor in man's relationship with the environment is his **attitude** to it. In Western culture man is seen to be apart from, rather than part of, nature. This tradition springs from the Book of Genesis, where 'God said unto them, Be fruitful, and multiply, and replenish the earth, and subdue it: and have dominion over the fish of the sea, and over the fowl of the air, and over every living thing that moveth upon the earth.' Even in the East, where ideally man is in harmony with nature, reality sets him apart from it. Although an increasing number of societies are embracing Marxism, this also has produced social attitudes which make population control more difficult and economic attitudes which see growth as progress and short-term economic gains as being more important than long-term environmental consequences. Until now, these attitudes have been acceptable because growth has been possible and the general condition of man has been steadily improving, but there is an increasing realisation that even if man is not part of nature, he must learn to manage the environment more carefully than has been necessary in the past.

This realisation has come about because it is clear that although man has affected the environment in many deliberate and positive ways, there are consequences of human activity which are accidental and uncontrolled and which could ultimately threaten life itself. Some idea of the complexity of the problem can be gained from an examination of the effects of human activity on world climate through interference with the heat balance (see *Physical Geography Made Simple*). The burning of fossil fuels such as coal and oil has increased the carbon dioxide content of the atmosphere, increasing its 'greenhouse effect' and trapping more heat within it. There is the risk that as a consequence world temperatures will rise, causing the melting of the ice caps and the flooding of densely populated lowland areas. On the other hand, the increasing amount of solid material being pumped into the atmosphere acts as a parasol, reflecting heat back into space. It has been estimated that high-flying jet aircraft have increased the cloud cover over the Atlantic by five per cent, and if this cover were world-wide, temperatures would fall to produce another ice age. Whether the one cancels the other out is not clear at the moment, but they are consequences of human activity that had not been foreseen.

The list of possible dangers is considerable and has resulted in a great deal of concern being expressed in recent years over the problems of **pollution**. So many dangerous substances are being introduced into the environment, whether deliberately as in the case of agricultural pesticides, or casually as in the case of industrial waste products, or incidentally as in the case of the lead content of motorcar exhausts, or accidentally as in the case of the poisoning of the River Rhine in 1969, that life itself may be under threat. The **exhaustion of resources** due to over-exploitation is considered by many people to be an equally serious threat and has resulted in calls for the conservation and management of resources before the situation becomes critical (Chapter Twenty-five).

Analysing the Man–Environment System

The interaction between man and environment therefore has two aspects: with environment influencing man, and man influencing environment. This might be seen as a simple **two-way system,** but reality is not so simple and consequences of this interaction are inevitable. Mismanagement of the environment by bad farming practices on the High Plains of the USA were compounded by a period of drought in the years 1933–8, and this produced disastrous consequences for man as strong winds blew away the exhausted topsoil in a series of 'black blizzards' to produce the notorious 'Dust Bowl' which covered 6·5 million hectares. In this area, the direct effect of human activity on the environment produced **feedbacks,** which are described as positive when they operate to amplify change, and negative when they operate to reduce change.

Large areas were made useless for agriculture by bad farming practice, but the national emergency caused by soil erosion had some beneficial effect on man's ability to manage the environment by the establishment of the US Soil Conservation Bureau and the National Resources Board, whose conservation practices provided **negative feedback** to reduce the damage. There was of course a time-lag between the occurrence of the damage and the effect of the policies, and this type of change is also described as 'lagged' feedback. On the other hand, the disaster had a harmful effect in causing mass migration to California, where good agricultural lands became overcrowded. Thus the **positive feedback** from events in Oklahoma and Texas was transferred to California, and such feedbacks in which one area pays for the actions of another are described as 'staggered'.

Far from being a simple two-way system, man's impact on the environment may be direct, but it is much more likely to result in feedbacks, which can be positive or negative, and lagged and/or staggered, depending on circumstance. As a result, the simple interaction model becomes a complicated system.

Attempts have been made to understand the interaction of man and environment by using a **systems analysis** approach. A system can be defined as 'a set of objects together with the relationships between the objects and between their attributes', and can operate at any scale, from atoms in a molecule to the universe itself. The relationship between man and environment can be viewed as an **ecosystem,** which is a term first used in ecology to describe the functional interactions among and between living organisms and their environment. The task of the geographer is to identify the various elements in the system, understand how they work, discover how they are related to each other and then study their interaction as a functioning whole. This is an attractive idea because form and process can be studied in a single, ordered framework and the various elements of the system can be measured to provide an explanation of man–environment relationships. The concept of the ecosystem is also useful in planning, since once the system is understood, the consequences of a change in any one part of it can be predicted and any necessary action taken. This would enable management of the ecosystem to take place to lessen the consequences of pollution and make the planning and conservation of resources possible.

However, there are two problems associated with the use of the ecosystem approach. The first concerns the scale and complexity of the system, which make it very difficult to analyse. The second concerns the role of man. The ecosystem implies some sort of balanced, functioning whole, but man is increasingly the dominant element in this system and may not even be an integral part of it, if it is accepted that man is not part of nature. Very complex socio-economic considerations are the most important factors affecting man's relationships with the environment, which is becoming increasingly man-made, and these have to be taken into account. A systems analysis approach is still useful, although systems are very difficult to analyse, but the ecosystem might better be replaced by the idea of a **control system** in which man controls negative feedback to maintain the stability of the system while using positive feedback to create change. In this system, man's role is not just ecosystem management, but positive socio-economic planning which can change the ecosystem to his advantage.

The Role of Culture in the Man–Environment Relationship

The idea that the man–environment relationship should be studied as a control system has found strong support among many geographers. The system provides a coherent framework within which the interaction between man and environment can be studied, but because of the problems of scale and complexity, it is difficult to isolate and quantify the various elements of the system.

However, there is one major element that must be analysed, since the notion of control emphasises man's role as an active agent in the system. This element is man's **culture**, since it is this that decides the form and process of human intervention, and acts through the socio-economic aims and technical abilities that go to make up culture.

The study of the role of culture in the man–environment relationship is not new in geography, but it has traditionally been a study of the forms produced by this relationship. Culture is the totality of human experience but it is made up of many different types of culture. Urban–industrial cultures have a very different set of relationships with the environment from rural–agricultural cultures and each has produced distinctive landscapes which divide the world up into a wide range of regional units. The study of the **cultural landscapes** produced by these different cultures has been a major area of study in human geography.

Cultural Landscapes

Cultural landscapes are produced by the interaction of man and nature in an area and they reflect the social and economic aims, and the technical abilities of the people living there. The task of the geographer has been to describe and analyse these landscapes in order to understand the imprint of man on the earth, and a large number of regional studies have been produced to achieve this. Attention has also been given to the ways in which landscapes change through time, and to the role that man plays in this change.

There are two aspects of the cultural landscape that must be considered. The first of these is the **functional** landscape which is produced by economic activity. The various economic activities of man have a distinctive imprint on the environment. Industrial activities produce quite different landscape forms from agricultural activities, and within agriculture itself the landscapes of viticulture, or intensive rice cultivation, or extensive wheat farming are quite distinctive.

However, man is not simply a functional creature. Although wheat farming in East Anglia is the same type of activity as wheat farming in the Paris Basin, there are considerable landscape differences that are not economically induced. The layout of settlement, house styles, field boundaries and so on are part of the **aesthetic** landscape shaped by man's preferences and prejudices during centuries of occupation. In some cases, such as the parkland of English country houses or the formal gardens of Versailles, landscapes are actually created to fit some current ideal or style. Even in recently settled areas with uniform environmental conditions such as the North American prairies, landscape differences are identifiable on either side of the American–Canadian border, which acts as a cultural as much as a political boundary, producing distinctive American and Canadian prairie landscapes.

The cultural landscape is the form produced by the interaction of man and environment, but in recent years much more attention has been placed on the processes of this interaction, especially on the role played by culturally produced **perceptions**. It is being increasingly recognised that man's relationship with the environment is indirect, in that it operates through the way that man perceives the environment, and the study of these perceptions and the ways in which they influence behaviour is currently a major area of interest for the geographer.

Conclusion

There are two main approaches to the study of human geography and these involve the analysis of two major systems, the ecological and the spatial. In this chapter the ecological system created by the interaction of man and environment has been examined and it appears that this can be best analysed as a control system with man the dominant element in it. The role of culture in the man–environment relationship has been emphasised since it is culture that influences the nature of human intervention in the system.

The operation of the ecological system produces an imprint on the land that can be described as a cultural landscape, and the study of these landscapes has been a major element in geography since the end of the nineteenth century. However, geographers are now giving increasing attention to process rather than form, especially the role that culturally produced perceptions play in man's evaluation and use of the environment, and these are examined in the next chapter.

Suggested Further Reading

Bryant, R., *Physical Geography Made Simple*, W. H. Allen, London, 1976.

Chorley, R. J., *Directions in Geography*, Methuen, London, 1973.

Detwyler, T. R., *Man's Impact on Environment*, McGraw-Hill, New York, 1971.

English, P. W., and Mayfield, R. C., *Man, Space and Environment*, Oxford University Press, New York, 1972.

Haggett, P., *Geography: A Modern Synthesis* (2nd edn), Harper and Row, New York, 1975.

Spencer, J. E., and Thomas W. L., *Cultural Geography*, Wiley, New York, 1969.

Taylor, G., *Geography in the Twentieth Century* (3rd edn), Methuen, London, 1957.

Thomas, W. L., *Man's Role in Changing the Face of the Earth*, Chicago University Press, Chicago, 1956.

CHAPTER TWO

ENVIRONMENTAL PERCEPTION AND BEHAVIOUR

The study of man's relationship with the environment has been increasingly concerned with explaining why man behaves as he does; why, among other things, he grows one crop rather than another, or chooses particular transport routes, or builds factories in specific places. Environmental behaviour is dependent on the ways in which the environment is perceived, and one of the major developments in geography since the mid-1960s has been the study of this environmental perception to explain behaviour.

Man's relationship with the environment is indirect in that environmental behaviour depends on the image of the world that each person carries inside his head. This image is therefore as important as the **objective environment** or 'real world' that geographers have traditionally studied and many geographers are now studying the **subjective environment**, or the environment as perceived by man, to better understand the man–environment relationship. This study of images, values, decisions and behaviour has produced a new emphasis in human geography. It is no longer the objects of human activity—farms, roads, factories—that are the focus of study, but man himself—how and why he behaves as he does. Human geography has become more human.

Before environmental behaviour can be explained, two basic questions have to be answered by the geographer. First, how does man perceive elements of space, such as distance, direction or physical space? Secondly, how does man perceive the features of the environment, such as resources, hazards or cities? The question of what is meant by environmental perception will therefore be examined.

Environmental Perception

The term environmental perception is used in two senses. First, it is the **process** by which an individual gains knowledge of the world by receiving stimuli from the environment through his senses. This stimulus/response is not a simple process since the individual receives eighteen separate visual images alone each second, and these are then filtered through his reason and emotions, which are themselves affected by past learning and motivation. As a result, different people respond to the same stimuli in different ways. Secondly, it is the **image of the environment** that each individual carries inside his head. This mental model is very important because it is the frame of reference within which man behaves, and is of considerable interest to the geographer.

The process of perception and its consequent mental model are affected by two basic considerations: the individual's personal view of the environment, and the influence of culture on this view. Each individual has his own view of the world and his own personal sense of space that is produced by his own inner feelings and drives. This personal space can be seen in Fig. 2.1, but of much more importance to the geographer is the influence of culture on the individual's view of the world, and the ways in which perceptions of the environment vary between cultures are a major focus of interest.

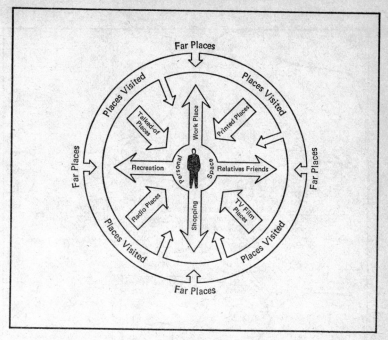

Fig. 2.1. A simplified mental map.

(from B. Goodey, *Perception of the Environment*, Centre for Urban and Regional Studies)

Because the real world presents the individual with so many images, choices and problems, a process of selection has to take place, and it is culture which enables him to choose certain stimuli and to arrange them into patterns which have meaning. As a result, reality is only perceived through a selective cultural filter which consists of philosophical considerations, social traditions, economic aims and so on. This cultural filter is learned, so that it is possible to identify cultural responses to the environment which are shared by all its individual members, and patterns of activity which are culturally recognisable, such as cultural landscapes, are produced.

Culture is the primary factor affecting the way in which man responds to the environment and since there is a wide variety of cultures, there is a wide variety of cultural responses, even to the same environment. For example, in the Fijian Islands of the Pacific, two distinct cultures can be identified, each with a different relationship with the environment. On the one hand there is the old Melanesian culture whose members utilise the environment to grow a small range of subsistence crops and whose wants are very limited. In contrast, there are the new Melanesians, largely Indian immigrants, who have a much more Westernised view of the environment, growing cash crops such as sugar-cane for export. Similar contrasts can be found throughout the world, between Chinese and Malay in Malaysia, African and European in Kenya, and Indian and Ladino in Mexico.

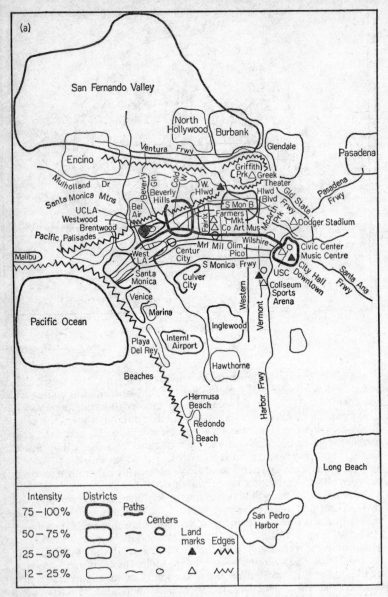

Fig. 2.2. Mental maps of Los Angeles.
Knowledge of the city held by: (a) Rich Whites from Westwood.

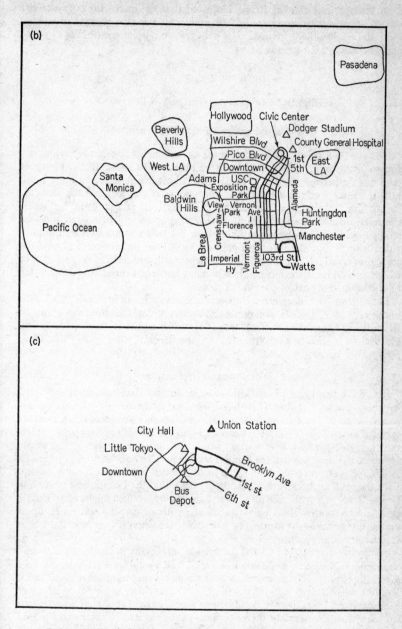

(b) Poor Blacks from Avalon.
(c) Spanish–speaking immigrants from Boyle Heights.

In the previous chapter it was indicated that the interaction of man and environment can be considered as a system, but it is now clear that between man and environment there exists a subjective environment of images which affects the way that man behaves.

Man

↑

Subjective environment (Images) ↔ Behaviour

↓

Objective environment (Real world)

The relationships between man, these environments and his behaviour are shown above and it is clear that there are two areas to be examined. First, the relationship between man and the real world must be studied to understand how the images of the subjective environment are created, and this involves identifying the process of perception, both personal and cultural. Secondly, the relationship between the subjective environment and behaviour must be studied, and this involves identifying how behaviour is affected by the individual's mental model. Most geographical work has been concerned with the second of these relationships and this chapter will concentrate on the ways in which behaviour is produced, but it must be remembered that both these relationships are part of the same process.

Each person therefore has an image of the environment inside his head. This image is produced by his own needs and desires, but much more important are the cultural influences affecting it. It is on this image that man's preferences, evaluations, decisions and ultimate behaviour depend, and the way that these operate are considered next.

Environmental Preferences

There are two types of environmental preference that have been examined by geographers. The first of these has been concerned with **landscape preferences**, in an attempt to understand the processes which produce particular types of landscape. It has been suggested that the English preference for neatness and order, and a love of the picturesque and rustic, have been a major influence in the creation of the English landscape. On the other hand, American landscape preferences are said to be for a pioneer or wilderness romanticism, with a special appreciation for the 'gigantism' that the Empire State Building or the Grand Canyon provides. The value of such studies might be to enable planners to modify the English landscape without causing too much upset among conservationist groups, or to enable recreation planners in the US to select successful vacation areas.

Secondly, the study of spatial preferences, especially in terms of residential desirability, has led to a considerable interest in **mental maps**. If a person were given the choice of living wherever he wished, in order to make that choice he would have to search through the image of the world in his mind, an image of landscapes and climates personally experienced, or read about in books or seen on television. Some might prefer to live in the near and familiar and some in the distant and exotic, but the image of space referred to can be considered that person's mental map, and attempts have been made to analyse these maps.

The maps are formed by the person's experience and the information he has received and so vary considerably from person to person, but despite this, there are common elements that can be identified.

Social class and education clearly affect a person's view of the world and this is confirmed in the maps in Fig. 2.2, where the amount of information about the city of Los Angeles possessed by three contrasting social groups has been collected and mapped. Rich Whites from Westwood, the area around the University of California campus, have a wide-ranging and detailed view of the city and its surrounding area, but poor Blacks from the inner city suburb of Avalon have a much more restricted view. When these factors are allied to a language barrier, thus restricting the passage of information, together with a short length of residence, the size of the Spanish-speaking immigrants' urban world is seen to be very small indeed, extending little from their central suburb of Boyle Heights.

It is not only who a person is, but also where he lives, that affects his perception of space, for the world looks different from different places. Twenty groups of schoolchildren in different parts of Britain were asked to rank the counties of England, Scotland and Wales in order of preference of where they would like to live and work, and some of the resulting maps are shown in Fig. 2.3.

Taken over-all, the south coast of England is considered the most attractive area of Britain, and attractiveness generally falls off northwards, with the exception of the Lake District. However, as can be seen from the maps drawn from preferences measured in Bristol, Liverpool and Inverness, views of Britain differ markedly from town to town. Although the method by which these maps were drawn has been questioned, the general conclusion is clear. A person's view of the world depends partly on the place in which he lives, and for a substantial proportion of people, their familiar home area is the one that they prefer.

A preference for a familiar home area is understandable, but the question has to be asked, how are **far places** perceived? Obviously, popular holiday areas are seen as desirable, but the perception of far places poses interesting problems. Perceptions of far places are often stereotypes, and it has been shown that children's views of Africa are considerably influenced by items such as Tarzan programmes on television. However, this is an important finding because it illustrates the fact that for the individual, the objective environment is often of less importance than his perceived image of it.

There is a great deal of uncertainty in the real world and the ways in which the perceived environment is used to evaluate the objective environment, often with serious consequences, are examined next.

Evaluating the Environment

Before the environment can be used, it has to be evaluated or assessed so that decisions about its use can be made. However, the environment is not always used rationally, because if it was San Francisco would not have been built in an earthquake zone or Brisbane in a flood area. The use of an environment depends on how it is perceived, and to understand patterns of land use or of spatial interaction, these perceptions must be understood.

It can be argued that the features of the physical environment do not have an objective reality for man because they are only significant in a cultural context. This is an interesting philosophical point that cannot be pursued here,

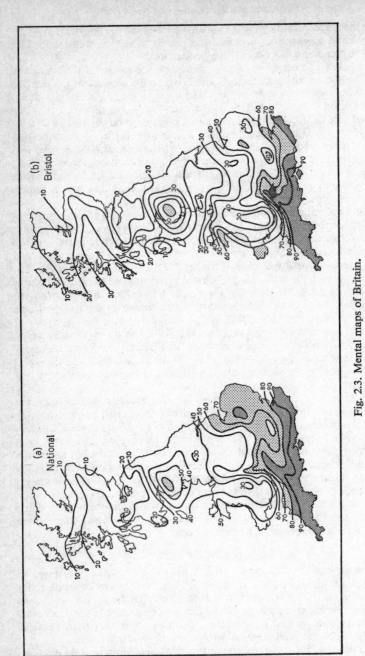

Fig. 2.3. Mental maps of Britain.

(from P. Gould and R. White, *Mental Maps*, Penguin)

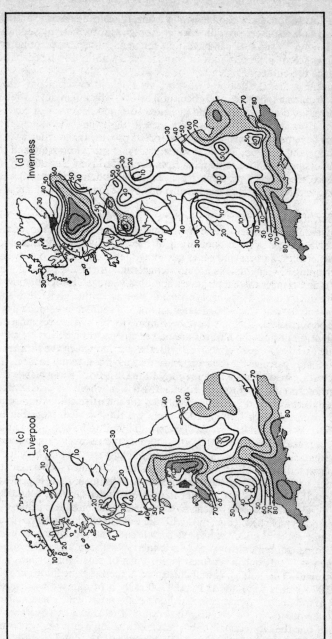

In (b), (c) and (d) the contours show the degree of preference of the groups living in the towns arrowed, while (a) shows the preferences of all the 20 groups surveyed. The most preferred areas have been shaded.

but as an illustration, snow can be seen as a hazard, causing damage and disruption, or as a resource, providing water storage and recreation. Similarly, the same amount of snowfall can have quite different consequences for human activity in different places. A foot of snow is barely noticed in Sweden, but brings chaos to southern England.

On another scale, the features of the New England environment which provided problems for the early agricultural settler—the mountainous relief, cool summers and cold winters, thin glaciated soils and heavy forest cover—have been given an entirely new significance in the twentieth century. The mountains have become 'scenery' and the forests provide the magnificence of the New England autumn. The cold winters provide snow for skiing and the cool summers provide a welcome relief from the heat of New York City. As a consequence, the farmers' problems have become abundant opportunities for the tourist, and New England has become one of the major vacation areas of the USA.

However, all environments have both positive and negative features. The most dangerous and unpredictable environments may also be the most desirable. Twelve per cent of the population of the USA live in potential flood areas, but fertility, flatness and other advantages are considered to outweigh the disadvantages. Geographers are now concerning themselves with finding out how man balances these advantages and disadvantages, especially how he copes with uncertainty. This has its problems, because although hazards such as drought and floods can be defined, human responses are much more variable. Nevertheless, attempts have been made to study these responses by an examination of how the hazards are perceived and evaluated.

One such study has been concerned with the ways in which the farmers of the Great Plains perceive the **drought hazard** they have constantly to face. This is an interesting area because the creation of the Dust Bowl was a classic case of the misinterpretation of the environment. An area whose major characteristics are uncertainty and variability was used for intensive cultivation rather than the extensive stock farming for which it is more suited. Research has shown that, despite past experience, farmers still tend to be optimistic about drought because, when asked, they overestimate the number of good years they have had and underestimate the number of bad years, so that even today their understanding of objective reality is distorted by their hopes. On the other hand, perception of the hazard increases with frequency and experience, but against this has to be set the fact that among older farmers, a fatalistic attitude develops and their awareness of the hazard becomes less acute.

Other studies have been concerned with the ways in which **flood hazards** are seen. On the whole, similar results have been found, and the dangers of flooding tend to be ignored unless damage is regular and recurrent, when adjustments such as flood control schemes, land zoning or payments for insurance cover are made. This point was well illustrated in the Brisbane floods of 1974, when 50,000 homes were affected and £100 million of damage was caused. Most of the damaged homes were in flood-plain areas which had suffered three similar floods in the nineteenth century. The area was known to be hazardous but the city council only prevented building in areas which had been affected by a smaller flood in 1931. Since the 1931 flood was the only serious hazard this century, the planners' perception of the flood hazard had been reduced, but this lack of caution has now to be paid for.

It might be argued that one disaster every century is an acceptable risk, but it emphasises the point that man has to take chances with the environment, that there is always a range of choices to be taken and that there is a constant degree of uncertainty to be faced. It is against this background that man makes the decisions that directly affect his behaviour, and the ways that these decisions are made are examined next.

Decision-Making and Behaviour

The study of environmental behaviour has two aspects, the study of behaviour itself, and the study of the consequences of behaviour. In the past, emphasis has been placed on the second of these, but this emphasis is now changing, and process rather than form is the focus of study. The decision-making process is the link between the ways that man perceives the environment and the ways that he behaves in it, and it is therefore necessary to understand how individual and group perceptions affect decision-making.

The study of how **individuals** make decisions is of considerable value in understanding how patterns of spatial interaction such as migration or shopping trips develop. In this area, a basic principle has been established: that people underestimate distances to places they consider desirable and overestimate distances considered less desirable. In other words, people move in perceived rather than objective space, and rationalise their choices by distorting reality. This is an interesting finding because it helps to explain why people do not always behave as rationally as some models of economic activity suppose. These tend to assume that because it would require less effort to shop at the nearest store, this is the one that a customer would use, but although this is a good general principle, different people see the effort involved in different ways, and shopping patterns are more complicated than the principle of distance decay would lead us to believe (see Chapter Twenty).

The general principle that decision-makers base their decisions on the environment as they see it, not as it objectively exists, is now well established. However, many decisions about resource use or location are not made by individuals but by **groups**, and particular attention has been given by geographers to the ways in which industrial location decisions are made.

Until recently, most explanations of industrial location (Chapter Sixteen) have assumed that location decisions are made by 'economic man', a mythical creature invented by economists, who always tries to maximise his profits and who is possessed of perfect knowledge. It is clear that behaviour is not as simple as this in reality, and as an alternative to this approach which sees man as an **optimiser**, it has been suggested that decisions are made which will produce returns which are not necessarily the optimum, but which will satisfy the decision maker. Whether man can be considered an optimiser or a **satisficer**, or, thirdly, an optimiser working within the constraints of imperfect knowledge and uncertainty is not yet clear, because the study of decision-making is at an early stage.

However, what is clear is the fact that to understand industrial locations, or patterns of resource use, or whatever, it must be realised that decisions are made by real people working within specific frameworks such as commercial practice or government policy. Attempts are now being made to understand the objectives and structures of decision-making organisations such as firms or government departments, and to understand the roles that individual and group perceptions and motivations play in decision-making. To understand how decisions are made, evidence will have to be collected as the decision-making process is taking place to see how information is assembled, chosen and evaluated, and the reasons for the final choice analysed. This is a very difficult process to study, and as an aid, **game theory** has been developed so that the ways in which people make decisions in situations of uncertain knowledge can be studied in simulated conditions (Chapter Twelve).

This then is the direction in which many geographers are moving, trying to explain behaviour by examining the influences and processes that produce it. Early attempts to explain behaviour resulted in determinism, but current behavioural studies emphasise the complexity of perception and behaviour, and the futility of seeking single-feature explanations such as determinism. Some have argued that the complexity is so great and human behaviour so erratic and unpredictable, that no general theory of environmental behaviour is possible, but research has shown that generalisations about human behaviour can be made so long as they are framed in **probabilistic** rather than deterministic terms. Unique factors and unexpected actions certainly abound but there is an overall pattern to human behaviour. If conditions a and b apply, then there is no certainty that condition c will result, but in many circumstances there will be a 90 per cent probability. If there are two shopping centres one and ten kilometres away from a village offering similar facilities, there is no guarantee that all the villagers will use the nearest one, but there is a very high probability that they will (Chapter Twenty).

The value of perception studies in understanding and predicting behaviour is likely to be of considerable value, and their application to planning problems is considered next.

Perception and Planning

In advanced countries there has been a growing concern for the quality of the environment, and planners have sought to maintain or improve this quality by controlling nuisance and promoting improvement. However, nuisance and improvement are not perceived alike by everyone. Some people enjoy living near motorways, while others dislike award-winning improvement schemes, but for planners to operate effectively, they must understand how the environment is perceived by the majority of the people and plan accordingly. Two areas are examined, urban planning and regional policy, where an understanding of perception processes would be of considerable value.

It is generally accepted that the redevelopment of many city centres has produced monuments to architecture and money rather than attractive urban environments, and there is now a call for building on a more human scale. Stress and even serious mental illness can be produced among people living in the glass and concrete deserts where high-rise buildings and elevated motorways dominate the townscape. It is being realised that for **urban planning** to be effective, there must be some understanding of the relationship between man and the urban environment, and the way that this understanding can be achieved is to study how the city is perceived by individuals and groups. The basic aim is to identify those features of the urban environment which people consider important or attractive, the landmarks with which people can identify, and to include such features in redevelopment schemes, while excluding as far as possible those features which are considered unattractive. Of course this presents difficulties because perceptions of the city vary from person to person according to age, sex, social class, education and so on, but there are many features that are considered significant by most people.

Work by Kevin Lynch in the USA on the images that residents have of their city has isolated five elements which are common to the mental maps of all of them. First are the **paths** along which people normally travel, mainly roads, which provide a framework around which the other elements are arranged. Secondly, are the **edges**, or barriers to movement, such as railway lines or beaches, while **nodes**, or centres of concentration, such as squares or busy road junctions form the third element. Fourthly, are the **districts**, which can be recognised as distinct sections of the city, and finally there are **landmarks**, which provide single outstanding reference points. In London, examples of these five features would be Oxford Street, the River Thames, Trafalgar Square, Soho and Buckingham Palace. Clearly, a city with ill-defined paths because of complicated traffic management schemes, or few landmarks because buildings of character had been replaced by uniform office blocks, would be likely to appear unattractive because people could easily get lost in it.

This realisation could be of considerable value to the planner since it would enable him to draw up redevelopment plans which would include attractive and easily recognisable elements in the city to create a coherent image. Of course, the planners already have their own image of the city, and a view, produced by their training, of what a city should look like, but it has been suggested that there is a gap between professional and public perceptions of the city that should be narrowed. Such a narrowing might help planning become more effective. As new towns have been built in Britain they have been divided up into neighbourhood units to help produce a sense of community, but when people in East Kilbride new town were asked, they had little or no realisation of the neighbourhood units in which they were living. Perhaps this was because the planners had not included those townscape features which enable people to divide and order space in their minds. If districts could be thus perceived, the neighbourhood idea might have had more meaning for the inhabitants.

In **regional policy**, a study of the perceived environment would be equally valuable. One of the problems facing the Development Areas in Britain is the poor image they have in the minds of industrialists in southern England who are being asked to move there. It is only slowly being realised that financial and other material incentives can only be part of the process of persuading industrialists to move to these areas, but increasing attention is now being paid to advertising which improves the image of the area wishing to attract industry. Wigan advertises itself as being 'next door to sea and country', Warrington tells industrialists that 'the pretty villages around the town contain some delightful homes', but it is Irvine in Scotland which unashamedly proclaims that 'it is a beautiful place to make money'. Irvine emphasises amenity as its major attraction: 'It is the only seaside New Town in Britain. A new development built around a charming centuries-old nucleus. A civilised environment with tremendous industrial and financial incentives. It is ringed by some of the world's finest golf courses and it enjoys sailing and swimming in some of the safest sea-waters in the world. The air is clean. The weather surprisingly mild. There are even palm trees growing in the grounds of Culzean Castle just down the coast.'

In developing countries, similar problems appear because officials are often reluctant to serve in difficult or unattractive areas. Since skilled manpower is at such a premium, it has been suggested that the mental maps of the country held by such officials should be drawn and analysed, to identify perceptual highs and lows, and higher salaries should be paid to officials prepared to work in areas considered unattractive. A scheme already exists in Sweden where salaries in the public sector are higher in the Arctic region than in the south of the country.

Conclusion

It is clear that the interaction of man and the environment is not a simple relationship between two elements, but is affected by an intervening image. This image is formed by the ways in which man perceives and stores information, and his preferences, evaluations, decisions and consequent behaviour depend on it.

It follows that the geographer must understand how the environment is perceived before he can understand behaviour, and there are two major areas of perception which are his concern. First, the way in which the features of the environment, such as resources, are perceived and utilised is a major consideration in the study of the ecological system. Secondly, the way in which space is perceived is a major consideration in the study of the spatial system. The ecological system was discussed in Chapter One, the structure and operation of the spatial system are examined in the next chapter.

Suggested Further Reading

Ambrose, P., *Analytical Human Geography*, Longman, London, 1969.

Davies, W. K. D., *The Conceptual Revolution in Geography*, University of London Press, London, 1972.

English, P. W., and Mayfield, R. C., *Man, Space and Environment*, Oxford University Press, New York, 1972.

Goodey, B., *Perception of the Environment*, Occasional Paper No. 17, Centre for Urban and Regional Studies, University of Birmingham, 1971.

Gould, P., and White, R., *Mental Maps*, Penguin, Harmondsworth, 1974 .

CHAPTER THREE

SPATIAL ORGANISATION

Man not only has relationships with the physical environment, he also has economic, social and political relationships as men interact with other men in the **social environment**. This interaction has produced a **built environment** which insulates an increasing proportion of the population, especially those living in towns and cities, from the direct effects of the physical environment. Human geographers are concerned with the spatial aspects of these relationships among men, and the forms, such as towns or transport links, resulting from their interaction.

The major theme in human geography in the 1960s was the study of the **spatial organisation** of society, with its emphasis on man-made environments and how they are affected by space. Sophisticated methods of analysing the distribution of man in space were applied and this approach formed the basis of the 'new geography' that was developed in the 1960s. The objective of the new geography has been to find some order in a complex world and to develop a body of theory which would explain locations and distributions. The search has been for a basis of explanation which would replace the discredited determinism, and it has been hoped that geography might be developed as a locational science.

As indicated in the previous chapter, this emphasis has changed recently to focus more on the study of the spatial structure of human behaviour, but the spatial emphasis still remains of basic concern for the geographer. The analysis of man in space now includes the study of the ways in which space is perceived and how these perceptions affect spatial behaviour.

Space is of interest for two main reasons. First, it is the place within which human activity occurs, and this aspect has been, and still remains, a basic element in geography. Geographers have been traditionally concerned with place as their focus of study and the subject has been popularly defined as being 'about maps'. A major objective before about 1950 was to divide space up into regions, in the same way that historians were concerned to divide time up into periods. The current concern with space is to examine the activity within it as a series of interconnected elements forming a complex **spatial system** that can be identified and analysed.

Secondly, space is an influence on human activity, and the **spatial environment** is the fourth component of the total environment (physical, social, built, spatial) within which men live and work. The study of the spatial structure of society and the processes producing it has become increasingly important in recent years and many see **spatial analysis**, the study of man in space, as the focus of geographical enquiry. The task is to identify regularities in the distribution of such elements as settlement or economic activity, and to relate these to the processes, such as the effects of distance and location, that produce them. Pattern and process are the basic elements of spatial analysis and will be examined next.

Spatial Patterns

One of the major traditions in geography has been a concern for the uniqueness of places. Attempts have been made in hundreds of regional studies to isolate the essential character of an area, and to explain why it differs from the regions around it. In recent years, however, the emphasis has changed to a search for similarities between places and features on the earth's surface in an attempt to discover whether or not there is any order in a complex world. Geographers have examined the built environment and the flows of goods, services and information between regions to see if this order exists, to find the pattern of man's arrangement in space.

Of course, distributions have always been of major concern and the map has been described as 'the tool of the geographer', but the new emphasis is on human geometry, the distribution of man in space, rather than simple mapping. Geometrical space has three characteristics—point, line and area—and these can easily be applied to geographical space. First, **locations** can be viewed as points, whether they be specific locations or general distributions. Secondly, the **interactions** between men take place along lines of communication. Thirdly, the division of space into areas takes place as men interact with other men and the environment to produce a pattern of **regions**.

The question to be answered is whether or not these spatial characteristics are distributed over the face of the earth in a purely random manner, or are arranged in any type of pattern. This question is not easily answered because the search for geographical order is complicated by the problem of scale. Processes may be random at one level, but ordered at another. In an analysis of shopping or migration patterns, for example, there are wide variations in the behaviour of individuals, but regularities can be observed among groups of people. In fact, many regularities have been identified in man's spatial behaviour, and their characteristics and causes are being examined.

Location

The distribution of settlement has been studied and statistical methods such as nearest-neighbour analysis have been developed to measure the pattern of settlement (Chapter Twenty-one). Using this technique, settlement distribution can be classified as being random, regular or clustered, and ideal examples are given in Fig. 3.1.

The ability to describe distributions in this way is of considerable value in the search for the processes that have produced them. The factors of colonisation and development that have operated to produce the pattern in Fig. 3.1a are probably associated with the processes of concentration and agglomeration described in Chapter Fifteen, and are quite different from those producing the pattern in Fig. 3.1c, which might be accounted for by the central place theory described in Chapter Eighteen.

Interaction

If locations can be viewed as points, the connections between them can be viewed as lines along which economic and social interaction is channelled. Differences between places on the surface of the earth, such as the availability of minerals, suitable conditions for agriculture, or scenic attraction, are the causes of spatial interaction (Chapter Nine), and a vast system of interchange

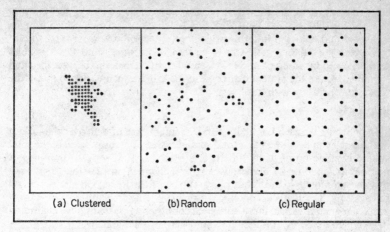

Fig. 3.1. Theoretical settlement patterns (after L. J. King).

has been developed. In this system, regions are linked in a complex interchange of flows as economic exchange takes place to enable the fruits of production to reach the consumer, and social interaction takes place between people in different places.

To simplify the complexity of this vast system, it is being studied as a **network**, or series of points and lines (Chapter Ten). This network can be analysed so that the basic elements of its structure, such as the extent to which each point is connected with all the other points in the network, and the ease with which it is possible to move through the network, can be determined. However, because the total network is so large, its component parts, which form systems in themselves, can be studied. International trade flows, the structure of national transport systems and even the geography of single firms can be analysed as networks (Fig. 3.2), and the principles there dis-

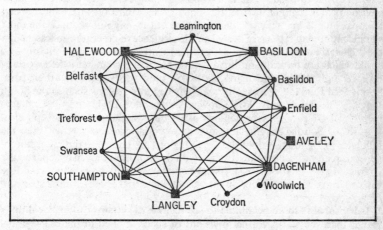

Fig. 3.2. The Ford manufacturing network in the UK in 1973.

covered applied to the total system. The movement of goods, services and information along these networks can be studied as **flows**, which can be measured and analysed in terms of content, direction, frequency and so on.

Viewing spatial interaction as a pattern of networks and flows enables regularities to be observed and the essential characteristics to be identified and simplified. Once the system can be described, it is much easier to study the processes operating within it.

Regions

In one sense, space is continuous and the interaction of man over the surface of the earth can be viewed as a total spatial system, but, as indicated, the total system is made up of many different subsystems. The world-wide transport network is made up of numerous smaller networks, so that the British rail system is complete in itself, but it is also part of the European and the world rail systems. The British economic or social systems are similarly constituent parts of a greater whole, but within each country such systems have characteristics which make them different from other national systems.

The reason for these differences is that although space is continuous, each part of the earth's surface has particular characteristics such as physical conditions or economic organisations which affect the spatial relationships that man has within it. Geographical space is therefore a divided continuum of complex interlocking spatial systems. In the same way, although it is possible to talk about the man–environment relationship as an ecological system, the physical environment varies so much that the relationship differs from place to place and there are many smaller ecological systems within the overall system.

The interaction of these smaller spatial and ecological systems operates to divide space up into distinctive units or areas which are known as **regions**, and which have long been of interest to the geographer. Before about 1950, the region was the major focus of study as geographers tried to classify space by dividing it up into sensible units. Under the influence of determinism, early attempts were made to identify natural regions where physical conditions could be seen to produce human responses, and these were really the major environmental regions such as the Equatorial, Monsoon or Mediterranean regions. This is one way of dividing space but it may not produce the most significant human regions. Even when the influence of determinism lessened in the 1930s, the emphasis remained on the identification of those divisions of space which are basically outlined by one particular characteristic, especially physical uniformity, and many textbooks used such regions as their base. South-East England, for example, was divided into regions such as the South Downs, The Weald and North Downs, the London Basin and the Chilterns (Fig. 3.3). Of course, such regions exist, but whether or not the physical features of South-East England give its essential character, rather than the influence of London, is doubtful. Such regions are known as **formal** or homogeneous regions because they are based on the uniformity given by a particular characteristic—in this case, physical conditions—but the country could be divided into different regions on the basis of industrial or agricultural structure or any other criterion.

It is probably more profitable to see regions as systems or **functional** units rather than the static, formal divisions of space implied in the old regional geography, and a great deal of attention has been given to the idea of the city

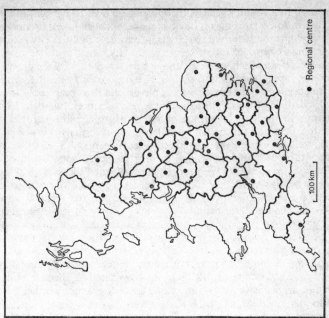

Fig. 3.4. Functional regions of England (after D. Senior).

• Regional centre

100 km

Fig. 3.3. Formal regions of England and Wales (after J. F. Unstead).

CENTRAL
UPLANDS
ENGLISH
LOWLAND
WELSH
PENINSULA
DEVON
PENINSULA

100 km

region (Fig. 3.4). In a country such as the UK, where over 80 per cent of the population live in towns, this makes obvious sense, but even in less urbanised parts of the world, the influence of the city is increasing rapidly. A city region is the area around a city which is both served by the city, which provides shops, employment, professional services, etc., and in turn serves the city, by providing food, water supply, labour and so on. The region thus operates as an integrated functioning whole, but it is very complex, and this complexity raises problems of measuring the extent of the city region (Chapter Twenty).

In the attempt to divide up the surface of the earth into significant units, the search is for regions which first have a central unity, be it formal or functional, given by the interaction of the spatial and ecological systems, and secondly are clearly different from the regions around them. However, attempts to divide space into such regions have not been entirely successful and the concept of the region must be seen as an ideal or model rather than an objective reality.

Two major problems arise from the attempt to make the regional ideal concrete. The first concerns the definition of regional boundaries. Even when defining formal regions, the boundary problem arises because features such as rainfall or vegetation do not change abruptly as lines on a map but rather shade from one region to another. Problems even arise over fixed features in the landscape such as mountain ranges or rivers, because although these may be barriers to movement and can therefore be considered as effective boundaries, it can be argued with equal conviction that they give unity rather than separation in many regions. Thus the River Danube gives a unity within its basin despite the barrier effects of political frontiers, while the Ural Mountains, because of the economic links with the Kusbas and the Donbas, can be said to join east and west Russia rather than separate Europe from Asia. The problem becomes even more acute when complex functional regions are involved since there is, for example, usually a considerable overlap between competing city regions. The area served by a city newspaper will not necessarily be the same as that served by its public transport or shops, and the boundary of the functional region will usually be a broad tract rather than a single precise line (Chapter Twenty).

The second problem concerns the question of scale. Depending on the criteria used, there are thousands of regions that can be defined, ranging from the major environmental regions to the region served by a single shop. In Britain alone there is a vast number of regions overlapping each other. If government is taken as the regional criterion, the London region is the entire country, but as far as everyday shopping is concerned, Greater London itself is made up of a large number of regions based on major centres such as Harrow, Croydon or Enfield.

However, despite these problems, the region is a very useful model for dividing space and, equally important, it has practical applications.

A third type of region can be identified, the **programming** region, which is designed to serve a particular purpose. One of the earliest programming regions was the Tennessee Valley Authority in the USA, which was designated in 1933 to coordinate the efforts of seven states in controlling flooding and soil erosion, and improving the prospects for industry and agriculture by providing power, navigation and irrigation in the valley of the Tennessee. Today, economic planning regions have been designated in many countries to help overcome damaging regional imbalances, and these will be discussed in

Chapter Twenty-three. In these cases, the geographer's task is not simply to identify existing spatial divisions but to suggest those divisions which will be the most significant and useful.

It can be seen therefore that a primary task of spatial analysis is to examine the patterns of point, line and area that exist in geographical space in order to be able to describe their structure and operation accurately. However, these patterns are not static but are constantly changing, and this change has also to be identified and measured. This is not always easy because records of past patterns are not always available. However, there are three kinds of evidence that can be used to examine change. Changes taking place at present can be studied by direct observation, but this can be very difficult if the changes are large or complex. Migration flows can be directly observed, but usually only on a sample basis, while for movements in the recent past, only periodic observation is possible through census or other statistical material. In the distant past, observation by inference must be used, and the origin and distribution of Dark Age settlers in England must be deduced from Anglo-Saxon and Scandinavian place names.

However, description is only the first step, since geography has become analytical and explanatory, and increasing attention is now being given to the spatial processes that produce these patterns.

The Spatial Environment

Once the spatial patterns of point, line and area, and the ways in which they change, have been identified, there are two closely related questions to be answered. What has produced these patterns, and what causes them to change? An attempt to answer these questions is made in subsequent chapters, but this must be prefaced by an examination of the spatial environment within which the interaction processes operate.

The basic framework within which human activity takes place is the physical environment, which differs considerably from place to place in the level of its resource endowment. The uneven distribution of agricultural and industrial resources over the surface of the earth is a basic factor producing the patterns of human activity described earlier, but the physical environment is only one component of the total human environment. Technology, in the form of efficient transport systems, has enabled man to bring resources together in convenient locations and to produce distribution patterns which are not directly dependent on the physical environment. The built environment is largely a product of the social environment within which it has been developed. However, the interaction necessary to overcome the problem of widely distributed resources takes place within the spatial environment and the characteristics of this environment, especially the effects of distance and location, have played an important part in producing the patterns of human activity of interest to the geographer. As a result, it is necessary to understand how space is perceived and measured.

The Importance of Distance

In any study of the spatial environment, distance must be a central focus because it forms the basic dimension of space and has a considerable influence on the operation of the spatial system. There are four ways in which spatial processes are affected by distance.

First, any movement of goods, people, services or information between places will involve a **cost**, which might be a bus fare or freight rate or simply the effort of walking. Secondly, this movement will take **time**, which is of considerable value, and which will limit the distance that items such as perishables can be sent. As a result, the interaction of cost- and time-distance raises obstacles to movement, and has two further consequences for spatial processes. Thirdly, distance limits the range of **opportunities** available to people, and shoppers in small provincial towns will normally have to make do with a limited range of goods locally while knowing of better opportunities in London, because of the time and cost involved in travelling to London to shop. Fourthly, available **information** is affected by distance, and people knowing more about their home area than about far places are likely to have many more local than distant contacts. The spread of information through space has been quite extensively studied and the **spatial diffusion** processes involved are discussed in Chapter Twelve.

It follows from this that distance is a friction that has to be overcome if movement is to take place, that a price has to be paid to overcome this distance, and that this will have the effect of constraining or stopping free movement over the surface of the earth. The decrease in movement as distance increases has been stated as the principle of **distance decay** and is discussed in Chapter Ten, but its precise nature is not easy to measure. However, its influence will be noted in the development of theories of industrial location, agricultural land use, settlement location and so on in later chapters, but when distance has to be measured in these theories, the question arises: what is really meant by distance?

Absolute and Relative Distance

This may seem a strange question, for geographical distance is usually regarded as an **absolute** measure. Distance separates places and is measured in conventional units such as miles or kilometres, and every schoolboy knows that the shortest distance between two points is a straight line. This is a rather simple view, however, and when questions are asked about the real world, problems arise.

What is the distance between London and Edinburgh? As a line on the map 'as the crow flies', the distance is about 530 km, but the distance by road is given by the Automobile Association as 600 km and the distance by rail is given by British Rail as 632 km, so even expressed in conventional units, different answers can be given to the same question. Furthermore, the shortest distance between two points on the earth's surface is not a straight line: we live in a 'curved universe' and a journey taken in a straight line from London to Edinburgh would involve digging a tunnel because of the curvature of the earth.

It is much more likely that if a person wished to travel from London to Edinburgh, the prime question would not be how many kilometres is it, but how long does it take to get there, how much does it cost and is it possible to get there easily?

It is clear from Table 3.1 that Edinburgh is a number of distances from London. By air the journey is a high cost but a low time–distance, by bus the journey is a low cost but a high time–distance, the car offers the greatest flexibility, while rail offers the greatest number of services. Thus the choice of transport method will depend on the purpose of the journey and the circumstances of the traveller. Distance is therefore **relative** rather than absolute and although time–distance and cost–distance are closely related to absolute distance in many ways, it is relative distance that affects the choice of transport method and this can be of a number of types.

Table 3.1. The Distances Between London and Edinburgh (May 1975)

Distance (km): Air—530 Rail—632 Road—600

Transport method	Travelling time (hr)	Cost (£)	Number of services/day
Road—Car[1]	7.30	9·00	—
—Bus	11.00	5·00	3
Rail	5.45–8.36	11·89[2]	11
Air	1.20	19·00	7

[1] 80 km/h at 50 km/gal. [2] Second class

First, there is **cost–distance** or economic distance, which is discussed further in Chapter Nine. It is very difficult to generalise about cost–distance because it differs considerably with the volume and type of goods carried, but it is not necessarily closely related to absolute distance. Transport costs are made up of terminal or handling costs, which are not related to distance carried, and line-haul costs which are. If handling costs are a major component of total costs as in the shipment of iron ore, the line-haul costs do not rise appreciably with distance carried, then distant sources of iron ore can be as attractive as nearby sources, and if, in addition, distant sources are rich in iron, they can be cheaper and therefore 'closer' than nearby ores.

Secondly, there is **time–distance** in which the measure of kilometres is replaced by the measure of hours and minutes. Time–distance is very important in mountainous country, for example, where distance measured on the ground is far less important than travel time, or in congested metropolitan areas where suburban commuters with a good train service may be 'closer' to their work than bus passengers who live many miles nearer.

Time–distance exhibits a number of characteristics which make it a very interesting measure. First, it is not constant in space, and the distance from A to B may not be the same as the distance from B to A. The air journey from London to New York takes two hours longer than the journey from New York to London because of the influence of westerly headwinds, and the situation is further complicated by the fact that long-distance east–west travel can involve time changes produced by the crossing of time zones. Secondly, it is not constant in time, and the distance at one time of the year may not be the same as that at another time. Time–distance can change seasonally. Because the St. Lawrence Seaway is closed in winter, the distance for seaborne freight from London to Montreal is less in summer than in winter when freight has to go via New York. In northern countries such as Canada or in Scandinavia, because of the severity of winter conditions and the closure of many roads and sealinks, time–distance is markedly different in summer and winter. Time–distance can also differ over much shorter periods in large cities and the time–distance of a journey across London is much greater at 5 p.m. than at 5 a.m.

A particular form of time–distance is **convenience–distance**, in which the ability to travel easily to a town 100 km away will bring it closer than a less well connected town 20 km away. Convenience–distance depends upon the frequency and reliability of transport services and places linked by an hourly service will be much closer to each other than those linked by a weekly service that is unreliable or hazardous, despite being many kilometres nearer.

As indicated in the previous chapter, increasing attention is being given to **perceived–distance**, or the distance we carry inside our heads. Time– and cost–distances are important considerations, but decisions to travel are also made by reference to how far we *think* places are, for all people carry mental maps that have a very important influence on their behaviour. In absolute terms. Amsterdam, Brussels and Paris are closer to London than Newcastle-upon-Tyne is, but most English people would regard these cities as foreign and therefore further away. Decisions to travel are also affected by how attractive the destination is seen to be, and migrants and tourists will travel great distances to areas considered attractive. In the USA, states considered attractive such as California and Florida have increased rapidly in population with migrants moving considerable distances despite the operation of distance decay. The task of administrators in depressed areas is to improve the image of the area so that the perceived–distance of industrialists who are seeking relocation of their factories is reduced, and this has formed a central theme in British regional policy which has, for example, emphasised the attractions of the National Parks near the Development Areas.

Another important form of relative distance is **social–distance**, which affects the amount of interaction between different social groups, Black and White, rich and poor. The absolute distance separating different social groups in cities may be quite small, and in London different social areas exist side by side, but the amount of interaction between such groups is generally small and the street separating them may be miles wide socially. On the other hand, Harrow-on-the-Hill and Highgate are 13 km apart, but are socially closer than Highgate and Holloway which are adjacent in absolute space. Because of higher levels of car ownership among higher income groups, the social space within which they move is much greater when measured in absolute terms than the social–space of poorer groups, and as a result the interaction patterns of different social groups vary considerably.

Absolute distance is clearly quite different from relative distance. Absolute distance is fixed, but relative distance changes locations, bringing some closer together but taking others further apart.

The Importance of Relative Distance

Absolute distance is important because it provides a standard and a framework for describing location. Coordinates of latitude and longitude can pinpoint a location and standard units of measurement can be used to describe the distance from one location to another. Absolute distance also strongly affects relative distance.

It is relative distance which affects behaviour, however, for decisions to move are made on a cost, time or convenience basis as perceived by people, and if distance is relative, then **space is relative**, since spaces are measured in distances. The study of relative space has been one of the most important developments in geography in recent years and the question 'Where?' has been given a new meaning since all locations are seen as being relative rather than fixed in space.

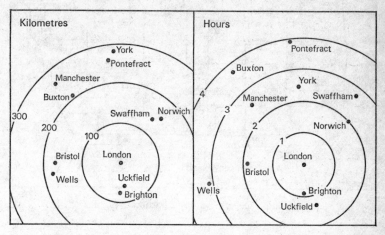

Fig. 3.5. Changing locations in (a) absolute and (b) relative space.

In Fig. 3.5 the distance from London of a group of towns is plotted in kilometres, and if an atlas is consulted the relative positions of these towns can be confirmed, but when the time–distance by public transport is plotted (Fig. 3.5) the position of the towns relative to London changes. A time–distance map could be drawn using each of these towns as the base, and the relative location of the other towns would be different for each of them.

This is not to say that maps of non-absolute spaces are new—the London Underground map, which only shows stations in relation to each other, has long been used—but that geographers are increasingly using them. A map in which absolute space is transformed into relative space is shown in Fig. 3.6 and can be compared with a conventional atlas map. This is a map of population space, but it is being realised that there are many surfaces overlying the earth's physical surface, such as the land-value and income surfaces discussed in Chapter Nineteen, and that the surfaces of social space, economic space and so on can be mapped and analysed. Such **transformations of space** are being used both to present information and as analytical tools.

The Dynamic Nature of Relative Space

One of the most interesting aspects of relative distance and relative space is that they are constantly changing, unlike absolute distance which changes extremely slowly even in geological time. Relative distance changes because of the development of **space-adjusting techniques** such as transport and communications, while education affects perceived distance by increasing knowledge of far places.

Relative distance changes principally as a result of technological change

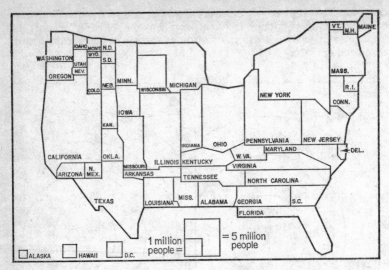

Fig. 3.6. Population space: USA in proportion to population, 1967.

and this is a steady process of development, occasionally accelerated, which is essentially making the world a smaller place despite the often increasing social distance between nations. The development of the steamship made the oceans much smaller by reducing the time it took to cross them while the development of refrigeration brought the northern and southern hemispheres together by 'abolishing the Tropics', thus making perishable food from the southern continents available in Europe and North America. Modern telecommunications have made it possible to transport information anywhere in the world almost instantly and because of television, Los Angeles is less remote than Wigan to many people living in London.

An attempt has been made to measure how fast places are coming together by D. Janelle in his theory of **time–space convergence** using the formula

$$\frac{TT_1 - TT_2}{Y_2 - Y_1} = \text{Rate at which places converge}$$

where TT_1 and TT_2 are travel times in different years, and Y_1 and Y_2 are the years in question. In 1776 it took approximately four days (5,760 minutes) to travel from London to Edinburgh, while 190 years later in 1966 it took only 180 minutes because of transport improvements. Using the formula

$$\frac{5,760 - 180}{190} = 29 \cdot 3 \text{ minutes}$$

it can be seen that between 1776 and 1966 Edinburgh was approaching London at a speed of 29·3 minutes a year. Obviously this rate cannot be held constant, and using rail travel time only the rate fell to only 3·4 minutes a year in the period 1850–1966, but it does provide an interesting method of showing how the world is shrinking.

Relative distance can also change rapidly as a result of the building of bridges or canals. When the Suez Canal was opened in 1869, Asia and Australia were brought much closer to Europe without moving an inch. Conversely, in 1967 the closure of the Canal took the oil fields of the Middle East further away from Europe by placing Africa in the way. London to Abadan via Suez is 10,500 km, but via the Cape it is 18,200 km, thus increasing the cost–distance. To reduce this distance, immediate steps were taken by the oil companies to increase the size of their tankers and thus carry more oil more cheaply per kilometre, and of the tankers being built in 1968 more than 65 per cent were of 150,000 tonnes and over compared with only one per cent over that size operating in 1967. An increase in scale was used to adjust space, and the operation has been so successful that there is a danger that the physical limitations of the Canal have made it obsolete for the supertanker. Another crisis in the Middle East in 1973 further intensified the effect of space as a barrier to movement when the price of petrol increased rapidly, but here a decrease in scale was suggested, in the form of smaller cars.

Conclusion

The study of the spatial organisation of society is a major theme in economic and social geography, and the interaction of man with man over and with the surface of the earth can be viewed as a spatial system. It is the aim of spatial analysis to explain this system by examining its structure and operation to identify the pattern and process of human activity in space.

The spatial patterns produced by this activity can be seen to have some regularity and are classified in three groups: locations, which are points on the earth's surface; interactions, which are lines of movement; and regions, which are areas or divisions of the earth's space.

The spatial processes producing these patterns are very complex but can be covered by the general term spatial interaction. Such processes include flows of goods and services, migration, short-term movements such as shopping or journey to work, social interaction, the diffusion of information, and will be discussed in later chapters. Increasing attention is being focused on the study of behaviour to explain these processes, especially how it is affected by the ways in which space is perceived.

Such patterns and processes are developed in a spatial environment which constrains interaction because of the friction of distance, but the space in which men behave is relative, because it is based on distances which are relative and which are constantly changing. The spatial environment has been given these qualities by man's success in developing methods of transport and communications which increase his ability to move goods, services, people and information over the earth's surface. By reducing time– and cost–distance, economic space can be adjusted to bring sources of supply and demand closer together, and telecommunications and education are adjusting perceived space. It might be argued that man has failed to reduce social distance sufficiently and that in many ways the world is moving further apart with the establishment of socio-economic blocks such as the EEC, NATO, COMECON and the 'Third World', but the analysis of space in these terms is an exciting consequence of the geographers' recent concern with relative space.

Suggested Further Reading

Abler, R., Adams, J. S. and Gould, P., *Spatial Organisation. The Geographer's View of the World*, Prentice-Hall, Englewood Cliffs, New Jersey, 1971.

Chisholm, M., *Human Geography*, Penguin, Harmondsworth, 1975.

Haggett, P., *Geography: A Modern Synthesis* (2nd edn), Harper & Row, New York, 1975.

Johnston, R. J., *Spatial Structures*, Methuen, London, 1973.

Minshull, R. M., *Regional Geography; Theory and Practice*, Hutchinson, London, 1967.

CHAPTER FOUR

THEORY IN HUMAN GEOGRAPHY

In the last twenty years, there have been significant changes in the study of human geography. Although the subject matter of the discipline has not changed very much, new questions have been asked about the pattern and process of man's economic and social activities over the surface of the earth, and new methods of analysis have been developed to answer them. These changes have been so great that they have produced what is now known as 'the new geography', and two 'revolutions' have been identified. The first of these is considered to have taken place between 1953 and 1963 and has been called the **quantitative revolution**. However, although the application of quantitative techniques was a major characteristic of the period, and the use of statistical methods has continued to provide an important analytical tool, the change was much more fundamental than simple quantification, and involved the application of scientific analysis to geographical problems and the building of a body of theory. The second, **behavioural revolution** began in the mid-1960s and is still taking place. As discussed in Chapter Two, this has involved a significant change in emphasis in human geography from the study of the products of human behaviour to the study of behaviour itself, especially the ways in which man perceives, evaluates and uses the environment, and how he behaves in earth-space.

Applying the Methods of Science

In the past, geography has tended to be largely descriptive, and regional description still forms a large part of many school geography syllabuses. There are many textbooks which present only a regional description, but although these are useful as works of reference, they do not go very far in explaining human activity, and **explanation** is the basic objective of science.

Dissatisfaction with this descriptive approach has been a major motive behind the recent changes, whereby human geography has become more analytical and explanatory, and these changes have been effected by the application of the methods of science to geographical problems in order to produce a body of theory which will explain man's activities over the surface of the earth. This trend has been most marked in the systematic branches of the subject such as economic and social geography, but even regional problems are now being studied within an analytical framework.

The Scientific Method

In order to become more scientific, human geography has become less descriptive and more problem-orientated, because the identification of a problem is the first stage in the application of the scientific method. A typical problem in economic geography might be 'What factors affect the distribution of wheat farming in England?', but since this is a very broad question involving a wide variety of factors, the problem might be more specifically framed in the form 'To what extent is the distribution of wheat farming in England affected by the distribution of lowland?'.

At this point, the second stage is begun with the formulation of a hypothesis, stated as 'The distribution of wheat farming in England is related to the distribution of lowland', and stated in these terms the hypothesis can be tested. A hypothesis is basically a potential answer to a problem, although in this case it will not provide a total explanation of the distribution of wheat farming. However, a more complex hypothesis could be formulated to include such factors as rainfall, soil type, economic conditions and so on, which could be similarly tested.

When the hypothesis has been formulated, the third step is to collect and classify information related to it, and here the problems of measurement first become apparent. The terms 'lowland' and 'wheat farming' must be defined. This might limit the area of investigation to those areas lying between sea-level and 100 metres, where wheat occupies more than 25 per cent of total cropland, but since there is no clear definition of these terms, different interpretations will give different results.

Serious problems also arise in the fourth stage when the hypothesis is tested against the real world and attempts are made to establish laws relating the distribution of wheat farming to the distribution of lowland. In the physical sciences, laws can be produced which are invariant, such as the law of gravity, but in the social sciences, relationships between phenomena are not so clear and laws are more likely to be probabilistic. Thus it might not be possible to say that wheat farming only takes place in areas below 100 metres, but it might be possible to say that there is a very high probability that it does. However, what degree of probability is acceptable before the hypothesis can be considered valid, and a law, even a probabilistic law, can be formulated? Does a hypothesis in the social sciences become a law if there is a 75 per cent correlation between two occurrences, or must it be 95 per cent and over?

Despite these problems, the formulation of laws is an essential step in the building of a body of theory in human geography, for the fifth and final stage in the scientific method involves combining a number of laws to produce a theory which defines and explains the interrelationships between a number of variables. If a number of laws could be established linking wheat farming to clearly identifiable factors such as landforms, climate and economic conditions, then a theory of agricultural land use might be proposed if similar relationships are found for other crops. Such a theory might not be as precise as theories in the physical sciences, since human activity is more complex and less predictable than the operation of inanimate elements, but the building of theory is an essential step in explaining human activity.

The Development of Theory

The current concern with theory is not an entirely new development in geography since attempts were made in the late nineteenth and early twentieth centuries to produce geographical laws. However, these were attempts to produce simple cause and effect laws which worked well in the physical sciences, but which resulted in the now discredited environmental determinism when applied to the complex and less predictable world of man. Possibilism was one reaction to this, but equally important, it produced a reaction against theory or generalisations of any sort. Emphasis was placed on the view that all places are unique, and that the task of the geographer is to describe and explain the differences that exist over the surface of the earth. This **ideographic** approach must be contrasted with the **nomethetic** approach which is concerned to find similarities between places and phenomena, and which is a necessary approach in the development of theory. The nomothetic approach is currently much more important, but the swing has not been complete and many geographers still believe that it is more important to explain how and why Paris is different from London than to explain how and why they are similar.

However, even at the time when explanation of the uniqueness of places was the dominant theme, there were attempts to develop generalisations about the location and distribution of economic and social activity. This early work was empirical and **inductive,** whereby a large number of actual locations such as factories were analysed, and specific conclusions from each were then drawn into general conclusions about industrial location. Recent trends have placed the emphasis on a theoretical, **deductive** approach whereby a problem is formulated, a set of basic assumptions about the problem is made, a theoretical answer to the problem is deduced, and this is then tested against real world conditions to check whether the assumptions, for example, about which factors affect the location of industry, are correct.

The basic aim of theory building is to connect ideas or laws to develop coherent theories which will explain geographical patterns and processes, and there are thus two main areas of investigation. First, regularities in the spatial organisation of human activity must be found, and patterns identified. Secondly, these regularities must be explained by examining the processes which have produced them.

The real world is an apparent confusion because of the volume of human activity over the surface of the earth, but a prime task of the geographer is to discover whether this reality is chaos or just complexity and diversity. The discovery of order and regularity is the first step in the development of theory because it suggests that common processes are operating in different places, and this order provides a standard against which the unusual can be measured. The nomothetic approach seeks to identify similarities rather than differences, to focus on the general rather than the particular, and in order to do this irrelevant information or 'noise' has to be removed to reveal the essential framework of man's spatial organisation.

Once a pattern has been identified, the second step is to analyse and explain the processes producing it, and two major types of theory have been developed to do this. The first of these is **normative theory**, which has been applied particularly to the spatial aspects of human activity. In this type of theory, idealised spatial patterns are produced using a set of simplifying assumptions which reduce the complexity of the real world to a flat, uniform plain inhabited by perfectly rational 'economic men'. The aim has been to establish what would happen under these ideal circumstances by the production of a norm, or standard, against which reality can be measured, but the theories developed by using this method have been very unreal.

A typical normative theory is agricultural location theory based on the work of von Thünen. This theory states that for every farm there is an optimal land use which will give the best profit to the farmer. Such a land use would be difficult to determine since the farmer would have to know the right level of capital and labour inputs, the cost of transport, market trends, soil and climatic conditions, and so on, but in the theory the farmer is assumed to be an economic man with perfect knowledge and the ability to use it (Chapter Twelve).

The theory postulates that if two crops were being grown near a market (M) and one had higher transport costs than the other because it was more perishable or bulkier, then their profitability curves would fall with increased distance from the market at different rates, as shown in Fig. 4.1a. In the

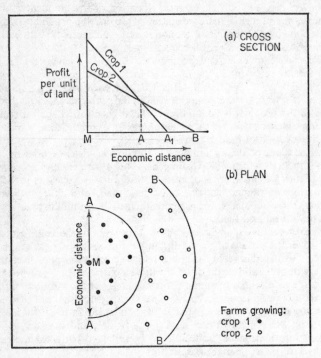

Fig. 4.1. Theoretical land use zones assuming profit maximisation (after A. Pred).

economic distance zone M–A, crop 1 would be the more profitable, with crop 2 the more profitable in the zone A–B, and as a result, if A and B were rotated around M, the pattern of optimum land use would be a number of concentric zones around the market. Part of this pattern is shown in Fig. 4.1b.

However, in the real world, farmers do not have total knowledge or perfect ability and **behavioural theory** has been developed to explain real world deviations from the theoretical norm, to take account of human motivation and behaviour. Real men do not behave like the economic men of normative theory, and the new theories are based on observed patterns of behaviour, focusing on the ways that environmental preferences, evaluations and decisions affect land use and location.

Fig. 4.1a shows that it is possible to make some, if not the best, profit from growing crop 1 in the zone $A–A_1$, or crop 2 in the zone M–A, and as a result the real world distribution of land use will probably be more like that shown in Fig. 4.2b. Many farmers will be satisfied with less than the theoretical maximum profit from their land, and the boundary between land use zones will be a zone of transition on either side of A where both crops are grown, rather than the definite boundary of normative theory.

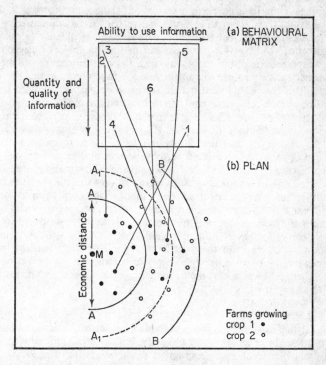

Fig. 4.2. 'Real world' agricultural locations linked to the behavioural matrix (after A. Pred).

Behavioural theory is concerned to find why sub-optimal decisions are made, and to help explain this, a **behavioural matrix** has been proposed by A. Pred. The matrix is shown in Fig. 4.2a and analyses the farmer's decision about which crop he will grow, in terms of the quality and quantity of information available to him, and his ability to use this information. In Fig. 4.2a the decisions of a number of farmers growing crop 1 have been plotted on the matrix and possible explanations of their decisions are offered. Farmer 1 has made the right decision by using good information well and he is similar to the economic man of normative theory. Farmer 2 has made the right decision purely by chance, however, since he has poor information and little ability to use it. Farmer 3 is similar but not so lucky, and the only important question to ask is how long will he stay in business? Farmer 4 is making a profit but not doing as well as he might because he has not been able to use the information available to him. Farmer 5 is in a similar position but for different reasons; he is very able but lacks the right information. Farmer 6 is an average farmer making a profit to the best of his ability and information.

Despite the fact that farmers growing crop 1 in the zone A–A$_1$ are not making the best possible profit from their land, they may be perfectly satisfied with the profit they are making, especially if a change to crop 2 required a major upheaval on their part. An objective of behavioural theory is to determine the extent to which man is a **satisficer** rather than an **optimiser**.

The problem with the behavioural matrix is that it is difficult to quantify. The number of Ministry of Agriculture information pamphlets received might be taken as a measure of the quality and quantity of information, but measuring a farmer's ability to use this information is much less certain. However, the concept of the behavioural matrix serves to emphasise the need for the study of how decisions about land use or location are made.

A second aim of theory building is to enable predictions to be made, and theory is an essential tool in planning. If every event or circumstance is considered to be unique, then it is impossible to plan ahead, but if a body of theory can be produced to explain current patterns and processes, then these can be projected forwards and the likely outcome of given circumstances can be predicted. Social and economic planning is very difficult because of the large number of variables involved, but a more serious objection to the idea that theories about human behaviour can be formulated is that such theories run against the ideas of free will and irrationality that are supposed to characterise people. However, although these characteristics do apply, human behaviour is predictable at the right level of generalisation, such as the behaviour of large groups. Although atoms in a molecule move in a random manner, there is nevertheless an overall order in the physical world that is not entirely lacking in society.

Models in Geography

Considerable use has been made of models in the application and development of theory in geography, and by the 1950s theoretical models were being used especially by economic geographers to explain patterns of location and interaction. However, the term model has been used so widely that its meaning is not precise, and it can be used to describe a hypothesis, a law, a theory and so on. Despite this, models and theories are very closely linked, and the definition of a model proposed by R. J. Chorley and P. Haggett is that it is 'a simplified structuring of reality which presents supposedly significant features or relationships in a generalised form'. This view of models recognises the fact that the world is so complex and diverse that it must be simplified before we can understand it, and models are built which are selective, structured, simplified approximations of reality, thus enabling its essential properties to be isolated and analysed.

Three basic types of model are used in geography, each one representing an increasingly abstract view of reality. The first type is the **iconic** model, such as an aerial photograph or a planner's model of a town redevelopment plan, in which the real world is represented simply by a change in scale. The second type is the **analog** model, such as a map in which real world properties such as population distributions are represented by other properties such as dots or shadings. The third type is the **symbolic** model, in which abstraction is further intensified and real world properties are represented by symbols, particularly mathematical symbols. Symbolic models in the form of mathematical models have become very important in geographical research and have formed a major element in the quantitative revolution. Such models can be further classified as either deterministic or probabilistic.

Deterministic models postulate direct cause and effect relationships and in the late nineteenth and early twentieth centuries produced environmental determinism. Despite the obvious problems, deterministic models were produced by economic geographers in the 1950s by eliminating human behaviour due to chance or irrationality. Following trends set in economics, models were built which assumed that locations were made by a perfectly rational 'economic man' who possessed perfect knowledge and who located his economic activities where the least costs would be involved. Such assumptions of least-cost behaviour led to an economic determinism which produced models not closely in accord with reality, but which represented an important first step in the development of theory.

There are four major areas where deterministic models have been developed to explain the location and distribution of economic activity. The first has been the development of central place theory, which seeks to explain the arrangement of market centres (Chapter Eighteen). The second has been the development of industrial location theory, which seeks to explain patterns of industrial location (Chapter Sixteen). The third has been the development of land rent theories to explain the distribution of urban and rural land use (Chapters Twelve and Nineteen). The fourth has been the application of the principles of least effort and distance decay to interaction models to explain movements over the surface of the earth (Chapter Ten). In all these models, consequences are determined by the operation of stated conditions, but because such models take economic man as the norm and take little account of real behaviour, a second type of model has been developed.

Probabilistic models have been developed to take into account the fact that human behaviour cannot be predicted with absolute certainty because of the wide range of variables producing it, many of which are influenced by chance or irrationality. These models are similar to deterministic models in that they assume that certain conditions will produce likely consequences, especially if group rather than individual behaviour is studied, but they do not assume an invariant causal link. To understand how random (or stochastic) processes affect patterns of human activity, **simulation** models have been developed in which the consequences of human behaviour are simulated by using mathematical laws of probability. Such stochastic simulation models have been principally applied to diffusion studies such as migration or the diffusion of agricultural innovation, in which an understanding of how people or ideas move in space is sought (Chapter Twelve). A game approach is used in which a basic set of rules is drawn up, based on observations of the real world, the probable consequences of these rules are worked out, and are then tested against reality. If the distributions produced are similar to reality, then the rules of the game are similar to real-life decision-making processes. Stochastic simulation models have been described as **Monte Carlo** models when chance alone determines the outcome of events, or **Markov Chain** models when each event is partially determined by previous events.

Simulation models are important because they are concerned with process rather than static patterns, but they do not explain the motivation behind spatial behaviour because they do not include the study of the ways that space is perceived or how perception affects behaviour. **Behavioural** models are now being sought to explain how man perceives, evaluates and uses space and the objects of the environment, but this study is only beginning. As mentioned earlier, a start has been made with the development of the behavioural matrix by Pred and this is further discussed in Chapter Sixteen.

Increasing use is being made of models in which the real world is viewed as a **system** or a set of interlocking systems. These models are based on the fact that each component of the real world has connections with other components and that one component is only important in relation to all the others. As a result, the focus of study is placed on the system of interrelated objects, on the whole rather than its parts, and systems analysis is employed to identify and analyse the component parts and functional relationships.

A system can be defined as 'a set of objects together with the relationships between the objects and between their attributes'. Such systems operate at various scales and different levels of complexity and are nested into each other to form a hierarchy of supersystems, systems and subsystems within the great universal system. In human geography, attention is focused on the analysis of two supersystems, the ecological system and the spatial system (Chapter One), which are made up of many systems such as agricultural or transport systems, which are themselves made up from many subsystems such as dairy farming or railway networks.

However, although models are very useful as an aid to our understanding of the world, there are three main problems in their use which arise from the complexity and diversity of reality. Models are simplifications of reality and are therefore very attractive, but there is a danger that they may be substituted for, or even preferred to, reality. The second problem is that reality can be simplified in many ways. Many types of model can be built and therefore any model must be considered as just one way of viewing reality. The third problem is perhaps the most important. Since the complexity and diversity of reality might be its most significant feature, there is a danger that the search for generalisation and order will obscure this.

Quantitative Analysis

The application of the scientific method to produce a body of theory in geography has greatly emphasised the need for precise measurement. As problems have been formulated in ways which can be tested, quantification has been the tool which has made this testing possible, and the old dictum that 'the map is the tool of the geographer' must now be modified to include statistical techniques. However, it must be remembered that quantification is only a tool and that the quantitative revolution could be more accurately described as the theoretical revolution.

This new emphasis does not mean that quantification is new in geography, for data such as figures of economic production or population size have always been used, but even for simple description the vast amount of data now being produced by public and private bodies has required a re-evaluation of methods of presentation. More important still, numerical data are now being used in the formulation and testing of hypotheses, and more rigorous techniques are possible in the new geography as sophisticated tools such as the computer have become available. Quantification has become especially important in the field of planning, where predictive models needing accurate data on which forecasts can be based have been developed.

There are many different statistical techniques being applied to geographical problems, but on the basis just described, they can be grouped into two categories. **Descriptive techniques** are used to summarise the vast range and amount of data available about economic and social patterns and trends, in order to make description and comparison possible. Because of the amount of data available it has to be condensed to manageable proportions and the first type of descriptive technique is concerned with producing a few representative figures which can be considered as typical. The most commonly used index is the average, such as the average size of farm in a region, but even here a knowledge of statistical techniques is needed, since there are three different measures of the average.

Table 4.1 shows the largest national oil tanker fleets in 1973, with three measures of the average. The most commonly used is the *arithmetic mean*, found by adding all the values together and dividing the total by the number of values, but the average might also be considered to be the *median*, which has an equal number of values above and below it, or the *mode*, which is the most frequently occurring value.

Table 4.1. National Oil Tanker Fleets 1973.
Countries over 1 Million Gross Registered Tons

Country	Million Gross Registered Tons	Average
Liberia	29·4	
Japan	14·2	
UK	14·1	
Norway	11·2	
Greece	6·4	Mean 7·1
France	5·0	
USA	4·7	
Panama	4·4	Median 4·4
USSR	3·6	
Italy	3·4	
Spain	2·2	
Netherlands	2·0	
Sweden	1·9	
Denmark	1·9	Mode 1·9
West Germany	1·8	

Source: *United Nations Statistical Yearbook*, 1973.

The second type of descriptive technique is concerned with measures of dispersion to find out how far the values in any set of data differ from the typical. The most important of these measures is the standard deviation from the mean which shows in a single measure the extent to which all the values in a set of data vary around the arithmetic mean value. Such techniques show just how typical the typical value is. In Table 4.1, where the size of tanker fleets ranges from 1·8 to 29·4 million tons, only Greece is close to the mean tonnage, the others being widely spread around this value, so the mean is not very typical and this is reflected in a high standard deviation figure of 7·2 million tons.

Such techniques enable accurate descriptions to be made and replace rather vague terms such as 'large' or 'unusual' with precise numerical values. More sophisticated descriptive techniques, such as nearest neighbour analysis, measure distributions so that they can be classified as random, regular or clustered (Chapter Three), while network analysis measures the degree to which points in a network are connected (Chapter Ten).

Inferential techniques are used for two main purposes. First, to test the extent to which a sample can be inferred to represent the whole. Because of the vast amount of data available about economic and social activity, sampling is essential, and the geographer has to know how to take a sample, how large it has to be, and the degree of accuracy of estimates based on the sample. Secondly, they are used to test hypotheses. Techniques are available to measure the existence and strength of relationships between variables from which it might be possible to infer an explanation. In the hypothesis of wheat farming discussed earlier, the strong correlation between the distribution of wheat farming and lowland in England would seem to imply that there is a cause–effect relationship. A number of techniques are used to measure correlations, such as simple regression, which measures relationships between two variables, or multiple regression, which measures relationships between a number of variables.

At the heart of inferential statistics is **probability theory,** which developed from interest in games of chance in the seventeenth century. A die has a one in six chance of landing on any one face, two dice have a one in thirty-six chance of landing on the same face, and, extending this principle, probability theory is concerned with forecasting the outcome of uncertain events. Any distribution could be produced by chance, and probability theory is used in geography first to determine the degree to which any distribution could be produced by chance, because if there is a high probability that it is, then significant relationships cannot be inferred. Secondly, probability theory is used to determine margins of error in sampling, with the ultimate aim of producing samples which are truly representative of the whole. Thirdly, probability theory is used in the development of theories and models to predict the outcome of human activity which is uncertain because of human irrationality or the operation of random factors.

The application of probability theory to geographical problems has been an important development, but the use of statistical techniques in human geography raises the problem of how to measure what may be immeasurable. This problem is particularly seen when techniques such as cost–benefit analysis are applied in planning. When an important new development such as an airport is planned, and before scarce resources can be allocated to it, the costs must be weighed against the benefits that the airport will bring, to establish whether or not it will be a worthwhile investment. Some costs, such as the construction costs, are easily measurable, but it is less easy to put a value on damage to the environment caused by increases in noise or air pollution. The problem of putting values on human variables in the development of theory is a major limitation to the development of models such as the behavioural matrix, but these variables do have values since alternative courses of action are balanced against each other when people make decisions, whether consciously or unconsciously. The task is to find acceptable values for loss of amenity when airports are built, for time saved when new roads are constructed, or for the 'psychic income' that people receive from living in areas that they consider attractive (Chapter Sixteen).

Despite these problems, quantification is an essential element in the understanding of geographical problems, for both description and explanation depend on it.

Conclusion

Since 1950 there have been two major developments in the study of human geography which have produced changes that many geographers consider to be revolutionary.

The first of these produced the quantitative revolution, in which the methods of science were applied to geographical problems and a wide range of quantitative techniques were used to test the hypotheses they produced. This revolution might more properly be called the theoretical revolution since the application of the scientific method and quantitative analysis was aimed at producing a body of theory to explain the form and process of human activity over the surface of the earth. This required a basic change in emphasis in geography, to identify and explain similarities between places rather than their differences, to study common rather than unique features. At this time, the main type of theory produced was normative theory in which the world is reduced to its basic essentials, an abstract space or isotropic plain inhabited by perfectly rational economic men, and this norm is then used as a standard against which the real world can be tested or measured.

However, the ideal conditions proposed in normative theory are inadequate to explain the complexities of the real world inhabited by men affected by irrational or random circumstance, and in recent years attempts have been made to explain human activity and the impact it has on the earth by understanding why man behaves as he does. The aim of this behavioural theory is to explain how man perceives the world and how this then affects his behaviour, taking into account the fact that man is not the optimiser of normative theory, but is a satisficer, or perhaps an optimiser with less than perfect knowledge and ability.

Probability theory is the main tool used to overcome the problems posed by irrational or chance behaviour, and probabilistic explanation is an essential element in behavioural theory. Behavioural theory has two main aspects. First, it is concerned with spatial behaviour, to understand how man perceives and uses space, and how space affects behaviour. Secondly, it is concerned with the ways that man uses the environment through a study of the perception and use of resources and attendant hazards. Now freed from a concern with environmental determinism, the study of the man–environment relationship has become once again a major focus in human geography.

Suggested Further Reading

Abler, R., Adams, J. S., and Gould, P., *Spatial Organisation. The Geographer's View of the World*, Prentice-Hall, Englewood Cliffs, New Jersey, 1971.

Chorley, R. J., and Haggett, P., *Socio-Economic Models in Geography*, Methuen, London, 1967.

Cole, J. P., and King, C. A. M., *Quantitative Geography*, Wiley, London, 1968.

Davies, W. K. D., *The Conceptual Revolution in Geography*, University of London Press, London, 1972.

Hammond, R., and McCullagh, P. S., *Quantitative Techniques in Geography: An Introduction*, Oxford University Press, London, 1974.

Pred, A., *Behavior and Location* (Part 1), Gleerup, Lund, 1967.

Toyne, P., and Newby, P. T., *Techniques in Human Geography*, Macmillan, London, 1971.

CHAPTER FIVE

POPULATION DISTRIBUTION

Until quite recently the systematic study of population had been largely neglected by geographers, in contrast with other fields of human geography such as agriculture, industry and settlement which have a long-established tradition of systematic analysis. However, in recent years there has been a growing awareness of the importance of population studies within the broad framework of human geography. Population geography has rapidly advanced from a peripheral position within the discipline to the stage where it has been claimed that 'numbers, densities and qualities of the population provide an essential background for all geography. Population is the point of reference from which all the other elements are observed and from which they all, singly and collectively, derive significance and meaning. It is population which furnishes the focus.' (G. T. Trewartha)

Population geography is concerned with the study of demographic processes and their consequences in an environmental context. It may thus be distinguished from demography by its emphasis on the spatial variations in the growth, movement and composition of populations, and its concern with the social and economic implications of these variations. The development of the subject has been severely limited by a lack of demographic data for many parts of the world, but, like other branches of geography, it is concerned with description, analysis and explanation, although a large part of the work to date has been concerned with population mapping and descriptive studies, simply in order to establish the data base which must precede analysis.

Sources of Population Data

One of the most difficult problems facing the population geographer is the varied quality of population data available for different countries and regions of the world. In general, the economically advanced nations have more accurate and detailed statistics than the developing countries, although in recent years the United Nations Organisation (UNO) has assisted many countries with the vital process of demographic data collection. The publications of the UNO have the advantage of compiling and collating dispersed and fragmentary material on a world basis. Thus, the reports and studies of the UNO, FAO, UNESCO and WHO provide vital documents for many aspects of population study.

At national level there are two main sources of population data: **census reports** and various **registers of population**. The latter involve the compulsory and legal registration of vital events such as births, deaths, marriages, divorces and adoptions. In most countries such registers have a far longer history than the national census, and it is generally agreed that national registers are more accurate and reliable than census returns. In addition, there are many specialised sources of information dealing with specific aspects of population. In the UK, for example, the Registrar-General's Quarterly Returns, reports of the Departments of Health and Social Security and Employment, the Central Statistical Office, Regional Health Authorities and so on, all provide useful information about various specific aspects of population.

A census has been defined as 'the total process of collecting, compiling, evaluating, analysing and publishing demographic, economic and social data pertaining, at a specific time, to all persons in a country or in a well-defined part of a country' (UNO, 1967). Although crude attempts were made to enumerate population in early times, modern census recording covers only a relatively recent time-span. The earliest modern censuses were organised in Scandinavia—in Sweden in 1748 and in Norway and Denmark in 1769. In fact, the Scandinavian countries still maintain a leading position in the collection of population statistics that are noted for their accuracy and detail. By contrast, the initial, though very imperfect, census of the USA was held in 1790, while it was not until 1801 that Britain held its first census.

Problems of Using Data Sources

Contrary to popular opinion, census statistics are subject to many errors and limitations. These result from omissions and double entries, either as a result of genuine error, illiteracy or with the intention to deceive for fiscal or political motives. National registers, while generally more reliable, also suffer from inaccuracies. In remote rural areas infants who die before registration may not be enumerated. It has been estimated, for example, that even in the USA almost 2 per cent of births still escape registration.

For the geographer working on census statistics there are many problems. Some of these result from breaks in sequence or the lack of a regular sequence in the census years. In the UK, for example, there was no census in 1941, while in France the rhythm of a supposedly five-yearly census interval was broken after the Second World War when enumeration was carried out in 1946, 1954, 1962, 1968 and 1974. Other states make no attempt at a regular census interval. Russia, for example, has held a census on five occasions only, in 1879, 1926, 1939, 1959 and 1970. In China, the first census was not held until as late as 1953, when almost one fifth of the world's population was brought into official statistics at a single stroke. Clearly, international comparisons of population statistics are made extremely difficult by such variations in census frequency.

It should also be appreciated that different countries employ different methods of data collection. In the UK, for example, individuals are recorded according to the place where they are found at the time of the census, whereas in the USA individuals are recorded according to their usual place of residence. However, a more serious problem is the lack of uniformity in the categories of data collected and the systems of classification employed in the published statistics. Various divisions are used for the classification of population into age groups; definitions of urban and rural population vary widely from country to country; definitions of occupational groups are similarly varied; migration statistics are notoriously unreliable, and lack international comparability owing to diverse methods of compilation and a lack of uniformity in the definition of temporary and permanent migrants. For some years the UN Statistical Office has sought to remedy these defects by encouraging countries to take their census in the same years and to follow an international scheme of data classification. Nevertheless, the problems remain. For many parts of the world no reliable demographic data whatsoever are available, and even in the more statistically advanced countries the amount of uncertainty is still considerable.

A further problem must be mentioned at this point. It will be apparent that the geographer working on census data is dependent on the size and shape of the areas for which the enumerations have been made. Frequently these censal divisions are based on administrative or even arbitrary boundaries which have little or no geographical significance. Furthermore, these censal units are subject to frequent changes and adjustments, thus invalidating comparisons of data over a long period of time. In this connection a proposal to replace the present irregular census divisions in the UK by a series of 100 m grid squares would be of great benefit to the population geographer. This would not only give statistical stability to the data base, but would also facilitate the computer processing of results.

World Distribution of Population

In 1973 the world's population was estimated at 3,866 millions. The distribution of this total, which inhabits 149 million square kilometres of land, is shown in Fig. 5.1. It is apparent that the distribution is extremely uneven with marked contrasts between vast areas of scanty population and highly crowded areas elsewhere. In fact, 80 per cent of the total population occupies less than 20 per cent of the land surface.

The main points of contrast are between the northern hemisphere and the southern hemisphere and between the Old World (Eurasia) and the New World. More than 90 per cent of the world's population is found in the northern hemisphere and over 85 per cent in the Old World. These facts are, of course, partly due to the inequalities of land area in the northern and southern hemispheres and in the Old World and New World, but even if one considers population densities rather than total numbers, the same essential contrasts are evident.

As may be seen from Fig. 5.1, three **primary concentrations** of outstandingly high population density (over 100 persons per square kilometre) are evident on a world scale; namely, South-East Asia, Europe and north-eastern North America. These three regions alone account for 70 per cent of the total world population. In South-East Asia more than 50 per cent of the world's population live on as little as 10 per cent of the world's land area; in Europe 15 per cent of the world's population occupy less than 5 per cent of the land area; while a further 4 per cent occupy the Atlantic fringe of North America. Various **secondary concentrations** of population may also be noted. These include California, eastern Brazil, the River Plate lowlands, North and South Africa and south-eastern Australia. These secondary concentrations account for a population of about 150 million, or 4 per cent of the world total. Finally, there are a number of smaller **tertiary concentrations** of population, often assuming the form of 'knots', such as the population clusters of the high basins of Mexico, or 'strings' such as the Nile Valley.

In contrast to these relatively densely peopled lands are the vast areas supporting densities as low as one person per square kilometre. These include high

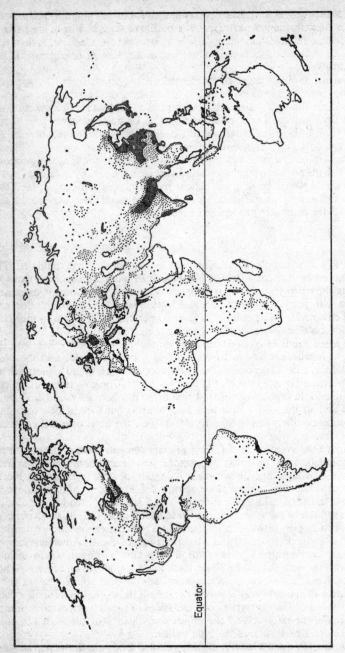

Equator

Fig. 5.1. World distribution of population.

latitude areas, especially the lands north of latitude 60° N, mid-latitude and tropical deserts, high mountain and plateau areas, and areas of equatorial forest.

Table 5.1. Population by Continents (1973)

	Population (millions)	Percentage of world total
Africa	374	9·7
North America	236	6·1
South America	309	8·0
Asia (excluding USSR)	2,204	57·0
Europe (excluding USSR)	472	12·2
USSR	250	6·5
Oceania	21	0·5
World	3,866	100·0

Source: *UN Demographic Yearbook*, 1973.

Ecumene and Nonecumene

Ecumene was a word used by the ancient Greeks to signify the inhabited portion of the earth's surface, thus distinguishing it from the remainder which was uninhabited. The term was revived by German geographers in the early nineteenth century and has been subject to slightly differing interpretations since that time. The term **nonecumene** is used to refer to the uninhabited, intermittently inhabited or very sparsely inhabited areas of the earth's surface. It has been estimated that approximately 60 per cent of the earth's land surface may be classified as ecumene and 40 per cent as nonecumene. However, it should be appreciated that such figures provide no more than a rough indication of the relative proportions.

The delimitation of ecumene and nonecumene is by no means easy. Areas of high population density merge gradually into low density areas. Within the ecumene are sparsely populated areas of parkland and farmland, while the nonecumene contains oases, mining camps and other small communities. In any case the boundary is not static. In earlier times an expanding ecumene was a characteristic feature of world history. This is less true at the present time when the settlement frontier shows signs of advance in a few areas but is static or retreating elsewhere.

In view of the past expansion of the ecumene, together with contemporary population pressures, it might be concluded that those areas which remain sparsely populated at the present time contain few resources or present the most serious obstacles to settlement. Alternatively, others would argue that man's assessment of these areas has tended to exaggerate the difficulties, and that on a world scale there is still considerable potential for settlement advance and expansion.

The concept of ecumene and nonecumene may be well illustrated by reference to Canada, the second largest nation in the world, yet containing a population of only 22 millions: 75 per cent of the Canadian population is concentrated within 150 km of the border with the USA, while vast areas in the north and west of the country remain largely uninhabited. Fig. 5.2 shows

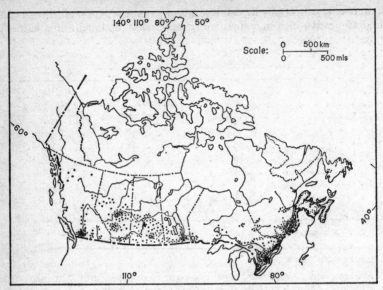

Fig. 5.2. Distribution of population in Canada.

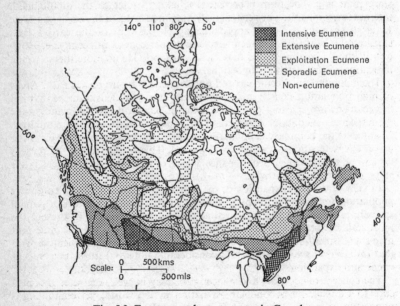

Fig. 5.3. Ecumene and nonecumene in Canada.

(from D. F. and R. G. Putman, *Canada: A Regional Analysis*, J. M. Dent and Sons (Canada) Ltd., 1970)

the distribution of population in Canada, while Fig. 5.3 presents a fourfold division of the ecumene according to the intensity of settlement and type of economy.

Table 5.2. Zones of the Canadian Ecumene

Zone	Characteristics
Intensive ecumene	Urban occupancy and industrial patterns, intensive agriculture, services and amenities.
Extensive ecumene	Mainly rural occupancy; extensive types of agriculture. Permanent planned forest production.
Exploitation ecumene	Systematic mining development with permanent transportation facilities and power supplies.
Sporadic ecumene	Very scattered economic activities.
Nonecumene	Empty space with no foreseeable development.

Source: D. F. and R. G. Putnam, *Canada: A Regional Analysis*, J. M. Dent & Sons (Canada) Ltd., 1970.

Influences on Population Distribution

From a brief examination of Fig. 5.1 it is tempting to conclude that environmental factors such as high altitude, extreme cold and aridity are the essential influences upon population distribution. However, closer consideration shows that such physical factors provide no more than a partial and deterministic explanation. As described in Chapter One, any attempt to define a climatic or environmental optimum for human habitation proves very difficult. Furthermore, man is by no means passive in his choice of areas for settlement and everywhere demonstrates an ability to exercise some control over his environment. Thus, the analysis of any population distribution, whether on a local, regional or even world scale, must inevitably take into account various social, demographic, economic, political and historical factors as well as purely physical influences.

It should also be emphasised that the factors affecting population distribution rarely, if ever, operate in isolation, but rather in combination. Thus, it is virtually impossible to evaluate the level of influence of any single factor. Typically, a whole range of influences is relevant, but their interplay is generally extremely complex. This is especially true of the economically advanced nations of the world. Indeed, it has been suggested that the role of physical factors in the spatial distribution of population declines in direct importance as civilisation advances in complexity.

Physical Influences on Population Distribution

It is obvious that population numbers and densities decrease with **altitude** in response to the increasing difficulties involved in the settlement of high-level environments. High altitude imposes physiological limits upon human existence through reduced atmospheric pressure and low oxygen content. Consequently very few permanent settlements are found in the Andes and Himalayas above 5,500 m, while La Paz, the capital of Bolivia, at a height of

3,640 m, is the highest city in the world. The decrease of population with altitude for the various continents is shown in Fig. 5.4.

The influence of altitude cannot, of course, be divorced from that of **latitude**. In low latitudes, high-plateau areas provide positive advantages and are often favoured for settlement on account of the climatic amelioration that they provide. Conversely, in high latitudes, areas of low ground are generally sought out by the scanty population of such areas. It is thus possible to refer to 'mountains that repel and mountains that attract'.

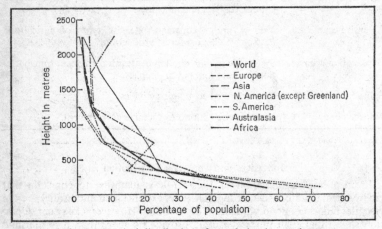

Fig. 5.4. Vertical distribution of population by continents.

(from J. Staszewski, Vertical Distribution of World Population, Polish Academy of Sciences, *Geog. Studies*, **14**, 1957)

Similarly, altitude cannot be disassociated from the factor of **relief** as an influence upon population distribution. Steep gradients, exposure and rugged terrain all tend to deter settlement by restricting movement and the possibilities of cultivation. Thus, an examination of population distribution maps will show that some of the most abrupt changes in population density occur at the junction of mountain and plain. However, within upland areas the pattern of valleys may have important effects. Certain valleys provide lines of penetration and favour communications and settlement, while cul-de-sac valleys remain isolated and sparsely populated. Similarly, on the more densely populated plains, rivers may exert either a positive or a negative effect. Most attract settlement, especially at crossing points, confluences and the head of navigation, but others may be liable to flooding and deter settlement.

Reference has already been made to the influence of **climate** upon population distribution and its effects on human activity (Chapter One). Such influences are extremely difficult to evaluate. Extremes of heat, cold, humidity and aridity all clearly deter settlement, but climatic optima are very difficult to define. It is of interest to note that two of the world's primary concentrations of population lie in middle latitudes, while the third is located mainly in the tropics. The difficulties of interpreting climatic influences may be further illustrated by the fact that virtually identical climatic environments support vastly different population densities. For example, the island of Java and the

Amazon Basin both experience an equatorial type of climate, but whereas Java has a population density of over 100 persons per square kilometre the Amazon Basin is one of the most sparsely populated regions of the world with an average density of less than 1 person per square kilometre.

In a similar manner, the influence of **soils** on population distribution is undeniably important but difficult to define as an isolated factor. Deltaic and alluvial soils frequently attract agricultural populations, while podzols and laterites, with their limited possibilities for cultivation, generally support only sparse populations. The attractiveness of particular soil types also depends to a large extent upon the agricultural technology of the population in question. Settlement of the American Prairies in the mid-nineteenth century, for example, was greatly encouraged by the development of the steel plough, the windmill and barbed wire.

World patterns of climate and soils strongly influence the distribution of major **vegetation** types, which in turn provide contrasting environments for a variety of agricultural activities. These are often associated with particular levels of population density. Consider, for example, the contrasting population densities of the ranching lands of the New World and areas of Asian rice cultivation. However, no firm rules can be established concerning the relationships between type of agricultural economy and population density.

The contemporary distribution of population in many parts of the world is also influenced to a large extent by the location of **mineral and energy resources**. For example, the population map of Western Europe reflects the distribution of coalfields and their associated industrial conurbations. In several instances these old centres of mining support densities of over 1,000 persons per square kilometre. The South African Rand, the Appalachian coalfields, the Donetz Basin and many other areas provide examples of population concentrations associated with the working of local mineral deposits. In the case of northern Canada and interior Australia the presence of minerals has attracted small settlements far beyond the limits of the ecumene. It will be appreciated that the influence of mineral and energy resources upon population depends on a whole range of related factors such as market demand, capital for development, availability of labour supply, presence of transportation links and cost of production. Indeed, all the physical influences outlined above should be evaluated in relation to the economic, social and political conditions in the area concerned.

Economic, Social and Political Influences on Population Distribution

It has already been implied that the density of population in a particular area depends to a large extent upon the **type and scale of economic activity** in that area. Technological and economic advances are usually associated with changes in population density and distribution. For example, the North American Prairies presented different opportunities for the Indians with their hunting economy, the nineteenth-century ranchers, the later settled agriculturalists and the modern industrialised and largely urbanised society. Each stage in the economic development of the region involved a growth of numbers and substantial changes in the distribution pattern. The Industrial Revolution has been a particularly potent force for change in many countries of the world. Pre-industrial agricultural populations, often fairly evenly distributed, were attracted to sources of energy, particularly coalfields, as well as lines of transport and communications and ports. Dense population concentrations replaced long-established patterns of dispersal and generally even distribution. On the whole, it is true to say that increasing complexity and diversity of economic activity encourages unevenness of population distribution.

In the present century, with increasing government control over economic activity, **political influences** have emerged as a significant factor affecting population patterns. In Communist countries, population may be directed to areas of social or economic need, while in the Western World various inducements may be offered to encourage or assist migration to new towns, development areas or simply away from overcrowded conurbations. Political events have also been responsible throughout history for mass migrations of population. The post-war movement of refugees into West Germany or the enforced expulsion of Asians from Uganda in 1972 provide examples of such a process.

Finally, it will be evident that **historical processes** must also be taken into account in any analysis of contemporary population patterns. The duration of settlement in any area is of fundamental importance. The relatively recent settlement of Australia is a basic reason for its low population density (2 persons per square kilometre), while the high density of India (175 persons per square kilometre) may be partly explained in terms of its long history of civilisation and occupancy. Nevertheless, it cannot be concluded that the highest population densities are found in the longest-settled regions. Numerous examples of formerly prosperous and densely populated regions, now only sparsely populated—such as parts of North Africa and Mesopotamia, the Yucatan Peninsula and eastern Sri Lanka—have led many historians and others to propose the idea of **cycles of occupation,** whereby population numbers and densities increase and then decline, only to be followed by a second cycle of population growth.

Measures of Population Density and Distribution

So far in this chapter the terms density and distribution have been used without definition, but, in fact, they do have precise and different meanings. **Distribution** refers to the actual pattern of spacing of units or individuals; **density,** on the other hand, is an expression of the ratio between total population and land area.

Measures of Population Density

Crude population density is a measure of the average number of individuals per unit area. For example, the UK has an average population density of 229 persons per square kilometre. As an average figure it suffers from all the limitations that this implies. A crude population density figure provides no information about extreme values within a territory, and comparisons of density figures are meaningful only for small areal units such as parishes and communes, but not for large units such as nations or continents. A crude density figure alone can never be used as an index of overpopulation.

Because of these limitations, various refinements of crude population density are sometimes employed. For example, densities can be calculated for inhabited or cultivated areas only rather than for 'gross' area. The latter is known as a **physiological or nutritional density.** Conversely, the density of certain sectors of the population can be calculated against total area. For example, it may be of interest to have a density figure for the industrial or agrarian sections of the population. The latter is referred to as an **agricultural density**. In urban areas where high-rise blocks of flats invalidate simple relationships between population and area, **room density**, or average number of persons per room, provides an index widely used by planners and sociologists.

Measures of Centrality, Dispersion and Concentration of Populations

Various techniques have been developed to express the central tendency of populations. Most have been concerned with the establishment of a theoretical central point within a given distribution.

The **mean centre** of a distribution is 'the point about which distances measured to all individuals of a population will, when squared, add up to a minimum value'. For grouped data such as the states or counties within a national territory it may be expressed as $\Sigma(pr^2)$, where p represents the population within a unit of area and r is the distance between the mid-point of the unit and the mean centre. Time-series maps showing changes in the position of the mean centre can provide an indication of the directional shifts in a changing pattern of population distribution. For example, the mean centre of the population of the USA has shown a steady shift westwards along the 39th parallel since 1790.

The **median centre**, or centre of convergence, is defined as 'the point where the whole population could be assembled with the minimum aggregate travel distance'. Using the substitutions noted above it may be expressed for grouped

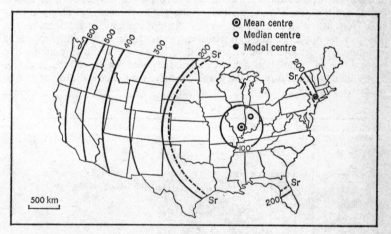

Fig. 5.5. Mean, median and modal centres of population in the USA
(after W. Warntz and D. Neft).

data as $\Sigma(pr)$. As with the mean centre, calculation of the location of the median centre is difficult and tedious, but at a regional scale it does have a practical application in the determination of optimum locations for centralised services such as schools, hospitals and hypermarkets.

The **modal centre** simply describes the point or area of maximum surface density within a distribution. Most countries are uni-modal; for example, London is the modal centre of the UK. A few countries are bi-modal, such as Canada with Montreal and Toronto, and Australia with Sydney and Melbourne, while a very small number of countries are multi-modal; for example, India with Bombay, Calcutta, Delhi and Madras.

When the location of these theoretical centres has been established, various statistical methods may be employed to analyse the extent to which population is dispersed around them. **Standard distance deviation** may be compared with the standard deviation of linear statistics, and is found by dividing the mean centre of population, $\Sigma(pr^2)$, by the total population, P, and then taking the square root of the resulting mean square

$$S_r = \sqrt{\frac{\Sigma(pr^2)}{P}}$$

Mean distance deviation is likewise the counterpart of mean deviation for linear statistics. It provides a measure of the mean distance of individuals from the median centre of population. It is found by dividing the median centre, $\Sigma(pr)$, by the total population, P

$$md_r = \frac{\Sigma(pr)}{P}$$

A point of particular interest in many geographical studies is the unevenness or degree of concentration of populations. Concentration is at a maximum in the hypothetical situation in which the total population is assembled at one point, and is at a minimum where each individual is located at an equal distance from his neighbour. The tendency of a population distribution towards one or other of these two hypothetical extremes can be measured by means of a graphical device known as a Lorenz Curve. This involves plotting cumulative percentages of population against cumulative percentages of area (see Fig. 5.6). Changes in the form of the graphical curve over time indicate increasing or decreasing concentration of population.

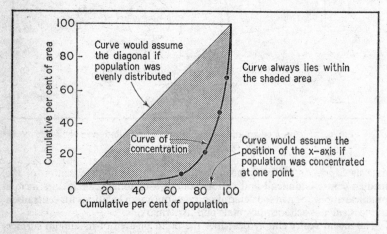

Fig. 5.6. Lorenz curve of population concentration in the USA in relation to density intervals on a county basis (after O. D. Duncan).

Conclusion

The systematic study of population constitutes a relatively recent and developing branch of human geography. At the same time its progress is hindered by serious quantitative and qualitative deficiencies in published demographic statistics. Population geography is concerned with the study of demographic processes in an environmental context and the spatial variations in population density and distribution which result from these processes. Explanation of distribution patterns involves consideration of a complex combination of physical, socio-economic and historical influences. Various quantitative measures and statistical techniques have been developed to give precision to comparisons of distribution patterns and to enable changes in a single distribution to be accurately measured. Population distributions are never static. The present distribution of world population is quite different from that of 1800, and doubtless will be different from that of a century hence. Such changes are the result of the interaction of the three components of population change: fertility, mortality and migration. These form the subject of the following chapter.

Suggested Further Reading

Beaujeu-Garnier, J., *Geography of Population*. Longman, London, 1966.

Benjamin, B., *The Population Census*, Heinemann, London, 1970.

Clarke, J. I., *Population Geography* (2nd edn), Pergamon, Oxford, 1972.

Demographic Yearbook, Statistical Office of the United Nations, New York (annually since 1949).

Hauser, P. M., and Duncan, O. D. (Eds.), *The Study of Population. An Inventory and Appraisal*, University of Chicago Press, Chicago, 1959.

Kosinski, L., *The Population of Europe*, Longman, London, 1970.

Petersen, W., *Population* (3rd edn), Macmillan, London, 1975.

Population Bulletin of the United Nations, United Nations Department of Social Affairs, New York (annually since 1951).

CHAPTER SIX

COMPONENTS OF POPULATION CHANGE

Patterns of distribution and density represent only a starting point in the geographical study of population. The dynamic aspects of the study, the changes in distribution patterns and the interaction of the demographic processes of births, deaths and migration, also form an important field of geographical study. A discussion of these processes, referred to collectively as the components of population change, forms the subject of the present chapter.

Fertility

The term **fertility** refers to the occurrence of live births among a defined population. In most parts of the world fertility exceeds both mortality and migration, and is thus the main determinant of population growth. At the same time, fertility is more difficult to analyse than mortality and is subject to greater short-term fluctuations. Whereas mortality is inevitable and involuntary, fertility can be controlled and is determined by a wide range of social, economic and political influences as well as physiological and psychological factors.

Various indices are employed to express fertility. The simplest, but in many ways the least satisfactory, is **crude birth rate**. This is simply the ratio between number of births (usually in one year) and total population (usually a mid-year estimate for the year in question). Thus the crude birth rate for the UK in 1973 was

$$\frac{779,000 \text{ (total number of births)}}{55,933,000 \text{ (1973 mid-year estimate of population)}} \times 1,000 = 13 \cdot 9 \text{\textperthousand}$$

Crude birth rate has the advantage of being easy to calculate and involves data that are generally readily available, if not always highly accurate. However, it fails to take into account the age and sex composition of the population, and this reduces its value for purposes of comparison. To overcome this deficiency other measures have been devised.

A **standardised birth rate** involves the calculation of what the birth rate for a region would have been if its age composition had been the same as that of the country as a whole. The computation is tedious but produces a rate which is directly comparable with that of other regions since variations in the number of births resulting from differences in age structure have been eliminated. Another useful index is the **general fertility rate**, which also avoids some of the deficiencies of the crude birth rate by changing the denominator from total population to the number of women in the reproductive age group, usually defined as 15–45 or 15–49.

The World Pattern of Fertility

In 1973 crude birth rates for the various nations of the world ranged from 10‰ (West Germany) to 52‰ (Niger and Swaziland). The highest levels of fertility, with crude birth rates in excess of 40‰, are experienced in most parts

of Latin America, Africa, the Indian subcontinent and South-East Asia. Very
few of the developing countries have achieved any success in making the
transition from high to low fertility. On the other hand, relatively low
fertility, with crude birth rates of less than 20‰, is typical of the developed
countries of Europe, North America, Oceania, USSR and Japan. These
facts have led certain writers to suggest that a decline in fertility is an inevitable
corollary of economic and social advancement.

Among those countries experiencing low fertility, the reduction of former
high birth rates has generally been achieved since the late nineteenth century.
An interesting exception is Japan, which more than halved its birth rate in
15 years from 35‰ in 1947 to 17‰ in 1962. Fig. 6.1 illustrates the decline in
crude birth rate for a selection of nations.

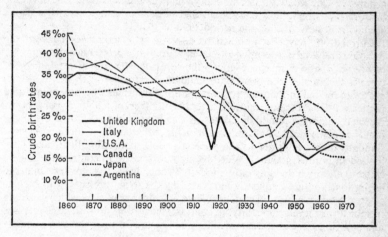

Fig. 6.1. Decline of birth rate in selected countries (1860–1970).

Detailed study of the population in those regions which have reduced their
crude birth rate figures shows that the apparent decline in fertility is in fact a
real one, and not simply a reflection of changes in population structure such
as a reduction in the number of women of child-bearing age. Furthermore,
although there is not complete unanimity on the point, there is nevertheless
general agreement that there has been no recent reduction in the fecundity of
populations in the world's economically advanced nations. In other words, we
are not considering an involuntary decline in fertility but rather a situation
in which a voluntary or controlled birth rate may be said to exist.

Factors Influencing Fertility Levels

Even in those parts of the world where the majority of the population has
passed from what may be termed a 'natural' birth rate to a 'controlled' birth
rate, human choice is not entirely free. Decisions concerned with family
limitation are both consciously and subconsciously influenced by a wide range
of moral, intellectual, financial and social motives. The changing status of
women in society, new attitudes towards children and marriage, the decline

of religious beliefs and superstitions in many parts of the Western World, and the prevalence of material ambition in modern society must all influence attitudes towards family size and thus indirectly affect birth rates.

Certain influences on birth control may be considered more closely. The factor of **religion** is important. Most of the world's major religions encourage family development and are opposed to birth control, sterilisation and abortion. Strongly religious communities thus tend to have high birth rates. Muslims, for example, especially those living in economically backward countries with a traditional society in which religious dogma remains unquestioned, are generally characterised by high birth rates. Algeria and Morocco, both predominately Muslim, had birth rates of 49‰ in 1973. In Western societies Catholic communities generally have higher birth rates than other religious groups. In Quebec, with its Catholic French Canadian population, the crude birth rate was one third higher than that of neighbouring Ontario, which is largely Protestant, during the period 1920 to 1950.

Correlations have been shown to exist in many countries between the duration and **level of education** and family size. It has been shown in a number of studies that the more advanced the level of educational attainment of parents the smaller the number of children per family. Such a situation is probably related to the negative correlation that has also been demonstrated between family income and the average number of children per family, especially among the middle classes. It has been said that limitation of the family is at its strictest where the difference between the actual and desired standard of life is greatest. The poorest people, possessing little, also have limited ambitions, and are typified by high birth rates. In contrast the middle classes, although having only modest means, have the greatest material aspirations and are frequently motivated by the social pressures which characterise modern advanced societies. Thus, it is this social class which generally has the lowest levels of fertility. In contrast, the well-to-do with large incomes and enjoying a social status which they can assure for their children generally have relatively high birth rates.

At national level, cycles of **economic prosperity and depression** appear to have a marked influence on marriage and birth rates. Correlations are not precise but in general terms it would seem that a sudden onset of prosperity favours an increase in family size, while a gradual rise in living standards has the reverse effect. The reasons for this are not altogether clear, but it may be that in the latter situation families become accustomed to improved living standards and do not wish to involve themselves with the expense and subdivision of income which children necessitate. On the other hand, economic depression, with accompanying unemployment, causes a sharp reduction in birth rates. These relationships are well illustrated by reference to statistics for the USA during the period 1920 to 1970 (Fig. 6.2).

During the present century **political influences** on population growth have emerged as a factor of some importance. Numerous examples exist of governments trying to influence their pattern of national population growth for economic and strategic reasons. During the late 1930s Germany, Italy and Japan all tried to increase their rates of population growth by offering financial inducements and concessions to those with large families; Australia has actively sought to boost its population by financing selective immigration. Conversely, the governments of India and Pakistan are promoting and encouraging programmes of birth control in an attempt to check their high rates of population increase, which have long counteracted economic progress.

It will be appreciated that these influences operate chiefly in societies where there is a high level of appreciation of economic change with appropriate responses and adjustments at the individual level. What then are the influences on birth rates in those parts of the world which have not made the transition from 'natural' to 'controlled' birth rates? What factors determine fertility levels in those parts of the world with crude birth rates in excess of 40‰?

Fig. 6.2. Birth rate, marriage rate and unemployment in the USA, 1920–70.

It is unfortunate that the nations of the world that experience the highest birth rates generally have the least complete and reliable statistical information. Nevertheless, there is sufficient evidence to suggest that **social customs and taboos** rather than physiological or environmental factors are the chief determinants. Concepts of marriage, monogamy or polygamy, variations in the average age of marriage, as well as religious proscriptions, all have an important bearing upon fertility levels. For example, in the Hindu society of India, girls marry on average at 16 years of age and produce their first child at 18. The Hindu religion places special importance on a male heir in a family, with the result that a large family may be produced before this is achieved. Furthermore, in order to ensure the survival of a male heir under conditions of high infant mortality, the family may be further increased. Thus, in many parts of India there is an average of seven children per family. In other words, reproductive behaviour is largely conditioned by social and religious customs which favour high fertility.

With the exception of the feeble reproductive capacity of people living in high-latitude regions, there is no evidence to suggest that climate or other environmental factors have any direct bearing upon fertility. Numerous localised studies of birth rates have revealed racial differentials, but there is no consistent pattern. For example, in Brazil the White population has a higher reproduction rate than the Negro population, while in the USA the reverse is true. It seems, therefore, that where such differentials exist they are probably a reflection of differences in social class and economic status, the effects of which have been noted earlier.

Relationships between fertility and **diet and health** have been examined by Josué de Castro in his book, *The Geography of Hunger*. He has drawn attention to the fact that the poorest and most undernourished people are usually characterised by the highest birth rates. This rapid increase in numbers further accentuates the poverty, thus creating a vicious circle which is extremely difficult to break. At the same time, of course, these underprivileged and impoverished people also suffer from the highest rates of infant mortality and lowest expectation of life, which partially counteract the results of high fertility rates.

Another factor which directly affects birth rates is **population structure**, especially the age composition of a population. Comparison of birth rates and fertility rates will reveal the importance of this factor. For example, in 1973 Japan and Spain had similar crude birth rates (19·4‰ and 19·2‰ respectively), but Japan's fertility rate was much lower (60‰) than Spain's (69‰) because her age composition was more youthful. In other words, areas with a high proportion of young adults may be expected to have high birth-rate figures. New towns, pioneer settlements and regions with high immigration rates tend to fall into this category. For the same reason urban areas often have higher birth rates than their rural neighbours, although their fertility rates may not be dissimilar.

We may conclude that the factors influencing the level of fertility in any area are largely economic, social and cultural rather than physical. Analysis is made difficult by the complex inter-relationships that exist between the factors concerned, and also, at a purely practical level, by the deficiencies and inaccuracies of much of the available data. It is fortunate that mortality statistics are generally more continuous and reliable than those relating to fertility, although again there are many uncertainties and problems.

Mortality

The term **mortality** is used to describe the occurrence of deaths among a defined population. **Infant mortality** is generally defined as the number of deaths of infants under the age of one year expressed per thousand live births. It has been described as 'perhaps the most sensitive barometer of the fitness of the social environment for human life' (Lewis Mumford). As a result of medical progress and improved health services, most nations have been characterised by declining mortality rates during the present century, a fact which contributes largely to the so-called 'population explosion' of modern times. The geographical study of mortality has attracted much attention since 1950 and medical geography, which concerns itself with the effects of environment on spatial variations in mortality, has emerged as an important field of specialised study.

As with fertility, a number of indices are employed to express levels of mortality. **Crude mortality rate** is simply a ratio between numbers of deaths and total population. Its manner of calculation may be demonstrated by the 1973 figures for the UK

$$\frac{669,475 \text{ (total number of deaths)}}{55,933,000 \text{ (1973 mid-year estimate of population)}} \times 1,000 = 12 \cdot 0‰$$

Crude mortality rates are greatly affected by the age structure of a population and a **standardised mortality rate,** calculated in the same manner as the standardised fertility rate referred to earlier, is essential for comparisons of mortality.

Life tables, which were first compiled for insurance purposes and are concerned with the effects of present mortality rates on the future age and sex composition of population, are also widely employed in the analysis of mortality. They involve following a hypothetical generation of births throughout life, subjecting it to varying mortality rates at different ages and plotting the number of survivors at each age. The **life table mortality rate,** which may be calculated from such a table, represents the probability of dying at a given age. It decreases to a minimum value at about the age of ten years and then increases steadily with advancing age. Another measure which may be extracted from life tables is that of **expectation of life** or average length of life. Expectation of life at birth is a particularly useful index since by its nature it is a standardised measure, unaffected by the age structure of the population in question.

The World Pattern of Mortality

Crude mortality rates in 1973 ranged from 4‰ (Guam) to 30‰ (Angola), with a mean value of 14‰. Countries with mortality substantially above the world average are located chiefly in South-East Asia, Africa and parts of Latin America. Populations in these parts of the world are generally characterised by high infant mortality (up to one third of all deaths may occur in the first year of life) and low expectation of life resulting from poor standards of diet, housing, hygiene and medical care. Conversely, low mortality rates are usually related to high living standards, good medical services, youthful population structure or a combination of these factors. It is interesting to note that virtually the same nations experience both the lowest mortality rates and the lowest fertility rates. Crude mortality rates of about 10‰ are typical of most countries of Western Europe, North America and Oceania, together with the USSR, Japan and certain countries of South America (Argentina, Uruguay and Venezuela). A number of small territories have also succeeded in reducing their mortality to surprisingly low levels; these include Fiji (5·0‰), Hong Kong (5·1‰), Kuwait (5·2‰), Singapore (5·5‰), Bahamas (5·7‰), and Puerto Rico (6·6‰).

A number of points should be emphasised at this stage. On a world scale the crude mortality rate is only about 40 per cent of the crude birth rate. In many countries the great gap that exists between fertility and mortality is producing an extremely rapid natural increase of population and placing a severe strain upon natural resources. This problem will be examined in Chapter Eight. At the same time world variations in mortality are smaller than variations in fertility. Among the economically advanced nations mortality decline has now been checked by the ageing of population caused by low fertility, while in many developing countries there have been spectacular reductions in mortality rates resulting from improved medical services, campaigns against infectious diseases and in some instances by economic progress and the raising of living standards. It has been said with some truth that there is now more equality in the face of death. If these trends continue, the influence of mortality on population growth will be further reduced and fertility will become even more firmly the main determinant of population growth.

Differential Mortality

The same basic influences on mortality which operate on a world scale, such as variations in standards of nutrition, medical care, hygiene and housing, also act as differentials within particular nations. In many instances they operate through differences in **social class**; that is to say, the underprivileged sections of a population are obliged to reside in substandard or slum housing and may be unable to afford an adequate, balanced diet, proper medical care and hospital treatment. Thus, the Black population of the USA has a substantially higher mortality rate at all ages than the White population, while in South Africa the level of infant mortality of the Black population is almost six times higher than that of the White population. In those countries which have a well-developed system of social security and welfare the class differential influences mortality less strongly. Workers enjoy the benefits of the same medical services as more fortunate individuals and may be housed in new towns or modern residential developments. Such concepts are fundamental in the planning of socialist and communist régimes.

Even in societies lacking extreme social differentials there are usually considerable internal variations in mortality. Although statistics are difficult to obtain, a number of studies have demonstrated the importance of **occupation structure** as an influence on mortality rates. It is obvious that certain occupations involve far greater hazards than others. Large mortality differences between husbands and wives will confirm that the essential influence is occupational rather than the product of living standards. Causes of death may also be indicative. Miners, for example, are vulnerable to a high level of accident risk as well as being prone to respiratory diseases such as pneumoconiosis and tuberculosis. Since many occupational groups tend to form residential concentrations it follows that occupation structure can constitute an important localised influence on mortality patterns.

Mortality also varies according to **place of residence**. Even after adjustments have been made for differences in age and sex structure, most urban areas still show higher mortality rates than rural areas despite their superior provision of medical services. This is especially true of large cities and conurbations. The reasons are not difficult to find; high population densities, crowded living conditions, high traffic densities, atmospheric pollution and the nervous strain of urban living all contribute to relatively high mortality rates. Mortality rates in the highly urbanised and industrialised regions of the UK, for example, are significantly higher than those in the rural areas.

Causes of Death

It is surprising to learn that even at the present time many countries make no attempt to compile detailed records of causes of death. In fact, countries that collect and publish such data represent less than half the total world population. Even the available data must be treated with great caution. Problems include vague declarations of cause of death such as 'senility', inaccurate diagnoses such as the presentation of a single cause when multiple causes operate, lack of uniformity in disease nomenclature which renders international comparisons difficult, and the fact that many causes of death have only recently been recognised, which invalidates historical comparisons. The World Health Organisation has sought to reduce these problems by the publication of its *Manual of the International Statistical Classification of Diseases, Injuries and Causes of Death* and by encouraging the compilation of accurate mortality statistics, but much remains to be done in this field of data collection.

Causes of death may be divided into two categories: **exogenetic** and **endogenetic**. The former are essentially the result of environmental influences and include infectious, pulmonary and digestive diseases associated with inadequate and contaminated food and water supply, and low standards of housing and hygiene. The latter, which are sometimes referred to as degenerative causes, are essentially biological and include congenital diseases and the gradual exhaustion of body functions.

A typical feature of demographic evolution is for a country to pass from a situation in which exogenetic causes of death predominate to one in which endogenetic causes are dominant; that is to say, where disease is little controlled, environmental causes hold sway, but with improved medical services these are gradually eliminated, leaving heart diseases and cancer as the main killers. Such an evolution may be demonstrated by reference to statistics for the UK (Table 6.1).

Table 6.1. **UK: Principal Natural Causes of Death**
(expressed per 1000 deaths)

Average 1848–72		*1970*	
Infectious diseases	321	Diseases of the circulatory system	506
Tuberculosis 146			
Scarlet fever 57		Heart diseases 306	
Typhoid 38		Cerebrovascular	
Respiratory diseases	148	diseases 137	
Bronchitis 66		Cancer	204
Pneumonia 57		Respiratory diseases	150
Diseases of the nervous system	129	Pneumonia 74	
		Bronchitis 50	
Diseases of the digestive system	83	Diseases of the digestive system	23
Diseases of the circulatory system	53	Diseases of the nervous system	13
Other causes	266	Infectious diseases	5
		Other causes	99

Sources: J. Beaujeu-Garnier, *Geography of Population*, Longman, 1966; *Annual Abstract of Statistics*, No. 108, HMSO, 1971.

In the mid-nineteenth century one person in three died from infectious diseases; in 1970 only one in two hundred. On the other hand, among the endogenetic causes, deaths from failure of the circulatory system, notably heart diseases, together with cancer have risen dramatically in recent decades and together accounted for over 70 per cent of deaths in 1970. A similar evolutionary process could be presented for most countries with mortality rates of less than 10‰. In most cases the changes have taken place over more than a century, but in a few instances the evolutionary sequence has been completed far more rapidly. Causes of death in Japan, for example, showed a complete reversal in the proportions of exogenetic and endogenetic causes between 1945 and 1970.

The struggle against death, which has occupied man since earliest times, appears to have entered a new phase during the present century. In most parts of the world there has been a definite reduction in mortality rates, usually accompanied by changes in the pattern of causes of death. The consequences of this development are clear: longer expectation of life and reduced infant mortality. Both have been hailed as successes, but at the same time they present new problems; namely, an increase in the number of elderly people and more mouths to feed. Unless success in the reduction of mortality rates is matched by resource development it must inevitably accentuate existing poverty and suffering.

Migration

Migration, the third component of population change, may be interpreted as a spontaneous effort to achieve a better balance between population and resources. Migration is defined here as a movement of population involving a change of permanent residence of substantial duration. Thus, no reference is made at this point to nomadism, transhumance, tourism, commuting or other similar movements which lie outside the scope of such a definition. Although there is an enormous diversity of types of migration in respect of cause, distance, duration, volume, direction and organisation, it will suffice for present purposes to draw a simple distinction between **international migration** and **internal migration,** the latter involving no crossing of international boundaries. A basic problem in the enumeration of migration relates to the distinction between short-term migrants and temporary visitors. How long must a visitor reside in a country before he is classified as an immigrant? Indeed, migration statistics must be treated with great caution, for definitions and methods of data collection vary widely from country to country.

From the evidence of those countries with reliable statistics it is clear that migration is generally a selective process; that is to say, there is a tendency for certain sections of the population to be more involved in migration than others, although this selectivity is less marked than formerly. Unless special circumstances operate, the majority of migrants tend to be young adults; international and long-distance internal migrants are predominantly male, while females are more involved in short-distance movements; single persons and married couples without children move more frequently than couples with children; professional workers are more mobile than unskilled workers.

Internal Migration

Very few countries have satisfactory data on movements of population within their boundaries. In Norway each commune has a register showing the destination of all those leaving the district and the area of origin of all newcomers, but such direct enumeration is extremely rare. More typically, internal movements of population must be inferred by indirect methods. For example, by comparing successive census totals it is possible to measure **net migration balance** by subtracting natural increase from total intercensal change. Alternatively, comparison of place-of-birth statistics with present residence may be suggestive of patterns of movement. However, such methods provide only a very incomplete and inadequate picture and in many instances geographers are obliged to conduct their own sample surveys.

Much attention has been directed towards the formulation of theories to explain patterns of migration. As early as the 1880s E. G. Ravenstein made a detailed study of migration statistics and presented papers on 'The Laws of Migration' in which the following principles were proposed (presented here in summary form):

1. The great body of migrants only proceed a short distance and consequently there takes place a universal shifting or displacement of the population, which produces 'currents of migration' setting in the direction of the great centres of commerce and industry which absorb the migrants.

2. Migration occurs in a series of stages. The inhabitants of a country immediately surrounding a town of rapid growth flock into it; the gaps thus left by the rural population are filled up by the migrants from more remote districts, until the attractive force of a rapidly growing city makes its influence felt, step by step, to the most remote corner of the Kingdom. Migrants enumerated in a certain centre of absorption will consequently grow less with the distance proportionately to the native population that furnishes them.

3. The process of dispersion is the inverse of that of absorption and exhibits similar features.

4. Each main stream of migration produces a compensating counter-current.

5. Migrants proceeding long distances generally go by preference to one of the great centres of commerce and industry.

6. The natives of towns are less migratory than those of the rural parts of the country.

7. Females are more migratory than males over short distances.

8. The incidence of migration increases with increasing technological development.

Subsequent studies have shown Ravenstein's broad generalisations to be basically correct and many of his concepts have been refined and expressed in more sophisticated forms. For example, the **Inverse Distance Law,** expounded by G. K. Zipf, states that 'the volume of migration is inversely proportional to the distance travelled by the migrants'. This may be expressed mathematically as

$$N_{ij} \propto \frac{1}{D_{ij}}$$

where N_{ij} is the number of migrants from town i to j and D_{ij} the distance between the two towns.

A number of studies have not only examined the relationships between volume of migration and distance, but have also considered the influence of 'opportunities'. In 1940, S. Stouffer proposed his **Theory of Intervening Opportunities**, in which he suggested that 'the number of persons going a given distance is directly proportional to the number of opportunities at that distance and inversely proportional to the number of intervening opportunities'.

$$N_{ij} \propto \frac{O_j}{O_{ij}}$$

where N_{ij} is the number of migrants moving from town i to j, O_j the number of opportunities at j, and O_{ij} the number of opportunities between i and j.

Stouffer defined 'opportunity' in terms of vacant houses, but others have interpreted it in terms of employment opportunities. Stouffer later refined his model by the addition of another variable, that of 'competing migrants at destination'.

Another interesting development has been the application of **gravity models** to migration analysis. Ravenstein's first law of migration implies that distance is a barrier to movement and that long-distance moves require exceptionally strong attractive forces. It may be argued, therefore, that variations in the size of destination centres will influence the strength of their attraction. At the same time, the volume of migration decreases with increasing distance from source, so that a nearby city may be expected to have a stronger attraction than a distant one of equal size. Such a situation may be expressed as

$$N_{ij} \propto \frac{P_i \times P_j}{D_{ij}^a}$$

where N_{ij} is the number of migrants moving from town i to j, P_i the population of town i, P_j the population of town j, D_{ij} the distance between towns i and j, and a is an exponent of distance.

According to the formula, the volume of migration between two towns i and is directly proportional to the product of the two populations and inversely proportional to an exponent of the distance between them. Thus, if we consider migration to London from Reading, Leeds and Cambridge it might be expected that the volume of the three migration flows would be in the ratio of $2 \cdot 1 : 1 \cdot 7 : 1 \cdot 1$.

	Reading	Leeds	Cambridge
Population (in thousands)	130	510	100
Distance from London (km)	61	306	87
	$2 \cdot 1$	$1 \cdot 7$	$1 \cdot 1$

If the actual value of any one of the migration flows were known it would be possible to estimate the other two. Numerous assumptions are, of course, implicit in such a model; for example, that apart from the friction of distance there is equally unimpeded movement between each source and destination, and the idea that members of each of the sending populations are equally attracted to the destination. In reality, as Stouffer has shown, variations in the availability of housing and employment complicate the model. Nevertheless, the basic formula can be weighted in various ways to give a closer approximation to reality. An example is given below.

$$N_{ij} \propto \frac{XP_i \times YP_j}{D_{ij}^a}$$

where X and Y might be values of $0 \cdot 5$ and $1 \cdot 0$ respectively to take into account the different levels of attraction of the two towns, low at i and high at j.

It could be argued that inequalities of one type or another are virtually preconditions of migration. Such an idea underlies the '**Push–Pull Theory**', which has long been implicit in much of the writing on migration. 'Push' factors are those influences which are thought to initiate migration flows; they are the adverse conditions which cause population to seek a living elsewhere and include, among others, low wages, poverty, famine, unemployment and natural disasters. 'Pull' factors are the attractions, real or imagined, of destination areas; they include high wages, cheap land, attractive living conditions and opportunities for economic advancement.

Many recent studies of migration have tended to accept a general background of 'push–pull' factors, but have also pointed out that any migration flow may also be interpreted as the aggregate result of numerous personal decisions about whether or not to move, when to move, and choice of destination. Thus, emphasis is increasingly being placed on the **psychology of decision-making**. D. J. Bogue, for example, has discussed migration-stimulating situations and examined the factors influencing choice of destination. One problem in such an approach is the fact that the decision to migrate may not necessarily be a rational one.

At the present time many studies are concerned with the construction of mental maps which attempt to represent the **perceived environment** rather than the real world situation. As pointed out in Chapter Two, the mental picture of an area may be of more geographical significance than reality. Such a line of argument is particularly relevant in migration studies, where choice of destination may be strongly influenced by the migrants' impression or perception of an area.

Types of Internal Migration

Detailed descriptions of the various types of internal migration lie beyond the scope of this book, but it may be of interest to draw attention to certain typical and recurrent types of internal movement. The importance of these various categories of movement depends to a large extent upon the stage reached in the social and economic evolution of the country concerned. For example, the development of rural settlement often shows phases of advance, stability, retreat and reoccupation. Similarly, rural–urban migrations often involve a phase of rapid urbanisation or concentration of population followed by a gradual diffusion from the urban centres.

Reference was made in Chapter Five to the ecumene–nonecumene concept, and it was suggested that an advancing settlement frontier was characteristic of earlier times. At present, extension of the inhabited world proceeds only slowly. Examples of recent **pioneer advance** may be noted in parts of the Soviet and Canadian Arctic, in certain desert areas such as the Negev, and in parts of the equatorial forest such as the Amazon Basin. Successful new settlement in such areas is inevitably government sponsored, for at the present time the individual pioneer is rarely able to confront nature singlehanded with success.

More typical at the present time are the numerous examples of **rural depopulation**. Decline of rural settlement by migration loss is generally most pronounced in the isolated or peripheral districts of a country or in areas of exceptional physical hardship. Under these circumstances the 'push' stimuli operate particularly strongly. The process may be well illustrated by reference to the North-West Highlands of Scotland, the high mountain valleys of the Alps, or the skerries and islands off the Norwegian coast; all are characterised by declining populations, largely as a result of a long-continuing negative migration balance. Because of the age-selectivity of migration, the process is cumulative. The younger sections of the population tend to move away, with the result that birth rates fall and death rates rise, thus accentuating the simple loss of numbers by migration.

The bulk of these rural migrants eventually find their way to the towns.

Indeed, the process of **urbanisation** is the most powerful and universally dominant form of internal migration at the present time. New towns are being created, large cities are becoming ever larger and groups of towns and cities are merging to form conurbations. The processes involved will be examined more closely in Chapter Seventeen. At this point it is sufficient to note certain of the results of the urbanisation process. In the UK, for example, the 1971 census classified 77 per cent of the population as urban. A comparable proportion of urban population is found in many other countries, including Australia, Israel, the Netherlands and Belgium. In Japan the proportion of town-dwellers rose from 22 per cent in 1925 to 72 per cent in 1970; in the USSR from 18 per cent in 1926 to 57 per cent in 1973; and in France from 46 per cent in 1921 to 72 per cent in 1974.

What, if any, are the limits to this process of urbanisation? Statistics indicate that in the case of many cities the limit may already have been reached. There is evidence to suggest that the congestion, overcrowding, inflated land and property values and health hazards of the inner districts of many cities have generated a movement of decentralisation or **suburbanisation**. A large proportion of those who actually work in the inner city can now only afford to purchase a house in the outer suburbs. Thus, between 1961 and 1971 all the Inner London boroughs maintained an established trend and showed a loss of population, while during the same period the outer suburban districts were all distinguished by vigorous population increase. A similar decentralisation is evident in most major cities in the UK and is indicative of the latest phase in the changing pattern of internal migration.

Many characteristic features of internal migration are revealed in Fig. 6.3, which shows the inter-regional balance of recent migration in Norway. North Norway, the region of greatest hardship, is characterised by a negative migration balance and loses population to all other regions. Conversely, the main centre of attraction is the country's most highly urbanised region, centred on the capital Oslo. A recent census revealed that over 60 per cent of Oslo's population were not born in the city, but had migrated there from other parts of Norway. Much of this drift to south-east Norway is in stages via other urban centres such as Bergen and Trondheim.

International Migration

Whereas internal migration merely alters the distribution of population within a country, international migration results in either a gain or loss in total numbers. A further difference lies in the fact that international migrants are generally involved in long-distance movements, often to a totally new physical and social environment, with the result that assimilation and integration are correspondingly more difficult.

Many of the causes of international migration are essentially the same as those which initiate internal population flows. The 'Push–Pull' theory, for example, can be readily applied to international movements, as illustrated by the great flow of migrants moving from Ireland, Scandinavia, Greece and southern Italy to North America during the late nineteenth and early twentieth centuries. At the same time it will be evident that analysis of international migration simply in terms of economic conditions in the areas of origin and destination or in relation to actual or perceived distance is complicated by the many legal restrictions, racial policies and political barriers which impede the

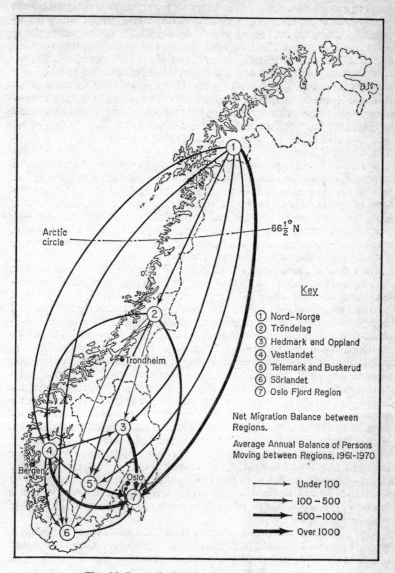

Fig. 6.3. Internal migration in Norway, 1961–70.

free movement of people on a world scale. Most restrictions on immigration are both quantitative and qualitative; that is to say, they are designed both to reduce total entry and also to exclude certain ethnic groups which for ill-defined reasons are considered undesirable. Examples of the latter type of restriction include the White Australia Policy, the quota system of the USA and the Commonwealth Immigration Policy of the UK. In contrast to these barriers to immigration there are also many examples of voluntary or enforced migration motivated by political, racial or religious persecution. Examples include the Jewish migration to Israel since 1948, the massive displacements of population following the partition of the Indian subcontinent in 1947, and the expulsion of Asians from Uganda in 1972.

The Results of Migration

The main **demographic** results of migration have been indicated earlier. Internal migration produces changes in distribution, whereas international movements cause changes in both total numbers and distribution. The selectivity of migration also produces changes in population composition. Sending areas become depleted of young adults, while receiving areas show a high proportion of population in this age group. Migration is also sex-selective, and in the following chapter examples will be given to show how it can produce a significant imbalance in the ratio between the sexes.

The **economic** consequences of migration are far less easy to evaluate and have been the subject of much discussion. A great deal depends on the economic conditions prevailing in both the sending and receiving areas, together with the 'quality' of the migrants. While it is quite clear that the movement of large numbers of people between two countries must have important repercussions, it is nevertheless impossible to establish firm rules or to predict the economic consequences. In the sending areas the loss of large numbers of people by emigration can cause an ageing of the population, loss of the most vigorous section of the population, and a slowing down of resource development. On the other hand, in small areas of extreme population pressure, the loss of numbers may be beneficial and lead to a rise in living standards. In the destination countries large numbers of immigrants may be either a burden or stimulus to development. Assessment must take into account the age, health, occupational skills and educational attainments of the immigrants, together with the economic needs of the receiving country and its ability to absorb increased numbers. Mention should also be made of the purely financial aspect whereby large flows of capital take place between immigrants and their homeland. Recent studies have shown this to be particularly important in respect of Italian and Greek immigrants in the USA, Chinese in the UK and Algerians in France.

Finally, mention must also be made of the **social** consequences of migration. In many parts of the world, problems of race, language and religion have their origins in an earlier pattern of migration. Migration has the effect of bringing different races, language groups and religious communities into contact, and all too often, into conflict. First-generation immigrants tend to settle in urban environments and to establish themselves in national or religious groups, thus forming urban **ghettos**, often overcrowded and with consequent social problems. Rural concentrations of immigrants also exist, such as the Dutch communities in Ontario, the Scandinavian settlements in the American Mid-West and the districts of German settlement in southern Brazil. On a larger scale, the early settlement of a country by different religious or language groups can be a source of continuing friction and conflict; consider, for example, the Afrikaaners and British in South Africa, or the French and British in Canada. On the other hand, there are those who take a more optimistic view, and, despite the problems, interpret migration as a vital process in the exchange of ideas between different cultures and the diffusion of knowledge in the complex web of civilisation.

Conclusion

Changes in population distribution and composition are the result of the interaction of the three components of population change: births, deaths and migration. Values for all three show marked regional variations. Birth rates, which are influenced by a wide variety of social and economic factors, generally exceed mortality and migration rates, and fertility is therefore the main determinant of population change, although a universal decline in mortality rates has contributed very largely to the rapid twentieth-century growth of world population. Patterns of migration, including their causes and effects, have long attracted the attention of geographers, and there have been many attempts to produce a theoretical framework to aid the understanding of the processes involved.

Suggested Further Reading

Barclay, G. W., *Techniques of Population Analysis*, Wiley, New York, 1958.
Benjamin, B., *Demographic Analysis*, George Allen & Unwin, London, 1968.
Cox, P. R., *Demography* (4th edn), Cambridge University Press, Cambridge, 1970.
Stamp, L. D., *The Geography of Life and Death*, Collins, London, 1964.
Thomlinson, R., *Demographic Problems*, Dickenson Publishing Co., Belmont, 1967.

CHAPTER SEVEN

POPULATION COMPOSITION

The composition or structure of a population at a given time may be regarded as the product of the processes of demographic change described in the previous chapter. The term 'population composition' is vaguely defined but is generally taken to include those characteristics of population for which quantitative data, especially census data, are available. Thus, studies of population composition normally include reference to the spatial variations of such factors as age, sex, marital status, family and household size, occupation, nationality, language and religion. In fact, the number of attributes which may be studied in this way is enormous, as reference to the wide range of population maps included in any good national atlas will indicate.

Broad distinctions are sometimes made between **physical** or **innate characteristics** such as age, sex and race, and **social** or **acquired characteristics** such as marital status and occupation. Many population characteristics such as social class, family and household structure, have received almost exclusive attention from sociologists, while geographers in practice have shown themselves to be interested in only a limited number of aspects of population composition, notably age and sex structure and ethnic and occupational structure. This chapter considers just the latter aspects.

Age Structure

The age structure of a population—that is to say, the number of males and females in each age group—is an expression of the processes of fertility, mortality and migration as they have operated during the lifetime of the oldest member of the population. It has been said that age structure records the demographic and to some extent the socio-economic history of a population over a period of about a century.

Since the average age of a population provides no indication of the wide distribution of ages about the mean, it has been found more useful to divide a population into three **age groups** and to consider the proportion of total population in each group. The three groups, which are variously defined, are as follows: children (0–14 or 0–19 years), adults (15–59, 15–64, 20–59 or 20–64), and aged (60 and over or 65 and over). Examination of age-group statistics for different parts of the world shows that the proportion of adult population is the least variable of the three groups. The chief regional differences lie in the proportions of children and old people. On the basis of these variations three **types of age structure** have been identified: namely, the West European type, with less than 30 per cent children and about 15 per cent aged population; the United States type, with 35–40 per cent children and about 10 per cent aged; and the Brazilian type, with 45–55 per cent children and only 4–8 per cent aged population. Most of the developing countries of the world fall into the last category. It should be noted that the proportion of adults is lowest in this type of age structure, in some cases only 40 per cent of the total population. Under these circumstances economic progress is difficult, for the economically active section of the population is relatively small and must support a large non-active population. Fig. 7.1 shows the age structure of various countries by means of a triangular graph, which is a commonly employed device for portraying age structure.

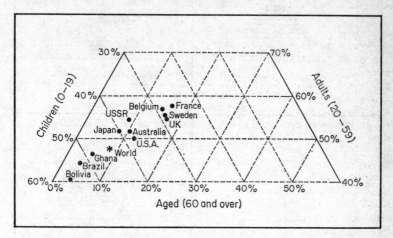

Fig. 7.1. Triangular coordinate graph showing age structure in selected countries. Percentages on each axis are of total population. The same type of graph may be used for showing intercensal changes within a single country.

The relative proportions of the three age groups may be clarified by the calculation and mapping of **age indices**. These simply express the total for one group as a percentage of the total for another group. Of the various age indices that may be calculated, the **old-age index** and the **dependency ratio** are the most widely used. The former is simply the number of aged people as a percentage of the adult population, while the latter is the combined total of children and aged population as a percentage of the adult population.

A more detailed picture of age structure than is possible with either age groups or age indices may be obtained by the construction of an **age pyramid**. Each age group of a population is represented by a horizontal bar, the length of which is proportional to the percentages of males and females in that age group. Males are arranged to the left and females to the right of a vertical axis, which is divided either into single years or intervals of five years.

The form of such a pyramid can indicate a great deal about the evolution of the population portrayed. A **stationary population**, with unchanging fertility and mortality rates over a long period of time, produces a regularly tapering pyramid; a **progressive population**, with an increasing birth rate and high mortality, produces a wide-based and rapidly tapering pyramid; a **regressive population**, with a declining birth rate and low mortality, produces a narrow-based pyramid. Many intermediate types may also be noted. Fig. 7.2 shows examples of the progressive, stationary, regressive and intermediate types of population pyramid.

With practice it is possible to elucidate the short-term effects of factors such as migration, war and epidemics from the form of age pyramids, as well as the

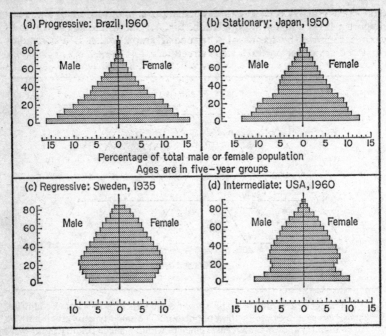

Fig. 7.2. Progressive, stationary, regressive and intermediate types of population pyramid.

more obvious long-term effects of fertility and mortality. The population pyramid for France illustrates this point very well (Fig. 7.3). During the First World War more than one million men of the generation born before 1900 were killed, a fact which, coupled with the longer life expectation of women, explains the asymmetrical shape of the upper pyramid. Another direct effect of the First World War was a marked reduction in births between 1915 and 1919, hence the deep indentation between the ages of 48 and 52 years. Furthermore, when the reduced generation of 1915–1919 reached the age of parenthood, a further drop in the birth rate occurred, which also coincided with the losses of the Second World War, thus creating a second indentation in the pyramid between the ages of 22 and 30 years. Post-war birth rates have been markedly higher than in earlier decades, hence the relatively wide base of the pyramid. However, in common with other West European countries, France has experienced a slight decline in its birth rate since 1965, despite the fact that the immediate post-war population 'bulge' had by then reached the age of parenthood, so that the lowest levels of the pyramid show a slight regression.

Sex Composition

Examination of published statistics shows that there are considerable regional and national differences in the proportions of the two sexes. These spatial variations are of interest to geographers in view of their social and economic implications. The ratio of the two sexes in a population is normally expressed as the number of males per 100 or 1,000 females, or vice versa.

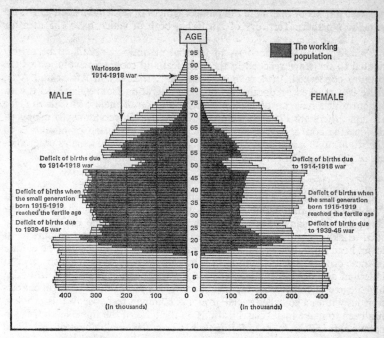

Fig. 7.3. Population pyramid for France (1968).

For reasons which are not clear, a feature of human populations is the fact that male births consistently exceed female births, although the degree of masculinity at birth varies from country to country. In the UK in 1973, 107 males were born for every 100 females. In developing countries infant mortality is markedly higher among males than females so that the excess of males at birth may be cancelled out within less than one year, as in the Ivory Coast where at the age of one year there are only 90 males per 100 females. Even in the economically advanced countries male mortality is higher than female mortality at all stages of life so that the excess of males at birth is progressively eliminated, until from about the age of 30 onwards there is an increasing predominance of females. On the other hand, in certain developing countries where women endure a deprived and subordinate role in society and often suffer high mortality rates in childbirth, the overall sex-ratio may show a deficit of females. For example, in India in 1971 there were 104 males per 100 females.

The sex-ratio of any area will be greatly influenced by the effects of migration as well as the preponderance of male births and the differential mortality rates of the two sexes. In earlier times international and long-distance migration almost always showed a marked predominance of males, thus creating a serious imbalance in the sex-ratio of both the sending and receiving areas. For example, in the USA in 1910, during the period of maximum immigration, there were 106 males per 100 females, while in Australia at the turn of the century there were 110 males to every 100 females. At present, areas with the greatest surplus of males are the pioneer fringes of settlement such as Alaska and the Northern Territory of Australia, both of which have 135 men for every 100 women.

The degree of sex selectivity of internal migration appears to be closely related to the stage reached in the technical and economic evolution of the country concerned. In developing countries, especially in Africa and Asia, there is a marked predominance of male migration from villages to towns. Indian towns have an unusually high proportion of males; in Calcutta, for example, there are 175 men for every 100 women. In economically advanced nations the converse is generally true. With the exception of migration to centres of mining and heavy industry, and military towns, females predominate in the process of rural depopulation and urbanisation.

Ethnic Composition

Consideration of the ethnic composition of populations raises the difficult problems of definition and classification of racial groups. Although man is a single species, many physical types are recognisable on the basis of criteria such as skin colour, hair structure and colour, eye form and colour, nasal form, head form, body form and size and blood group. In the case of certain of these criteria, such as stature, it is not always easy to distinguish between inherited and acquired characteristics. Furthermore, it is unusual to find a high degree of coincidence between more than a few of these physical characteristics within a so-called racial group. A common response to this problem has been to make racial classifications on the basis of the single factor of skin colour alone. Even more unfortunate has been the employment of social and political factors such as language, religion, nationality and country of birth, as indicators of race. The whole subject of race is, of course, bound up with myths of racial superiority and the evils of racial segregation and discrimination. Nevertheless, the geographer frequently has need to distinguish 'ethnic groups', for ethnic differences are frequently associated with demographic differences as well as economic, social and political problems in many parts of the world.

Plural Societies

Nearly all societies contain some degree of ethnic diversity, especially in their largest towns and cities. In many instances, multi-racial or plural societies have their origins in the period of European overseas expansion and colonisation. In regions subjected to this process, one generally finds four types of ethnic group: the indigenous population, such as the Amerindians, Bantu and Melanesians who occupied the area prior to the arrival of the Europeans, the descendants of the European colonists, a non-indigenous coloured population brought in by the Europeans as slaves or indentured labourers to replace or supplement the indigenous population for manual work, and people of mixed race, often forming distinctive groups such as Cape Coloureds, Creoles, Mestizos and Anglo-Indians.

Racial diversity is not necessarily a cause for social or political division, but where minority groups in a multi-racial society have reduced opportunities for economic advancement or restricted liberties and rights, then the problems created are very great indeed. Such problems tend to be least where integration is most widely accepted and practised, as in Latin America, and most serious where social segregation is practised, as in South Africa with its system of apartheid.

On a more local scale the existence of urban ghettos is a serious social problem in many countries. The term ghetto refers to the segregated areas of large cities occupied by minority groups. In the USA, for example, the majority of Negroes, Puerto Ricans and Mexican–Americans are forced by various social and economic pressures to reside in areas in which they themselves are dominant, and it has been noted that not one of the hundred largest urban areas in the USA can be said to be without a ghetto. Such areas are characterised by low incomes, high unemployment, substandard housing, neglected amenities and high levels of delinquency and crime. The development and growth of Negro ghettos in the USA has been analysed by R. L. Morrill by means of a probabilistic simulation model incorporating factors such as the birth rate of the ghetto population, the rate of Negro immigration into the ghetto and the prejudice of local White residents and their resistance to movements of Negroes out of the ghetto into adjacent areas. He concluded that 'integrated residential living appears to be a remote possibility. Even if Negroes achieve equality in education and employment, housing integration will probably lag several decades behind. Thus, existing ghettos are likely to continue to expand.' According to Morrill, the best short-term hopes of improvement lie in the upgrading of conditions in the existing ghettos, and the prevention of the establishment of new ghettos.

Ethnic Minorities in the U.K.

In the UK there are no official statistics concerning the size or distribution of racial minorities. This is because it has long been felt that the process of distinguishing minority groups by including questions in the census on colour, religion or other such factors would not only be extremely difficult to operate but would also hint of discrimination. On the other hand, it might be argued that racial minorities face special social problems, and that basic information about their numbers and distribution is an essential prerequisite for the provision of social services appropriate to their needs. The census does, however, collect data on place of birth, and this can provide some guide in the estimation of total numbers. Table 7.1 shows the country of birth of immigrants in the UK in 1971 according to the census of that year.

Table 7.1. Country of Birth of Immigrants in the UK (1971)

New Commonwealth	India	322,670
(Independence and Commonwealth membership	West Indies	302,970
since 1945)	Africa	176,060
	Pakistan	139,445
	Cyprus	72,665
	Others	143,355
Old Commonwealth (Australia, Canada, New Zealand)		145,250
Irish (excluding Northern Ireland)		720,985
Non-Commonwealth and non-Irish immigrants		1,076,935
Total		3,100,335

Source: UK Census, 1971.

In considering these figures a number of points must be borne in mind. First, not all of those born in 'New Commonwealth' countries such as India, Pakistan and the various countries of the Caribbean are coloured people. For example, there are an estimated 100,000 White people born in India now resident in the UK. Secondly, many of those enumerated, especially the Africans, are not permanent citizens, but students and others who might be expected to return to their country of origin. On the other hand, coloured children born in the UK are not included in these totals. Thus, no more than a rough estimate of the size of the coloured population is possible with present data sources. However, most expert estimates of the total coloured population of the UK lie between 1·0 and 1·2 millions, or approximately 2 per cent of the total population. Thus, where racial problems exist, they stem from the uneven distribution and local concentrations of coloured population rather than total numbers.

Numerous studies have been made of the distribution of specific minority groups in the UK. For example, C. Peach in a detailed analysis of West Indian migration to the UK prior to the restrictions imposed by the various Commonwealth Immigrants Acts of the 1960s demonstrated that the volume of migration to the UK rose and fell according to the demand for labour from year to year. He also noted that on arrival West Indians tended to settle predominantly in urban areas, especially the old, depressed inner city districts which had long been losing population by the normal processes of internal migration. In other words, the West Indians acted as a replacement population in many of the least desirable districts of London, Birmingham and other major cities. Other studies, notably those of the Chinese and Indians in London, have emphasised the close community ties which exist within these immigrant groups, but have also drawn attention to their low level of social interaction with the population as a whole. Although Britain has avoided the worst manifestations of racial discrimination and prejudice, its various minority groups are still far from fully integrated into society.

Occupational Structure

Size and Sex Composition of Working Population

The economically active section of any population is generally defined as 'those who are engaged in remunerative occupations and who seek a livelihood in such occupations'. Excluded from this definition are children under working age, retired persons, students, housewives and those living from investment income. The size of the active population in relation to total population is determined not only by purely demographic factors such as age structure, but is also greatly influenced by economic and social considerations. The 'active' proportion of the total population ranges from about 30 per cent in developing countries to about 50 per cent in the economically advanced countries. According to official statistics, values range from 22 per cent in the Ivory Coast to 54 per cent in the USSR, although some doubt may be cast on the accuracy of the extremely low figure for the former country.

Variations in values appear to be largely due to differences in the level of female employment; whereas the proportions of 'active' males range from 50 per cent to 70 per cent of the total male population, the equivalent figures for females are from 1 per cent to 50 per cent. The proportion of active females tends to be highest in predominantly agricultural countries or in advanced countries which have preserved a strong rural way of life. In many such countries, over 80 per cent of the female working-population is employed on the land. Traditions and social customs also play their part; the lack of female emancipation in Muslim societies, for example, is reflected in figures for Iraq and Pakistan, where only 1·6 per cent and 3·8 per cent respectively of the female population are economically active. Political régime may also exert an influence. In communist countries a high proportion of women have been liberated from domestic work by the provision of crèches, nurseries and other social services, so that in the USSR, for example, 50·5 per cent of the female population is economically active, a figure exceeded only by Romania with 52·7 per cent. Similarly, Albania, Bulgaria, Czechoslovakia and Poland all have values of over 40 per cent.

In countries with a high proportion of children and/or old people, the proportion of working population is correspondingly small. The point is particularly true of advanced countries where there may be compulsory education up to the age of 16 years and widespread opportunities for further education, and where compulsory retirement in many occupations is at the age of 65 or even earlier. France, which has one of the highest percentages of old people in the world, provides a good example of this situation. In 1970 there were only 2·5 active persons for each retired person (see Fig. 7.2). The economic implications of this can be seen in the fact that in 1970 the French National Railways had to pay out three times as much in pensions as in wages.

Variations in the relative size and sex composition of the active population generally exist between urban and rural areas. In the towns there are better opportunities for further education and vocational training, and employment opportunities are more varied and rewarding for women. Urban employment usually provides the security of pension schemes for the elderly so that the length of working life is generally shorter than in the country, where many agricultural workers are in employment for virtually the whole of their life. Thus, there are radical differences in the employment structure of town and country areas.

Variations in Employment Structure

The statistics published by various countries relating to the composition of their working populations present many problems of interpretation. An enormous variety of occupations is found in any country, and many different schemes of classification are employed in the presentation of this information. There is, in fact, an urgent need for a uniform system of classification to facilitate international comparisons of data. The UN Statistical Commission has proposed a system of data classification based on nine categories. The suggested groupings are as follows: 1. agriculture, forestry, hunting and fishing; 2. mining and quarrying; 3. manufacturing industries; 4. building and construction; 5. electricity, gas, water and sanitary services; 6. commerce, insurance and banking; 7. transport, storage and communications; 8. other services; 9. not classifiable elsewhere.

An alternative form of classification reduces the above categories to three major groups: **primary activities**, including agriculture, forestry, hunting, fishing and extractive industry; **secondary activities**, including manufacturing industry, building and construction work and power industries; and **tertiary**

activities which are non-productive of material goods and which include transport, communications, commerce, administration and other services.

The proportion of working population engaged in these three groups varies markedly in different countries according to their level of economic development. In developing countries more than 80 per cent of the working population is generally engaged in primary activities, with approximately 5 per cent in secondary and 15 per cent in tertiary activities. Many of those in the latter group are involved in domestic service or petty trading. An important phase of economic and social development in many countries has been characterised by the processes of industrialisation, rural depopulation and urbanisation. This is reflected in a marked increase in the proportion of working population engaged in secondary, and to a lesser degree tertiary, activities, at the expense of the primary group. In the most economically advanced countries a further phase of development has been marked by increasing complexity and diversification of secondary activities and a transference of labour from the primary and secondary sectors to the tertiary sector, so that in the USA, Canada, UK, Australia and New Zealand, for example, more than 45 per cent of the working population is employed in various types of service activity. It has been calculated that for every 100 industrial workers in these countries there are at least 130 others in supporting ancillary services. Largely on the evidence of the USA, where the tertiary sector accounts for 59 per cent of the working population, it has been suggested that these trends may continue until approximately 70 per cent of the working population is engaged in service activities, a complete reversal of the occupation structure found in developing countries.

Recently, certain writers have distinguished and defined a group of **quaternary activities**, using the term to refer to 'the more intellectual occupations . . . whose task is to think, research and develop ideas'. Although statistics are lacking for such a group, it is suggested that in the most economically advanced nations these quaternary activities involve a small but growing proportion of the population, characterised by the highest incomes and a high degree of mobility in the process of career advancement.

Despite certain limitations, figures for the three main groups of economic activities serve as a useful basis for distinguishing between primitive economies dominated by primary activities, especially agriculture, and complex industrial–commercial economies in which employment in tertiary services exceeds even manufacturing industry. Between these extremes are many intermediate types.

Unemployment

In any country or region a certain proportion of the potentially active population will be out of work at any given time. Changes of residence and employment inevitably produce a form of unemployment which involves 2 per cent to 3 per cent of the potentially active population. Where unemployment is maintained at this minimum level a country would normally be regarded as experiencing full employment. Indeed, it might be argued that unemployment levels below 2 per cent are indicative of a shortage of labour, for, with relatively small numbers seeking work, employees may be unable to fill specialised job vacancies.

Consideration of the nature of unemployment will show that precise definitions and enumeration are by no means easy, for it may take many forms. It may be persistent and general as in the USA during the 1930s, when 14 per cent of the labour force was out of work, or it may be cyclic, as in regions which rely heavily upon seasonal activities or in high-latitude regions where winter conditions impose restrictions upon levels of economic activity, causing unemployment levels to increase by up to four times. Alternatively it may be structural, affecting only certain industries or groups of industries. The term concealed unemployment is also used to describe a situation in which employees are working on 'short-time' or otherwise operating at less than full capacity. Data on unemployment must therefore be approached with caution. There is general agreement among experts that the published statistics for most countries tend to understate the true level of unemployment and completely ignore the existence of underemployment.

There is a delicate balance between labour requirements and the availability of labour. The equilibrium can be upset by a variety of factors, both economic and demographic, including fluctuations in economic prosperity, changes in international trade, government policy, technological developments such as automation, as well as changes in the size of the labour force. In essence, the equilibrium is concerned with the relationships between natural and human resources, and these are further discussed in Chapter Twenty-Five.

Conclusion

Almost any attribute of a population, either physical or social, which is capable of measurement and enumeration may be regarded as constituting part of the composition or structure of that population. In this chapter four such factors—age, sex, race and occupation—have been examined, and it has been shown that these attributes are subject to significant spatial variations at regional, national and international level. These variations are the result of particular interactions of the basic processes of demographic change examined in the previous chapter. Factors of population structure may have important social, political and economic implications.

Suggested Further Reading

Allen S., *New Minorities, Old Conflicts: Asian and West Indian Migrants in Britain*, Random House, New York, 1971.

Barton, M., *Racial Minorities*, Collins, London, 1973.

Coates, B. E., and Rawston, E. M., *Regional Variations in Britain*, Batsford, London, 1971.

Field, F., and Haikin, P., *Black Britons*, Oxford University Press, London, 1971.

Hill, C., *Immigration and Integration: A Study of the Settlement of Coloured Minorities in Britain*, Pergamon, Oxford, 1970.

Jones, E. A., *The Social Structure of Modern Britain* (2nd edn), Pergamon, Oxford, 1972.

Kwee Choo, N., *The Chinese in London*, Oxford University Press, London, 1968.

Peach, C., *West Indian Migration to Britain. A Study in Social Geography*, Oxford University Press, London, 1968.

Rose, H. M., *The Black Ghetto. A Spatial Behavioural Perspective*, McGraw-Hill, New York, 1971.

Trewartha, G. T., *A Geography of Population: World Patterns*, Wiley, New York, 1969.

CHAPTER EIGHT

POPULATION GROWTH

In Chapter Five the point was made that patterns of population distribution are never static. Any map of population distribution is simply an approximate representation of that distribution at a particular time. Although most countries contain certain regions which have shown a loss of population in recent years, almost all the nations of the world are currently characterised by an overall increase in numbers. Indeed, during the present century the world's population has increased at a rate unprecedented in the history of mankind, so that world population growth has become one of the most urgent problems of the present time.

Population growth may be expressed in various ways. The term **natural increase** refers simply to the difference between the numbers of births and deaths. More useful is **natural increase rate**, which is calculated by subtracting deaths from births and dividing by the total population for a specific year. However, natural increase rate ignores the age composition of the population and is not a measure of replacement. For example, a population with a high proportion of young adults in the reproductive age group might have a positive natural increase rate and yet still be experiencing low fertility and lack of replacement.

Reproduction rates attempt to utilise data about present birth rates as a means of predicting future levels of population replacement. **Gross reproduction rate** is defined as the number of female babies born per 1,000 women in the reproductive age group. A refined version of this measure is **net reproduction rate**, which takes into account the fact that not all the female babies born survive to reproductive age and not all survivors will in turn have children. A net reproduction rate of 1,000, or 1·000 as it is usually expressed, is taken to mean thàt a population will maintain itself at its existing level. Indices above or below this figure suggest increasing or declining populations respectively.

None of these measures takes into account the effects of migration upon numerical changes of population. This is incorporated in the most basic measure, **annual rate of increase**, which simply expresses the annual increase in numbers as a percentage of the population at the beginning of the year. Such a measure involves easily accessible data, but is adequate for only very generalised comparisons of population growth. The usefulness of all of these measures is, of course, subject to the quality and reliability of the census returns or population estimates upon which they are based.

Population Projections and Estimates

In recent years there has been an increasing demand for estimates of future populations. Such information is required by both national and local governments and other institutions concerned with economic and social planning, as well as by business companies making estimates about the size and composition of future markets and labour force. Despite the increased demand on their services, demographers are well aware of their limitations in this field.

Population experts are unable to forecast or predict future population size or composition with a high degree of precision or certainty. An obvious analogy may be made with the predictive ability of the meteorologist. To make this clear, demographers refer less ambitiously to population estimates or projections.

It is generally agreed that the term **population estimate** refers to a short-term forecast usually based on reliable data concerning past and present births, deaths and migratory movements, whereas a **population projection** ranges further into the future and is based on certain assumptions about fertility, mortality and migration. In fact, it is normal for a set of projections to be calculated to show the effects of various assumptions. The results are not averaged; each is presented individually, together with a statement of the assumptions upon which it is based, and the user is left to make his own assessments.

Although the computation of future populations is mathematically complicated and beyond the scope of this book, it should be remembered that the validity of the calculations involved depends on the reliability of the assumptions made about the input data. The main problem generally lies in the estimation of future trends in fertility, the chief long-term determinant of population growth. Nor can projections take into account special direct influences, such as wars, famine, disease or major advances in medical science, or indirect influences, such as social and economic change within a country. It is not surprising, therefore, that comparisons of past projections with the actual populations enumerated on the forecast dates show a disappointingly low level of correlation, even in those countries where the data involved are reasonably accurate. For example, population projections for the UK published in 1937, 1942 and 1944 gave predicted totals for 1951 of 45·0, 47·5 and 46·1 millions respectively. The actual 1951 figure was 48·8 million. A 1921 projection for the USA predicted a population of 190 millions by the year 2000, a figure which was exceeded by the mid-1960s. Projections of world population have been subject to even more massive errors. In 1951, UN demographers forecast a world population of between 2,976 and 3,636 millions for 1980. Even the highest of these figures was reached towards the end of 1970, ten years ahead of the predicted date. These examples serve as a cautionary note when considering the following sections which deal with world population growth and predictions of population growth to the end of the century.

World Population Growth

Total world population in 1975 was estimated by the UNO as 4,000 millions. This may be compared with figures of 2,486 and 2,982 millions in 1950 and 1960 respectively. Over the past decade the increase in world population has been at a rate of approximately 70 million persons per year. This figure is equivalent to a population larger than that of the UK or about one third of the population of the USA. It represents a monthly addition to the world's population equivalent to about half that of Greater London, or a daily addition equal to the population of Swansea or Sunderland. If such a growth rate were to continue, world population would double by the end of the century.

Contemporary growth rates can best be appreciated by placing them in their historical context. The first thousand million of population was reached by about 1820, the second about 1930, the third about 1960, and the fourth about

1975. That is to say, after requiring hundreds of thousands of years to achieve the first thousand million, a second thousand million was added in just over a century, a third in about three decades, and a fourth in just 15 years. The five and six thousand million marks are expected to be reached in 1986 and 1995 respectively. United Nations demographers, who have always been rather conservative in their population forecasts, are currently estimating a total world population of between 6,000 and 7,000 millions by the end of the century. As a UN Population Bulletin of 1951 pointed out, 'it took 200,000 years for the world's human population to reach 2,500 million, it will now take a mere 30 years to add another 2,000 million'.

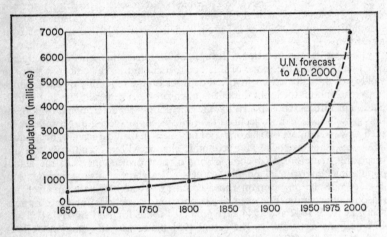

Fig. 8.1. World population growth since 1650.

Clearly this rate of increase cannot continue for more than a very limited period without creating drastic dislocations in the world pattern of settlement and economic activity. Among demographers there is universal agreement that uncontrolled human increase is a luxury that the world can no longer afford.

Historical Background to Contemporary Growth Rates

The present rate of world population growth is a relatively recent phenomenon. Although accurate and reliable data are not available for earlier times, it nevertheless seems clear that the spectacular acceleration of population growth dates from the mid-seventeenth century. It is thought that the annual rate of population growth doubled during the period 1650–1850, doubled again between 1850 and 1920, and yet again between 1920 and 1970. Total world population in 1650 has been variously estimated by historical demographers as being within the range of 470 and 545 millions, increasing to 1,091–1,175 millions in 1850, and 2,486 millions in 1950.

The distribution of this overall growth has been very uneven during the past two centuries. The greatest influence on total world growth has been the increase in numbers of the Asian population, from an estimated 257 millions in 1650 to 2,204 millions in 1973. The Asian share of total world population has long shown a steady increase to its 57 per cent in 1973. During the eighteenth and nineteenth centuries Europeans also contributed very strongly to the total world growth, both in Europe and in areas to which they emigrated. However, Europe's rate of increase has slowed down very considerably during the present century, and Europe, excluding the USSR, now accounts for only 12 per cent of the total world population, compared with 18 per cent in 1920. Both North and South America have increased their numbers by more than ten times since 1800. The population of Africa, which long remained constant at approximately 100 millions, has also experienced a rapid increase in the last 100 years. The distribution of world population by continents in 1973 is shown in Table 5.1 (page 55).

A Model for Population Evolution

Despite the inadequacy of the population data available for earlier times, various attempts have been made to formulate a general model of population growth. It should be appreciated that such models of demographic evolution are largely based upon the European experience, and that it does not follow that other types of region will necessarily pass through the same pattern of evolution, or that the timing and sequence of stages will be comparable from one region to another. Indeed, from the evidence available from developing countries it would appear that the western experience is frequently 'telescoped' as a result of economic aid programmes and technical assistance. In other words, it is possible to establish only a very general model of demographic evolution against which particular trends and patterns of growth may be assessed.

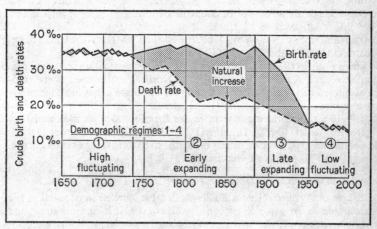

Fig. 8.2. A model of demographic evolution.

The most simple model involves four stages of population growth. In Stage One, referred to as a **primitive demographic régime**, fertility and mortality both stand at very high levels, but are subject to considerable short-term fluctuations. Population growth under these circumstances is slow or intermittent. Such a situation is typical of countries with low levels of economic development, low expectation of life, and lack of both birth and death control. It is the type of situation which persisted in Britain until the early eighteenth century, and which is still common in parts of tropical Africa and South-East Asia, where birth and death rates both exceed 30‰.

Stage Two is the **expanding or youthful demographic régime**. This stage is marked by a sharp decline in mortality rates, while fertility remains high. The result is a very rapid natural increase of population. This is accompanied by an ageing of the population; that is to say, an increasing proportion of old people. This second stage prevailed in Britain until about 1870. Statistics suggest that many countries of the world are currently in this type of situation, many having acquired these characteristics very suddenly and within the last two decades. Abrupt declines in mortality rates without any corresponding decline in birth rates have produced a number of startlingly high natural increase rates; for example, those of Kuwait (38·1‰), Colombia (35·1‰), Mexico (34·1‰), Iraq (33·8‰), Paraguay (33·8‰) and many others. To appreciate the significance of these figures it should be noted that a consistent increase rate of 30‰ will cause a population to double in less than 25 years. Also included in this group are a large number of countries with less spectacular, but nevertheless very high, natural increase rates, such as Ghana (28·8‰), Liberia (28·8‰), Brazil (28·3‰), Uganda (25·6‰) and Tanzania (25·1‰).

The Third Stage, which may be termed a **late expanding demographic régime**, is characterised by medium fertility (birth rates approximately 20‰) and low mortality (mortality rates approximately 10‰). Population growth is less rapid than in the previous stage, but since many of the countries concerned have by this stage acquired very large populations, the absolute increase in numbers produced by even a modest growth rate is very considerable. Included in Stage Three are a number of countries of southern Europe, such as Spain (10·7‰), Yugoslavia (9·3‰) and Portugal (9·0‰), as well as the USSR (9·0‰) and many New World countries such as New Zealand (12·0‰), Australia (10·4‰) and Canada (8·1‰).

Stage Four in the model is referred to as a **low fluctuating or mature demographic régime**. A number of countries of North-West Europe may be said to have entered this final stage of demographic evolution. They are characterised by low birth rates (approximately 12‰) and low mortality rates (approximately 10‰). Natural increase rates are therefore low, as indicated by the figures for Austria (0·6‰), Belgium (1·2‰), UK (1·9‰) and Sweden (3·0‰). A few countries even have an excess of deaths over births; for example, Luxembourg (−2·1‰) and West Germany (−1·6‰).

Population Growth in the Developing World

It is generally agreed that a small manageable increase in population is not undesirable in an expanding economy. However, it is clear that beyond a certain level, population increase may become excessive, so that the economy is sapped and the problems associated with overpopulation such as poverty, malnutrition and starvation reach serious proportions. The problem lies in assessing when the optimum population for any given economy has been reached, or the point when population growth becomes excessive. Although the determination of optimum population is difficult, it nevertheless seems clear that most of the developing nations have already passed this point.

In the case of these countries it it often argued that the expansion of education, the introduction of economic and technical aid and the development of industry can relieve or even solve the problems. This idea appears to be based on the suggestion that industrialisation and urbanisation will create the same pattern of demographic evolution experienced in Western Europe as described earlier. Closer examination of this proposition shows that the situation in the developing world is, in fact, different in many respects from that which prevailed in Europe in the late eighteenth and nineteenth centuries. The developing countries start with a much larger population base than the European countries had at that time; their present rate of increase is much greater than that of nineteenth-century Europe, and they lack the outlets for massive overseas emigration which did so much to relieve population pressure during Europe's period of most rapid growth. Even if one holds to the view that the European model of demographic evolution will, in fact, be reproduced in the developing world, it should be noted that most of the developing nations are only just entering Stage Two, and there seems little prospect that, even if the European experience of 150 years could be 'telescoped', Stages Three and Four could not be reached until well into the next century. Clearly the outlook for the next 50 years is very serious indeed.

It is appropriate at this point to examine very briefly certain of the most critical areas of contemporary population growth. India, with a population of over 575 millions and an average density of 175 persons per square kilometre, demonstrates the problems facing many developing countries. Its death rate has declined steadily from 44‰ in 1890 to its 1973 level of 16·7‰, while an excessively high birth rate has fallen only very slowly in recent decades from 45‰ in 1930 to 42·8‰ in 1973. The 'gap' between births and deaths is thus widening and the population is currently increasing at a rate of 2·2 per cent, or almost 13 million per year. All economic progress is thwarted by the rapid growth of numbers. The various post-war development plans designed to increase production have barely kept pace with the growing demand for food, and as Premier Nehru pointed out in 1959, 'population control will not solve all our problems, but other problems will not be solved without it'.

China, with an estimated population of 814 million in 1973, is another country with both a massive population total and a very rapid rate of increase. Latest figures show a birth rate of 33·1‰ and a death rate of 15·3‰, giving an annual increase of approximately 2 per cent, or 15 million per year. If such rates were maintained, China's population would be approximately 1,850 million by the end of the century. Since 1948 a great deal of labour in China has been absorbed in agricultural collectivisation programmes and public works such as irrigation schemes, afforestation and road-building. Until recently this produced a sense of optimism which suggested that production could absorb population growth, but the latest information available indicates that China is examining the need for an official birth-control policy.

A rather different problem is presented by the countries of tropical Latin America. These nations have much smaller base populations, but even higher rates of natural increase than either India or China. Between 1950 and 1970 the population of tropical Latin America almost doubled from 84 to 155 million. The cause of this increase was the familiar 'gap' between birth rates and death rates. At the present time birth rates are generally over 40‰ and mortality rates around 10‰, producing annual increase rates of 2·8, 3·2, 3·4 and 3·1 per cent in Brazil, Colombia, Ecuador and Peru respectively. At the same time it is known that this part of the world has a rich endowment of natural resources. It is critical, therefore, that resource development should proceed rapidly before economic progress stagnates under the burden of overpopulation. At present rates the population of these countries will double within 25 years. Tropical Latin America requires immediate population control before the problems of overpopulation become too deep-rooted and the crisis of the Far East is duplicated there.

Population Growth: Attitudes and Interpretations

The various interpretations and theories of population growth have been divided into three broad categories: biological, cultural and economic. **Biological theories** suggest that the influences on human population growth are essentially the same as those regulating the growth in numbers of plants and animals. It has been argued, for example, that fertility diminishes and is regulated by increasing population density. **Cultural theories**, on the other hand, regard demographic growth as unique and emphasise the importance of man's reason and intellect in influencing his growth in numbers. The declining birth rates of the economically advanced nations are seen as evidence of man's ability to control his growth in numbers. **Economic theories**, especially those of Marxist–Leninist economists, emphasise the importance of economic factors, notably the demand for labour, as being the essential influences on growth rates, patterns of migration and population distribution.

Thomas Robert Malthus

Any comments on the interpretation of population growth must inevitably make mention of the writings of the Reverend Thomas Malthus (1766–1834). Malthus first expounded his ideas in his *Essay on the Principle of Population*, published in 1798. He was convinced that man would always be faced with the basic problem that his numbers increase more rapidly than food production. In his original book he suggested that population has a tendency to increase in a geometric ratio (1,2,4,8,16,32, . . .), while food production tends to increase in an arithmetic ratio (1,2,3,4,5,6, . . .), the former subject to population checks such as war, disease and famine, and the latter subject to the introduction of new developments in agriculture. Five years later he revised and modified his theory. His mathematical progressions were given less emphasis, although not abandoned, and more prominence given to 'moral restraint' as a check on population increase. Nevertheless, Malthus remained the supreme pessimist and saw little prospect of man controlling his growth in numbers.

Neo-Malthusianism

In his time, Malthus could not have foreseen the effects of the Industrial Revolution, the nineteenth-century improvements in transportation, or the opening up of the New World grain lands and ranching areas. For a long period, therefore, his fears seemed unfounded and his ideas were largely rejected or neglected. More recently, in the light of the changed demographic circumstances of the twentieth century, many individuals and groups have started to re-examine his ideas, to apply them to countries in the second stage of demographic evolution, and more especially to modify and re-interpret his concepts to fit the contemporary situation.

The view is frequently expressed, for example, that foreign aid to developing countries aggravates rather than relieves the problems of overpopulation, because, it is argued, according to the Malthusian principle, population will simply increase to meet the improved level of subsistence. All that is gained is an even bigger problem in the form of an increased population. Other neo-Malthusian groups advocate massive birth-control programmes in order to slow down rates of increase, although it should be noted that Malthus himself never sanctioned birth-control, which he regarded as a vice. Nevertheless, it is true to say that many Malthusian concepts underlie the pessimistic views of those who regard the contemporary growth of world population with fear and alarm.

The Marxist Viewpoint

Most Marxist–Leninist economists argue that overpopulation and its asso-ciated problems are the result of the maldistribution and poor organisation of resources within and between countries. Overpopulation and poverty are seen as the results of a capitalist system of economic organisation. If society and economy were reorganised on socialist lines, it is argued, the problems could be solved. It is suggested that the labour of man is the basis of all wealth and, therefore, the greater the population, if organised on socialist lines, the greater the common well-being. On this basis the problems of overpopulation are dangerously oversimplified. For the USSR, with its vast lands and rich resources requiring manpower for development, the Marxist ideas might have some degree of relevance and validity. An expanding population might pro-duce increased wealth under Soviet conditions, but this argument is not valid under the conditions prevailing in China or in most other parts of the com-munist world.

Population and Resources

From the preceding remarks it will be evident that the ability of a country to absorb a large increase in population depends upon a number of factors, including its size, endowment of resources, social structure and especially the stage reached in its economic development. Rates of population growth and population density should always be considered in relation to a nation's resources and economy. At the same time it is clear that such resources are not easily measured or evaluated. Different societies and cultural groups have different needs, traditions and aspirations. Consequently there are no simple indices of overpopulation, optimum population or underpopulation. Optimum population in one country may be overpopulation in another, depending on the level of economic development in the countries concerned. Similarly, changing social and economic conditions mean that optimum population today may be overpopulation tomorrow.

Optimum Population

Optimum population has been defined as the size of population enabling maximum per capita output and the highest possible living standards under given economic and technological conditions. For example, a decline in the population of the UK to 30 million would necessitate the abandonment of many resources and a reduction in public services, with a resultant decline in living standards. Conversely, an increased population of 80 million could not be supported at present living standards with the current level of resource development. Optimum population lies somewhere between these two extremes, but to say exactly where is extremely difficult. Expert opinion suggests that the present population of 55 millions in the UK is probably close to, or even beyond, the optimum figure, and there is a growing feeling that the Government should formulate an official population policy, although population growth in the UK has slowed down very substantially since 1970.

Overpopulation

Overpopulation exists where there is an excess of population over utilised or potential resources. It may result from an increase in population or a decline in resources; that is to say, overpopulation occurs when resource development fails to keep pace with population growth. While there is no simple measure of overpopulation, it is usually distinguished by low per capita incomes, low and declining living standards, high levels of unemployment, pronounced outward migration and high population density. In extreme cases its symptoms may be hunger, famine and malnutrition. Inevitably overpopulation strikes hardest at those occupying the lowest levels in society—the landless, the smallholders, the unskilled and semi-skilled workers.

Underpopulation

Underpopulation exists when a population is too small fully to utilise its available resources, or where resources could support a larger population with no reduction in living standards. Examples of underpopulation are found in certain regions of low technical development such as areas of pastoral nomadism and shifting agriculture, but are uncommon among the economically developed nations of the world, although examples include the Canadian Prairies, parts of Australia, New Zealand and Argentina, all regions of extensive, temperate agriculture.

A World View

Many of the concepts described above have been applied to the problem of world population growth, and there is a large and growing literature devoted to the relationships between world population growth and the world's present and potential supply of food and other resources. The viewpoints and interpretations are varied. There are those who point with dismay at the present levels of hunger and malnutrition in the world, and predict a deterioration of the situation.

Regional outbreaks of famine strike the headlines with distressing regularity. Bihar, Biafra, Bangladesh and Ethiopia have been among the worst disaster areas in recent years. Less striking, but equally insidious, is the spread of malnutrition, causing impaired health and vitality and producing **deficiency diseases** among a very large proportion of the world's population. Deficiency diseases are caused by two main dietary gaps, protein–calorie malnutrition and vitamin–mineral deficiencies. They include kwashiorkor, nutritional marasmus, anaemia, trachoma, beri-beri, pellagra, goitre and many other diseases. In addition to these specific deficiency diseases, malnutrition also lowers resistance to many other diseases and infections, including yaws, bilharzia, tuberculosis, leprosy and malaria. It is estimated that over half the world's population have suffered at some time from one or more of these diseases, which produce a sapping of energy and initiative and an inability to cope with physical and intellectual effort. These effects are most serious in the developing world where such qualities are most urgently required. Any deterioration in the present situation would clearly have disastrous consequences for the future economic prospects of all nations.

On the other hand, there are those who hold a more optimistic view. They believe that large-scale birth-control programmes can at least check the present excessive rate of world population growth, and also suggest that many opportunities exist for increasing world food supplies. They draw attention to the possibilities for increasing yields from existing farmland, successfully extending the agricultural frontier into marginal areas, developing new sources of protein, and reducing loss and wastage by more efficient storage and distribution.

Whichever viewpoint is held, there is some hope to be gained from the fact that there is now a growing awareness of the serious nature and enormous scale of the problem. It is now realised that the accommodation at reasonable living standards of even the most modest forecasts of population growth to the end of the century will require massive efforts by all nations and international cooperation on an unprecedented scale.

Conclusion

Various indices may be employed for measuring population growth and replacement. None is entirely satisfactory for comparing growth rates in different parts of the world. Even more caution is required in the interpretation of population estimates and projections, which have a history of unreliable and inaccurate prediction. Despite these limitations it seems clear from even the most modest estimates that the world's population is likely to double by the end of the century, most of the increase occurring in the developing nations, especially those of South-East Asia and tropical Latin America.

The twentieth-century population explosion has brought us up against a number of harsh ecological facts. Man is now pressing hard on his environment and resources. There is an increasing imbalance between the world's population and its material resources. 'To stop this process means planned conservation in place of reckless exploitation, regulation and control of human numbers, as well as of industrial and technological enterprise, in place of uninhibited expansion. And this means an ecological approach. Ecology will become the basic science of the new age. . . . The aim will be to achieve a balanced relation between man and nature, an equilibrium between human needs and world resources.' (Julian Huxley)

Suggested Further Reading

Clarke, J. I., *Population Geography and the Developing Countries*, Pergamon, Oxford, 1971.
De Castro, J., *The Geography of Hunger*, Gollancz, London, 1952.
Lowry, J. H., *World Population and Food Supply*, Arnold, London, 1970.
Malthus, T. R., *Essay on the Principle of Population* (1798), Dent, London, 1973.
Park, C. W., *The Population Explosion*, Heinemann, London, 1965.
Stamp, L. D., *Our Developing World*, Faber, London, 1960.

Taylor, L. R. (Ed.), *The Optimum Population for Britain*, Academic Press, London, 1970.
Trewartha, G. T., *The Less Developed Realm. A Geography of its Population*, Wiley, London, 1972.
Young, L. B., *Population in Perspective*, Oxford University Press, London, 1968.
Zelinsky, W., *Prologue to Population Geography*, Prentice-Hall, Englewood Cliffs, N.J., 1966.

PART THREE: ECONOMIC GEOGRAPHY

CHAPTER NINE

TRANSPORT: ADJUSTING SPACE BY REDUCING ECONOMIC DISTANCE

The exchange of goods and services is a central feature of economic activity, but since natural resources, manufacturing capacity and markets for products are not all located at the same place, this exchange involves movement. To link areas of demand with areas of supply, transport facilities have to be provided, and the history of transport is the development of increasingly effective methods of overcoming the friction of distance by the invention of new forms of transport, new methods of propulsion, new construction techniques and so on. This process has been very successful and the world economy today is characterised by the vast transfer of a wide range of goods and services on a global scale as areas of shortage are supplied by areas of surplus in an attempt to bring supply and demand into equilibrium.

The study of the patterns that this inter-regional transfer has produced is an important element in transport geography and has two aspects. First, the transport links themselves can be seen as a **network** which can be analysed to measure accessibility, and this concern with lines makes transport geography different from other aspects of the subject which are more concerned with points or areas. Secondly, the volume of traffic on these transport links can be measured as **flows** which produce a complicated pattern for study of a few principal and a large number of subsidiary routes. Transport flows and networks will be examined in the next chapter.

Transport geography is also concerned with the study of transport as a space-adjusting technique. Man adjusts space to suit his needs, bringing sources of supply and demand together by reducing the distance between them, and the analysis of **economic distance** is a second important aspect of study. The reduction of economic distance is important because it is not only a response to the market forces of supply and demand but can itself help economic development, in the way that the provision of the railways in the nineteenth century stimulated the development of the central USA. Transport as a space-adjusting technique will be examined in this chapter.

Transport Costs and Economic Distance

The transport of goods from areas of surplus to areas of deficiency increases their value, so that iron ore commands a much higher price in Tokyo than it does in Western Australia, but the transport of the iron ore involves a cost, and for movement to take place the cost of transport must be less than the increase in the value of the iron ore. The point where transport costs become greater than the increase in value is the maximum **economic distance** that any commodity can be carried and this varies considerably between commodities. A £500 camera can be carried much further than £500 worth of cement because of the difference in the transport costs involved.

Transport costs vary for a number of reasons. First, they vary with distance, so that a journey of 1,000 km will cost more than a journey of 100 km in the same carrier. Secondly, they vary with the type of terrain to be covered, so that it is more expensive to cross land than oceans and more expensive to cross mountains than plains. Thirdly, they vary with the type of carrier, so that petroleum can be carried more cheaply per tonne by pipeline than by road tanker. Fourthly, they vary with the type of commodity to be carried, so that it costs more to transport a tonne of beef which has to be refrigerated than it does to transport a tonne of coal. Finally, they vary with the degree of competition from other carriers, so that where a number of carriers operate on the same route, transport rates are usually lower than where one carrier has a monopoly. From this it is clear that transport costs will vary depending on the particular type, origin and destination of a cargo, but they will be made up of two basic elements which the customer or shipper has to pay. These two elements are the operating costs involved in the actual movement of goods, and the profits that the carrier expects when he determines his rates. The level of these costs is important to the shipper because they will affect his total costs and thus the market price that he sets in competition with other producers. Transport costs must therefore be minimised.

Operating Costs in Transport

Three types of operating cost can be distinguished in the transport of goods: **line-haul costs**, which are incurred in the process of moving and which are made up principally of fuel costs and wages; **overhead costs**, which represent the cost of equipment involved such as terminal facilities, ships or railway track, repair shops, offices and so on; and **transfer costs**, which are made up of indirect costs such as insurance cover for the cargo.

Table 9.1. Comparative Transport Costs per Tonne–Kilometre Between Methods

	Method	Cost (*Rail transport* = 100)
Land	Man	1,800–7,000
	Horse and cart	1,800
	Road	430
	Rail	100
Water	River	28
	Ocean	14
	Great Lakes	7
Air	Aircraft	1,500

After Van Royen, W. V., and Bengtson, N. A., *Fundamentals of Economic Geography* (5th edn), Prentice-Hall, Englewood Cliffs, New Jersey, 1964.

To move a wide range of goods over the far from uniform surface of the earth, many different forms of transport have been developed, each with its own cost structure and suitability for certain types of cargo. The costs of movement have been simplified in Table 9.1, which uses some US statistics to compare the cost of transporting one tonne of goods for one kilometre between different methods of transport, and using rail transport as the base (100) significant differences appear. These costs differ because, first, line-haul and terminal costs differ between various methods of transport and, secondly, because of the differing proportions of these costs in the make-up of total costs. As a consequence, some forms are more suited to particular distances than others.

In Fig. 9.1 the terminal and overhead costs of road, rail and ocean transport are shown at T_1, T_2 and T_3, and it is clear that the terminal costs of ocean transport—which needs the expensive provision of ports with elaborate handling facilities—are very high when compared with the terminal costs of road transport, where goods can be loaded at the kerbside. On the other hand,

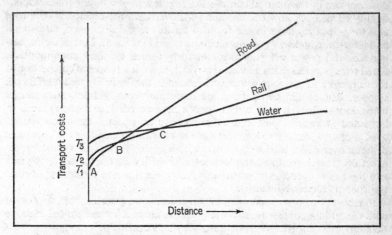

Fig. 9.1. The cost structure of different methods of transport.

the line-haul costs of road transport rise rapidly with distance because only relatively small loads are carried and the costs therefore have to be spread over a few items of cargo, while ocean line-haul costs rise very slowly with distance because costs are spread over much larger cargoes. Rail transport can be seen to occupy an intermediate position. Road transport is therefore cheapest over short distances (A–B), rail over medium distances (B–C) and ocean transport over long distances (beyond C), but this is a generalisation that is affected by many other advantages and disadvantages that the different forms of transport have.

Land Transport

Land transport is very important because most movement takes place overland but until relatively recently it was difficult to move bulky or large amounts of goods. The revolution in land transport came with the building of the **railways** after 1830, which radically altered space by linking many places, by bringing towns closer together and by opening the continental interiors to commercial agriculture and mining. Today the railways are less important than formerly but they still have many advantages for both goods and passengers. Passengers can be moved very quickly between large cities because trains travelling on their own routes can be timed to provide a regular and reliable service avoiding the congestion and delay which is often found on the roads, while goods, especially heavy goods, can be carried efficiently for medium and long distances because line-haul costs are lower than for other forms of land transport. On the other hand, high terminal costs, the inflexibility of routes, the problems of gradients, awkward loads and track maintenance have meant that competition from road transport has attracted goods traffic away from the railways, and over long distances, air transport can be attractive to passengers.

The **roads** have been the principal form of competition for the railways and since 1900 there has been a second revolution in land transport with the development of the internal combustion engine and new motor roads. Good-quality roads have now become almost universal in the developed countries and long-distance links in the form of motorways, autobahnen, autostrade and inter-state highway systems facilitate rapid movement. Lorries of increasing size and power carrying loads of forty tonnes are now commonplace. Road transport has many advantages which make it a powerful competitor to the railways and these are principally related to the flexibility that it offers the shipper. Routes and destinations are more numerous and deliveries can be made door to door, a wide range of goods can be carried from small parcels to large and awkward loads, and although road transport is most competitive over shorter distances, the increase in vehicle size is extending the economic distance over which lorries can operate. This flexibility has had a considerable effect upon settlement and the location of industry during the last fifty years and the general process of suburbanisation owes much to the spread of road transport (Chapter Nineteen).

In recent years a very specialised form of land transport has been developed with the building of **pipelines**. These pipelines are much more limited in scope than any other form of transport since they only operate point to point in a set route and are capable of carrying only a small range of goods, principally oil, natural gas and chemical products. For these products, however, pipelines are very efficient in cutting transport costs and they are being built to carry oil across Alaska, natural gas across Britain and in many other places where large flows are expected. It has been suggested that other commodities such as coal could be mixed with water and pumped through pipelines but whether or not this is taken up, pipelines have become an important link in the transport systems of many countries, especially the USA where they carry about 17 per cent of all freight per tonne–kilometre.

Water Transport

For most of man's history water transport has been the cheapest and most convenient form of transporting bulky or large quantities of goods, and today **ocean transport** still provides the longest binding links of the world economy. The great advantage of ocean transport lies in its low line-haul costs, achieved because a ready-made interconnected route is available, little friction has to be overcome thus reducing fuel costs, large carriers of up to 500,000 tonnes can thus be used spreading costs thinly over a large cargo, and the result of this advantage is that distance is relatively unimportant On the other hand, terminal costs are high because of the need for transhipment at ports where land and ocean meet, and since ocean shipping is relatively slow-moving it is largely used for the long-distance movement of bulk cargoes.

In recent years considerable changes have been taking place in ocean transport to make it even more efficient. The size of bulk carriers such as oil tankers and ore ships has been increasing, since larger ships are cheaper per tonne to build, cheaper per kilometre to operate and can carry cargo more cheaply. To take these large ships, special ore ports such as Port Talbot and tanker terminals such as Bantry Bay have been built, and many established ports have had to build outports near deeper water, such as Rotterdam-Europort.

The consequence of this activity has been the bringing of previously remote sources of minerals, especially iron ore, within economic distance of the consuming nations, often at the expense of closer but poorer deposits. Specialised ships such as liquefied gas carriers and container ships have also been built and the increasing use of containers which are packed and unpacked away from the port has led to an increase in the speed and safety of handling general cargo, but has also led to a reduction in the number of jobs in the ports and an increase in competition between ports for the container traffic.

Water transport has also been important inland where rivers, lakes and canals have been used. In Britain, canals played an important part in the Industrial Revolution, carrying bulky materials in the great canal age from 1760 to the beginning of the railway age in 1830, but British canals are too short and narrow to compete effectively with road and rail transport, and their future, unless renovated for leisure craft, is limited. Canals in Europe, however, together with navigable rivers, continue to provide a cheap if slower form of transport for the carriage of bulky articles, and an extensive water network links the major industrial centres. In North America, rivers and canals, especially the Mississippi–Ohio and the St. Lawrence Seaway also carry vast quantities of goods.

Air Transport

Air transport is the most recent development in man's efforts to reduce distance and it differs from other forms of transport in that it is only concerned with the rapid transport of high-value goods and passengers. The principal drawback to air transport is its cost. Aircraft are expensive to build and operate, they carry only small cargoes, and require elaborate provision in the form of airports and controlling systems. On the other hand, light valuable cargoes can be moved rapidly on a world-wide scale and long-distance passenger traffic is now almost entirely carried by air. In difficult areas such as Brazil or northern Canada air transport is often the only way of moving easily, and although other forms of transport have to be provided if bulk cargoes such as minerals have to be moved, air transport plays an important role in development.

There have been two recent changes that might revolutionise air transport itself: the development of supersonic transport aircraft such as Concorde, which will bring New York within three and a half hours of London, and, more important still, the development of wide-bodied 'jumbo jets' capable of carrying large loads. It seems improbable that air transport will ever be a prime mover of anything other than people, but in the passenger transport field aircraft have radically rearranged space.

This brief review illustrates the fact that each form of transport so far developed has its own cost structure that gives it advantages and disadvantages, making it attractive to some commodities and not to others, but costs alone do not determine how attractive a transport method is to a shipper because the freight rate that he pays must also include the profit of the carrier.

Profits and Freight Rates

Freight rates are thus made up of costs and profits, and the level of profit that the carrier takes depends on a number of considerations. In a simple situation this is based on what the carrier thinks he can get and what the shipper is prepared to pay, and in the heyday of the canals in Britain very large profits were made. Some indication of the profits to be made can be gained from the fact that freight rates of 2s 6d (12½p) per ton fell to 4d (1½p) per ton on the Loughborough Navigation in 1836 when its monopoly was challenged by the railway. **Competition** between different carriers on a route is a major factor determining the level of profit. The railway–canal conflict is nicely reversed today in the USA where the presence of the New York State Barge Canal has held down railway freight rates between New York and the Great Lakes so that freight is carried more cheaply from Chicago to New York (1,446 km) than from Chicago to Philadelphia (1,309 km). Competition is therefore a major factor affecting the level of profit of a carrier but it is not the only consideration and the structure of freight rates is extremely complex.

The basic factor determining the level of a freight rate is the **commodity** to be carried and quite different rates are charged for carrying a tonne of iron than for carrying a tonne of cameras. The lowest rates are charged for non-breakable, non-perishable commodities such as coal or iron ore because such materials can be loaded and unloaded by bulk methods and they can travel in open wagons at low speeds without deteriorating. Many commodities need much more careful handling, however, and the extra costs that this involves are reflected in the freight rate. Milk must be carried in special containers that can be transported quickly and cleaned easily, and many non-perishable items such as precision instruments or passengers need special care in transit and elaborate provision has to be made for secure or comfortable journeys. As a general rule, manufactured goods are charged a higher freight rate than raw materials or semi-finished products because, being of higher value, they can bear a higher transport charge and this has had a marked influence on the location of industry. Raw materials are carried for less per tonne-kilometre than for finished products, so that the economic distance that raw materials can be carried is greater than finished products and this has meant that market locations have been possible for many industries, despite the need to carry large amounts of raw materials.

Distance is a second factor affecting the level of freight rates, although as indicated, economic distance is more important than absolute distance. Fig. 9.1 shows that the cost of transport, although varying between methods, does not rise in direct proportion to distance, and that a journey of 1,000 km need not be twice as expensive as a journey of 500 km. Costs fall off per tonne-kilometre with distance because terminal costs can be spread over more kilometres, and rates often reflect this **long-haul advantage**. On the other hand, if the journey is broken and transhipment has to take place, the additional terminal costs at this **break-of-bulk point** can increase costs considerably, although some carriers give **in-transit privileges** to shippers by carrying raw materials at long-haul rates to a break-of-bulk point where the shipper has a processing plant, and continuing those rates for the product that leaves the plant. Grain from the Prairies of Canada that is milled into flour enjoys this privilege which is given by the carrier to attract business.

A third factor affecting the level of freight rates is the **quantity and frequency of movement** of commodities. Commodities that are moved in large amounts can be given low rates since a small profit per unit gives a large cumulative profit. On the other hand, small cargoes which do not fill a lorry or railway wagon involve the same line-haul costs as a full load and these must be spread over fewer items. Similarly, favourable rates are given to regular shippers for both goodwill and because profits, although smaller, are assured.

Other concessions can also be made to shippers by carriers; if a carrier has a major commodity flow from A to B he may offer special rates from B to A to avoid his containers being returned empty. Such **back-haul rates** are given on the return of grain flows from the Prairies to the Atlantic ports of North America.

On the other hand, freight rates are not all based on concessions and it has already been seen that higher rates may be charged for fragile or perishable cargoes. Premiums may also be charged for special services. These are clearly seen in the passenger field where premium rates are charged on the fastest Inter-City trains in Britain; similarly, the fare for a supersonic flight is higher than that for a normal flight.

Governments and Transport Policy

It would be a mistake to assume that the study of economic distance only involves an examination of the costs and profits that go to make up freight rates, for there is a third factor affecting the provision and pricing of transport facilities; namely, the transport policies of national governments, which often override purely economic considerations.

Governments are taking an increasing interest in transport decisions for three major groups of reasons: economic, political and social. Transport is of vital **economic** importance to a country because it constitutes a major part of the infrastructure within which economic activity takes place, but infrastructure investments usually require such large amounts of capital and bring only long-term or indirect returns that governments are often the only agents capable of financing them. In financing the provision of transport, however, governments can use the new transport links as instruments of policy and one of the objects of the motorway building programme in Britain has been to facilitate the dispersal of industry from the South-East by making the Development Areas, established as part of a general regional policy (Chapter Twenty-Three), accessible to and from the major market areas of the country. Governments have also used pricing policies to concentrate industry in chosen areas, and in Germany freight rates were set lower for iron ore than for coal by successive governments before 1945 so that French and Swedish ore could be imported more cheaply than coal could be exported; this helped produce a concentration of industry in the Ruhr despite the fact that more ore than coal had to be moved to produce a tonne of steel.

Often closely associated with economic factors, **political** factors are important considerations affecting government involvement in transport policy, especially where this concerns pricing. In order to place foreign goods and commodities at a disadvantage by making them more expensive, tariffs are often placed on imports. An extreme example of this existed in Western Europe until 1956, when artificial barriers in the form of double handling charges on fuel and ore crossing international boundaries were removed by the ECSC. The provision of transport facilities has also been a factor of political or strategic importance, and the trans-continental railways of the USA and Canada were considered vital elements in the creation of coast-to-coast political units because they provided the necessary binding links.

Increasingly, transport is considered a vital **social service** rather than a profit-making business, and as a result government involvement or control has become as important a factor as competition. Uneconomic railway lines are often kept open and bus services are provided in remote country areas. Two kinds of subsidy are used to pay for these services: either direct cash grants to cover losses, or indirect subsidies in the form of uniform rates imposed over the whole transport system to enable high-profit routes to support those that make a loss. In this way British Rail is able to provide services in isolated rural areas such as East Anglia or the Scottish Highlands. Governments must also exercise controls to ensure that the transport system operates as far as possible for the public good by preventing restrictive practices such as price fixing by monopoly groups and yet must avoid unnecessary competition.

There is a growing realisation that even more control on private transport may be necessary in the developed countries because of congestion in the road system, and proposals such as subsidies for the railways to attract traffic away from the roads, the restriction of parking places in towns and special charges for driving in the centre of large cities have been suggested, but such controls are politically difficult to apply.

Conclusion

Man's attempts to adjust space to suit his needs by the reduction of economic distance are very complex because they involve the movement of a wide range of goods over a large number of routes within complex economic, social and political frameworks. Nevertheless, improvements in transport technology and changes in supply and demand have produced a constantly changing economic world. Economic distance continues to be reduced within the great movement system that transport provides, and this system is examined in the following chapter.

Suggested Further Reading

Appleton, J. H., *The Geography of Communications in Britain*, Oxford University Press, London, 1962.

Benson, D., and Whitehead, G., *Transport and Distribution Made Simple*, W. H. Allen, London, 1975.

Paterson, J. H., *Land, Work and Resources*, Arnold, London, 1972.

Taafe, E. J., and Gauthier, H. L., *Geography of Transportation*, Prentice-Hall, Englewood Cliffs, New Jersey, 1973.

CHAPTER TEN

TRANSPORT: FLOWS AND NETWORKS

The resources that man uses are distributed over the earth in an uneven and discontinuous pattern and to bring these resources together in places where they can be used, many methods of transport have been developed to form a complex system that plays a central role in economic activity. The previous chapter indicated that the basic purpose of transport is to overcome the effects of the physical separation of areas of supply from areas of demand by reducing the economic distance between them, and that movement will take place if this distance is not too great. However, this is only a part, although an important part, of the explanation of how the movement system operates.

The development of a transport system carrying flows of goods and services is the result of many complex decisions involving two closely related groups. First, the transport users who decide which routes they will use and the volume of traffic that will flow along them, and secondly, the transport agencies who provide the transport links that make this movement possible. Using this basic distinction this chapter will examine the nature of the flows of goods and services that characterise economic activity and the framework within which such movement takes place.

Flow Theory

Conditions Affecting Flows

Transport systems develop in response to demands for movement, and the conditions that affect the development of transport systems have been ordered into a simple model by E. L. Ullman, who identified three basic factors affecting interaction between regions: complementarity, intervening opportunity and transferability.

Interaction between regions will not take place unless two conditions are met. First, there must be a demand in one region that can be met from another region, and secondly, as a corollary to this, the area of demand must be able to pay for the supply so that a two-way movement develops. In this way the two regions can be said to be complementary and this **complementarity** is the basis for interaction between them. Complementarity was once seen as a simple interaction between environmentally different areas, with mid-latitude industrial areas exchanging manufactured goods for primary produce from the Tropics, but the term has been widened to include movements between similar environments. Nevertheless, complementarity is still produced by differences between regions, and if each region was self-sufficient no movement would take place, but regional specialisation is a characteristic of industrial economies and flows of machinery form an important element in world trade.

Complementarity is such an important factor in producing interaction that it results in the large-scale movement of low-value bulk cargoes such as iron ore, grain or petroleum over many thousands of kilometres, but interaction does not take place simply because regions are complementary. English pubs do not normally sell beer brewed in Milwaukee or Pilsen despite their

109

complementarity. Buyers and sellers have alternative courses of action open to them and a buyer can always buy from another source, buy another product, produce it himself or do without.

Interaction between complementary regions will only take place if there are no **intervening opportunities** for buyers or sellers to get what they require more easily. English people buy French wine because little wine is produced in England, but they do not buy French bread because English bakeries present an intervening opportunity between English buyers and French bakeries. Interaction patterns are constantly changing because intervening opportunities appear or disappear. The development of synthetic rubber as an industrial product has reduced the amount of interaction between the Tropics and the middle latitudes as demand for natural rubber has lessened, while on the other hand the depletion of the Lake Superior iron ore deposits has resulted in the use of South American and African ores in the USA, and complementary regions much further apart have been able to interact. The principle of intervening opportunity, used here in an economic context, can be compared with its use in the field of migration studies (Chapter Six).

Interaction between complementary regions will also only take place if the product can be moved. To some extent this depends on the nature of the product and although there is a demand for Spanish sunshine among British holidaymakers it is not transferable unless demand travels to supply, but in commerce the **transferability** of a product is largely determined by the costs of movement. Movement will only take place if the cost, or economic distance, is not too great, because if it is the buyer will then take an alternative course of action. It follows from this that transferability decreases as economic distance increases and any intervening opportunity will be taken if it reduces this distance. Since economic distance and intervening opportunity are not constants, transferability will change considerably from time to time.

The development of transport systems must be seen as a process in which complementarity, operating to encourage movement between regions, is balanced against intervening opportunity and transferability, which operate to discourage movement. This distinction between these factors has been incorporated into a simple theory of interaction using a gravity model similar to that discussed in Chapter Six.

The Gravity Model

The impetus to develop theories of interaction comes from the fact that flows are not random but appear to have some regularity which can be observed and analysed. It was noted in the nineteenth century that migration flows were related to the size of the groups involved and the distance separating them in the same way that bodies in the universe are attracted to each other according to Newton's Law of Universal Gravitation and this physical law is being applied to the geographical attractions that Ullman called complementarity.

Newton's Law states that bodies are attracted to each other in proportion to the product of their masses and inversely as the square of their distance, so that large bodies have more attraction for each other than small bodies, but that this attraction decreases as the distance between them increases. Applying this law to economic geography, complementary regions attract each other and flows of goods will take place from areas of surplus to areas of deficiency, and the greater the attraction, or demand, the greater the flow will be. Movement will take place as long as the value of the goods in the area of demand is greater than the cost of their purchase and transport from the area of surplus, but as distance increases and transport costs rise, interaction will decrease. The volume of movement will depend on the amount of goods needed to reduce the price difference between the two areas to the level of the transport cost, when no further movement will take place.

Using the gravity model the geographer should be able to predict the amount of interaction between two regions by multiplying the mass of the two regions and dividing the result by the distance between them, but how are mass and distance to be measured?

Using population statistics, the size of a population may be considered as its mass, but the amount of economic interaction will not depend on its numerical size, but on its economic size as measured by its purchasing power, and a rich country such as Sweden will be involved in world trade to a much greater extent than Cuba, which has a similar population size. A mass such as purchasing power is difficult to define precisely and therefore it is not always easy to measure complementarity.

Nor is it easy to measure distance, which operates to discourage movement, because economic rather than geographical distance governs interaction between regions. Nevertheless, attempts have been made to identify the nature of the relationship between distance and interaction and this has resulted in the establishment of the general principle of **distance decay**. This states that the amount of interaction between two places decreases as the distance between them increases, so that the amount of contact between people living in two towns of similar size five kilometres apart will be much greater than between two towns fifty kilometres apart. Attempts to measure this relationship have shown that it is difficult to be precise about the way in which contacts decrease with distance except that the general pattern is that contacts fall off rapidly over a short distance and then decline much more slowly over longer distances. The form of the distance-decay curve is shown in Fig. 10.1. and work on

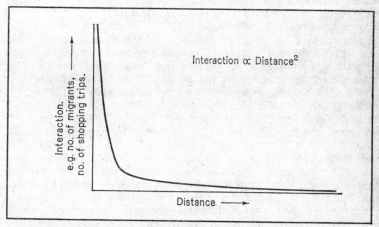

Fig. 10.1. The form of the distance-decay curve.

migration in Sweden suggests that as in Newton's Law, the number of contacts declines inversely as the square of the distance, so that the number of contacts at 20 kilometres ($1/20^2 = 1/400$) will only be a quarter of those at 10 kilometres ($1/10^2 = 1/100$). Despite the problems of measurement, gravity models provide an attractive, if simple, explanation of interaction, and with refined measures of mass and distance could be used to predict the consequences for traffic flows of the establishment of any new mass such as an airport, shopping centre or oil field.

Whatever the causes of interaction, flows of goods, services and information within or between regions are a central part of economic activity, and the next section will examine the development of the international flows of world trade.

The Development of the Network of Interchange

Trade arises mainly from regional economic differences and serves to balance production and consumption by moving goods and services from areas of surplus to areas of deficiency. The flow of goods that constitutes trade must be conveyed by transport methods and to enable trade to take place, extensive transport networks have been developed. International trade has been an important factor in the development of the advanced economies and there is a strong relationship between volume of trade and standards of living, but archaeological evidence shows that early man was already travelling considerable distances to obtain raw materials and exchange goods, and the history of trade is the development of an increasingly complex network of interchange.

Throughout history sophisticated systems of exchange have existed, from prehistoric trade in stone axes and amber to our present massive commodity transfers. Phoenician, Roman, Viking, Arab, Venetian, Spanish, Portuguese, Dutch and British traders have all played an important role in the trade of Europe, and as early as Roman times, European and Asian traders linked almost all of the Eastern Hemisphere from Spain to China. However, as long as goods were costly to transport and could be shipped only in small quantities, trade was confined to goods of small bulk and high value such as spices, silks, wine and honey that could bear the costs and risks of carriage. There were exceptions such as the Roman trade in grain from North Africa, but the cargo revolution did not really begin until the late eighteenth century.

Before that time, however, there was a **network revolution** that began in the Great Age of Discovery in Europe. Western European traders wished to take part in the long-established trade with the East, having seen the wealth of the Arab traders during the Crusades, but the fall of Constantinople to the Turks in 1453 and the Venetian monopoly of eastern trade prevented this. During the Renaissance, the revival of Greek ideas of a spherical earth, navigational aids such as the compass, and improvements in ship design encouraged the search for alternative routes to by-pass the Mediterranean. India was reached by sea in 1498, China in 1513, the Americas in 1492 and Magellan's expedition sailed round the world in 1519–22. The consequences of these discoveries were considerable, for Western Europe changed its position in relative space from the edge of the world to its centre, while previously important trading areas such as the Baltic and the Mediterranean became culs-de-sac.

New patterns of trade emerged from a combination of economic and climatic factors, most notably across the Atlantic. The world's wind systems played an important role in the organisation of the trade network until the advent of the steamship in the nineteenth century, and the Atlantic passage used the trade winds south of latitude 30°N westwards, and the westerlies north of latitude 30°N eastwards. This circular movement developed into the famous, or notorious, triangular or quadrangular Atlantic trade in manufactured goods from Britain to West Africa in exchange for slaves to the West Indies or American colonies in exchange for sugar, rum, cotton and tobacco back to Britain. The type of cargo also changed during the three centuries after the beginning of the Great Age of Discovery with new products such as tea, sugar and tobacco entering world trade, but trade was still essentially in high-value, low-bulk goods.

The **cargo revolution** came in the nineteenth century when the character of international trade changed radically to the large-scale transfer of bulk cargoes. A new trading system was developed, exchanging manufactured goods for raw materials and foodstuffs, and the pattern of trade also changed as London became its centre. The basic cause of this change was the process of industrialisation using steam power and mechanical methods of manufacturing to increase production, creating a demand for large quantities of raw materials and a supply of manufactured products. Complementarity increased enormously. Population also grew rapidly in the nineteenth century and the rising standard of living of an increasingly urbanised population demanded large imports of foodstuffs. To enable the system to operate, new methods of finance were introduced such as the extension of credit by the new commercial banks. The philosophy of Free Trade stimulated interchange by removing tariffs, and improved methods of transport reduced costs and made possible the large-scale transfer of commodities. European settlers developed the agricultural and mineral resources of the Americas and Australasia, creating new sources of supply and demand, and the 'Scramble for Africa' in the later nineteenth century was part of the constant search for materials and markets.

All this activity had a marked effect upon the nature and structure of world trade but the nineteenth-century trading system broke down under the impact of two World Wars and the Depression of the 1930s, and since 1945 a new system has emerged.

Current Flows of International Trade

At present, international trade flows are characterised by their considerable volume, large range of commodities and wide geographical extent.

Volume of Trade

World trade is constantly changing and one of its major characteristics has been a growth rate of more than 8 per cent per annum since 1950, which has greatly increased the volume of trade. Table 10.1 shows that goods worth 23,500 million dollars were traded in 1938 but that this figure had been multiplied over seventeen times to 412,400 million dollars in 1972, and even when allowance is made for currency inflation there has been over a fivefold increase. The reasons for this increase are not hard to find because the period since 1945 has been one of rapid economic growth. During the Second World War the productive capacities of much of Europe, the USSR and Japan were destroyed and the process of recovery generated much trade, but this recovery has been to levels far higher than those of 1939 as these areas have shared in the great economic upsurge that has characterised all advanced economies, war damaged or not. Trade has also been facilitated by a reduction in tariff barriers since 1945. International trade differs from domestic trade primarily because governments interpose obstacles to international trade that do not apply to domestic trade, in the form of tariffs on imports, currency exchange controls and even the direct prohibition of trade with those countries with whose policies they disagree. These restrictions are major factors increasing the economic distance between countries, especially tariff barriers which operate directly to increase movement costs, but since 1945 the trend has been to reduce tariff barriers, at least on manufactured goods.

Table 10.1. The Value of Goods in World Trade 1938–72
(Exports in millions of US Dollars)

	1938	1948	1958	1968	1972
Developed market economies	15,100	36,600	71,200	168,400	297,200
Developing market economies	6,000	17,200	24,900	42,700	72,600
Centrally planned economies	2,400	3,700	12,100	27,000	42,600
World total	23,500	57,500	108,200	239,100	412,400

Source: *UN Statistical Yearbook*, 1973.

Trade has also been stimulated by the growth of population since 1945, and more particularly its economic growth as standards of living have risen and demand has expanded. This expansion of demand, together with the increasing sophistication of products using a wide range of materials gathered on a world-wide basis, has increased the volume of trade considerably.

However, growth has not been uniform, and Table 10.1 shows the considerable differences in the extent to which the three major types of economy are involved in world trade. The dominance of the advanced industrial countries, which had 72 per cent of world trade in 1972, is quite clear, and what is more, since these economies had only 64·3 per cent in 1938, this dominance is increasing. Despite an overall growth of trade in the planned economies of the Communist World, especially between the USSR and its satellites, their share of world trade has remained remarkably constant over the past 35 years, increasing from 10·2 per cent in 1938 to 10·3 per cent in 1972. In the developing economies of the Third World, the period from 1938 to 1972 was marked by a drop in their share of trade from 25·5 per cent to 17·6 per cent and the overall situation is made worse by the fact that there are some very rich mineral exporters such as Libya in this group which contribute a disproportionate share of this figure, whereas many of the agricultural subsistence economies such as that of Ethiopia play a negligible role in world trade (Chapter Twenty-four).

Composition of Commodity Flows

Not only is the volume of world trade increasing but the type of goods entering world trade is changing and since 1945 there have been two complementary trends.

First, there has been an increase in the importance of manufactured goods, which now make up the largest and fastest growing component of trade, comprising 67 per cent of its value in 1972 compared with only 46 per cent in

1938. The recent increase in the proportion of manufactured goods in world trade is the result of two major groups of factors. First, the period of economic growth since 1945 has been led by an expansion of the products of manufacturing industry and most international investment has been in industry rather than in primary production. Secondly, tariff barriers to the import of manufactured goods have been progressively reduced since 1947 under the General Agreement on Tariffs and Trade (GATT), and even those countries in the Third World who are trying to develop their industries behind the protection of tariff walls still find a need for the import of sophisticated machinery.

The second trend, closely related to the first, has been a decrease in the importance of primary products in world trade, together with a change in the type of primary product exchanged. In 1938 primary products accounted for half of the value of world trade but this figure had fallen to one third by 1972. The type of commodity has also changed during this period and wool, rubber and fruit were no longer in the top twenty products in 1972 while coal and cotton had fallen drastically in importance. On the other hand, some primary products such as tin, lead and zinc have increased in importance and petroleum has constituted over one half of the tonnage of world trade since 1960.

These changes in the proportion and composition of primary products in world trade came about because of changes in demand, largely as a consequence of technological change In some instances demands have increased as new industries or products have evolved, requiring 'new' commodities such as aluminium or petroleum, but elsewhere demand has decreased. The development of synthetics for rubber, silk and cotton has reduced the demand for the natural product and the application of scientific methods to agriculture in the developed countries has increased production and resulted in a lessened demand for many imported foodstuffs. At the same time, population increases in the food-exporting countries have meant that less food is available to enter world trade and many developed countries have continued to protect their agriculture by tariffs on imports despite the GATT.

Direction of Commodity Flows

As the volume and balance of world trade has changed there has also been a significant change in the direction of commodity flows from the pattern established in the nineteenth century, when manufactured goods from the developed countries were exchanged for the foodstuffs and raw materials from the less developed. Now most trade is in manufactured goods between developed countries and 60 per cent of trade takes place between two leading areas, Anglo-America and Western Europe, although there are important traders such as Japan elsewhere.

Since 1945 a number of trends have become apparent in the geography of world trade. First, there has been a decline in Britain's share of exports, especially to Latin America, and a decreasing share of exports even to Commonwealth countries such as Australia and New Zealand has reduced London's role as the hub of trade, although the City still provides important services. Secondly, there has been the development of other exporters to fill this gap, especially the USA which is now the world's leading exporter with extensive markets in Europe, Japan and Canada; West Germany, which has been able to increase its exports because of the removal of tariff barriers in the EEC; and Japan, which has pursued aggressive trade policies in the USA and more recently in Europe. Thirdly, trade has increased between the USSR and its European satellites with smaller increases to Western Europe and the developing countries. Fourthly, there has been an increase in the trade of a small number of primary products, but this has been largely restricted to mineral products, especially petroleum from the Middle East, North Africa and Venezuela. Finally, the trade of the Third World has decreased as the developed economies increasingly trade among themselves.

Since the late 1950s the formation of duty-free areas made up of several countries has been an important influence on the pattern of trade and the formation of the European Economic Community in 1957, the European Free Trade Area in 1959, the Central American Common Market in 1959 and the Latin American Free Trade Association in 1960 has produced a redirection of their trade. What the long-term effects of such unions will be remains to be seen, but it seems probable that they will increase trade between members, restrict trade between members and non-members and encourage trade between non-members. Thus British food imports from Europe have increased following Britain's entry into the EEC in 1972, imports from traditional suppliers such as New Zealand have decreased and New Zealand is directing its exports to new markets such as Japan.

Flows of international trade are therefore large and complex and are constantly growing and changing and this is reflected in the complex transport **networks** that have been built to make these exchanges possible. These networks pose interesting problems of analysis for the geographer who must explain their structure and location and develop theories which will help to make them more efficient.

Network Analysis

Attempts to explain the structure and location of transport networks have involved two approaches. First, emphasis has been placed on the study of the parts of the network, and secondly, the network as a whole has been studied.

Single Routes

A network is made up of many single routes which link together two or more centres and to explain why these are located where they are, economic, strategic and social reasons must be sought. In a free enterprise economy transport facilities will be provided if they are profitable, and to determine this, the transport builder must decide whether or not the potential revenue is greater than the costs of providing a service. This can be quite difficult since there is a large number of factors to be considered and there are many examples of poor decision-making producing failure. The building of the last major railway line to London in the period 1893–99, the Great Central Railway from Sheffield, can be considered such a failure since it never paid a dividend, but on the other hand there are many links carrying large flows of traffic such as the Panama Canal or the new motorways that reflect successful decisions. Strategic factors can also account for the presence of transport facilities, from the building of the Roman road system to the building of the trans-continental railways in North America and Russia. Social factors are important in accounting for the smaller links in the network such as paths and local roads which help local interchange, but with the recent increase in leisure travel in the developed countries, transport facilities play an increasing social role and affect location decisions.

The actual location of the route that is chosen will normally be the one that gives the greatest benefits, and in economic terms these will be measured by the size of the profit. To achieve profitability, costs must be minimised and revenues maximised, but in reality the choice of the 'best' route will involve a compromise between a number of considerations.

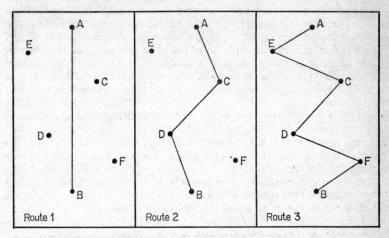

Fig. 10.2. The problem of finding the best route (after P. Haggett).

In Fig. 10.2 the least-cost route between two major centres A and B is the direct Route 1. However, there are two important secondary centres C and D which provide plenty of traffic, and although Route 2 costs more to build because it is longer, the increased revenues from C and D make it worthwhile. But, as has been indicated, there are considerations other than economic profits in route selection and although E and F are only minor economic centres which generate little commercial traffic, F is an important strategic centre protecting the whole region and E is an economically depressed area, politically unstable, which must be integrated into the national economy. The government might therefore choose Route 3 as the 'best' route, with five links connecting six centres. Such networks are increasingly being studied by geographers.

Networks

Transport networks are integrated structures that link centres or **nodes** such as towns or cities and each **link** in the network not only connects two nodes but is part of the whole system of connection between many other pairs of nodes. A three-stage hierarchy of networks can be identified, with the individual network such as a road or rail network at its base, above which is the regional network comprising all the individual networks, and at the top is the network which links all the regional networks and combines them into the global network.

To analyse these networks, **graph theory** is used in which all routes and centres are reduced to a system of links and nodes, ignoring the route characteristics of different networks and the flows passing along them. Graph theory is used to evaluate the accessibility of the nodes in the network by measuring the degree to which they are connected with each other in two ways.

First, it is possible to measure how any one node is connected with the rest of the network by calculating the number of nodes with which it is directly connected and the minimum number of links it would be necessary to travel along in order to visit all the other nodes in the network. This is useful when new links are being planned in the network because the effects of alternative routes on the accessibility of various nodes can be calculated. In Fig. 10.2, if the government decided to build an ordnance factory at E to reduce unemployment and to provide arms for the strategic centre at F, what would happen if traffic was so heavy that a new route had to be built? A new direct route from E to F would serve only one purpose and would be more expensive to build than an extension of the routes ECF or EDF, but if CF was built what would the effect be on D? C and F would become the best connected nodes in the network and if traffic on route EC became so heavy that a new route AC was built to relieve it, C would become the most important node in the whole system. This is a simple case, but this type of analysis can be applied to very complicated networks.

Secondly, the connectivity of the whole system can be measured by finding the ratio between the number of links and the number of nodes. This ratio is called the Beta Index (B.I.) and in Fig. 10.3 as the number of links between six

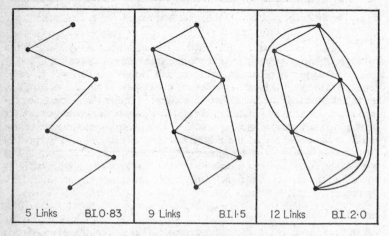

5 Links   B.I. 0·83   9 Links   B.I. 1·5   12 Links   B.I. 2·0

Fig. 10.3. Using the beta-index to measure connectivity.

nodes increases from five, which is the minimum number of links necessary to connect each node, to nine, which is the number of direct non-intersecting links, to twelve, which is the maximum number of non-intersecting links, the Beta Index increases from 0·83 to 1·5 to 2·0. The value of this measure is that it has been shown that a high degree of connectivity as measured by the Beta

Index is correlated with advanced economies (France 1·42) while developing economies have a low index (Sri Lanka 0·76).

Finally, to return to the distinction made at the beginning of the chapter between transport users and transport builders, it must be noted that quite different networks would be developed to suit these two groups, as shown in Fig. 10.4. Users wish to minimise their costs, and the ideal user network

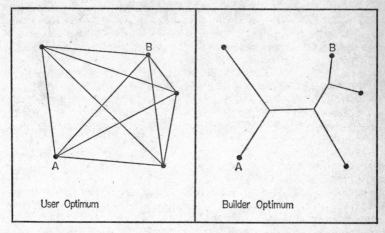

Fig. 10.4. Alternate shortest path networks connecting five centres
(after W. Bunge).

between five urban centres would be ten direct links, but to minimise building costs the builder pattern would involve only seven shorter links with interchanges away from the urban centres. A journey from A to B would be much shorter on the user network but the overall length of the network would be high, while the journey on the builder network would be longer but on a reduced network. It must be noted that the trend of network patterns is towards the shorter builder pattern as railway networks contract and concentrate on a few major routes and as new motorway systems are built, and this may have implications for settlement patterns as new interchanges away from the towns attract industry as they are beginning to do on Britain's motorways.

Conclusion

The development of methods of transport to overcome the physical separation of sources of supply and demand by reducing the distance between them, and the establishment of transport networks to make interchange possible, are of basic importance to man's economic activities, forming the binding links of the world economy. They also enable social interaction to take place by making contact between people easier, so that transport improvements have made the world a smaller place in many respects. Transport is very important and plays a central role in all the activities discussed in the following chapters.

Suggested Further Reading

Cox, K. R., *Man, Location and Behaviour*, Wiley, New York, 1972.

Haggett, P., and Chorley, R. J., *Network Analysis in Geography*, Arnold, London, 1969.

Thoman, R. S., and Conkling, E. C., *Geography of International Trade*, Prentice-Hall, Englewood Cliffs, New Jersey, 1967.

CHAPTER ELEVEN

AGRICULTURE: PROCESS AND PATTERN

Spatial patterns of agricultural activity have long attracted the interest of economic geographers. However, apart from a few notable exceptions, most agricultural geographers prior to the 1950s displayed a preoccupation in establishing simple correlations between crop and livestock distributions and factors of the physical environment such as soil, climate and relief. The economic aspects of agricultural production were largely ignored.

It is now widely appreciated that the **physical** environment imposes certain broad limits within which particular crops may be successfully cultivated or certain types of livestock profitably reared, but that the scale, intensity and extent of production within these physical limits is determined by **economic** considerations such as the cost of production, market demand, competition between different land uses, and government support policies and subsidies. Unfortunately something of the earlier approach still persists. The cultivation of rubber in Malaysia, for example, is still explained in a number of textbooks by considering the physical requirements of the rubber tree, *Hevea brasiliensis*, and then demonstrating the extent to which conditions of soil and climate in Malaysia match up to these requirements. What is overlooked in such an approach is that no rubber is cultivated commercially in many other parts of the equatorial region which possess virtually identical physical conditions. Furthermore, conditions in Malaysia would allow the successful cultivation of a dozen or more commercial crops. Why then should rubber be grown in preference to coffee, rice, sugar-cane, cocoa, oil-palm or coconuts? Such questions can only be answered in economic terms, in particular by reference to the principle of **comparative advantage** (Chapter Fifteen). This suggests that 'a product tends to be produced by those farmers whose ratio of advantage in the production of it is higher than that of other products' and that 'the choice of crop or livestock enterprises or combination of enterprises tends to be determined by comparative advantage in terms of profit or net return'. Thus, a better financial return may be obtained from an indifferent crop of rubber than from an excellent crop of rice, depending on differences in demand and costs of production for rubber and rice.

While factors of the physical environment such as average length of the growing season, average length of the frost-free period or the total amount and seasonal distribution of precipitation impose basic limits upon agricultural production, they alone will not adequately explain patterns of agricultural land use, whether it be in India, Iowa or Ireland. The point was neatly summed up by the economic geographer, R. O. Buchanan, in his study, *The Pastoral Industries of New Zealand*, in which he stated that 'in industries organised on a commercial, as distinct from a subsistence basis, geographical conditions express themselves, if at all, in economic, mainly monetary, terms . . . and the nature and extent of the influence of the geographical conditions are themselves dependent on the precise nature of the economic conditions . . . and that the geography of production must be a study of the interaction of geographical and economic conditions in an area and for the products concerned'. Thus, in his study Buchanan examined not only such physical factors as climate, soil, drainage, vegetation and accessibility, but also the relative fluctuations in world prices for wool, meat and dairy products, quotas, tariffs and other forms of protection operated by the industrial countries of Europe and the way in which they react on the price level of the world market and thus indirectly on the agricultural geography of New Zealand. The geographical analysis of agricultural location is thus concerned with both physical and economic factors, although the emphasis in recent years has been placed much more firmly on the process of interaction between these two sets of factors.

Physical Influences on Agriculture

The physical influences on agricultural activity can be divided into three main groups; climate, soils and relief. Of these, climate is the chief determinant of agricultural patterns. Soil characteristics are largely the product of past and present climates, while the effects of relief are expressed in large measure through variations in climate.

The Influence of Climate on Agriculture

All plants need **water** in order to survive, but their requirements vary widely, as well as their ability to extract water from the soil. Since plants derive the bulk of their water requirements through their root systems, water must be available in the soil in the appropriate quantities. A continued deficiency or excess of soil-water will ultimately cause the destruction of crops. Excessive precipitation may also cause problems of rill, gully and sheet erosion of the soil cover, as well as flooding of fields and serious crop losses in lowland areas. Heavy and prolonged falls of snow in winter may also have serious consequences upon agricultural production. In many parts of Scandinavia and Canada, for example, work on the land virtually comes to a standstill during the winter months. The spring snow-melt may also cause problems of waterlogging of fields and crucial delays in the start of the annual round of work on the farm which, in any event, is concentrated into a critically short period of intense activity. However, on the credit side a prolonged snow cover does have an insulating effect and reduces frost penetration into the ground so that certain cereal crops may be sown in the autumn without risk of frost damage.

Suitable **temperature** conditions are also essential for the successful germination of seeds and plant growth. Again requirements vary, but most plants need a minimum temperature of 5–7°C before growth commences. The average number of days per year with temperatures above this threshold level provides a rough guide to the length of the available growing season. A more precise indication may be provided by the calculation of **accumulated temperatures**: the amount by which each day's temperature exceeds a threshold figure is added throughout the growing season to give a cumulative temperature figure. For example, wheat, which has a threshold figure of 5°C, requires approximately 1,300 day-degrees of accumulated temperature in order to give optimum yield.

In marginal areas of cultivation where the length of the growing season is scarcely long enough for the successful cultivation of particular crops, serious damage may be caused by spring and autumn **frost**. For example, in Finland, which lies at the northern limit of grain farming, there is always a considerable risk of failure because of killing frosts or an unusually short summer. Severe killing frosts causing complete crop failure throughout the country occur on average every fortieth year, or once in the lifetime of every generation of Finnish farmers. Less severe crop failures occur once every ten years, and regional crop failures due to frost once in every four years. It appears that many Finnish farmers adopt an over-optimistic view of the frost hazard and underestimate the risks of failure involved (Chapter Two). On a local scale, the incidence of frost-hollows may be an important influence on patterns of cultivation, especially fruit crops, which are particularly susceptible to frost damage.

Light is also essential for plant growth, and sufficient amounts of sunshine are necessary for the ripening of crops. In temperate regions the ripening and harvesting of crops may be delayed during unusually cloudy summers, while in parts of the equatorial region, where temperature conditions encourage rapid plant growth, persistent cloud cover and reduced amounts of direct sunshine may prevent the double-cropping which would otherwise be possible.

Wind is another element of climate which affects farming activities in many ways. One obvious effect of this particular hazard is the damage caused to mature cereal crops by storm winds. Cold local winds such as the Mistral of southern France may cause serious crop losses, while hot, dry winds such as the Sirocco of southern Italy and Malta may have a desiccating effect upon crops. Less obvious is the fact that constant strong winds increase evapo-transpiration from crops and lead to increased water requirements to compensate for this fact. The loss of valuable topsoil by wind erosion, especially in areas of **dry farming** where crops are grown under semi-arid conditions without irrigation, is also an extremely serious problem in many parts of the world. Reference was made in Chapter Two to the way in which problems of crop failure and soil erosion during the 1930s in the Dust Bowl of the USA resulted from a misinterpretation of the agricultural potential of the Great Plains.

Soil and Agriculture

Any study of farming activity must make reference to the soil, since it is the essential material upon which all agriculture is based. It contains minerals such as nitrogen, phosphorus, sulphur, potassium, magnesium, calcium and iron, as well as minute quantities of trace elements such as boron, iodine and cobalt which are necessary for plant growth. All forms of agriculture, whether arable or pastoral, remove certain of these minerals and trace elements from the soil, so that fertility and crop returns will ultimately diminish unless these essential constituents are replaced. Soil fertility may be maintained by fallowing, scientifically based crop rotations, and the application of manure or chemical fertilisers.

A companion volume, *Physical Geography Made Simple*, includes reference to the processes of soil formation (pedogenesis), describes variations in soil texture and composition, and comments on the methods of soil classification. The suitability of any soil for agriculture depends upon its composition, texture and depth, and is determined by a variety of factors, including the nature of the parent material, past and present climatic influences, relief and vegetation, soil organisms, as well as man's use of the soil which may have the effect of either converting naturally infertile soils into good farmland by manuring, deep-digging, draining and liming, or initiating soil erosion by bad husbandry. It takes nature from 300 to 1,000 years to build up 25 mm of fertile soil. Man by wanton misuse can destroy 200 mm in one or two generations. Justifiably, therefore, soil quality has been described as a response to management.

Loam soils are often regarded as ideal soils because of their richness in plant food, good drainage without waterlogging and general ease of working, although heavier clay soils may be more suitable for certain crops, provided that drainage is adequate. Sandy soils are generally infertile, although they may respond to heavy applications of fertiliser.

Relief and Agriculture

Three elements of relief—altitude, aspect and gradient—influence patterns of agricultural activity. As mentioned earlier, the effects of **altitude** are chiefly expressed through climatic modifications, notably the decrease in temperature with increased height. Thus, in southern Scotland the length of the growing season decreases from about 240 days at sea level to about 180 days at 330 m and 135 days at 600 m. In middle latitudes other adverse effects of increased altitude generally include higher precipitation, strong winds and a deterioration of soil quality. High altitude therefore restricts the number and types of crops that may be grown. Where arable farming is practised, reliance tends to be placed on hardy cereals and fodder crops, but in many upland areas pastoral farming is the dominant type of agricultural activity.

On the other hand, in the tropics, increased altitude provides some relief from the excessively high temperature and humidity of the lowland plains, and provides an improved environment for many crops. In Java, for example, the best crops of tea are grown at heights of 1,200–1,800 m, while in Kenya the main coffee growing belt is located at elevations of 1,400–1,800 m.

On a local scale another important element of relief is the **aspect** or orientation of slopes. In the northern hemisphere, south-facing slopes receive longer

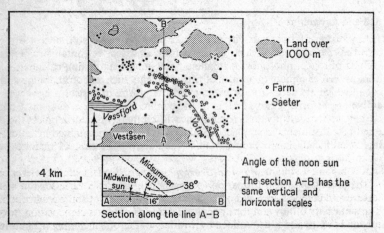

Fig. 11.1. Aspect control in Hemsedal, Norway.
(from A. C. O'Dell, *The Scandinavian World*, Longman)

periods of more intensive sunshine than their north-facing counterparts. Numerous studies have been made of this effect in deeply cut, east–west orientated valleys in Norway, Austria, Switzerland and elsewhere. Although the temperature differences between the sunny (**adret**) and shady (**ubac**) slopes of such valleys are quite small, they are nevertheless sufficient to cause significant differences in the land use and settlement patterns of the two opposing valley sides. Cultivation extends to higher levels on the south-facing slopes; most villages and farms are found on the sunny side of the valley, whereas the shady, north-facing slopes are often heavily forested and devoid of settlement and cultivation. Fig. 11.1 shows the influence of aspect on the distribution of farms and saeters in a west Norwegian valley.

Finally, the **gradient** of slopes imposes an important control on the type of agriculture and methods of cultivation that may be practised in any area. Not only is the risk of soil erosion greater on steep slopes than on gentle ones, but steep gradients also greatly restrict the use of heavy machinery. For example, the use of combine harvesters is normally restricted to slopes of less than 10° with a soil whose structure will not deteriorate under the weight of such heavy machines. In many parts of the world, especially in South-East Asia, complex systems of **terracing** have been developed to allow steep hillsides to be brought under cultivation. Table 11.1 indicates correlations between gradient and land use in the UK.

Table 11.1. Gradient and Land Use in the UK

Gradient (degrees)	Gradient (ratio)	Description	Comments
3°	1 in 20	Gently sloping	Farming operations easily carried out.
6°	1 in 10	Moderate slope	No serious obstacles to farming. Easily cultivated.
11°	1 in 5	Fairly steep	Limit for ground ploughed and cut annually.
18°	1 in 3	Steep	Maximum slope under cultivation. Ploughing difficult and hazardous. Generally permanent grass.
25°	1 in 2	Steep	Too steep for cultivation. May be forested if soil is present.

Source: D. R. Macgregor, Some Observations on the Geographical Significance of Slopes, *Geography*, Vol. 42, 1957.

The physical factors outlined above should not be thought of as absolute controls which impose rigid, unchanging limits on agricultural production. Soils can be modified and improved by the application of fertilisers designed to compensate for specific mineral deficiencies, inadequate soil drainage can be improved by tile drains, ditches and pumping, farming can be extended into areas of low and unreliable rainfall by **irrigation** schemes, and the geographical limits of particular crops extended by plant breeding. In the latter context great success has been achieved in developing short maturing varieties of wheat and hybrid maize whereby the cultivation of these cereals has been extended into previously marginal and unsuitable areas. Almost complete control over the physical environment is achieved in farming practices such as the rearing of battery hens, the raising of dairy cattle in large buildings in which the animals are constantly housed and fed, and the cultivation of market-garden crops in soil-less cultures under glass. However, these developments can only be achieved at enormous cost. This in turn implies a strong demand and high returns for the products in order to justify the capital expenditure involved.

The flexibility of environmental constraints may be illustrated by a simple model in which a single physical factor exercises a dominant influence on crop distribution, in which the farmers' information and decision-making are assumed to be perfect, and in which transport costs have no effect.

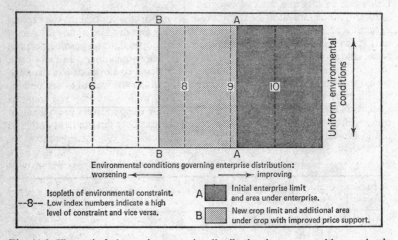

Fig. 11.2. Theoretical change in enterprise distribution in an area with one simple environmental variable and variations of price support assuming perfect conditions.

(from W. B. Morgan and R. J. C. Munton, *Agricultural Geography*, Methuen)

In Fig. 11.2 values for the dominant physical control—which might be length of growing season, frost incidence or soil quality—are shown by a series of isopleths. Under certain conditions of market demand the area under cultivation of a particular crop might extend to the margin, A–A. However, if demand should increase, or if the government increased the level of its price support for the crop, it is possible to imagine an extension of the cropped area to a new suboptimal margin at B–B. With falling prices or the withdrawal of price support, the margin of cultivation might recede towards, or even beyond, A–A. In each instance the limit of cultivation correlates with a different isopleth value. In other words, physical factors determine the shape of the crop area, while economic factors determine its extent.

Social and Economic Influences on Agriculture

So far attention has been directed to the purely physical influences on agricultural production. As mentioned earlier, social and economic influences are scarcely less significant in determining the type and methods of farm production in any area and the spatial patterns of agricultural activity. It is these factors which are examined next.

Land Tenure

Land tenure is one of the most fundamental influences on agriculture. Among primitive peoples land is owned by the community and the concept of individual ownership is unknown. It is in the more economically advanced farming regions of the world that various forms of land tenure are to be found. These include freehold ownership, various forms of tenancy and communal and state ownership. As well as determining the amount of income which must be set aside to meet mortgages or rent, the form of tenancy also influences the extent of the farmer's participation in planning and policy, the degree to which he is dependent solely on his own resources in developing the farm, and the ease with which operations can be expanded or contracted by the purchase or letting of land.

Freehold ownership is the dominant form of land holding in most advanced farming nations, although the UK, with a majority of tenant farmers, is an exception to this. It is frequently suggested that freehold ownership offers the strongest incentives for efficient farm management and allows the greatest freedom and flexibility in decisions about farm policy, although the outcome of these decisions will ultimately depend on the experience and knowledge of the farmer. On the other hand, the owner-occupier is free to subdivide his holding between his heirs, and, if local custom favours gavelkind (equal inheritance between all heirs) rather than primogeniture (inheritance by the eldest child), this can lead to a reduction in unit sizes and a fragmentation of holdings which is unlikely to occur under a system based on tenancies.

Two forms of tenant farming may be noted. The most common is **cash tenancy**, in which a fixed cash rent is paid to the landowner. The second form is **share-cropping**, or métayage, whereby the tenant cultivates the land and gives the owner an agreed share of the farm produce. Under the former system the farmer has a fixed outgoing in rent, but a fluctuating income from the land. He may also be restricted in his farming operations by conditions in his lease, which in extreme cases even stipulate particular cropping rotations. Security of tenure depends on the length of the lease, and this in turn influences farming methods. With a long lease the farmer will be more willing to invest capital, perhaps in conjunction with the landlord, in farm improvements, but with a short lease there is a danger that he will avoid making capital improvements and seek to maximise his profits by over-cropping or over-grazing, to the long-term detriment of the land.

In share-cropping, the farmer's annual payments to the landowner are related to the return from the farm, and to some extent he is protected from fluctuations in yield and income. However, in many instances the share due to the landlord is fixed at an excessively high level so that he is left with a very meagre income for his labours. In parts of the USA where the practice still persists, 'share-croppers' generally form a very impoverished section of the agricultural community. In Europe share-cropping still survives in parts of France and Italy.

State ownership of both land and the capital equipment of agricultural production represents another form of tenancy which has been established in most countries of the Communist World. Ideological considerations apart, state control of agriculture may be seen as an attempt to rationalise and modernise agricultural production, achieve economies of scale and eliminate many of the problems common to peasant cultivators, such as small size and fragmentation of holdings. However, the collective farms (*kolkhozy*) and state farms (*sovkhozy*) of the Soviet Union have not been an unqualified success. It has been suggested that 'the yield or fertility of the soil has not been very materially improved, although the productivity of agricultural labour has been considerably increased'. Thus, the USSR, with a very favourable ratio of land to population (one sixth of the earth's land area but only one fifteenth of the world's population), is unable to produce enough food to support its own population, and since the mid-1950s has been a major importer of grain from North America. State farms are also found in many countries of Eastern Europe—East Germany, Czechoslovakia, Hungary, Romania, Bulgaria and Albania—as well as in China, where the traditional pattern of small peasant holdings was reorganised after 1950, first into collective units, and later into large 'communes'.

Scale of Operations

In most studies of **farm size** and its effects on productivity, land area is taken as the sole criterion of farm size. Yet land is only one of many farm resources, and in theory other measures of unit size such as the number and size of buildings, labour inputs or value of production might also be employed. However, information on land area is most readily available, compared with data on farm output or labour inputs, and for this reason it is widely used as an index of size.

The economic viability of a farm of a given size is difficult to assess, and depends on the type, method and intensity of production as well as the economic aspirations of the farmer and the social context within which the farming is carried out. Under the system of intensive, subsistence rice-growing practised throughout much of South-East Asia one hectare of land is sufficient to support a family, whereas on the drier parts of the Great Plains of the USA a farm of 200 ha is considered small and would scarcely support a family. However, despite the problems of defining a minimum or optimum farm size, it does seem clear that in many parts of the world there is an excessive number of small, inefficient farm units.

The main constraint imposed by small size lies in the lack of choice of alternative types of production open to the farmer. In order to achieve an adequate return, small enterprises must produce a high return per hectare by intensive production methods. In Britain this generally means dairying or the growing of cash root crops, often supplemented by the rearing of pigs and poultry. It has been noted that in the UK many farmers stay in milk production because their holdings are not large enough to make cereal growing a profitable alternative and because capital is 'trapped' in dairy buildings and cannot be transferred to tractors, drills and combine harvesters.

In many parts of the world, because of the limited returns available from small farm units, farmers frequently engage in a secondary occupation to supplement the farm income. In Scandinavia, for example, many farmers also work in forestry and fishing, while in many parts of France, the Low Countries, Germany and Poland many **worker-peasants**, or '5-o'clock farmers' as they have been termed, combine the running of a smallholding with a full-time job in a nearby urban centre. Indeed, part-time farmers of this type are common in the various agricultural systems of both the developed and developing world.

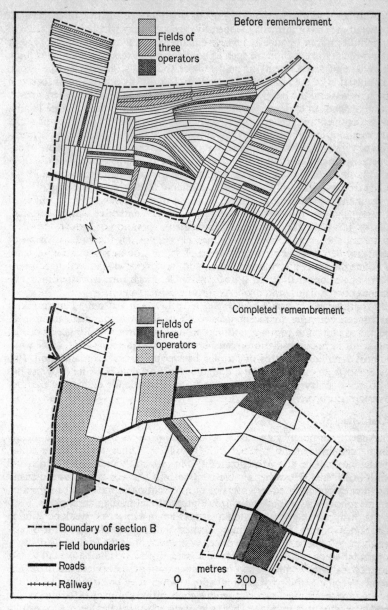

Fig. 11.3. The effect of remembrement in the commune of Vézelise
Meurthe-et-Moselle.

(from I. B. Thompson, *Modern France*, Butterworths)

Another response to the problems of small unit size is that of **cooperation** between groups of farmers. Cooperative schemes vary widely in their scale of organisation, but frequently involve communal purchase and usage of major items of capital expenditure such as combine harvesters and grain silos, bulk purchase of seeds, fertilisers and animal foodstuffs, as well as the group organisation of the marketing of produce. In this way economies of scale can be achieved and the bargaining power of farmers in relation to buyers greatly strengthened. In countries such as Denmark, the Netherlands and Finland, where cooperative schemes have been encouraged and financed by the state, the organisation embraces agricultural education, quality control and processing of products, as well as marketing and advertising. Extreme forms of cooperative organisation are found in Israel in the form of the *moshavim*, in which small family farms share centralised cooperative services, and the *kibbutzim*, which involve complete communal ownership of the land.

In many instances the economic problems of small unit size are accentuated by **fragmentation** of holdings into numerous small, and often widely scattered, plots. Such a situation may result from the preservation of former open-field patterns, the operation of inheritance laws involving the equal division of property between heirs, or the piecemeal acquisition or reclamation of land. Fragmentation is a serious problem, and in extreme cases mechanisation of farm operations is difficult, if not impossible, much time is wasted in movement between fields, and property disputes are common.

Programmes of **farm consolidation** have been carried out in many West European countries in recent decades. This involves the amalgamation of scattered plots into compact holdings around farmsteads. In France an official policy of farm consolidation (**remembrement**) was started in 1941, since when almost 7 million hectares of farmland have undergone reorganisation. Fig. 11.3 shows an example from a commune in Lorraine. Striking progress has also been achieved in West Germany, the Netherlands and other parts of Western Europe.

Marketing

Apart from purely subsistence economies, patterns of farming are greatly influenced by demand for particular products. Other things being equal, preference will be given to commodities for which there is a strong demand with high profit. However, simple relationships between supply and demand are greatly complicated by government intervention in the form of subsidies, tariffs, quota restrictions and various international trading agreements.

As mentioned earlier, individual farmers are in a relatively weak position in relation to buyers. There are more farmers than merchants, so that it is relatively easy for buyers to dictate prices. Moreover, after the harvesting of crops or the fattening of livestock, the farmer generally has no alternative but to sell. In most cases he cannot retain his produce until market prices are high. The economic vulnerability of the individual farmer may be strengthened by the formation of growers' associations or cooperative groups for the processing and marketing of produce. This type of arrangement has been successfully applied to cheese-making in Switzerland and the Netherlands, wine production in France and bacon-curing in Denmark.

Many agricultural commodities deteriorate rapidly or require expensive and specialised equipment for processing. Under these circumstances government marketing boards or agencies are frequently set up. In the UK, for example, the Milk Marketing Board was set up to reduce the transport costs of milk collection from farms and its distribution from dairies to market centres. The British Egg Marketing Board, with almost 400 egg-packaging stations, attempts a similar function. In the case of British sugar-beet production, acreages and prices for the crop are determined by the government and it is grown under contracts made each year between the farmer and the British Sugar Corporation.

In recent years large companies involved in the freezing, canning, drying and packaging of produce, and large firms owning supermarket chains have bought increasingly large quantities of fruit, vegetables and poultry direct from farmers. One important result of these developments is for processing to be carried out in enormous, factory-like units, the location of which in turn exercises a profound effect upon patterns of agricultural land use. This is true of most advanced farming nations. In such countries the small local livestock market, abattoir and dairy now play a relatively insignificant role in the pattern of agricultural marketing.

Transport

Transport provides the essential link between agricultural producer and buyer, as well as the means of moving various material inputs such as seeds, fodder and fertilisers to the farmer. Historically, the impact of transport developments on agriculture has been enormous. In North America, railway construction converted ranching land on the interior plains into vast grain producing areas. The advent of refrigerated shipping in the 1870s transformed the farming face of Australia, New Zealand and Argentina by permitting the movement of frozen beef and mutton to European markets. In many parts of Africa the construction of new roads and railways has been the essential prelude to the opening up of new farming districts.

Most geographical studies of the influence of transport on agriculture have concentrated on transport costs, although, as described in Chapter Nine, there are many other factors which go to make up economic distance, such as **speed** of movement, **frequency** of services and the availability of **special facilities** for the preservation of perishable goods. However, it is the cost factor which is undoubtedly the dominant influence upon patterns of agricultural land use. Indeed, the cost of transporting produce to market forms a central theme in von Thünen's classic theory of agricultural location (see Chapters Four and Twelve).

In the case of international trade in agricultural produce, transport costs may include not only freight charges, but also insurance, customs charges, transhipment costs, packaging and handling costs and storage charges. The costing of internal movements of produce is less complicated, and is essentially a product of weight and distance. Thus, bulky and heavy crops such as potatoes and sugar-beet tend to be grown close to urban markets and processing factories respectively. On the other hand, less bulky, high-value commodities may be able to withstand high transport costs and can be profitably grown at a great distance from the market. For example, costly airfreight services are even used to transport early-season crops of fruit, vegetables and flowers from the Channel Islands, Scilly Islands and various Mediterranean areas to the London market. Transport improvements and reductions in transport costs may be instrumental in extending the area of production for given markets.

Labour

Different crops and different types of livestock vary greatly in their labour requirements as well as in the seasonality of their labour demands. Labour requirements for a selection of crops and livestock in England and Wales are given in Table 11.2: note the wide range of values.

Table 11.2. Standard Agricultural Labour Requirements:
England and Wales (1971)

Crop	Man-days per hectare	Type of livestock	Man-days per head
Permanent grass	1·2	Broiler hens	0·05
Wheat, barley	4·9	Upland sheep (over 1 year)	0·5
Turnips, swedes	22·2	Lowland sheep (over 1 year)	1·0
Potatoes	37·0	Pigs (over 2 months)	1·0
Orchard crops	56·8	Beef cattle	3·0
Glasshouse crops	3210·0	Dairy cattle	10·0

Source: Ministry of Agriculture.

Availability and cost of labour will obviously play an important part in determining the farmer's choice of crops and livestock. Low population densities and shortage of labour in a region will tend to restrict agriculture to forms and methods requiring little labour in relation to land, such as extensive, highly-mechanised grain cultivation or stock ranching. Conversely, a high population density and abundance of labour will favour labour-intensive forms of production such as the cultivation of paddy-rice or market-gardening.

Almost all forms of agricultural production are typified by marked seasonal variations in labour demand. During periods of intensive activity such as harvesting this demand may be met by the regular work force working overtime, by the use of part-time personnel, the recruitment of casual labour, or even by the subcontracting of certain jobs. At times of the year when there is relatively little activity on the farm, the regular labour force may be underemployed and reduced to short-time working. However, this constant adjustment of the labour force to the amount of work in hand presents many problems, and certain writers have even suggested that the extreme variability in the length of the working week and the resultant fluctuations in weekly earnings has been an important contributory factor to the drift of labour from the land in Britain (Chapter Twenty-one).

In many advanced farming nations there has been a marked reduction in the size of the agricultural labour force in recent decades. In the UK the combined total of full-time and part-time agricultural employees fell from 843,000 in 1950 to about 350,000 in 1970. Low wages, dissatisfaction with working conditions, better job opportunities and prospects in industry, and the increasing mechanisation of many aspects of agricultural production have all contributed to this reduction in the size of the work force.

The substitution of machinery for manual labour occurs when a farmer considers that capital investment in machinery, including purchase costs, running costs and depreciation, will increase profits through a reduction in labour costs. It has been estimated that 'in 1830 the production of wheat on one hectare, using the ordinary plough, harrow, sickles and flails, took 144 man-hours. In the United States in 1896, with the aid of machines in use at that time, this had been reduced to 22 man-hours; in 1930, when using tractors and combine harvesters, the time was brought down to $8\frac{1}{4}$ man-hours.' Thus, by the development of increasingly efficient and sophisticated machinery enormous savings in both time and cost were effected.

Another result of mechanisation has been to bring into cultivation areas that were previously considered unsuitable. The introduction of the Otto-meyer plough, capable of ploughing to depths of 1·8 m, has been instrumental in bringing parts of the Dutch and West German heathlands under cultivation, while in Australia the development of the so-called 'stump-jump' plough has allowed areas not completely cleared of tree-stumps and roots to be brought into production.

Capital

From the preceding remarks it will be evident that the increasing mechanisation and modernisation of farming in many parts of the world has involved very profound changes in both methods and organisation. 'In advanced commercial economies farming as a way of life is retreating before farming as a business. The development of agribusiness with its capital intensive and vertically integrated production systems is reducing the relative significance of land and labour and emphasising the importance of capital deployment and marketing skills.' (W. B. Morgan and R. J. C. Munton)

In developed economies capital may be raised by privately negotiated loans from finance or mortgage companies, from clearing banks or from cooperative banks dealing specifically with agricultural business. Old and middle-aged farmers generally have more difficulty than young farmers in obtaining capital for improvements, but on the other hand are usually less willing to innovate and often require less capital than their more youthful counterparts. In some instances government grants and loans may be available for improvements to land and buildings. In this case the question of the farmer's knowledge and information about the grants available and his attitude and response to such grants becomes an important factor. The spread or diffusion of information of this type has, therefore, attracted the attention of many geographers in recent years (Chapter Twelve).

In developing countries funds are less readily available to farmers. Peasant farmers, living close to the margin of subsistence, have an income from the land which fluctuates from year to year according to crop yield and market price, while on the other hand family expenditure and outgoings remain relatively fixed. Periodically income falls considerably below expenditure, and to cover this deficit the peasant farmer frequently resorts to the money-lender. Thus, debts at cripplingly high interest rates are contracted in bad years in anticipation that they will be discharged in good years, but in fact few peasants manage to free themselves from such repayments. **Rural indebtedness** of this type is prevalent among peasant farmers in south-east Asia, the Middle East and southern Europe. The effect of indebtedness is to reduce further the small profit margin on which the farmer and his family must live, and to reduce the capital available for farm improvements and modernisation. Agricultural progress is thus retarded if not completely prevented.

Government Influences

In most countries there has been a marked increase in the level of government control over agriculture during the present century. It is an obvious point that stable government tends to promote stable economic conditions, which in turn encourage capital investment in agriculture as in other forms of economic activity. However, this may be regarded as an incidental influence. More specifically, government policies and attitudes towards land taxes, food prices, wage levels, freight rates and food imports all have a profound and direct influence on agricultural production.

Government action operates at two distinct levels: first through policies affecting the internal organisation of agriculture, and secondly through controls on external trade. **Internal organisation** finds its most extreme and direct form in the collective agriculture of the Communist World, in which the government plans and controls virtually all aspects of agricultural production. In the Western World policy decisions are more typically implemented by means of financial incentives such as grants, loans, subsidies and tax allowances. Low interest-rate loans may be available for the purchase of machinery and for land improvements. Land reclamation schemes may be financed by the government. Agricultural research and education may be advanced by the establishment of colleges and research centres. Guaranteed prices and other forms of subsidy may be used to influence the level of production of particular commodities. Subsidies may also act as a means of protecting high-cost home producers from competition with low-cost foreign producers.

External trade is generally controlled by means of tariffs and quotas on food imports. In the EEC, USA and other high-cost producing areas, the effect of such trade restrictions is to allow small, inefficient farms to shelter behind tariff barriers. 'As long as the small farms persist, sheltered by tariffs and supported by subsidies, a variety of crops and livestock will be maintained, some of which would disappear if truly competitive conditions prevailed. In the low-cost producing countries, access to wider markets at remunerative prices would encourage greater intensification of agriculture, though it is less easy to visualise the landscape changes that would follow there.' (L. Symons)

The Pattern of World Agriculture

Having considered the ways in which both physical and economic factors influence the type of farming in any area, we now examine the patterns produced by these processes.

Problems of Delimitation and Classification

It is obvious that the farms in any area will have an almost unlimited number of attributes such as size, form of tenure, degree of fragmentation, size of labour force, type of production and value of output, to name just a few. Since it is highly unlikely that there will be complete spatial correlation in the degree of variation of these attributes, it may be argued that for any given area there are a number of sets of agricultural regions, depending on the criteria selected. The sets will not necessarily coincide. Such agricultural regions are termed single-feature or **special-purpose regions**. Alternatively, it can be argued that while all the attributes of the farms are unlikely to co-vary exactly, they can be reduced to a single index figure and agricultural regions delimited according to the distribution of these index values. Working in this way it is possible to produce a system of multiple-feature or **general-purpose regions**.

Either approach can be applied to small areas for which there are comprehensive and detailed statistics, but unfortunately such information is lacking for most parts of the world other than the UK and USA with their parish and county statistics respectively. Thus, while geographers have made great progress in recent years in developing procedures for delimiting small agricultural regions (Chapter Twelve), the lack of an adequate data base has prevented the application of new analytical techniques on a world scale. The approach that has generally been adopted in the past is for a number of agricultural types to be assumed *a priori* to exist, and then for each part of the world to be allocated to one particular category on the basis of the scanty cartographic information, inadequate statistical data and vague descriptive accounts that are available.

Most schemes of classification of world agriculture attempt to formulate a system of general-purpose regions, although care must be taken to employ criteria which are capable of quantification and which emphasise elements or characteristics of the farming system rather than factors of the physical environment. Thus, the use of climatic factors or soil types is unsatisfactory since it presupposes rather than proves their influence on farming practices. Several early classifications of world agriculture, such as that proposed by H. Engelbrecht in 1930, consisted of little more than a map of world climatic regions with the substitution of an agricultural nomenclature.

In a recent study of the problems involved in identifying agricultural types and classifying world agriculture, D. Grigg recommended a number of basic criteria which should be taken into account. These were degree of commercialisation, type of tenure and scale of enterprise, intensity of farming, crop and livestock combinations and methods of farming. These factors provide a logical basis for agricultural classification, but in practice their application poses many problems. For example, in recent years peasant farmers in many parts of the world have turned increasingly to the cultivation of cash crops, so that the traditional distinction between subsistence and commercial farming is now far less clear than formerly. Intensity of farming is difficult to define, measure and compare. Dairying in the UK and rice-growing in South-East Asia are both intensive systems of agriculture, but in different ways: one is capital-intensive, the other labour-intensive. Methods of farming constitute one of the major differences between regions, but level of agricultural technology is difficult to reduce to a single measurable and mappable factor. Even the seemingly simple question of crop and livestock combinations is not without difficulties of application. India, for example, has almost 20 per cent of the world's cattle, but produces negligible amounts of milk and meat. Should the presence of 160 million cattle in India be taken into account, therefore, in allocating the country to a particular agricultural category? However, lest the problems of classification and delimitation appear insoluble, one of the more successful systems of classification will be examined next.

World Agricultural Regions: A System Examined

Evaluated on the basis of the points raised by D. Grigg, one of the most satisfactory, and also one of the earliest, attempts to formulate a classification of world agriculture was that proposed by D. Whittlesey in 1936. He employed five criteria for his definition of world agricultural regions: namely, crop and livestock combinations, intensity of land use, processing and marketing of farm produce, degree of mechanisation and types and associations of buildings and other structures associated with agriculture. Assessment of these factors appears to have been subjective rather than quantitative.

His scheme, shown in Fig. 11.4, involves 13 main types of agricultural region, with a further category for land virtually unused for farming. Although a particular type of production dominates in each one, it is possible to carry on other types of farming at higher cost by using larger inputs of capital and labour and accepting a smaller profit margin. Thus, in each of Whittlesey's regions various other forms of agriculture are also found. Nevertheless, his basic classification still provides the foundation for many current atlas maps and most textbook descriptions of world agriculture. Accounts of the farming organisation and chief crops grown in each of the various agricultural regions can be found in several of the books listed in the Suggested Further Reading at the end of this chapter.

A problem inherent in any scheme of regional classification is that of agricultural change, especially the evolution and modernisation of traditional systems under the influence of Western technology, finance and management. Agricultural developments during recent decades have tended to reduce the differences between various parts of the world. For example, there has been a blurring of the distinction between commercial and subsistence farming. There has also been some reduction in the diversity of tenurial systems and a spread of state or communal ownership in many parts of the world. Diversification of former monocultural systems has led to greater emphasis being placed on livestock in many farming systems. Differences in regional productivity have also been reduced to some extent by efforts to improve farming efficiency by increased mechanisation and the greater use of fertilisers. As a result of such changes, various revisions and modifications of Whittlesey's early scheme were undertaken by economic geographers during the 1960s, notably by R. S. Thoman and D. Fryer in 1962 and 1965 respectively, although the original scheme was modified in detail only.

Conclusion

The type of agriculture practised in any area is determined by both physical and socio-economic factors. The environmental factors of climate, soil and relief impose certain restraints and limitations upon the range of crops that may be successfully cultivated and the types of livestock that may be profitably reared in an area. However, within any particular environment many choices and options are normally open to the farmer, and the actual farming pattern is determined by the farmer's evaluation of the possibilities offered by the environment as well as various social and economic factors. These include farm size, type of tenure, consumer demand, transport and marketing facilities, the availability of capital, and government subsidies and support policies. The physical limits of production are relatively stable and can only be extended within fairly narrow limits, but the economic margin of production fluctuates according to demand. During periods of strong market demand and high profits, production may be extended into physically marginal areas, even though this usually involves lower yields and a greater risk of crop failure.

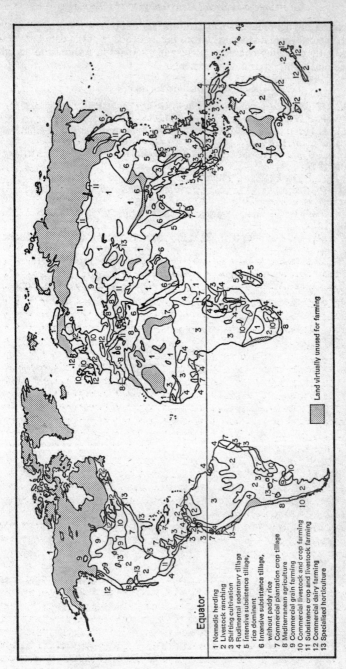

Equator

1 Nomadic herding
2 Livestock ranching
3 Shifting cultivation
4 Rudimental sedentary tillage
5 Intensive subsistence tillage,
  rice dominant
6 Intensive subsistence tillage,
  without paddy rice
7 Commercial plantation crop tillage
8 Mediterranean agriculture
9 Commercial grain farming
10 Commercial livestock and crop farming
11 Subsistence crop and livestock farming
12 Commercial dairy farming
13 Specialised horticulture

Land virtually unused for farming

Fig. 11.4. Principal types of world agriculture (after D. Whittlesey).

Classification and delimitation of agricultural regions on a world scale presents many problems. These arise chiefly from the inadequacy of the data base and the constantly changing character of farming activity in response to social, economic and technological developments.

Suggested Further Reading

Coppock, J. T., *An Agricultural Geography of Great Britain*, Bell, London, 1971.

Courtenay, P. P., *Plantation Agriculture*, Bell, London, 1965.

Duckham, A. N., and Masefield, G. B., *Farming Systems of the World*, Chatto & Windus, London, 1970.

Dumont, R., *Types of Rural Economy. Studies in World Agriculture*. Methuen, London, 1957.

Gourou, P., *The Tropical World* (4th edn), Longman, London, 1966.

Gregor, H. F., *Geography of Agriculture: Themes in Research*, Prentice-Hall, Englewood Cliffs, New Jersey, 1970.

Grigg, D., *The Harsh Lands. A Study in Agricultural Development*, Macmillan, London, 1970.

Morgan, W. B., and Munton, R. J. C., *Agricultural Geography*, Methuen, London, 1971.

Shanin, T., *Peasants and Peasant Societies*, Penguin, Harmondsworth, 1971.

Symons, L. J., *Agricultural Geography*, Bell, London, 1966.

Webster, C. C., and Wilson, P. N., *Agriculture in the Tropics*, Longman, London, 1966.

CHAPTER TWELVE

AGRICULTURE: THEORY AND ANALYSIS

In the previous chapter attention was directed towards a consideration of the main physical and socio-economic influences on patterns of agricultural production. The aim of the present chapter is to examine an early, but still important, theory of agricultural location, and to demonstrate certain of the techniques more recently developed by geographers for studying decision-making in the agricultural context, changes in the spatial patterns of agriculture and the classification and delimitation of various types of agricultural region. A considerable degree of selectivity has been involved in the choice of techniques for inclusion—this chapter is by no means exhaustive—but the material gives some indication of the modern geographical approach to the study of agriculture.

A Theory of Agricultural Location

Von Thünen's Isolated State

One of the earliest attempts to explain agricultural land use patterns in economic terms is contained in a model of agricultural location proposed by J. H. von Thünen in the early nineteenth century. Von Thünen himself was a prosperous and successful owner and manager of a large estate in Mecklenburg, and his major work, 'Der Isolierte Staat' (The Isolated State), published in 1826, was based in part on his observations of farming practices in that locality. Thus, although von Thünen's work was quoted in Chapter Four as an example of a normative model, it was based in part upon empirical evidence relating to economic conditions in the early nineteenth century.

His theory of agricultural land use is based on the concept of **economic rent**, which had been described earlier in 1817 by the economist, D. Ricardo, although von Thünen was unaware of Ricardo's work and arrived at the same conclusion quite independently. The economic rent of an area is the return which can be obtained above that which can be got from land which is at the **margin of production**.

In Fig. 12.1a, A is an area of cultivation close to a city (O). The yield for a given crop is 2·0 tonnes per hectare. As the city expands and its market for produce increases, cultivation is extended to area B, which is located further from the city and is regarded as having a lower fertility. At B the yield is 1·5 tonnes per hectare. In this situation the economic rent of A is 0·5 tonne per hectare converted to a monetary value. If area C is brought into production and yields 1·0 tonne per hectare then the economic rent of A and B will be 1·0 and 0·5 tonnes respectively. Ricardo based his ideas on economic rent on fertility differences of the soil, but von Thünen showed that exactly the same situation arises if the 'quality' of the land varies not with respect to fertility, but with respect to location. Thus in Fig. 12.1b the land is assumed to be of uniform fertility and crop yields equal in all areas, but the return on agricultural produce (XY) declines with increasing distance from the city (O) due to

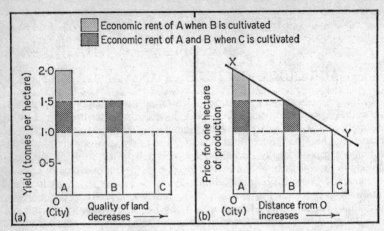

Fig. 12.1. (a) Ricardo's concept of economic rent based on the assumption of declining soil fertility with increasing distance from the city (O). (b) Von Thünen's concept of economic rent determined by the increase in transport costs with distance from the city.

the greater cost of transporting crops to the market. In the diagram the shaded portions of the columns represent the economic rent of A and B if the next distant location is farmed.

The idea may next be extended to two crops, potatoes and wheat. Fig. 12.2 shows the decline in returns over distance for the two crops. Potatoes yield a larger bulk per hectare than wheat, and are more costly to transport. The return from potatoes therefore shows a steeper decline away from the city

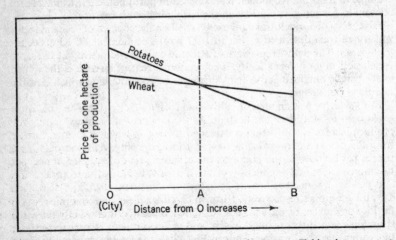

Fig. 12.2. Economic rent for two crops: wheat and potatoes. Taking into account transport costs, potatoes are most profitably grown between O and A, and wheat between A and B.

market than that of wheat. Under these circumstances potatoes will tend to be grown between OA and wheat between AB. By rotating the axis OAB through 360 degrees a concentric zonation of land use will result.

This principle was applied by von Thünen to a hypothetical area which he described as an 'isolated state', surrounded by an uncultivated wilderness and having no trade connections with outside areas. Within this hypothetical state he also assumed the terrain to be completely uniform in respect of relief, soil, climate and all other physical conditions (an **isotropic surface**). His theory was developed on the further assumptions that all surplus produce was sold in a single central city upon which all communications converged, that a single form of transport was used (horse-drawn carts), and that transport costs were directly proportional to distance. Under these conditions von Thünen envisaged that the pattern of agricultural land use would consist of a series of concentric zones of differing production around the city as shown in Fig. 12.3a.

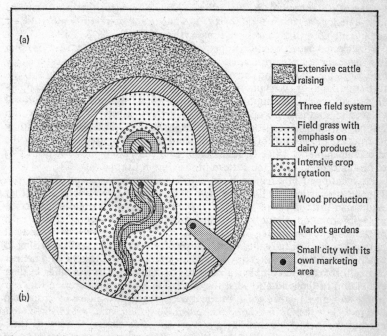

Extensive cattle raising

Three field system

Field grass with emphasis on dairy products

Intensive crop rotation

Wood production

Market gardens

Small city with its own marketing area

Fig. 12.3. (a) Concentric zonation of land use in von Thünen's isolated state. (b) Land use modified by two variables: a navigable river and a second market centre.

The presence of a forest belt close to the city deserves comment. It should be remembered that in the early nineteenth century timber was in strong demand for building and fuel, produced high returns, was both difficult and costly to transport and therefore represented a logical land use close to the city under the economic conditions of that time. Having examined the anticipated pattern of land use in his highly idealised and isolated state, von Thünen then proceeded to use his model as a yardstick for studying the causes of deviations from the theoretical pattern and the effect of particular variables. For example, the modified diagram (Fig. 12.3b) illustrates the distortions produced by the presence of a navigable river and a second urban centre and market.

The Application of von Thünen's Model

Von Thünen's model has been dismissed by various writers as being anachronistic and of no relevance to the contemporary economic situation. However, von Thünen himself went to some length to point out that his work was essentially a method of approach to the complex subject of agricultural location, and that while his findings had no claim to universality, the methods by which they were obtained could be applied generally. Changes in transportation since the early nineteenth century have done most to destroy the symmetry of the land use systems around central markets. Modern transport and refrigeration now enable city markets to receive perishable goods from a variety of distant suppliers. Nevertheless, 'while transport costs continue to form a major part of the total costs of producing and marketing crops, at least some semblance of a concentric zonal system remains'. (J. R. Peet)

A neglected aspect of von Thünen's model is that of its scale. M. Chisholm has suggested that the principles may be applied to the land use on a single farm or estate, to the land surrounding a village, or to the patterns of agriculture at national or even continental scale. In other words, the model is applicable at all scales. Chisholm himself quotes several examples of agricultural villages in southern Europe around which the intensity of land use varies inversely with distance from the settlement. At national level a recent study interpreted the pattern of agricultural land use in Uruguay in terms of the von Thünen model, while O. Jonasson attempted to apply the basic principles to an understanding of the pattern of farming in Europe.

As mentioned in Chapter Four, normative models such as that of von Thünen are particularly limited by two of their basic assumptions. First, they assume, in the context of agricultural location, that all operators have complete information about crop yields and prices, and secondly, that each operator makes completely rational decisions to maximise returns in the light of that knowledge. In reality crop yields vary from year to year according to weather conditions, market prices fluctuate according to demand, and neither can be forecast with complete accuracy. Furthermore, farmers differ in their evaluation of the land and what they regard as a just remuneration for their work, and may neither make rational decisions about choice of crops and livestock, nor seek to maximise the return from their land. All of these facts combine to distort the symmetry of von Thünen's circles. In view of these problems much attention has been directed in recent years to the question of decision-making at the level of the individual farmer.

Game Theory

Game theory has been applied to studies of economic activity in order to achieve a better understanding of the decision-making process. It is concerned with the problem of making rational decisions in the face of uncertain conditions, so that in the context of agricultural geography a 'game' is set up whereby the farmer is playing his environment in some form. The environment has a number of 'gambits' that it can play. It can produce a dry year, a wet year, or average conditions, each of which affects crop yields. The farmer likewise can make various moves. He can grow different crops, some of which yield well in wet years and others which do well in dry years, or he can compromise by growing a combination of crops or growing a crop that gives only a moderate return under either of the two extreme weather conditions.

A simple example will serve to illustrate the approach. In the Chanda district of eastern Madhya Pradesh Province in India, the local farmers' choice of crops is influenced by the variability of the rainfall. In a wet year rice gives the best yield per acre, but in dry years the rice yield is very low, and jowar (sorghum) gives a better return. A **pay-off matrix** with sample figures for yield can be drawn up to illustrate this situation (Table 12.1). This is the most ele-

Table 12.1.   Pay-Off Matrix for Man Versus Environment Game

	Environment		
	Wet year	Dry year	
Farmer's ⌠Rice	63	43	Figures represent units of crop yield per
choices ⌊Jowar	28	58	unit area

Table 12.2.   Solution for Man Versus Environment Game

	Average yield ($\bar{x}$)	Variation $\Sigma(x-\bar{x})$	Percentage of total variation	Percentage of crops grown
Rice	53	20	40	60
Jowar	43	30	60	40
Total variation		50		

Source: M. H. Yeates, *An Introduction to Quantitative Analysis in Economic Geography*, McGraw-Hill, New York, 1968.

mentary form of matrix in which the environment and the farmer each have only two 'strategies'. It is known as a two-person-two-strategy-zero-sum game. The solution is found by calculating the variation from the mean for each crop, expressing it as a percentage of the total variation for both crops, and assigning the result to the alternate strategy (Table 12.2).

Rice has the smaller variation in yield and should be the dominant crop, but some jowar should be grown as an insurance in dry years. In this example rice should be grown 60 per cent of the time and jowar 40 per cent of the time in order to achieve the maximum return or pay-off over the long term. These proportions raise the question of how the solution should be interpreted. Should the farmer plant rice six years out of ten and jowar four years out of ten, mixing the years in random fashion, or should he plant the two crops in these proportions each year? The answer is that in the long term it makes no difference, but in fact in an area of food scarcity it is probably better to take the short-term view and plant the appropriate proportions each year, thereby avoiding the catastrophic situation produced by the cultivation of jowar alone in a wet year.

The same basic approach may next be extended to a more complicated example. P. Gould has described the situation in another area of uncertain rainfall, the Middle Zone of Ghana, where the farmers may grow the following crops, each with varying degrees of resistance to drought: yams, millet, cassava, maize and hill rice. In this instance a pay-off matrix for a two-person-five-strategy-zero-sum game can be constructed as shown in Table 12.3.

Table 12.3. **Pay-Off Matrix for Five Crop Choices Versus Two Environmental Conditions**

		Environment	
		Wet year	Dry year
Farmer's choices	Yams	82	11
	Maize	70	49
	Cassava	12	38
	Millet	43	32
	Hill rice	30	71

Figures represent units of crop yield per unit area

Source: After P. R. Gould, Man Against his Environment: A Game Theoretic Framework, *Annals of the Association of American Geographers*, Vol. 53, 1963.

A pay-off matrix such as this, in which one opponent has only two strategies, can always be reduced to a two-by-two game. This is done by a simple graphical device. Two vertical axes are drawn to represent wet and dry years. Values for each of the farmer's strategies are plotted on the appropriate axes and the pairs of values connected. The lowest point on the uppermost boundary of the

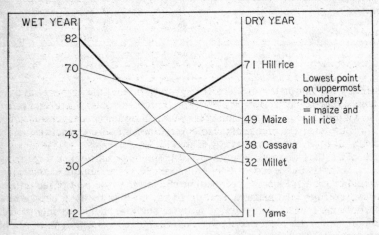

Fig. 12.4. Graphical solution to assign critical pair of strategies in a two-person-five-strategy-zero-sum game (after P. R. Gould).

diagram indicates which two crops—in this case maize and hill rice—should be grown (Fig. 12.4). The proportions of the two crops which will give the maximum pay-off can then be calculated in exactly the same way as for the first example. In this case 33·9 per cent hill rice and 66·1 per cent maize should be grown.

The solutions to the two examples described above assume that the choice of strategy should be on the basis of the 'best possible worst position', the so-called maximum–minimum solution. The farmer examines the worst outcome for each of his alternate strategies and selects the least risky. He is planning for the worst but has no idea how likely it is to occur. It has been suggested that this type of solution is best for subsistence farmers who must ensure a certain minimum yield to avoid starvation, and for farmers who are not prepared to take even the slightest risk. However, a number of other approaches and alternative solutions are also possible depending on how much risk the farmer is prepared to take.

Table 12.4. Pay-Off Matrix for Man Versus Environment Game

		Environment		
		Wet year	Dry year	
Farmer's	Maize	70	49	Figures represent units of crop yield
choices	Hill rice	30	71	per unit area

Table 12.5. Solution for Man Versus Environment Game

	Average yield ($\bar{x}$)	Variation $\Sigma(x - \bar{x})$	Percentage of total variation	Percentage of crops grown
Maize	59·5	21·0	33·9	66·1
Hill rice	50·5	41·0	66·1	33·9
Total variation		62·0		

Source: After P. R. Gould, Man against his Environment: A Game Theoretic Framework, *Annals of the Association of American Geographers*, Vol. 53, 1963.

Thus, game theory provides a number of abstract, deterministic solutions to the problem of decision-making in the face of risk and uncertainty. If the farmer attempts to reduce the element of risk in his cropping programmes, it is almost inevitable that he will have to be content with sub-optimal returns. P. R. Gould has noted that the mathematically derived solutions from game theory raise a number of interesting questions for the geographer. 'Does the land use pattern in any area approach the ideal? And if not, why not? If the land use pattern does not approach the ideal, does this imply a conscious departure on the part of the people, or does their less-than-ideal use of the land reflect only the best estimate they can make with the knowledge available to them, rather than any degree of irrationality? . . . If one were in an advisory position, would this help to make decisions regarding the improvement of agricultural practices? . . . Thus, the usefulness of the tool is not so much the solving of the basic problem, but the host of questions it raises for further research.'

In many of the more advanced farming nations government subsidies and compensation for full or partial crop losses provide some security against the uncertainties of crop yield resulting from climatic variation. To obtain this safeguard the farmer must obviously have full knowledge and information about the government assistance and grants available to him. There are, of course, other uncertainties apart from climate. Crop failures and livestock losses may result from the spread of plant and animal diseases. Again, the progressive farmer will be fully aware of disease prevention measures such as crop spraying and livestock vaccination which can do much to reduce these risks. Farmers themselves vary in their perception of the risks involved, in particular agricultural practices, and in their willingness to accept new techniques and innovations that can reduce the element of uncertainty in their means of livelihood. The whole question of environmental perception was discussed in Chapter Two. In the following section attention is directed to the ways in which new ideas and innovations may be introduced into an area, are first accepted by the most progressive farmers, and then spread more generally throughout the farming population.

The Diffusion of Innovation

The study of diffusion processes, especially the formulation of **simulation models**, which aim to re-create patterns of diffusion, has engaged the attention of many geographers in recent years. This field of study has its origins in the work of the Swedish geographer, T. Hägerstrand, who, during the 1950s, developed a technique for simulating the patterns of diffusion of a variety of innovations.

Hägerstrand identified a set of rules which he believed to govern the spread of ideas or information among a population. All other factors not included within these rules were considered to influence the diffusion pattern in a completely random manner. The inclusion of this random element is important, for, in a sense, it represents man's non-rational, non-economic behaviour which is difficult to accommodate in any model or technique of analysis (Chapter Four). Hägerstrand assumed that information among farmers would be spread by face-to-face contact, and his first basic rule was that the probability of contact between individuals would depend on the distance separating them. Near neighbours would be more likely to meet than distant individuals. Working on the diffusion of farming innovations in the Asby district of Central Sweden, Hägerstrand based this distance-decay function on empirical data showing the decline of migration over distance for the local population. Assuming the probability of social contact between individuals to be the same as the probability of migrating over a given distance, he showed how it is possible to construct a **mean information field**. This represents the probability of someone at the edge of the area having contact with someone at the centre.

In his study of the Asby district Hägerstrand divided a 25 × 25 km area into 25 squares or cells, each one measuring 5 × 5 km. In Fig. 12.5a the distance-decay values (based on migration data) have had their point of origin set on the centre cell and have been rotated through 360° to give point values for the centre of each cell. In Fig. 12.5b these values have been multiplied by 25, since the distance-decay values were based on the number of migrating households per square kilometre and each cell covers 25 km². The **probability of contact** for each cell with the centre cell can now be calculated by dividing each cell value by the sum of all values. The result of this procedure is shown in Fig. 12.5c. Thus, a cell with its centre point 10 km from the centre of the middle cell has a probability of

$$P_i = \frac{V_i}{\sum\limits_{25} V_i} = \frac{4\cdot17}{248\cdot25} = 0\cdot0168$$

where V_i is the point value of the ith cell and P_i is the probability of the ith cell having contact with the centre cell. Finally, as shown in Fig. 12.5d, the contact probability values can be converted into a series of intervals, the sizes of which are determined by their respective probability values. The latter procedure makes possible the use of **random numbers**. The cell intervals are large near the centre of the grid and there is a strong chance that a randomly

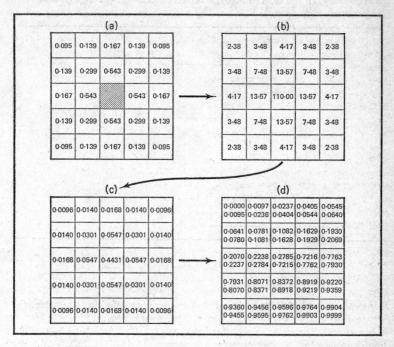

Fig. 12.5. Calculation of the mean information field for Asby, Sweden
(after T. Hägerstrand).

drawn four-figure number would fall within one of the intervals near the middle of the grid, whereas in the outer cells the interval is small and the chance of a random number falling within one of these ranges is only slight. Once constructed in this way the mean information field can be used as an overlay or floating grid to enable the simulation of patterns of diffusion. The grid can be centred over an underlying cell containing a 'teller' or farmer ready to pass information to a potential 'receiver' or adopter of the innovation. By using random number tables and the lattice of the probability intervals it is possible to select a grid cell to which the information is passed.

Hägerstrand's early work on the Asby district was concerned with the diffusion of a government subsidy which was introduced in Sweden in 1928 to encourage farmers to improve their pastures and discourage them from allowing cattle to forage in open woodland. The study area was gridded into 5×5 km cells and 22 original acceptors located as shown in Fig. 12.6. This pattern was taken as the starting point for the simulation model, and the floating grid placed in turn over each of the 22 acceptors. The assumption was made that when contact had been made between a 'teller' and a 'receiver' in the manner described above, the information would be immediately accepted and adopted by the 'receiver'. Thus, if the information is transmitted over a number of intervals or 'generations', the number of acceptors should increase geometrically. In the case of Asby, with 22 original acceptors, the number of

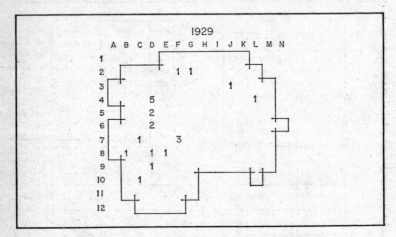

Fig. 12.6. Distribution of original acceptors of a farming subsidy in the Asby district of Central Sweden, 1929 (after T. Hägerstrand).

farmers informed of the subsidy and taking advantage of it should theoretically increase from 22 to 44, 88 and 176 over three generation intervals. In fact this is not exactly the case; two 'tellers' may pass the information to the same 'receiver', one 'teller' may pass the information to another 'teller', and some contacts may be made with farmers outside the study area. The rate of diffusion is, therefore, rather less than a geometric ratio. However, underlying the model is the basic principle that the possibility of an informant and adopter being paired depends on the distance between them as defined by the mean information field.

In Fig. 12.7 a comparison is made between the actual pattern of diffusion of subsidy acceptors in the Asby district and the simulated pattern. Although there are minor differences between the two, the closeness of fit is remarkable. The differences are probably due to the assumption that the decay of contact over distance is the same in all directions. In reality one is not dealing with a uniform surface. For example, around Asby numerous lakes break up the land surface and act as barriers, so that contacts are directed more strongly in some directions than others. Also the assumption of immediate acceptance of the subsidy by all farmers is unrealistic. Nevertheless, the model provides important insights into the spatial diffusion of ideas and information through time.

The basic approach has been extended and modified to fit various situations. Highly sophisticated diffusion models with various barriers to movement and

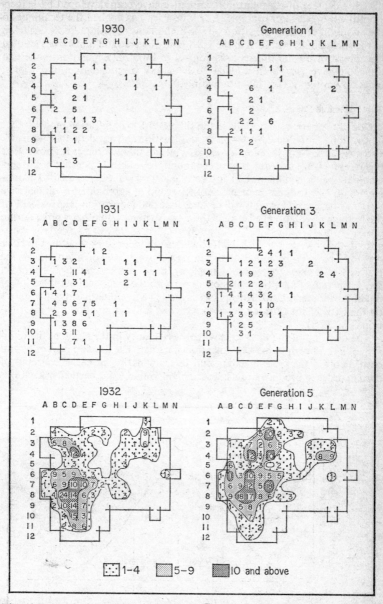

Fig. 12.7. Comparison of Hägerstrand's simulated diffusion (right-hand diagrams) and the actual diffusion (left-hand diagrams) of the acceptors of a farming subsidy in the Asby district of Central Sweden (after T. Hägerstrand).

differing degrees of resistance to acceptance have been developed by Hägerstrand and others. For example, L. W. Bowden has applied the technique to
the adoption of pump irrigation on the high plains of Colorado, Z. Griliches
to the spread of hybrid corn in the USA, and Hägerstrand himself has studied
the spread of bovine tuberculosis control in Sweden. Simulation models of
diffusion have also been applied to a variety of non-agricultural topics,
especially in the field of migration study.

The Diffusion Curve

One of the basic assumptions in the simplest form of diffusion model is that
innovations are adopted as soon as information is passed to the 'receiver'.
From research into the adoption of agricultural innovations it is known that
this is, in fact, not the case. It has been found that about 16 per cent of farmers
who may be termed **innovators** and **early adopters** will be prepared to experi-
ment with new techniques, while another group of approximately similar size
who may be termed **laggards** will resist change and innovation. The **majority** of
the farming population lie between these two extremes. In other words, during
the early stages in the diffusion of an innovation there will be a certain resistance to the new ideas involved which will result in a rather slow start to their
spread. This will be followed by an accelerating rate of adoption as the
majority of farmers follow the example of the innovators and early adopters.
Later, the rate of adoption will slow down with the approaching saturation of
potential adopters. E. M. Rogers has suggested a fivefold division of adopters
on the basis of the time-lag between receiving and acting upon new information (Fig. 12.8).

The question of the time-lag emerges very clearly in the study of the diffusion of hybrid corn in the USA mentioned earlier. The development of hybrid
corn involved the cross-breeding and interpollination of earlier varieties of
corn in order to produce strains of seed highly suitable for particular locations

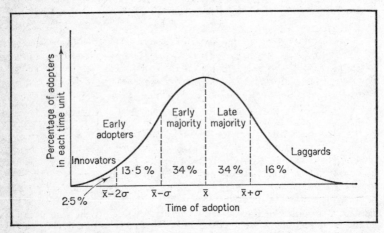

Fig. 12.8. Distribution of adopters of an innovation with time.
(from E. M. Rogers, *The Diffusion of Innovations*, Free Press, N.Y.)

and greatly superior to the varieties originally grown. The development of hybrid strains has been the chief factor underlying the dramatic increases in corn yield per hectare in the USA since the mid-1930s. In Fig. 12.9 the upper limit of the graph is 100 per cent, indicating that the whole of the area under corn was planted in hybrid varieties. The diagram shows that Iowa, one of the leading producers of corn in the so-called Corn Belt, was the first to accept the new strains of seed. By 1942 the farmers of Iowa had achieved almost total acceptance of hybrid corn before even 45 per cent of the corn lands of the USA as a whole were under hybrid varieties, while in the same year the farmers of Texas and Alabama had scarcely introduced the new strains of

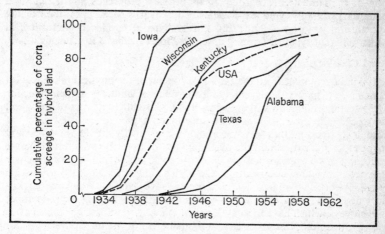

Fig. 12.9. Cumulative percentile diagrams (Ogive curves) illustrating the progressive adoption of hybrid corn in the USA and five selected states.

(from Z. Griliches, *Science*, 132, 1960, copyright 1960, American Association for the Advancement of Science)

seed. These differences between the rate of acceptance of the Corn Belt states and the Southern states were not the result of a limited supply of the new seed, but rather differences in the demand for it, which in turn reflected differences in the importance of corn in the cropping pattern and the size of the profits to be gained from adopting the innovation. Thus, the use of hybrid corn tended to spread from the centre to the margins of production.

In the context of agricultural geography, the study of diffusion processes clarifies the nature of the constant changes and adjustments in the patterns of farming activity in response to economic and technological developments. Geographers have also concerned themselves with the development of techniques both for describing farming patterns at any given point in time, and for analysing these changes through time. These techniques form the subject for the final section of this chapter.

Classification and Regionalisation

In geographical studies there is no essential difference between the operations of classifying data and establishing regional divisions. The geographer's variables on which he divides his data are spatial variables, and consequently each of the classes produced from these variables has a spatial extent and becomes a region. In the previous chapter reference was made to the distinction between special-purpose or single-feature regions and general-purpose or multiple-feature regions. It was also pointed out that, while the classification of agriculture on a world scale had been hindered by a lack of data, many techniques had been developed for the delimitation of smaller scale agricultural regions.

In the field of agricultural geography three main types of classification may be noted: first, **land classification**, which involves the evaluation and classification of the land itself according to its physical properties and agricultural potential; secondly, **land use classification**, which is based upon the existing agricultural use of the land; and thirdly, **type of farming classification**, in which different types of farming enterprise form the basis for classification.

Land Classification

It will be apparent from the earlier discussion of the physical influences on agriculture (Chapter Eleven) that different tracts of land vary in their value for agricultural production and in their suitability for different types of crops and livestock. With growing population pressure on a more or less fixed supply of land, it is important that these variations in land quality should be studied and mapped in order to obtain the maximum return from this valuable resource. Indeed, it has been said that 'no country can be considered to be adequately mapped until a land classification map of this kind on a sufficiently large scale is available' (L. J. Symons). The need for surveys of land potential are particularly urgent in the Tropics, where such information is lacking for wide areas. Soil surveys, which have been undertaken in many countries, go some way to meeting this need, but, of course, soil quality is not the only physical factor affecting the productivity of the land. Ideally, evaluation of the agricultural potential of any area should also make reference to elevation, gradient, aspect, drainage and susceptibility to soil erosion, as well as climatic factors.

In the UK the first major attempt to classify the land in terms of its physical properties followed the publication in 1942 of the Report of the Committee on Land Utilisation in Rural Areas (The Scott Report). The Scott Committee asked the Land Utilisation Survey to prepare a classification of land according to its inherent fertility and **potential productivity**. Three main categories of agricultural land were identified—good, medium and poor quality—with various subdivisions in each group. Table 12.6 shows details of the scheme together with values for the 1940s. The figures have not been subsequently revised, but with improved farming techniques a contemporary classification would probably place a higher value on many areas such as the chalklands of south-east England.

An interesting scheme for land classification was published in 1960 as a basis for land administration and land use planning in Ontario. In this scheme land was divided into seven categories according to the nature of the problems and **costs of development** for commercial agriculture. Yet another, more restricted, classification was developed in the USA by the US Soil Conservation Service whereby the land was divided into eight classes according to its **susceptibility to soil erosion**.

It should be appreciated that in each of the schemes mentioned above the approach was to evaluate and classify individual parcels of land. These were not formalised into regions, but simply mapped as they stood with no attempt at generalisation. Thus, the land classification maps produced by the British Land Utilisation Survey, for example, are characterised by complex mixtures of land classes within quite small areas. A further limitation is that a high degree of subjectivity is involved in the designation of land to a particular category, and no attempt is made to relate one class to another on a quantitative basis.

Table 12.6.   Land Classification, England and Wales

Main category	Subcategory	Percentage of total area of England and Wales	
Good	1. First-class	4·1	
	2. Good general purpose farmland	20·2	
	3. First-class land: restricted use	2·2	37·9
	4. Good but heavy land	11·4	
Medium	5. Medium light land	4·8	
	6. Medium general-purpose farmland	19·8	24·6
Poor	7. Poor heavy land	1·6	
	8. Poor mountain and moorland	31·7	
	9. Poor light land	1·5	35·2
	10. Poorest land	0·4	
Residue	11. Built-up area	2·3	2·3

Source: L. D. Stamp, *The Land of Britain: Its Use and Misuse*, 1948.

Land Use Classification

Modern techniques for classifying land use and delimiting relatively small-scale agricultural regions have stemmed very largely from the work carried out by J. C. Weaver during the mid-1950s on the crop and livestock patterns of the American Middle West. Weaver recognised that in almost every farming system several crops are grown in combination, and only very rarely does a single crop assume complete dominance. He noted that 'far too consistently American geographers have been content to draw dot or isopleth maps of individual crops and to study the revealed distribution patterns as more or less detached phenomena. Overgeneralised agricultural regions have been labelled with over-simplified crop names, such as Corn Belt, Cotton Belt or Spring Wheat Belt, and little realistic appraisal has been made, for example, of the fact that within the so-called Corn Belt, corn is not a uniformly pre-eminent crop in a universally similar crop association' (J. C. Weaver). In the light of such criticisms Weaver developed the technique of **crop-combination analysis** in order to clarify multiple crop patterns and provide a quantitative method of delimiting crop regions and measuring changes in crop distributions through time.

Weaver's original study involved an examination of agricultural land use in over 1,000 counties in various Mid-West states. For each one he calculated the area devoted to particular crops as a percentage of the total cropped area. These actual values were then compared with a set of values derived from a series of model situations. He argued that in a system of monoculture 100 per cent of the cropland would, by definition, be devoted to a single crop; in an ideal two-crop system, 50 per cent of the land would be given over to each crop; in a three-crop system, 33·3 per cent of the land would be devoted to each of three crops, and so forth, as shown in Table 12.7.

Table 12.7. **Theoretical Values for Various Crop Combinations**

Type of combination	Area of total cropland devoted to each crop	
Monoculture	100% of total cropland	
2-crop combination	50% devoted to each of 2 crops	
3-crop combination	33·3 %	3
4-crop combination	25%	4
5-crop combination	20%	5
9-crop combination	11·1%	9
10-crop combination	10%	10

Source : After J. C. Weaver

In order to determine which of the theoretical values listed above corresponds most closely with the actual percentages recorded, the technique of standard deviation (σ) is applied to the actual data. Thus

$$\sigma = \sqrt{\frac{\Sigma(d^2)}{n}}$$

where d is the difference between the recorded crop percentages and the appropriate percentage in Table 12.7, and n is the number of crops in the combination. In fact, since relative rather than actual values are significant, the square root is not extracted, and in practice the actual formula employed is

$$\sigma^2 = \frac{\Sigma d^2}{n}$$

A worked example taken from Weaver's study will serve to demonstrate the technique. Percentage areas under different crops in Keokuk County, Iowa, were recorded as follows: corn 54, oats 24, hay 13, soybeans 5 and wheat 2. The procedure for comparing the actual cropping pattern with the theoretical values is shown in Table 12.8. It will be seen that the deviation of the actual

Table 12.8. **Calculation of Variances for Keokuk County, Iowa (1949)**

	Mono-culture	Two crops		Three crops			Four crops				Five crops				
	C	C	O	C	O	H	C	O	H	S	C	O	H	S	W
Percentage cropland occupied	54	54	24	54	24	13	54	24	13	5	54	24	13	5	2
Theoretical percentage	100	50	50	33·3	33·3	33·3	25	25	25	25	20	20	20	20	20
Difference (d)	46	4	26	20·7	9·3	20·3	29	1	12	20	34	4	7	15	18
d^2	2116	16	676	428	86	412	841	1	144	400	1156	16	49	225	324
Σd^2	2116	692		926			1386				1770				
$\Sigma d^2/n$	2116	346		309			347				354				

Source: J. C. Weaver, Crop-Combination Regions in the Middle West, *Geographical Review*, Vol. 44, 1954. C = corn, O = oats, H = hay, S = soybeans, and W = wheat.

percentages from the theoretical percentages is lowest for the three-crop combination. Keokuk County is therefore interpreted as a three-crop combination area dominated by corn, oats and hay.

Working in this way, Weaver drew boundaries round blocks of counties with the same combination of crops. The ranking of crops within a given combination was ignored, so that areas dominated by corn, oats and hay, or hay, oats and corn, were reduced to a common crop-combination region. A striking feature of the maps thus produced was that they were at considerable variance with the subjective and impressionistic, but long-accepted crop regions described by earlier geographers. Fig. 12.10, which shows the changing pattern of crop-combination regions in Iowa over a period of 30 years, demonstrates the application of crop-combination analysis to the study of agricul-

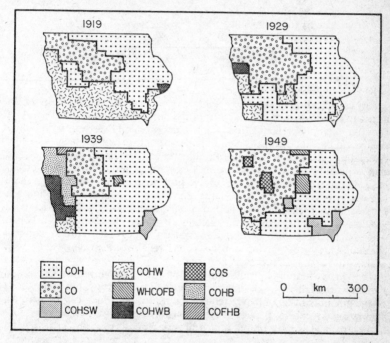

Fig. 12.10. Crop combination regions in Iowa (1919–1949): C—Corn, O—Oats, H—Hay, W—Wheat, S—Soybeans, B—Barley and F—Flax.

tural change and evolution. Notice the decline of the four-crop combination (corn, oats, hay and wheat) in south-west Iowa. In the north-west of the state the area under corn and oats was extended at the expense of other combinations, while in the south-east a new five-crop combination developed after 1929. Such changes are clearly revealed by the technique of crop-combination analysis.

The technique has been applied with various modifications to the study of land use patterns in many parts of the world. The same essential method has also been used to study livestock combinations. The various types of livestock are generally reduced to **standard livestock units** on the basis of feed requirements and then each type is expressed as a percentage of the total livestock units for an area.

Table 12.9.   Livestock Conversion Units

Type of livestock	Number of livestock feed units
Cattle (over 2 years old)	1·00
Cattle (1–2 years old)	0·66
Cattle (under 1 year old)	0·33
Breeding ewes	0·20
Other sheep	0·06
Pigs	0·14
Poultry (over 6 months)	0·02
Poultry (under 6 months)	0·005

Source: J. T. Coppock, *An Agricultural Atlas of England and Wales*, Faber, 1964.

Type of Farming Classification

Any classification of areas according to type of farming should be based on as many characteristics or attributes of the farming system as possible. As a very minimum, reference should be made to crops and livestock, both individually and in association. As mentioned earlier, crops can be standardised by calculating each as a percentage of total cropland. Similarly, livestock can be standardised by converting the various types to standard livestock units on the basis of feed requirements. However, the problem remains of combining these two elements in some way. Indeed, the central problem in the formulation of a type of farming classification is that of standardising disparate agricultural variables so that they can be combined in a common classification procedure.

One standardisation procedure is to reduce all types of farm production to a common base by employing **standard labour requirements**. Using values such as those in Table 11.2, it is possible to make quantitative comparisons between diverse types of farming production on the basis of labour inputs. Crops and livestock are evaluated, not in terms of the land they occupy, but on the basis of the amounts of labour they require. Other factors which can be used as, standardised measures include **gross output value** and **gross margin value**. The latter is defined as gross output minus all variable costs of seeds, fertilisers and labour, but excluding fixed overheads. Data on labour inputs are generally more readily available than information on the value of farm inputs, and for this reason standard labour requirements have been more widely used as a standardisation index than either of the monetary values. Assuming standard labour requirements to have been used as a conversion factor, the resultant data can be presented in two ways. The first involves mapping and regionalisation on the basis of the leading enterprise, while the second employs Weaver's technique of mapping combinations of activities, using in this instance enterprises on the farm as percentages of the total standard man–day units. A worked example for a hypothetical unit (farm or parish) will serve to illustrate the method of identifying the leading enterprise or appropriate combination of enterprises. Assuming the area to contain 50 ha under wheat, and 250 pigs

200 dairy cattle and 1,000 lowland sheep, the following procedure would be adopted. On the basis of these figures the unit under study would be classified as a single enterprise area dominated by dairy farming.

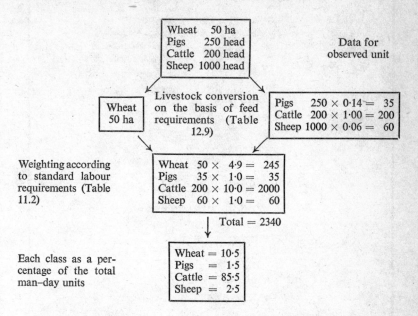

During the early 1960s J. T. Coppock employed the techniques of crop and livestock combination analysis as well as enterprise combination analysis in the preparation of the *Agricultural Atlas of England and Wales*. Coppock's work was based on statistics for the 350 National Agricultural Advisory Districts for England and Wales. In delimiting types of farming regions he employed the procedures outlined above, and examined the various combinations of five types of enterprise: dairy cattle, sheep and beef cattle, cash crops, horticultural crops (fruit and vegetables), and pigs and poultry. Fig. 12.11 shows both the leading enterprise and enterprise combinations for each of the Agricultural Advisory Districts.

Conclusion

In this chapter some indication has been given of the various ways in which it is possible to approach the study of agricultural activity. Von Thünen's model is concerned with an optimal pattern of land use within the constraints laid down by various assumptions concerning production and transport costs, and market demand. In view of the complexities of the environmental and socio-economic influences on production, and the often irrational nature of decision-making, such an optimal model is hardly realistic, although the economic principles underlying it are worthy of serious study. Game theory provides certain insights into decision-making under conditions of environmental uncertainty and risk with which all farmers have to contend. The methods adopted by the most successful and progressive farmers in any area will tend to

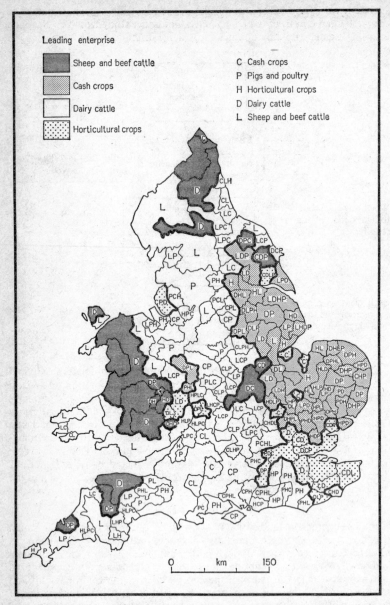

Fig. 12.11. Enterprise combinations (five enterprises) for the National Agricultural Advisory Districts of England and Wales. The leading enterprises are shown by the shading and the others in the combination systems by the overprinted letters.

(from J. T. Coppock, *An Agricultural Atlas of England and Wales*, Faber, 1964) spread throughout the remainder of the farming population, and diffusion models have been developed to aid the understanding of this process of agricultural change. Finally, the efforts which have been made to regionalise the variables related to agricultural activity indicate the importance which continues to be placed on the concept of the region in geographical studies.

Suggested Further Reading

Bowden, L. W., *Diffusion of the Decision to Irrigate*, University of Chicago, Department of Geography Research Paper 97, Chicago, 1965.

Chisholm, M., *Rural Settlement and Land Use* (2nd edn), Hutchinson, London, 1968.

Coppock, J. T., *An Agricultural Atlas of England and Wales*, Faber, London, 1964.

Found, W. F., *A Theoretical Approach to Rural Land Use Patterns*, Arnold, London, 1971.

Hägerstrand, T., *Innovation Diffusion as a Spatial Process* (translated by A. Pred and G. Haag), Chicago University Press, Chicago, 1968.

Hägerstrand, T., 'On Monte Carlo Simulation of Diffusion', in *Quantitative Geography* (Part I: Economic and Cultural Topics), Eds. W. L. Garrison and D. Marble, Northwestern University Press, Evanston, Illinois, 1967.

Hall, P., (Ed.), *Von Thünen's Isolated State* (translated by C. M. Wartemberg), Pergamon, Oxford, 1966.

Rogers, E. M., *The Diffusion of Innovations*, Free Press of Glencoe, New York, 1962.

Tarrant, J. R., *Agricultural Geography*, David & Charles. Newton Abbot, 1974.

Von Neumann, J., and Morgenstern, O., *Theory of Games and Economic Behaviour*, Princeton University Press, Princeton, 1953.

Yeates, M. H., *An Introduction to Quantitative Analysis in Human Geography*, McGraw-Hill, New York, 1968.

CHAPTER THIRTEEN

MINERAL RESOURCES AND THEIR EXPLOITATION

The mining and quarrying of rocks and minerals symbolises both the old and the new in economic activity. On the one hand, man's use of metals can be traced back several millennia to the Bronze Age when the techniques of metal smelting and alloying were discovered and metals first used in the manufacture of tools and implements; on the other hand, the large-scale exploitation of mineral resources did not take place until the time of the Industrial Revolution some 200 years ago. The changes initiated at that time were based essentially on the use of iron as a raw material and coal as a source of power. During the present century the volume and value of mining production has risen to unprecedented levels and shows no signs of slackening. Indeed, the depletion of many non-renewable mineral resources is a matter of serious concern, and the impending exhaustion of many known reserves means that new sources must be discovered if industrial activity which is based directly or indirectly on mineral resources is to continue unimpaired (Chapter Twenty-five).

The distribution of mining activity in any region does not correlate simply with the distribution of known resources. The extent to which the resources are exploited depends on the economic need and incentive to mine or quarry them, as well as the technical knowledge and ability to extract, process and convert them to useful ends. In this chapter attention is directed chiefly to the occurrence and mining of metal ores, together with some reference to materials used for building and construction, and to industrial raw materials used chiefly in the chemical industry. Fuel minerals are considered separately in the following chapter.

The Mode of Occurrence of Minerals

The term **ore** is used to describe an accumulation of any mineral in sufficient concentration to warrant commercial exploitation. The relative ease with which mineral ores may be mined or quarried and the resultant cost of extraction are determined largely by the type of formation or structure in which they are found. It is important, therefore, for the economic geographer to have some appreciation of the main types of formation in which minerals occur.

Igneous Ore Bodies

Many important mineral deposits are contained within major igneous intrusions. During earlier geological periods large bodies of molten rock or magma were intruded into the crustal rocks in many areas. As these cooled, different constituents frequently separated to form **magmatic ore deposits**, often of great commercial importance. Examples of such deposits include the iron ore (magnetite) of Kiruna in North Sweden, the copper and nickel deposits of Sudbury, Ontario, and the iron, nickel, chromite and platinum formations of the Bushveldt complex in South Africa.

Associated with the intrusion of large bodies of igneous material, liquids and gases were often forced upwards through cavities and fissures towards the earth's surface, cooling and crystallising as they ascended to form **veins** and **lodes**. The various mineral constituents solidified at different temperatures and tended to accumulate at definite depths below the earth's surface. Thus, veins and lodes tend to display a zonation of minerals with depth. In the mines of Cornwall, for example, copper ore is often replaced by tin as depth increases. Other mineral ores solidified at a similar temperature and are frequently found in association; silver with lead and zinc, copper with nickel, and iron with manganese. In many old mines the continuation of working depends on the value of the secondary minerals being extracted.

Although they include some of the world's most famed ore deposits, and have yielded vast treasures of gold and silver, as well as much of the world's supply of copper, lead, zinc, tin, tungsten and mercury, lode and vein formations are generally difficult and costly to mine. They follow irregular courses through the rocks, thin and subdivide at random, and their mineral content may suddenly change.

In many cases the 'country rock' adjacent to large igneous ore bodies, as well as veins and lodes, may have been impregnated with mineral-bearing fluids and gases by a process known as **pneumatolysis**. The effect of this is to produce what are known as **contact-metasomatic deposits**, finely divided ores which are also difficult and costly to mine.

Sedimentary Ore Deposits

Sedimentary or bedded ores are characterised by their occurrence in level sheets, often of considerable thickness, rather than in veins or irregular masses. In some cases they were formed by a process of deposition on the bed of former lakes and seas. A notable example is the 'Minette' iron ore (limonite) of Lorraine in eastern France. Sedimentary iron ores are also mined in Luxembourg, West Germany, the USSR, South Africa and Brazil. Other important sedimentary ores formed in this manner include the manganese deposits of Georgia and the Ukraine in the USSR, and the phosphate beds of Algeria, Tunisia and Morocco. Another group of sedimentary minerals, including gypsum, potash and rock-salt, are known as evaporites, and owe their origin to a process of evaporation from former shallow seas. Others, including certain bedded iron ores, were formed by the solution, downward percolation and redeposition of minerals at depth. Another mode of formation involves the decomposition of surface rocks, usually under tropical conditions, and the removal of soluble constituents, leaving a residual mass of naturally concentrated ore. Bauxite and certain types of iron, manganese and nickel deposits fall within this category. As well as the minerals mentioned above, many sedimentary rocks, such as limestone, chalk and clay, have important commercial uses for building stone, cement production and brick-making respectively.

Alluvial Deposits

Certain minerals may occur as alluvial deposits in the sands and gravels of valley floors and piedmont areas. Under favourable circumstances, heavy minerals, removed from their parent rock by weathering and erosion, may settle in stream beds in commercially attractive concentrations. The minerals found in such deposits, which are known as **placer deposits**, are generally confined to those which resist corrosion by water. Among the most important are gold, diamonds and tin.

Oceanic Mineral Resources

The water of the oceans contains vast quantities of minerals, but most are so widely diffused as to be of no economic significance. It has been estimated for example, that it would cost £10 million to extract the £2 million worth of gold contained in a cubic kilometre of sea water. On the other hand, certain minerals attain a sufficient concentration to warrant the processing of sea water. Thus, about 30 per cent of the world's supply of common salt, 60 per cent of magnesium and 70 per cent of bromine are derived from the oceans. The sediments of the sea bed are also known to contain significant concentrations of minerals in many areas, but the technical difficulties of extraction have so far limited working to shallow inshore waters. Furthermore, despite an impending shortage of many minerals, large-scale working of sea bed resources appears unlikely in the near future.

Factors Influencing Mining Activity

The extraction and preparation of minerals for industrial uses generally involves a number of distinct processes. The mine itself may assume various forms depending on the nature of the ore and its mode of occurrence. Sedimentary or bedded ores, if they lie close to the surface, are frequently worked by **opencast** methods. Where deposits outcrop on an escarpment or valley side, **adits** or tunnels driven into the hillside may be the most economical method of extraction. Lodes and veins inevitably require a complex arrangement of **shafts** and **galleries**. Placer deposits are normally worked by the **pumping** or **dredging** of mineral-bearing sands and gravels. In some instances soluble minerals such as rock-salt, potash and sulphur, may be worked by the **Frasch process**, whereby the minerals are dissolved in superheated steam and the solution forced to the surface by compressed air.

In the case of metal ores, the valuable minerals are interspersed with waste material of no economic value which is referred to as **gangue**. For example, copper ores containing less than 1·0 per cent metallic copper are worked in many parts of the world and ore containing 6 per cent copper is considered exceptionally rich. Because of the low metallic content of such ore, it will not stand the cost of long-distance haulage and must be at least partly processed close to the point where it is mined. Thus, an important stage of production is **ore-dressing**, which involves crushing the ore and separating the valuable minerals from the gangue by gravitation, flotation or chemical processes. In some instances the ore thus separated may be smelted and pelletised prior to being transported to the point of demand. Recent improvements in the techniques of ore-dressing have made profitable the working of low-grade ores which were previously uneconomic, and, in some instances, even the spoil heaps of former mines. It has been said that 'the history of mining is, largely, one of the increase in efficiency of ore-dressing. The waste heaps of one generation have been reworked with profit by a later' (N. J. G. Pounds).

Physical Influences on Mining Activity

It was indicated earlier that the form of occurrence of different minerals greatly affects their cost of extraction. The relative ease of working is greatly influenced by the **depth** of the deposit. Opencast working is cheaper than underground working, which involves the sinking of shafts, the cutting of tunnels with roof supports, the installation of winding gear, pumping equipment and underground railways, as well as the costs of ventilation and lighting. Generally speaking, igneous ores are more costly to mine than sedimentary ores due to their irregular forms of occurrence.

The **quality** or grade of ore is also an important consideration. Given a hypothetical situation in which a number of deposits of equal quality and ease of working are assumed to exist, those near to major markets will be exploited first. In reality, the choice is almost always between alternative deposits of varying quality. Under these circumstances it may be profitable to work low-grade deposits close to the market, while distant resources must be of high quality in order to bear the costs of transportation. Thus, despite the high costs of iron mining in the harsh Arctic environment of Swedish Lapland and the great distance of this area from the main iron and steel producing centres of Western Europe, the Swedish mines at Kiruna and Gällivare are able to offer iron ore at a competitive price in these markets. This is largely due to the exceptionally high quality of the ore, which contains 55–70 per cent iron. It is unlikely that iron ore of the quality found in Lorraine in eastern France (24–35 per cent iron content) could be economically worked so far from its market destination.

Sweden's Arctic sources of iron ore have a further advantage; namely, the large size of the reserves. The outcrop of iron ore at Kiruna, for example, has been traced to depths of over 1,000 m, and at present rates of extraction the mines there have every prospect of an extremely long life. Due to the high level of capital investment in modern mining operations, **size of reserves** is an extremely important consideration. Indeed, there is a growing tendency for the size of reserve to outweigh all other factors. Ore deposits which offer possibilities for large-scale methods of extraction and resulting economies of scale, irrespective of the quality of the ore, are increasingly being developed in many parts of the world. This trend has been described as 'the new philosophy of large-scale, low-grade mining'.

Economic Influences on Mining Activity

Even if the physical characteristics of a given ore body make it suitable for potential working, a number of economic conditions must be fulfilled before exploitation takes place. The same conditions will also determine the active life of any mine or quarry.

Demand for particular minerals is, of course, the necessary stimulus for the initiation or continuation of working. In this connection it should be appreciated that the pattern of demand for minerals is constantly changing in response to technological developments. For example, the growth of demand for copper during the present century has been largely due to its increasing use in the electrical industry; in similar manner the growth of demand for bauxite can be related, in part, to the rise of the aircraft industry. Conversely, other metals have been replaced by plastics and other synthetic materials in many industrial products, thereby causing demand to fall. Changing demand affects price, which in turn determines the profitability and economic margins of mining enterprises. The point is well illustrated by the reopening of a number of Cornish tin mines in recent years. Since the early 1960s there has been a serious world shortage of tin, causing the price to rise from £890 per tonne in 1961 to £3,190 per tonne in 1975. With this steep rise in price, together with improved methods of extraction and ore-dressing, it has been profitable to reopen a number of the old Cornish tin mines, re-work certain of the associated spoil heaps and set up plant to extract stream-tin from various alluvial deposits. As a result, the output of Cornish tin doubled between 1970 and 1973. Most tin mines in Cornwall fell into disuse in the late nineteenth century, not because the ore had been completely worked out, but because the price of tin fell as low as £90 per tonne in the 1870s, at which level working was no longer economic.

The availability of **capital** is also essential for successful mining operations. The opening of a modern mine involves high levels of capital investment in prospecting, surveying, the installation of mining gear, pumping equipment, ore-dressing plant and transport systems. It has been estimated that 'a big new mine may cost $100 million to $300 million or more to develop with no return for perhaps five years and a very uncertain price situation when production begins so far ahead' (K. Warren). Such expenditure is justified only if the mine has a potentially long and profitable life, and for this reason large ore bodies tend to be worked before small ones, even if the latter have much to recommend them.

Labour supply is another important factor. Not only does the wage bill for the work force constitute a large part of the production costs of any mine, but the availability of suitably skilled and qualified workers is an essential consideration in the planning of any new mining operation. Mining is often carried out in remote areas of great physical hardship, such as high latitudes, deserts and mountain areas. Examples include Arctic Canada, the Great Australian Desert and the high Andes. Not only is the local population sparse in such areas, but is also generally untrained for the highly technical and specialised work which is characteristic of modern mining activity. Thus, it is often necessary to attract qualified staff and operators into remote and unattractive areas by inducements such as high wages, the provision of social and recreational amenities, and in some instances by the construction of entire planned settlements or company towns such as Schefferville in Quebec and Lynn Lake in Manitoba.

The availability of **transport** systems to link areas of mining activity with their markets is another essential condition. Road transport is rarely suitable for the movement of large volumes of heavy, bulky materials, and the opening up of many of the present major mining districts of the world had to await the coming of the railway. Katanga in Central Africa, Kiruna in Arctic Sweden, Schefferville in Central Labrador, Cerro de Pasco in Peru and Broken Hill in Australia are all major mining centres where the presence of large ore bodies had long been known but had to await the construction of railway links before large-scale modern development could proceed. Indeed, the railway network in Central Africa, as in many other parts of the world, can be explained largely in terms of the distribution of minerals and the need to link them with various coastal transhipment points.

The cost of transport may also play a significant role in determining patterns of mining production. A good example is afforded by the sand and gravel industry in the UK. Because of the decentralised nature of the sand and gravel industry, its importance is often underestimated, despite the fact that, measured in terms of its volume of production (142 million tonnes in 1973), it is the largest single category of mineral production, even exceeding coal output. The wide scatter of more than 1,300 relatively small sand and gravel workings in the UK, and the absence of major sand and gravel producing regions, are largely explicable in terms of transport economics. The greatest single factor influencing the location of the industry is accessibility to markets. Sand and gravel is a low-value commodity, and the cost of transport is a major element in the market price of the material. In 1975 the value of medium-quality gravel at the point of extraction in South-East England was £1·50 per tonne. Not only is the material of low intrinsic value, but is characteristically moved in small loads to a variety of changing destinations as building and construction projects are started and completed. The lorries used for the movement of sand and gravel have a capacity of about 16 tonnes and can therefore carry only about £24 worth of material. The distance over which such a load can be economically transported is very small. In fact, with the addition of transport costs, the market price is doubled at a distance of about 20 km from the point of extraction. Thus, since each quarry can economically supply only a very limited market area, it is necessary to have a large number of widely scattered production points. Nor can centralisation of the industry be achieved by using alternate forms of transport, for the lifespan of a sand or gravel quarry is seldom long enough to warrant the laying of railway lines, as for a coalmine or limestone quarry. In any case, the constantly changing market destinations also necessitate the use of road transport.

New assessments of the profitability of ore deposits must continually be made in the light of changes and improvements in the **technology** of mining, ore-dressing and metal smelting. Reference was made earlier to the way in which more efficient methods of ore-dressing have enabled previously uneconomic, low-grade ores to be brought into production. Thus, in recent years increasing use has been made of the deposits of taconite, a very low-grade iron ore, found in the Lake Superior Highlands of the USA. Of much greater importance was the invention of the Bessemer Converter in 1856 and its later improvement by Gilchrist and Thomas in 1879. As a result of these developments, iron ore containing small amounts of phosphorus which had previously been unusable was brought into production. It has been remarked that no discovery has done more to change the geography of the iron industry, allowing as it did iron ore deposits of Lorraine, Swedish Lapland and many other areas to be exploited for the first time. More recently, improved methods of steel-making and the development of alloy steels has stimulated a demand for metals such as chromium, nickel, cobalt and tungsten. The development of furnaces allowing the increasing use of scrap iron in steel production has also had important implications. In countries such as Japan and Italy which are deficient in iron ore, very heavy reliance is placed on the use of scrap in iron and steel production. This recycling of scrap metal is a conservation measure of great significance and tends to have the effect of stabilising ore prices. When scarcity threatens, ore prices rise, and with them the price of scrap. This provides an incentive for the collection of scrap metal, which in turn prevents prices rising to excessive levels.

Finally, mention should be made of various **political influences** on mining activity. Because of the vital importance of many minerals in the functioning of modern industrial economies, the possession of supplies of essential ores is of great strategic importance, especially in times of war. Thus, many countries have sought to reduce their dependence on imported ores either by stockpiling, promoting research into the development of substitute materials, or by working low-grade ore deposits which would scarcely be considered economic under normal circumstances. For example, during the First World War, Germany, cut off from its Chilean source of nitrates, developed techniques for producing nitrates from atmospheric nitrogen, which in turn broke Chile's virtual monopoly of nitrate production and had extremely serious consequences for the mining industry there. During the 1930s, for the same strategic reasons, Germany also started to mine iron ore deposits containing as little as 20 per cent iron at Peine and Salzgitter. In these ways normal economic principles may be subordinated to political considerations.

The Effects of Mining on Landscape

A notable effect of mining activity is the initiation of rapid landscape changes in the areas concerned. Such changes include not only the permanent marks and scars of the mining itself, but also the rapid growth, and the often equally rapid decline, of associated settlement. J. Brunhes has remarked that 'the essential characteristic of mineral exploitation is that it fixes man's labours suddenly and for a time being only, at one particular place on the earth's surface'. The most spectacular growth and decline of mining settlements has been associated with the working of lodes of gold, silver and other precious metals. Typical of such boom towns is the Canadian settlement of Dawson on the Klondyke River. In 1897, after the discovery of gold in the area, this northern outpost of settlement became a tent-camp for some 1,500 prospectors and miners. A year later it was a flourishing township with a population of almost 40,000, but within five years of the first gold strike it was a ghost town of a few hundred people. Similar ghost towns are a feature of many mining districts in the Rocky Mountains of the USA. They illustrate the fact that mining often takes place in areas where no alternative or supplementary economy can be practised. Once the ore is worked out, or if the demand for the ore ceases, then the population is obliged to move elsewhere. A recent example of this process is provided by the Canadian township of Elliot Lake, a modern planned settlement built at enormous cost in the mid-1950s following the discovery of uranium in 1953 in the Blind River district on the southern edge of the Canadian Shield. The development was based on an initial order by the USA for uranium to the value of $1,000 million. However, following the discovery of uranium in New Mexico, the USA announced in 1959 that it would not take up its options on further deliveries of Canadian ore after 1962. The population of Elliot Lake declined from a peak of about 25,000 in 1958 to a mere 5,000 three years later, leaving what has been described as 'the first nuclear-age ghost town, and undoubtedly the handsomest one anywhere in the world' (I. M. Robinson). At the same time it should be appreciated that the effects of mining on settlement are not always of a transitory nature. Reference to a settlement map of Western Europe will illustrate the way in which large industrial centres and conurbations have grown up on the main coalfield areas.

However brief the period of mining activity in any area, and whatever the effects on associated settlement, the working of minerals inevitably produces distinctive landscape features in the form of disused shafts, adits or quarries, surface subsidence in many areas, dumps and spoil heaps of waste material, vegetation destroyed by air and water pollution, disused mineral lines, and derelict mining gear and ore-processing machinery. Almost all areas of former mining or quarrying activity have been permanently scarred in this way. South Wales has its slag heaps, Bedfordshire its old brick-clay quarries, the Colne Valley its disused gravel pits, Cornwall its kaolin spoil heaps and Snowdonia its slate tips.

In recent decades much attention has been directed to the problems of **landscape restoration** in mining areas. For example, since 1952 a condition which has been frequently attached to the granting of planning permission for opencast mining or quarrying is that the topsoil and overburden must be replaced when mining is complete, and the land restored to its former condition. In Northamptonshire many former iron workings have been successfully restored in this way. Elsewhere old sand and gravel pits have been turned into a positive amenity with facilities for angling, sailing, waterskiing or swimming. However, in many of the old mining areas where exploitation pre-dated the modern concern for landscape restoration, serious problems still remain. It has been estimated that there are over 100,000 hectares of derelict land in the UK, to which a further 1,400 hectares are being added each year. In many of these areas, spoil heaps of toxic waste stubbornly resist colonisation by vegetation, old quarries remain unused and unfilled and degraded landscapes bear witness to the former exploitation of mineral resources without regard for future generations.

Conclusion

The exploitation of mineral resources is influenced by both physical and economic considerations. The physical characteristics of any ore formation, such as its size, depth and quality, determine not only the method of extraction, but also the relative ease and cost of working. However, the mere presence of potentially workable minerals in any area does not necessarily mean that mining will take place. A number of economic conditions must also be fulfilled. There must be a sufficient demand for the ore, an adequate supply of labour and sufficient capital to develop the mine or quarry and establish the necessary infrastructure, especially the essential transport links between mine and market. Costs of production tend to increase with the age of any mine, until a point is reached where production costs exceed the market value of the product. The mine is then economically worked out, although a favourable movement of prices may lead to its reopening. Mining activity often produces important landscape changes. These include the growth, and in some cases the decline, of associated settlement, as well as the creation of derelict land.

Suggested Further Reading

Barr, J., *Derelict Britain*, Penguin, Harmondsworth, 1969.
Bateman, A. M., *The Formation of Mineral Deposits*, Wiley, New York, 1951.
Bateman, A. M., *Economic Mineral Deposits* (2nd edn), Wiley, New York, 1950.
Blunden, J., *The Mineral Resources of Britain. A Study in Exploitation and Planning*, Hutchinson, London, 1975.
Burton, I., and Kates, R. W. (Eds.), *Readings in Resource Management and Conservation*, Chicago University Press, Chicago, 1965.

McDivitt, J. F., *Minerals and Men*, Johns Hopkins, Baltimore, 1965.
Open University, *The Earth's Physical Resources* (Blocks 1–6), Open University, Bletchley, 1973.
Park, C. F., and MacDiarmid, R. A., *Ore Deposits*, Freeman, San Francisco, 1964.
Riley, C. M., *Our Mineral Resources*, Wiley, New York, 1959.
Skinner, B. J., *Earth Resources*, Prentice-Hall, Englewood Cliffs, New Jersey, 1969.
Warren, K., *Mineral Resources*, David & Charles, Newton Abbot, 1973.

CHAPTER FOURTEEN

ENERGY RESOURCES: FUEL AND POWER

The movement of goods, services, people and information, and the development of commercial agriculture and large-scale industry are all dependent on the availability of supplies of energy to provide heat and motive power. Throughout history, man has used energy in the form of animal, wind and water power to supplement his own limited abilities, but in the last 200 years, technological advances have enabled him to tap the stored energy of the earth by burning its fossil fuels and to harness water power more effectively by converting it into electricity. At present, the demand for energy from **fuels** such as coal, oil, natural gas and nuclear materials, and from **power sources** such as falling water is so great that there is a prospect of their being exhausted or fully utilised, and the search is now on for new energy sources such as the sun, the tides and the heat of the earth's interior.

Energy Consumption and Standards of Living

The considerable energy thus released has been applied to intensifying man's use of the earth and has been a major factor contributing to the growth of the advanced Western economies. The increased productivity achieved by the labour force using this energy in the form of mechanical processes has contributed much to the high standards of living enjoyed today in areas such as Western Europe and North America.

Table 14.1 shows the high degree of correlation that exists between a

Table 14.1. Gross National Product per Head, Energy Production and Energy Consumption in Selected Countries (1965)

Country	GNP per capita ($)	Energy production (million tonnes coal equivalent)	Energy consumption (per capita kg coal)	Energy consumption (per $1 of GNP equivalent)
USA	3,515	1,633	9,671	2·75
Canada	2,658	134	8,077	3·04
Denmark	2,333	1	4,149	1·78
Switzerland	2,331	3	2,699	1·16
West Germany	2,197	184	4,625	2·11
Japan	2,122	62	1,926	1·58
France	2,104	70	3,309	1·57
UK	1,992	194	5,307	2·66
New Zealand	1,970	3	2,603	1·32
Australia	1,910	38	4,697	2·46
Czechoslovakia	1,561	74	5,870	3·76
USSR	1,340	925	3,819	2·85
Venezuela	882	247	3,246	3·68
Cyprus	702	—	927	1·32
Libya	542	76	613	1·13
Chile	497	7	1,119	2·25

Source: Manners, G., *The Geography of Energy* (2nd edn), Hutchinson, London, 1971.

country's consumption of energy and its standard of living, expressed as the Gross National Product (GNP) per capita, and it has been estimated that the USA uses as much energy on central heating and air-conditioning alone as China uses for all purposes. However, this simple correlation between energy consumption and the GNP must be modified by three main considerations.

First, by the level of economic development and type of industry in a country: the consumption of energy in industry produces wealth, but in developing countries such as Venezuela and Chile, a considerable amount of energy is needed to establish the manufacturing system and much energy has to be invested in future production facilities such as heavy industry. Secondly, by the availability of energy resources in a country: countries with small energy reserves need to import supplies, and the costs of buying and transporting fuel will reduce the proportion of the GNP available for consumption. Thirdly, by world climatic variations: in middle and high latitudes, a considerable amount of energy is simply consumed for non-productive heating purposes.

Nevertheless, economic development and energy consumption are so closely linked that, as a general rule, one can be used to indicate the other. The importance of these links is dramatically demonstrated when energy supplies are cut or curtailed. The disruption of oil supplies caused by the Middle East wars of 1956, 1967 and 1973, and the coal miners' and electricity workers' strikes in Britain in 1971 and 1974, emphasised the essential role of energy supplies in industrialised and urbanised societies as industrial production was reduced and power cuts affected the life of the nation.

However, despite the threat of disruption of supplies, one of the principal characteristics of energy consumption is that it is rising rapidly and Table 14.2 shows past and projected increases in world energy consumption.

Table 14.2. World Energy Consumption 1925–1980

Year	Million tonnes of coal equivalent
1925	1,485
1950	2,611
1970	6,821
1980 (est.)	11,195

Source: *UN Statistical Yearbook*, 1973.

The current rate of increase is estimated at about 5 per cent per annum, but the demand for energy in the economically advanced countries is expanding more rapidly than this, despite rising costs. As yet, the developing countries consume comparatively little, but there is a very high potential for growth if they sought to match consumption in the advanced countries. In Japan, for example, oil consumption was 34 million tonnes in 1960, but this increased by 16 per cent per annum to 261 million tonnes in 1974, and the problem is that world-wide increases on this scale could not be met from existing energy reserves.

Capital and Income Energy

Energy resources can be classified in two groups: fuel, which is used to generate heat; and power, which is used to provide a motive force. These purposes are not entirely separate, since heat from coal can be turned into steam to power a locomotive and water power can be used to produce electricity which produces heat, but they form a useful distinction in the discussion of energy resources.

Fuels form the principal source of energy in use at present, but the fossil fuels of coal, oil and natural gas, and the nuclear fuels of uranium and thorium must be regarded as the earth's **energy capital** that is being used rapidly and, once used, cannot be replaced. There have been great successes in the discovery of new reserves of oil in the North Sea and at Prudhoe Bay, Alaska, and large new reserves of coal have been found at Selby in Yorkshire. Although such discoveries extend estimated reserves, capital energy has definite limits that will eventually be reached.

Income energy comes from the continuing activity of the sun and gives man much better long-term prospects because it is a renewable resource. However, at the moment, renewable resources such as sun, wind and water power are little used, and only water power in the form of hydro-electricity makes any significant contribution to the world's energy supply. The limitation on the widespread replacement of fossil fuels by hydro-electricity is primarily economic, since electrically generated heat is much more expensive than that produced from fossil fuels, but there are also technological problems to be overcome if the heat of the sun is to be used as a direct form of energy.

As a result of the situation in which energy supplies are of vital importance to economic growth and the maintenance of living standards, while at the same time the earth's energy capital is being seriously depleted by increasing demand, ways of utilising the earth's energy income more efficiently will eventually have to be found. A geographical study of this complex energy situation involves four main considerations. First, the various sources of supply and demand must be identified. Secondly, the complex energy transport networks and the flows which overcome the spatial differences between supply and demand must be analysed. Thirdly, attention must be paid to the factors affecting the decision-making process in energy use. Finally, consideration must be given to the imbalance produced in the man–environment system by the over-use of resources. These resource management problems will be examined in Chapter Twenty-Five.

Sources of Supply and Demand

The world's known supplies of fuel and power are distributed in a very uneven pattern, as can be seen from Fig. 14.1, and it has been estimated that 90 per cent of coal reserves and 80 per cent of oil reserves lie north of latitude 20° N, while 80 per cent of the potential hydro-electric power sources lie south of this latitude.

In many ways, the absolute location of energy sources is less important than their location in economic space, especially their location relative to markets, since interest is usually focused on the most easily exploitable deposits. However, demand is growing so fast and political problems affect such a high proportion of the world's oil reserves that most known sources of fuel are utilised.

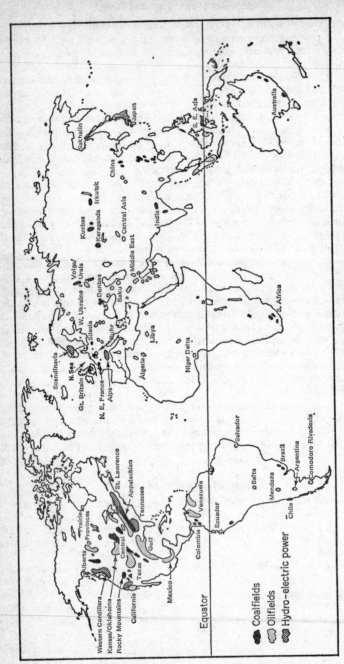

Fig. 14.1. World distribution of coal, oil and hydro-electric power.

Coalfields
Oilfields
Hydro-electric power

Western Cordillera
Kansas/Oklahoma
Rocky Mountains
California

Alberta
Prairie
Provinces
Texas

St. Lawrence
Central
Gulf

Appalachian
Tennessee

Mexico

Colombia
Ecuador
Venezuela

Salvador

Balta
Mendoza
Brazil
Chile
Argentina
Comodoro Rivadavia

Equator

Scandinavia
N. Sea
Gt. Britain
N. E. France
Alps

Silesia
Ruhr
Algeria
Libya
Niger Delta

W. Ukraine
Donbas
Baku
Middle East

Volga/
Urals

Kurzbas
Karaganda
Central Asia
India

Irkutsk
China

Sakhalin
Japan
S. E. Asia

S. Africa

Australia

Coal

The major coalfields of the world lie in the middle latitudes of the northern hemisphere, principally flanking the highlands of the Hercynian mountain system, and have provided the setting for the development of Western industrial civilisation. Coal was the first fuel used on a large scale and is associated with many revolutionary developments. The Newcomen steam engine, Darby's experiments in smelting iron, Watt's conversion of vertical motion into rotary motion and Stephenson's application of steam to transport were all milestones in the Industrial Revolution.

Coal is a dirty, bulky material which is difficult and costly to transport. Because inefficient early machines needed vast amounts of coal, industry moved to the coalfields, which have subsequently developed as the world's principal manufacturing regions (Chapter Fifteen).

All developed coalfields have seen the progression from a large number of small mines on the most accessible seams, to fewer larger and deeper mines. The winning of coal makes great demands on the labour force but in Europe and North America there have been considerable advances in mining technology. The first fully automated British colliery at Bevercotes in Nottinghamshire went into production in 1966 and it is estimated that by the late 1970s, 100 million tonnes of coal will be taken by automated machinery from British mines each year. Mechanisation has already doubled the coal output per man shift, and although the labour force has fallen, there has not been a corresponding fall in output. However, not all coalfields are easy to mechanise, and mines with heavily faulted or thin seams are difficult and expensive to work. In Britain, the Yorkshire, Nottingham and Derby Coalfield, with thick, level and continuous seams, can compete with other fuels, but there has been a general trend for cheaper fuels to be substituted for coal, and coal has faced increasing competition, especially from oil.

Coal consumption in Britain and Western Europe has declined, and remains about steady in the USA, as coal is being used for a smaller range of

Table 14.3.   Coal and Lignite—Estimated Reserves and Production in 1972
(million tonnes)

	Coal		Lignite	
	Reserves	*Production*	*Reserves*	*Production*
World total	6,641,200	2,144	2,041,400	806
USA	1,100,000	535	406,000	6
USSR	4,121,603	451	1,406,380	152
China	1,011,000	400	700	n.a.
Poland	45,741	151	14,862	38
UK	15,500	120	—	—
West Germany	70,000	103	62,000	110
India	106,260	75	2,063	3
South Africa	72,465	58	—	—
East Germany	50	1	30,000	248

Source: *UN Statistical Yearbook*, 1973.

purposes. Today there are two principal users of coal as a fuel in these areas. In Britain and the USA more than half the coal consumed is used for the production of electricity in thermal power stations, which have the advantage that under closely controlled conditions the efficiency of burning coal can be increased and pollution decreased. Coal also retains its traditional market in the smelting industry, where coking coal is still an essential raw material in the production of iron and steel. In addition, coal is important as a raw material in the chemical industry, where it is used for a range of products as diverse as aspirin and nylon.

In the newer industrial and developing countries, however, the story of declining production and consumption does not apply. In the USSR, China, India and Australia, for example, consumption is rising as heavy industries are developed and coal holds a similar position in the economy as it did in nineteenth-century Europe.

Petroleum

Petroleum is very much the fuel of the twentieth century. The first oil well was drilled at Titusville, Pennsylvania, in 1859, but only a small proportion of the crude oil was then used. The principal product was kerosene which was used for lighting, and until about 1900 more than half the crude oil was discarded as useless, but since 1900 changing demand and advances in refining technology have meant that almost all of the oil is now usable. The increase in demand has been enormous, as first, the use of the internal combustion engine has become universal, and secondly, oil has become the raw material of the petrochemical industry. Since 1913, world output has increased thirty times while coal output has barely trebled.

Like coal, petroleum is a fossil fuel, but unlike coal, it cannot be used as it comes out of the ground, and the petroleum industry has two aspects, production and refining. The distribution of the petroleum-producing countries is shown in Fig. 14.1, and production figures are given in Table 14.4. It is clear that the producing areas are different from the areas of coal production,

Table 14.4. **Leading World Petroleum Countries—Reserves, Production, and Refining Capacity in 1972**

(million tonnes)

Known reserves		Production		Refining capacity	
World	76,800	World	2,527	World (excl. USSR, China)	2,559
Saudi Arabia	18,685	USA	467	USA	672
Kuwait	10,197	USSR	400	Japan	204
Iran	8,515	Saudi Arabia	286	Italy	196
USSR	5,716	Iran	248	France	145
USA	4,899	Venezuela	168	West Germany	133
Iraq	4,433	Kuwait	151	UK	124
Libya	3,184	Libya	106	Netherlands	99
UAE	2,654	Nigeria	91	Canada	85
Venezuela	1,978	Canada	73	Venezuela	76
Nigeria	1,729	Iraq	71	Belgium	44

Source: *UN Statistical Yearbook*, 1973.

and since the major industrial economies were largely coal based, this means that oil has to be transported to markets there. Petroleum is shipped from the producing areas in the form of crude oil since the refining industry is now in the industrialised countries, and with the great increase in consumption, petroleum now forms the most important commodity, in terms of tonnage, in world trade.

Oil refineries could be located on the oil field, near the market or at some intermediate transhipment point, and in the early days of the industry, a location at source was the most economic. Since only a small part of the crude oil was used and between 6 and 10 per cent of the oil was used as refinery fuel, transport costs were avoided if refineries were built on the oil fields, but since 1945 there has been a major movement towards market locations, and as can be seen from Table 14.4 most refining capacity is now in the consuming countries of Western Europe, North America and Japan. These refineries are mainly located at transhipment points within these areas, especially in coastal locations, in order to handle imported oil.

The **relocation of the oil-refining industry** since 1945 has been brought about by the interaction of many factors, and clearly illustrates the complexity of the influences affecting spatial processes. First, there have been changes in the size, location and nature of the market. Between 1913 and 1974, world oil production increased from 55 million to 2,869 million tonnes under the influence of rapidly rising demand. Before 1945 this demand was largely concentrated in the USA, but since 1945 the growth areas have been Western Europe and Japan, and because of the size of this increase in demand, large-scale refining has become an economic proposition in these areas. This trend has been strongly reinforced by changes in the nature of demand. Before 1939, the principal demand in Europe was for petrol, and since Middle East oil yields only about 20 per cent petrol, a great deal of waste would have had to be carried to market refineries. Since 1945, a demand has grown for the full range of petroleum products (diesel fuel, heating oils, heavy oils) and crude oil can now be economically carried to Europe and Japan where it is almost all usable.

Secondly, the more efficient use of petroleum has been brought about by advances in refining technology which, as well as making nearly all of the crude oil usable, has meant that petrol can be produced from it almost regardless of its quality. As a result, refineries have been 'freed' from locations on certain types of oil field and, more important still, a refinery located near the market can draw crude oil from several different fields, with all the advantages that this gives. A third factor has been improvements in transport methods, and pipelines and supertankers are now capable of moving large quantities of crude oil cheaply over long distances. Moreover, it is cheaper to move the crude oil in bulk than it is to move finished products, and market locations have thus become more economic. Fourthly, the costs of building and operating a refinery are enormous, and the oil companies have considered it more sensible to make such large capital investments near to the markets, which are likely to remain, than on oil fields, which may become exhausted. Also, as a fifth factor, the oil from some fields may cease to become available because of political problems. Most of the world's oil fields are in rather politically unstable areas such as South America or the Middle East, and since the threat of nationalisation presents a major problem for the oil companies in some producing countries, large-scale capital investments are considered too risky there.

A final factor has been the activity of governments in the consuming countries, which has encouraged home locations by applying preferential tariffs to make it easier and cheaper to import crude oil rather than finished products. The aim has been to develop a refining industry to help safeguard fuel supplies as far as possible, to save foreign exchange (since crude oil is cheaper than finished products), and to provide a profitable export industry in finished petroleum products. There has also been an increasing demand for refineries to provide the raw material for the rapidly developing petro-chemical industry.

The interaction of these factors has radically altered the distribution of the oil-refining industry since 1945, and 80 per cent of capacity is now concentrated in Western Europe, North America and Japan. However, this separation between supply and demand poses serious problems for the consuming countries. Oil has been a cheap fuel until recently, and it proved such an attractive substitute for coal in transport, heating and electricity production that the industrialised economies have become very dependent on oil. However, the decisions of the Organisation of Petroleum Exporting Countries (OPEC) to raise the price of oil in 1973 and 1974 have now made it a relatively expensive fuel. Problems also arise for the consuming countries in that their fuel supplies are under outside control. Already, the rise in the price of Middle East oil is making previously uneconomic sources of oil look attractive. Exploration and production is now going ahead in very difficult conditions in the North Sea and Alaska and the geography of oil production is likely to change considerably in the next few years.

Table 14.5. Natural Gas—Reserves and Production 1972
(thousand million cubic metres)

Known reserves		Production	
World	54,100	World	1,140
USSR	18,633	USA	638
USA	7,535	USSR	221
Iran	5,656	Canada	83
Algeria	3,964	Netherlands	58
Netherlands	2,209	UK	27
Saudi Arabia	1,540	Romania	26
Canada	1,499	Mexico	19
UK	1,303	Iran	17
Venezuela	1,165	West Germany	17
Nigeria	1,161	Italy	14

Source: *UN Statistical Yearbook*, 1973.

Natural Gas

Natural gas can be found independently or in association with petroleum and this is reflected in Table 14.5, which shows that the distribution of world reserves includes oil-producing countries such as Saudi Arabia and Kuwait among others such as the Netherlands and the UK. However, production of natural gas is largely concentrated in North America, where it has long been used as a major source of energy, and Europe, where its development has been more recent, following large-scale discoveries in and around the North Sea.

Natural gas has considerable advantages as a fuel because it is clean and can be closely controlled for heating purposes. Government policies in the USA and Britain have regulated the price of gas and this has enlarged its markets in these countries.

Electricity

Electricity is a form rather than a source of energy because it is produced by man and not taken directly from nature. It is produced by two quite separate industries, each with its own locational requirements, although the end product is identical. **Thermo-electricity** is produced from a wide range of fuels which power steam turbines or internal combustion engines to drive generators. **Hydro-electricity** is produced by generators driven by turbines powered by the force of running water. Thermo-electricity is providing an increasing share of world production and the industry is the most rapidly expanding market for the primary fuels.

Production of electricity is largely concentrated in the developed countries, although much of the hydro-electric potential, already being utilised in Brazil, is in the developing countries (Table 14.6).

Table 14.6. Electricity Production by Leading Countries (1972)
(thousand million kilowatt-hours)

Total		Thermal		Nuclear		Hydro	
USA	1,853	USA	1,522	USA	54	USA	276
USSR	857	USSR	735	UK	29	Canada	178
Japan	429	Japan	331	France	14	USSR	123
West Germany	275	West Germany	252	Japan	9	Japan	88
UK	264	UK	230	West Germany	9	Norway	67
Canada	238	France	101	Canada	7	Sweden	53
France	163	Italy	86	Italy	4	France	48
Italy	135	Poland	75	Sweden	1	Brazil	43
Poland	76	East Germany	71			Italy	43
East Germany	73	South Africa	59			Spain	37

Source: *UN Statistical Yearbook*, 1973.

Electricity is unlike other power sources because it cannot be stored, but on the other hand it can be transmitted by cable to a maximum distance of 800 km. Within this distance, electricity is a flexible power source, easily distributed, and therefore attractive to industry and for domestic use, but the inability to store it makes the industry very susceptible to varying demand. Not only are there seasonal peaks of demand, but through 24 hours demand has peaks and lows, and generating capacity must be capable of matching demand at all times. At less than peak demand, equipment is under-used and uneconomic, and to overcome this problem, various solutions have been sought. Since peak times vary in England and France, a cable has been laid between the two countries so that one may supplement the other, and at a more local scale, night-storage heaters have been produced in which blocks of concrete are heated at off-peak times to release their heat slowly during periods of peak demand. As a result of these characteristics, electricity production tends to take place near to the market, or, in the case of hydro-electric power stations, which have to be located near the supply of water power, industries such as aluminium smelting which use vast amounts of electricity are attracted to the electricity source.

The construction of **thermo-electric** power stations is one of the world's major growth industries. Electricity can be generated from a wide range of fuels such as peat, lignite, nuclear fuels or the heat of the earth, but most is produced from coal and oil. The great advantage is that fuel can be converted efficiently and with little pollution. However, the principal location factor for a thermal generating station is not fuel, but the need for water to produce steam and for cooling purposes. A nuclear power station needs 160 million litres of water an hour, which largely explains why most of them are located on the coast, and even a conventional station needs about 14 million litres an hour per turbine.

As **hydro-electric** power stations use freely available running water to generate electricity, it might be supposed that hydro-electricity is the cheapest form. However, this is not the case, for free water power has to be balanced against the high costs of developing it, and very large capital investments have to be made in the form of dams and power stations.

The physical requirements for hydro-electric power generation include a sufficient head of water, a reliable water source throughout the year, a valley that can be dammed and bedrock that is stable and impervious. Such conditions occur very widely in the world, but a site will only be developed if capital is available to cover the immense installation costs, and if there is a market for the electricity which is often not the case in the underdeveloped countries. The market is a critical factor since the plant needs to run at full capacity to operate economically. In some cases, the market can be created, as for example, by the construction of the aluminium smelter at Kitimat in British Columbia, but much potential is currently unusable because there is no demand close at hand.

On the other hand, there is a trend for large-scale water control schemes to be multi-purpose, and large dams such as Aswan on the Nile are also concerned with flood control and irrigation, but despite this, very little electricity is produced outside the advanced industrial economies.

The Transport of Energy

To overcome the spatial differences between the sources of supply of fuel and power and the areas of demand, complex transport networks have been developed. Several methods of transport are used to move the different types of fuel to their markets and to distribute power in the form of electricity, and they can be classified under two headings.

The Continuous Media

One basic difference between the two classes of transport lies in their degree of flexibility. The continuous media of pipelines and transmission cables provide transport over fixed routes and each carry only one product. As a result of this inflexibility and because the installation of pipelines and cables involves heavy capital outlays, continuous media networks are only economically viable if supply and demand are large and constant. Their initial installation must also be carefully planned because subsequent changes are likely to involve heavy expenditure.

This creates problems in the case of electricity since it can only be carried by the continuous media, and consequently, simple cost factors are not the only ones operating. Social and political considerations are involved in programmes such as rural electrification, and consumer costs may be lowered by government subsidies. Additional costs can also be incurred for social reasons when cables are carefully routed or buried underground to preserve areas of outstanding natural beauty such as the National Parks in Britain. Despite these problems, electricity has become so important in the industrial and domestic life of the advanced economies that extensive electricity transmission networks have been established and even remote rural areas have supplies.

Pipelines are used principally for the transport of oil and natural gas, and differ from transmission cables in that the products can be carried by alternative methods. In fact, many pipelines are just one link in a network of movement where oil is carried from the oil field to the coast by pipeline, from port to port by tanker, and from port to refinery by a second pipeline, although pipelines often directly connect producer and consumer. Pipelines are particularly well developed in the USA, where they carry about 17 per cent of all freight per tonne–kilometre, and are also very important in Canada, the USSR, the Middle East and Venezuela. Their importance has increased in Europe in recent years with the development of North Sea oil and gas deposits and the relocation of much refinery capacity away from the coast in Germany.

The Discontinuous Media

Although large amounts of fuel can be pumped economically between fixed points by pipeline, other forms of transport are more flexible because routes, types and quantities of fuel can be changed to take account of changes in supply and demand. The disadvantage of the discontinuous media of shipping, road and rail is that each break in a journey involves additional costs, particularly if transhipment is necessary.

Despite this problem, and the expensive berthing facilities that they require, tankers offer the lowest rates for the long-distance movement of large quantities of oil, and over half the world's shipping is employed in oil transport. Water has always been the cheapest medium of transport for bulky goods but recent increases in tanker size have meant that rates can be further reduced because the costs of running a large ship can be spread over a large cargo so that each tonne of cargo carries only a small proportion of the transport cost. However, the movement of such large quantities of oil is not without risk either to the ship, where the fire hazard is considerable, or to the environment, as was demonstrated by the devastating effects of the wreck of the *Torrey Canyon* on the beaches of Cornwall and Brittany in 1967. In the case of the transport of natural gas, additional costs are involved because the only practical way of moving gas outside pipelines is to liquefy it, and the extremely low temperatures that are needed require expensive, technically advanced, refrigerated ships. Pipelines are therefore a better method of transporting gas, but as in the case of the shipment of Algerian gas to Britain, ships are the only practical proposition.

Coal remains an important element in world trade but only about 5 per cent of coal mined is exported. The principal reason for this is that the coal-fields and the industrial areas are closely linked, and although large amounts of coal are transported, unlike oil, most movement is over short distances within countries. Most coal is moved by rail (over 70 per cent in the USA), but road and water transport are also important, and one of the principal characteristics of the discontinuous media is that a journey may have a number of different links. In some cases coal is used as a substitute cargo in preference to ballast and in the USA the volume has been sufficient to fuel an industrial region on the southern shores of Lake Erie. Originally, ports such as Cleveland, Ashtabula, Erie and Toledo were simply transhipment points for iron ore coming from Lake Superior to the iron and steel industry located on the coalfield around Pittsburgh. Instead of returning from Pittsburgh empty, however, barges and rail-cars carried coal back to the lakeshore and the presence of both coal and iron ore led to the establishment of an iron and steel industry there. Industrial areas based on similar return arrangements are found in the USSR and Australia.

It must be remembered that although the discontinuous media are more flexible than the continuous, this flexibility is still constrained. The flexibility of rail transport is limited by the nature of the rail network, and fuel has to compete with flows of other commodities, but installations such as power stations requiring large and regular deliveries of fuel can overcome these problems by having special rail links. The most flexible form of land transport is by road and this is increasingly providing the final link in the journey from producer to consumer, but problems arise from the presence of large vehicles on roads which were not designed for them, and there is a strong environmental lobby to keep down the size of lorries despite the economic advantages that they afford.

This is an important issue. Except in the case of electricity where no alternative is available, a number of methods can be used to transport fuel and the decisions about which method is used will depend on a wide range of factors, social and political as well as economic. Increasing attention is being given to the ways in which such decisions are reached, including the study of how various sources of energy are chosen for particular purposes.

Choosing an Energy Supply

There are five main considerations that affect decisions about which type of fuel or power is used in industry, transport and so on, but they do not operate independently and a final decision will normally result from a balance of advantage against disadvantage.

The **availability** of an energy source is a prime factor in its use, and availability has varied considerably through time and space in the past. However, change has been a major characteristic in the story of the supply of energy, and sources have not only increased in size and number, especially since the late nineteenth century, but have also become available in much wider areas than formerly. Increasing demand for energy and technological advances that enable supplies to be exploited and distributed have been the causes of this increase in availability and this has produced considerable geographical consequences. The first great power source, coal, originally tied industry very closely to its areas of production, and because coal was not available in many areas and was difficult to move, industry became very localised. The subsequent development of energy sources has had a liberalising effect on industrial location. Petroleum and its refined products are more easily distributed than coal and this flexibility has been massively reinforced by the effect that the development of the internal combustion engine has had on transport. Electricity has also contributed greatly to the widespread distribution of industry as it is readily available at the end of a power line. New industrial landscapes have been produced by the widespread availability of electricity and the rural factories of the Central Lakes Region of Sweden contrast markedly with the older, coal-based industrial regions of Germany and Britain.

The **suitability** of an energy source for a particular purpose will also affect whether or not it is chosen. In the field of transport, various forms of energy can be used in some operations, and railway locomotives can be powered by wood, coal, oil, electricity and even grass. In this case, availability is often the critical factor, but in others the choice is much more restricted, and although some road vehicles are electrically powered, the overwhelming majority are powered by petrol and diesel engines since petroleum is the most suitable fuel. In industry, the degree of control needed in an operation will affect the choice of fuel. The large-scale smelting of iron is fuelled by coal, but for special steels, electric arc furnaces are more suitable for maintaining high, even temperatures at critical periods. Similarly, aluminium smelting needs large amounts of electricity and the industry is generally restricted to hydro-electric power sites which produce it. However, technical suitability is only one consideration since a choice of energy supplies can often be made, and economic suitability plays a more important role.

The **cost** of an energy source, if available and technically suitable, will usually be the deciding factor in its use, but cost is rather a difficult factor to assess. The costs of an energy source are made up of three main elements: production costs, transport and distribution costs and various tax costs. These three elements vary in importance from fuel to fuel and also from time to time for each fuel. As a result, the advantage that one fuel has over another is not constant, and this can have considerable consequences for the pattern of production. A rise in the cost of one fuel can give another fuel an advantage and allow previous uneconomic sources to be worked profitably.

Recent changes in the cost of oil illustrate the problem well, for until the mid-1960s oil was a cheap form of energy, and in industrial Europe, Middle East oil was pricing coal out of important markets such as the generation of electricity. The closure of the Suez Canal in 1967 immediately caused prices to rise because of the increase in transport costs, but the development of the supertanker and increased refinery efficiency helped to keep prices down, and oil still remained a cheap fuel. This situation was radically changed by the decision of the OPEC bloc in 1973 to raise crude oil prices substantially, and thus alter the position of oil compared with other energy sources. Coal has again become competitive in Europe for electricity production and the high-cost North Sea and Alaskan oil fields have become economically as well as politically attractive.

The type of market will also affect decisions about which source of energy is chosen. For a large, concentrated market, oil and gas costs can be cut by increasing the size of tankers and pipelines, but distribution to a number of widely scattered industrial settlements raises different problems, and in this case, electricity may be most easily distributed. Different markets also have different patterns of demand and where there are considerable fluctuations, the advantage lies with coal and oil which can be stockpiled, and with gas production which can be regulated. Electricity cannot be stored, and as a result the development of hydro-electric schemes requires detailed investigation of the market potential at the planning stage.

The interaction of these four factors produces the use of a variety of fuels, and this is described as the **fuel mix** of a country, but the composition of this mix is unlikely to reflect only economic and technical factors. Political factors also play a major role. Fuel and power are vital in a modern industrial economy, and this importance is reflected in the extent of government intervention in a nation's energy policy. The supply of energy is a matter of public concern, and in Britain, coal, gas and electricity production is undertaken by public organisations, while the government has shares in oil companies and influences the consumption of oil through taxation. Governments intervene directly in energy policy, especially in sensitive areas such as the building of nuclear power stations, and in equalising prices between different fuels such as natural and coal gas. Indirectly, legislation such as Clean Air Acts also affects the use of fuel, especially for heating in cities, and has been a major element in the change from coal to oil fired boilers.

Conclusion

The supply of fuel and power is a vital element in economic activity, making production possible and enabling distribution to the consumer to take place. Its importance increases in all sections of the economy as a country develops, as much in primary production such as fishing or agriculture as in manufacturing industry, and its role is vital in transport, which forms the binding link of national economies within the international economy. The importance of energy supplies is greatly emphasised when they are disrupted, either by wars or industrial disputes, or by significant changes in their price, and 'the energy crisis' which developed in 1974 is likely to remain a major preoccupation of the industrialised countries.

In view of the vast energy inflow to the earth from the sun each day, this may seem a surprising problem, but it arises from the fact that at present it is the capital energy of the earth, stored in the form of coal, oil and so on, which is mainly used. Some use is being made of income energy in the form of hydro-electric power, but only a minute proportion of the potential is presently being tapped. In the future, this form of energy must supply man's needs since the capital energy is finite, and it is hoped that advances in technology will produce new energy sources such as solar batteries, or enable old sources such as windpower for shipping to be used more effectively.

Suggested Further Reading

Estall, R. C., and Buchanan, R. O., *Industrial Activity and Economic Geography* (2nd edn), Hutchinson, London, 1966.

Guyol, N. B., *Energy in the Perspective of Geography*, Prentice-Hall, Englewood Cliffs, New Jersey, 1971.

Manners, G., *The Geography of Energy* (2nd edn), Hutchinson, London, 1971.

Odell, P. R., *An Economic Geography of Oil*, Bell, London, 1963.

Odell, P. R., *Oil and World Power: A Geographical Interpretation*, Penguin, Harmondsworth, 1970.

Simpson, E. S., *Coal and the Power Industries in Postwar Britain*, Longman, London, 1966.

CHAPTER FIFTEEN

THE LOCATION OF INDUSTRY

The questions 'where?' and 'why there?' are basic in geography, and in any study of industry, the location of industry and the reasons for that location need to be identified and analysed.

Finding the Location of Industry

The first task of the industrial geographer is to collect and organise the necessary data so that specific locations and general distributions can be mapped. This task is not as simple as it might at first appear, for there are a number of problems to be solved.

Defining and Classifying Industry

It would be useful at the outset to explain what is meant by the term 'industry', since there is often confusion as to what it includes. This confusion arises from the fact that the fishing industry, the steel industry, the tourist industry or even the 'pop' industry are talked about in general terms, but each of these 'industries' represents a different type of economic activity.

Fishing, forestry, agriculture and mining are **primary** activities, concerned with the production of raw materials for both foodstuffs and industrial use, while the processing, fabrication and manufacture of these primary products are known as **secondary** activities. These activities are linked by the **tertiary** activities, which are basically concerned with the distribution of primary and secondary products through systems of transport, wholesaling and retailing. This group also includes the provision of personal services through the service trades and professions. In recent years, as economic organisation has become more complex, a further subdivision has become necessary, and it is now recognised that there is a **quarternary** group concerned with education, research and communication activities. This sector is especially concerned with research and development, and is developing in science-based industrial complexes such as Boston, Massachusetts, and the Palo Alto/Bay area in California.

Faced with this range of activity, the term 'industry' is usually used by the geographer to describe those activities in the secondary sector, and is particularly concerned with **manufacturing**. An account of the distribution of industry in Australia, for example, would not include agriculture, even though sheep farming produces an industrial raw material.

Unfortunately, there is now the problem of defining the term 'manufacturing', since this term also can include many things. The United Nations defines manufacturing as 'the mechanical or chemical transformation of inorganic or organic substances into new products, whether the work is performed by power-driven machinery or by hand, whether it is done in a factory or in the worker's home, and whether the products are sold wholesale or retail'. This is a very wide definition, however, and 'manufacturing' is more usually restricted to modern manufacturing industry with its sophisticated products and elaborate structures. Characterised by complex methods, the specialisation of labour, the use of machinery and inanimate power, modern manufacturing employs a large proportion of the working population, and its vast output has enabled the industrialised countries to develop a distinct and very favoured type of economy.

In view of the complexity of modern manufacturing, it is impossible to describe the specific characteristics of each industry in an area, and classes must be used, grouping together industries which are 'almost' alike. Many **industrial classification systems** have been developed, such as the British Census Classification and the US Standard Industrial Classification, but while these systems work within countries, there is the difficulty of achieving comparability among nations having various classifications. Industries such as iron smelting and oil refining do not create many problems, but imprecise groups such as engineering leave scope for wide interpretation. The problem has been tackled by the United Nations and there is now the International Standard Industrial Classification of all Economic Activities, but good comparability between nations of data collected for their own purposes will be difficult to achieve. This means that caution must be used when interpreting maps showing international distributions of even single industries.

The Problem of Measuring Industry

The answer to the question 'where is industry located?' includes not only a consideration of the type of industry, but also of how much industry is in a particular location. This also creates problems, for there are several criteria that can be used to measure industry, and different methods of measurement give different results.

Of these measures, the simplest is the **number of factories**, since this information is the most readily available. It does have limitations, however, because it takes no account of size, and a factory employing 5,000 men with a wide range of products is given the same ranking as a one-product factory employing 50 men.

The most widely used measure is the **number of employees**, since the information is usually available and is easily understood. Its major disadvantage is that it takes no account of mechanisation, and a small workforce with modern machines can be much more productive than a large workforce.

Attempts have been made to find some more significant measure than simply total numbers. The number of production workers has also been used, but the underlying assumption that these can be separated from a non-productive administrative, research and service staff is unrealistic. A measure which can be used to show the relative importance of industry in an area is the **percentage of the labour force** engaged in manufacturing, but like all relative measures, its weakness is that it takes no account of absolute employment and a small area with a high proportion of industrial workers may appear more important than a major industrial area with a large tertiary sector.

In addition to measures of size and relative importance, there are a number of **value** measures that can be used. One of the least useful is the value of **raw materials** going into a product since it only measures amounts being used and not the amount of manufacturing that takes place, but this can be overcome to some extent by measuring the value of the **finished product**. Unfortunately, many products—cars, for example—are made up of components made in different factories and these may be counted many times over. The best value measure is probably **value added**, when the difference between the value of the materials used and the value of the finished product is measured, representing the approximate value added in manufacture. This is the best indicator of the relative economic importance of manufacturing in different industries and different areas. If the value of **labour**, as represented by wages and salaries, is isolated from this figure, comparison with other areas will show geographical differences in the contribution that labour makes to production. This can also be related to the value of **capital invested**, which is the best indicator of mechanisation in industry, although it must be emphasised that factories do not always run to capacity and much capital may be idle.

Useful as they are, all these value measures share a number of disadvantages. Comparisons through time are very difficult since value is expressed in money terms, which vary with inflation and deflation, and since there is no world currency, international comparisons are difficult. There is also a practical difficulty in that much information is confidential and therefore unavailable.

Since the prime objective of industry is production, it might seem that the most obvious measure to use when assessing the size of industry would be its **physical output**, but although it is useful in comparing factories within the same industry, comparisons between industries are impossible.

Identifying Industrial Regions

With such a wide range of criteria available to measure the amount of industry, each with its advantages and disadvantages, it is difficult to say with precision how much industry is located in an area. Yet it is a problem that must be solved if we are to be able to identify concentrations of manufacturing as **industrial regions**.

Many attempts have been made to analyse the location of industry using the measures discussed, especially in studies aimed at delimiting the manufacturing belt of the north-eastern USA. A wide range of single criteria have been used, such as the number of production workers or the amount of value added, but there has been an increasing emphasis on the use of more than one criterion. Several single criteria have been mapped and the individual distributions have been superimposed on one map, for example. Other criteria have been expressed as simple ratios, such as the ratio of total employment to manufacturing employment, while much more complicated multiple-criteria systems have been developed to produce indices of magnitude, intensity and concentration, location quotients, coefficients of localisation and location coefficients.

Nevertheless, despite these attempts, there is still no single way to measure the distribution of industry, and any map reflects the peculiarities of the criteria on which it is based. Work published in 1961 suggested that there was an answer, when it was found that all but one of thirteen single measures of manufacturing in the USA were highly correlated, suggesting that it makes little difference which measure is employed since they all give the same result. Unfortunately, recent work on the measurement of manufacturing in Argentina and Australia has not found such high levels of correlation, and has reopened the question of what is the most suitable measure.

The World Distribution of Industry

Despite the fact that the location of industry cannot be measured with precision, it is an observable fact that there are parts of the world with much more industry than others, and there are some areas where industry is so concentrated that they must be classified as industrial regions. These areas are shown in Fig. 15.1, although it must be remembered that they have been identified with as much subjective judgement as objective measurement.

The five main centres of industrial development are the north-eastern USA, Europe, the western USSR, northern India and eastern Asia, and although there are some minor concentrations outside these areas, there are large areas devoid of any industry. The distribution pattern of world industry as shown on the map exhibits some interesting features. Most industrial development is located in the middle latitudes and is closely associated with coalfields and areas of European settlement. The tropical belt is characterised by an almost total absence of industry.

Explaining the Location of Industry

When the general distribution of industry has been mapped, the next task is to explain why industry is located where it is, a process that involves the explanation of both specific locations and general distributions. It must be known, for example, not only why the Spencer steelworks was built east of Newport and not west of it, but why it was built in South Wales and not in Scotland or Lincolnshire or any of the other sites that were considered and rejected.

Approaches to the Problem of Location

Industrial locations can be explained in two ways: first, by explaining why certain areas are attractive to industry; and secondly by explaining why certain industries are attracted to particular areas. These two approaches are of course complementary, but they involve differences in emphasis.

The first approach places the emphasis upon the region and the various industries within it, and seeks to identify the advantages that the region offers. This **regional approach** operates at various levels, for there is not only the problem of the world distribution of industry, but also of the distribution of industry within a country, within a region or even within a town. In each of these units there is a pattern that needs to be explained.

The advantages that an area offers fall into a number of categories. The presence in an area of suitable sites, favourable climate, easy access to sources of power and raw materials and nearness to large markets can be considered as **natural advantages**, which are reinforced as the area develops by **acquired advantages**. These include good transport facilities, commercial services, skilled labour, market organisation and the development of subsidiary services. In themselves, however, natural and acquired advantages are not sufficient to explain why industry is located in a region, because regions with similar advantages do not necessarily have the same industries. For an industry to be located in a region, it must enjoy a **comparative advantage** over other industries similarly attracted but unable to compete for limited resources. For example, commerce has a comparative advantage over industry in the central areas of

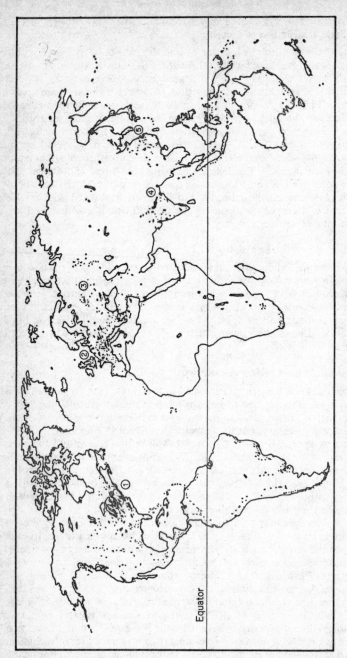

Fig. 15.1. World distribution of manufacturing.

cities, and as a result, industry is being forced out (Chapter Nineteen). Finally, once an area has started to expand, **cumulative advantages** develop as people begin to move in and new industries are attracted to serve the growing market.

The greater the number of advantages an area possesses, the greater will be its attraction for industry, and the major industrial areas of the world can be seen as concentrations of advantages.

The second approach to the problem puts the emphasis upon the explanation of the distribution of particular **industries**, and attention is given to the various regions in which it is located. An attempt is made, for example, to explain why some industries are located on coalfields while others are found in ports, or why some industries are highly localised while others are widely distributed. A study of the car industry would seek to explain why the industry is widely distributed in many regions and why it has particular locations within those regions, by isolating the factors that affect the costs of car production and examining them in relation to the locations chosen.

Both these approaches are complementary in that they are concerned with the identification of the factors that affect the location of industry.

The Factors that Affect the Location of Industry

From the studies of manufacturing regions and industries that have been made, it is apparent that there are many factors operating to affect the location of industry. Many geography textbooks divide these factors into geographical and non-geographical factors, but although historical, economic, social or political factors can be identified, it is not so easy to say what is meant by a **geographical factor**.

Geographical factors are usually taken as being those which in themselves are of a geographical nature, such as relief, climate, raw materials and so on, while non-geographical factors include government activity, management and human factors. This tends to produce a deterministic view of location (Chapter One), and reflects the geographers' attempt to explain location in terms of **absolute** values operating at a particular place. As an example, the location of the Lancashire cotton industry has often been explained in terms of the presence of a humid climate, soft water, abundant coal and the position of Liverpool in the Atlantic trade. Insufficient attention has been paid to the existence of these conditions elsewhere, such as South Wales or Scotland, where large-scale cotton industries did not develop, and point to the fact that the development of the Lancashire cotton industry must be explained in **relative** terms. It is much more satisfactory that there should not be a distinction between geographical and non-geographical factors, but that factors that have **geographical consequences** should be sought.

In attempting to explain the location of industry, therefore, it is necessary to isolate the factors that have operated to produce these locations, but before this is done, there are a number of points that must be emphasised. First, these factors, although isolated in this chapter, have not operated in isolation, but in combination in a complex system of inter-relationships with other factors that makes it difficult to assess the importance of any one factor. Secondly, the relative importance of these factors varies from time to time, from area to area, from industry to industry, and within different types of economy, making it difficult to draw general conclusions. Thirdly, it must be remembered that not all the influences that have operated have been favourable, and that most good locations have been those where the number of favourable factors have outweighed the unfavourable ones. In reality, an optimum location is a relative term.

Assembly, Processing and Distribution

The first and most important group of factors that affect the location of industry are those associated with the assembly, processing and distribution of materials and products.

Despite the difficulties associated with the use of the term geographical factor, it might be applied to **distance**, which is one of the most important factors explaining patterns of economic activity. The desire to reduce distance means that **transfer costs** are central to the problem of industrial location. These transfer costs are largely made up of the direct costs of transporting goods from place to place, but they also include the indirect costs such as insurance, damage in transit and clerical costs.

Distance is not simply a question of kilometres, although this is very important, as a comparison of moving goods in the Andes with moving goods on the Prairies will show. As discussed in Chapter Nine, it is much better to talk in terms of **economic distance**, which is affected by other considerations such as the type of transport, the type of commodity, freight rates and so on. The basic concern of the manufacturer is to reduce economic distance, and transport plays a central role in location.

All industries use **materials**, and therefore must be in a location to get them economically. In the early period of manufacturing, raw materials were very important because of the transport problem, and even today there are industries in which raw materials play an important role. In industries which lose either bulk or weight in the manufacturing process, such as copper smelting, it is obviously undesirable to carry waste, or in industries where the raw material is perishable, such as fruit canning, there is the danger that the material will become unusable, and processing takes place near to the raw material. Raw materials are becoming much less important as a location factor for a number of reasons. First, as transport has developed and special handling facilities have become available, the movement of raw materials has become easier. Secondly, as industry has become more complex, fewer and fewer firms are raw material based, and in the USA about 80 per cent of manufacturers start with semi-processed or even finished products. Thirdly, technological improvements have intensified the use of materials so that there is less waste in manufacture, and materials themselves are being improved at source to enable them to be transported. Fourthly, as other factors such as markets and labour supply have gained in importance, raw materials have declined relatively.

Energy is used to generate heat and provide a motive force, and energy for industry is provided by various sources of fuel and power (Chapter Fourteen). Historically, **energy sources** have had a considerable effect on the location of industry, and there is still a strong correlation between industry and coalfields. This came about because energy was almost immovable in the early period of manufacturing, and because of the inefficiency of the processes by which materials were transformed into energy, large amounts of coal were required. Because costs are still involved in the transport of energy, industries using large amounts, such as the electrochemical and electrometallurgical industries, are still located near to sources of cheap electricity.

Energy, like raw materials, is nevertheless declining in importance as a location factor. Fuel efficiency has been improved considerably, and whereas eight or ten tonnes of coal were needed to smelt a tonne of pig iron in the eighteenth century, the present figure of less than one tonne makes a coalfield location less essential. The grip of the coalfields has also been weakened by the possibility of substituting other forms of fuel and power, especially as new sources have been made available through the development of electricity grids and oil and gas pipelines, and the energy requirements of the modern growth industries are much less locationally demanding.

Although still not a major factor, **water supplies** have become of increasing importance in recent years. Water is used in most industrial plant for processing, steam raising, or cooling, and in considering the location of industry, both the quantity and the quality of the water supply must be considered. It is not usually appreciated how much water is used in industry, but the production of a tonne of steel may take 200,000 litres, and even a litre of beer involves the use of over 240 litres of water, much of it of a high level of purity. Water supply will play an increasing part in industry, and in southern California, for example, one of the fastest growing areas of the USA, further growth is being seriously threatened by the shortage of water, despite the development of large-scale water supply projects.

Closely associated with the problem of water supply is the problem of **waste disposal.** The most common method of disposing of industrial waste is to dump it in rivers, but as demand for water increases, this must be seen as an undesirable activity, and sites with expensive disposal problems are not likely to attract industry.

Much more important as a factor at the moment is the cost and availability of labour. The **cost of labour** is not easy to ascertain, because true costs are not what one has to pay, but what one gets back, and assessing the productivity of a labour force is more than a simple consideration of wage rates. Measuring productivity entails balancing wages against output, and this balance can be affected by many considerations such as absenteeism, turnover rates and labour relations which all affect the costs of production. These costs vary geographically, and therefore have locational consequences, as also do differences in the **availability of labour.** Such differences are found not only in the quantity of labour available, but also in the quality of labour, as represented by the skills that an area can offer. In an automated age, craft skills are obviously becoming less important, but an area with a skilled and versatile labour force remains attractive. How attractive depends to a large extent on the type of industry, for oil refineries employ few men and can almost afford to ignore labour as a factor, especially when it is balanced against more critical factors such as access to deep water, but, in contrast, the clothing manufacturer in a labour-intensive industry is far less free to choose.

The real difficulty in evaluating the role of labour in location concerns the **mobility of labour.** Labour can be mobile either between jobs or between areas, and the degree to which it is mobile will affect its locational power. If labour were completely mobile, for example, it would have no locational power because workers would move to jobs, while an immobile labour force would attract industry. At the moment it seems that labour is relatively immobile, but mobility is increasing, especially among young professional and skilled workers.

A very specialised form of labour is **management**, and many locations can only be understood in terms of management decisions. Historically, the entrepreneurs who provided the initiative and enterprise in many industries were considered so important as to constitute the fourth factor of production. With the development of the limited liability company, this special status is no longer given, but good management is still an important factor in the choice of sites, and especially in keeping a firm in business. The manufacturer must ask whether an area is likely to produce good managers, or whether a chosen area can attract such men, and one of the major obstacles to industrialisation in the underdeveloped countries is the shortage of management skills.

Another historically important factor was the local availability of **money capital**. With the development of banking services, however, money capital has become much more mobile, and within a country has little locational effect. Internationally, money is much less mobile, especially to unstable areas with high risk and uncertain returns, and the availability of money, either as loans or aid, can play an important role in the underdeveloped countries.

In considering the role of these factors, it must not be forgotten that the purpose of industry is to produce goods for sale, and therefore the **market** is an important locational consideration. Indeed, as the pull of materials and energy sources has declined, the market has become the prime consideration. Markets are attractive to industries whose products increase in weight, bulk or fragility in the manufacturing process, such as beer, cars or radios, because a market location for these industries will reduce transfer costs. Perishable goods such as newspapers and bread benefit from a market location, as do clothing industries, where there is need for direct contact between producer and customer, while some industries are attracted to the market because it provides materials such as steel scrap. The market is also a concentration of labour and a concentration of spending power, and the larger it is, the greater the attraction it exerts. Some industries cannot operate economically below a certain level because of the need for economies of scale, and modern blast furnaces which operate in million tonne per annum units must increasingly be in market locations.

Geographical Inertia

In explaining the present distribution of industry, not only is it necessary to discover the facts that operated to attract industry initially, but also those facts which explain why industry has remained in that location, often after the initial advantages have disappeared. This second group of factors consists of those encouraging **inertia**.

Capital can be divided under two headings—money capital and physical capital—and although it has been indicated that money capital is quite mobile, physical capital such as factories, machinery and homes is not. Physical capital can be mobile between uses, and cotton mills in Lancashire are now being used for light engineering, but geographical mobility is rare and it is usually cheaper to modernise or expand an existing location rather than move to a new site. This **capital immobility** is therefore a major factor encouraging inertia.

Inertia is also encouraged by the development of many **secondary advantages** that arise from the presence of industry in an area. These may offset the loss of the original attractions, and it can be argued that the ability of an area to keep its industry is as important as the ability to attract it. The presence of some of the factors already examined, such as good transport, labour, economic and social facilities and services, is important in encouraging inertia, but there are other factors resulting from the advantages that a firm can get from being in association with other firms in an area. Some industries can be regarded as location leaders either because they provide materials for other industries, as steel attracts engineering, or because they require specialist firms to supply parts, as cars attract components. These **linkages**, together with the advantages that accrue from the economies that can be gained in areas where factories are in close association with the factories around them, result in the **concentration** of industry in certain areas. Industry attracts industry, and when they are reinforced by the development of specialised services, these concentrations have considerable staying power.

Environment

It is being realised that one of the consequences of the increasing mobility of labour, in an age of increasing leisure, is that new industries must be located in areas that can attract labour, especially skilled and professional labour. As a result, a third group of factors, associated with the physical attractions of an area, must be considered.

In the USA the state with the greatest rate of population growth in the period 1960–70 was Nevada, followed by Florida and Arizona, reflecting an increasing demand for congenial living conditions. In one study, it was found that 25 per cent of firms had selected Colorado and Utah because of the climate, and **climate** has been a factor affecting location in a number of ways. In the USA, for example, the warmer states have a comparative cost advantage over the colder states, and a southern industrial worker who needs to spend less on clothing and home heating will accept a salary of 10 or 20 per cent less than his northern counterpart. The aircraft industry has moved to the South-West partly for the climatic advantage as hangar heating costs have been reduced and good flying weather increased.

Government Intervention

Until now, the assumption has been made that manufacturers are free to locate wherever they think they can get acceptable returns, but there is a fourth group of factors, external to the manufacturing process, which has to be considered. In particular, there are those factors by which **governments** encourage or restrict development. In planned economies, the location of industry is strictly controlled, but even in free enterprise economies government influence is being increasingly felt. Most Western countries operate mixed economies, and use a mixture of compulsion and inducement to influence industrial location (Chapter Twenty-three).

There are a number of reasons why governments seek to affect location. Economic and social considerations are important since it is the duty of government to ensure that a country's resources are used to the best advantage and that there are no great inequalities in the distribution of wealth. Political considerations are also important, in that inequalities such as those arising from persistent unemployment are a threat to political stability, and most governments, at least in Western Europe, have regional planning policies aimed at reducing serious regional imbalances. Finally, strategic considerations must be taken into account, especially in times of war when key industries are moved to 'safe' locations.

There are factors operating at the local level also. Variations in regulations concerning working conditions in federal countries can be important and were a factor encouraging the movement of the US cotton industry from New England to the South because women there could work the night shifts that were illegal in New England. Local rates and taxes also vary, and though not a major factor, played a part in the location of the Chicago steel industry across the state line in Indiana rather than in Illinois. Local authorities also use inducements to attract industry by establishing industrial estates or offering tax incentives, and the operation of local planning controls, especially the practice of zoning areas for specific purposes, has a strong influence on the precise location of industry.

The Human Factor

Finally, it must be remembered that industry does not just grow, but develops as the result of **human decisions**, and although these decisions are greatly affected by economic considerations, the ultimate choice of location is taken by men (Chapter Two). As a result, precise locations are often the result of fortuitous circumstance. One of the best-known examples of this is the location of the car industry in Oxford, which began there because William Morris bought the school in which his father had been taught for his first factory. On a wider scale, the world distribution of industry and its correlation with areas of European settlement reflect something in the social and economic systems of Europe which, unlike Asia, encouraged innovation and provided a climate of opinion in which change was possible.

The Dynamic Element in Location

Geography is not only concerned with existing locations: it is also concerned with change, and one of the most important features of industrial location is that it is dynamic. The factors that affect location are constantly changing as new sources of supply are discovered, new demands develop, new forms of production are introduced and methods of transport improve. As a consequence, locational relationships are always relative and subject to change through time. Major trends of change must therefore be identified and their locational consequences examined.

First, there has been a considerable **increase in industrial output**. It can be seen from Table 15.1 that using output in 1963 as the base, the index for the production of manufactured goods increased by 77 per cent in the ten years to 1972. This is partly due to the fact that industry has expanded in many of the developing countries, but the real growth has been in those countries already industrialised, especially the USA. In these major industrial countries, not only is total output rising, but more significantly, the rate of growth is accelerating as growth becomes cumulative.

Secondly, industrial organisation and production is becoming more complex. Technical change has always been a factor affecting location, but in recent years the **rate of innovation** has increased rapidly. This has been a major element in the growth of output with innovations such as the basic oxygen techniques and computer-controlled processes in the steel industry greatly affecting production. Industry is increasingly science-based, and shortages of technical know-how in the underdeveloped countries will cause them to fall even further behind.

Table 15.1. Indices of World Production, Trade and Population Growth 1963-72

	1963	1964	1965	1966	1967	1968	1969	1970	1971	1972
Manufactured goods	100	108	116	126	132	142	153	158	165	177
Minerals	100	106	111	116	120	127	133	142	145	148
Agriculture: food	100	104	105	110	114	118	119	122	125	124
Agriculture: non-food	100	101	103	106	107	109	112	114	115	119
World trade	100	110	118	127	134	152	169	184	193	211
Population	100	102	104	107	109	111	114	116	119	122

Source: *UN Statistical Yearbook*, 1973.

As new types of materials are required and existing sources of traditional materials are exhausted, industry will need **new sources of supply**. Table 15.1 shows that there has been a steady increase in the production of minerals, and with it there have been many geographical changes. In recent years, for example, the geography of iron ore production has changed as beneficiation techniques have been developed for concentrating ores, and bulk carrier ships have increased in size. As the southern hemisphere has become a major source of ore, the average length of iron ore haul has increased dramatically, and by 1967 ore shipments to West Germany averaged 4,800 km, to Japan 11,250 km, and some ores were being carried 19,000 km.

The **nature of demand** is also constantly changing. As standards of living increase in the developed countries, the relative importance of industries producing the basic necessities of life has declined. The index of world production in the food industries only rose by 51 per cent, and textiles by 42 per cent in the period 1963-72, while, in contrast, metal products rose by 95 per cent, and chemicals and petroleum/coal products rose by 124 per cent.

With the growing complexity of technology, the increasing volume of demand and the growth of international business organisations, the **size of the manufacturing unit** has grown. As competition has grown, it has become uneconomic to think in terms of iron and steel plant of less than one million tonnes annual capacity, and giants with twelve million tonne capacities are so cutting their costs of production that the small producer cannot compete in world markets. In order to effect the necessary economies of scale, many firms are now internationally based, and the development of the international corporation, with large financial and technical resources, is becoming common.

This international approach is part of an **increasing interdependence** among countries for sources of supply of materials, energy and markets for manufactured goods. In many ways the world is growing smaller, and this is reflected in the trade figures in Table 15.1 where it can be seen that world trade increased faster than any of the other indices shown. International cooperation is also reflected in the increasing concern about pollution as it is realised that the products of industry, intended and unintended, are having global consequences, many of which threaten our existence.

Paradoxically, this increasing interdependence is accompanied by an **increasing division** of the world into rich and poor countries, and the gap is widening rapidly. Increasing technical knowledge allied to industrialisation has not only enabled the rich countries to increase production, it has also meant that many of the products supplied by the poorer countries have been replaced by substitutes. Table 15.1 shows that non-food agricultural products, for example cotton, many of which were the staple exports of the underdeveloped world, have increased only slowly. Fortunately, food production is increasing at a faster rate than population, but these increases are unevenly distributed, and world poverty and hunger remain serious problems (Chapters Eight and Twenty-four).

Thirdly, and finally, accompanying the changes in output, the **pattern of production** is also changing. Much of the increase has been absorbed by the old industrial areas, but even here there have been changes. Many of the old industrial areas such as Lancashire or New England have seen a decline in their staple industries, and have subsequently been involved in the process of **industrial readjustment**, whereby attempts have been made, with mixed success, to attract new industries. Other areas have been affected by the process of **suburbanisation** as industry has moved from city centres to outer suburbs, repelled by costs and congestion, attracted by more space and better conditions, and encouraged by the development of good transport systems, power supplies and services.

There have also been developments in new areas. In the USA, for example, there has been a remarkable growth of industry in the Pacific states and on the Gulf Coast, while in Canada, although Toronto and Montreal have grown, the greatest recent increases have been on the Prairies and around Vancouver. In Europe, similar movements can be seen as industry moves south in Britain, France and Germany. Unfortunately, the pattern of industrial production has not changed to include much of the underdeveloped world. Many countries have developed some industry but it has usually been on a small scale with little impact on world trade. Even India, with large industrial concentrations around Bombay and in the Damodar Valley, has a very small per capita output, and most of the underdeveloped world is an industrial desert.

Conclusion

The problems of finding the location of industry, explaining why industry is located where it is and explaining why locations change are complex. The considerable diversity that is found between industries and areas could not make it otherwise. Yet major trends are discernible in the geography of industry, and it is the task of the geographer to bring order to the apparent chaos of reality.

In this chapter the results of empirical work have been used to isolate the factors which affect the location of industry. The next chapter turns to the problems of organising these factors into a general explanatory theory.

Suggested Further Reading

Alexandersson, G., *Geography of Manufacturing*, Prentice-Hall, Englewood Cliffs, New Jersey, 1967.

Estall, R. C., and Buchanan, R. O., *Industrial Activity and Economic Geography* (3rd edn), Hutchinson, London, 1973.

Jarrett, H. R., *A Geography of Manufacturing*, Macdonald and Evans, London, 1969.

Miller, E. W., *A Geography of Manufacturing*, Prentice-Hall, Englewood Cliffs, New Jersey, 1962.

Riley, R. C., *Industrial Geography*, Chatto and Windus, London, 1973.

Thoman, R. S., Conkling, E. C., and Yeates, M. H., *A Geography of Economic Activity* (2nd edn), McGraw-Hill, New York, 1968.

CHAPTER SIXTEEN

INDUSTRIAL LOCATION THEORY

Since the mid-1950s there has been a significant change of emphasis in industrial geography, from observation and description to the development of theory. Until that time, industrial geographers were largely concerned with case studies of particular industries or industrial regions, but the desire to make geography more scientific made necessary a theoretical approach (Chapter Four). Theories are needed to **explain** the location of industry, and also to **predict** suitable locations for future developments.

The Search for Order

The real world is apparent confusion, and one of the basic questions to be answered in geography is whether this reality is chaos or just complexity. Is the distribution of industry simply random, or is it arranged in an ordered pattern? Increasingly, the search for an explanation of the location of industry has taken the form of a search for order in a complex world, and this has resulted in a movement away from the study of the unique and the particular to a search for generalisation and theory.

The distribution of industry is not, in fact, totally random, as can be seen from the world pattern of manufacturing (see Fig. 15.1), since it tends to form clusters in certain latitudes. This tendency for industries to come together is such a marked feature that J. H. Thompson has suggested that a **concentration theory** can be formulated, identifying a hierarchy of concentrations (Fig. 16.1).

The members of the hierarchy are basically classified according to the

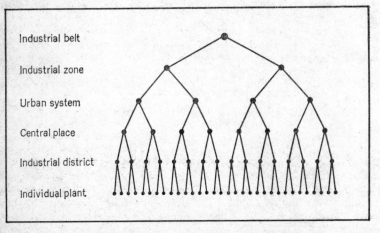

Fig. 16.1. A hierarchy of industrial concentrations.

amount and density of manufacturing that takes place, and also in terms of function and linkage. The basic unit is the individual plant or factory, which, when concentrated in an area such as an industrial estate, forms an industrial district. Two or more districts form a central place, usually a manufacturing town such as Swindon, and two or more central places form an urban system or small conurbation such as Portsmouth–Southampton. Two or more urban systems form an industrial zone, such as South Lancashire, and at the top of the hierarchy is the industrial belt of Western Europe or North America.

The idea of concentration is carried further and an **agglomeration theory** is suggested which takes account of the fact that the amount of manufacturing in conurbations increases as a country develops economically. Thompson sees the very large urban systems getting very much larger in advanced economies, but it must be remembered that there will come a time when the benefits of agglomeration will be balanced by the penalties of congestion and a process of dispersal will follow.

The location of particular industries is not totally random either, as can be seen from the fact that many industries have similar locations in different countries. Oil refineries are largely situated on coastal or waterway sites, especially in the large oil-importing countries of Western Europe or Japan, despite a recent trend towards market oriented, pipeline based, inland sites in Germany. Some industries such as flour-milling, shipbuilding, sugar and vegetable oil refining show such a marked locational pattern that they have come to be known as 'port industries'.

Order and Theory

This tendency for industries to come together and for certain industries to have 'typical' locations is the combined result of thousands of individual decisions, and represents a common response to certain attractions. These **decisions** are taken within the framework of a set of conditions which limits the range of activity of manufacturers in some directions and encourages it in others. These conditions constitute the physical, economic, social and political environments which were examined in the preceding chapter as a set of variables affecting the location of industry.

The importance of these factors affecting the location of industry varies from industry to industry, from area to area and from time to time. The basic problem to be solved is whether or not these variables can be ordered into some sort of theoretical framework that will help to explain present distributions and also help in the choice of sites for industrial growth that will develop successfully in the future.

Attempts to develop such a theoretical framework have been made by both geographers and economists, with the geographer using a largely **inductive** approach, drawing general conclusions from his case studies. However, most work has been done by economists using a more theoretical, **deductive** approach, in which a number of basic conditions are stated and from which conclusions can be deduced. For the future it may be hoped that economic geographers can marry the theory to the real world situations, although the relative simplicity of the theories and the complexity of reality make reluctant partners.

Optimum Locations

A central theme in the development of industrial location theories has been the concept of **optimum location**; that there is for each factory a 'best location'. In a real world that is constantly changing, the existence of such a place seems improbable, but the concept has value in theory because it represents a standard against which reality can be measured.

The question arises of what is meant by the best location, since the term 'best' could be interpreted in economic, social or political senses. Since location theory has been largely developed in capitalist societies, the best location is taken to be that which gives the best **profits**. The best location is therefore where costs are lowest and revenues are highest, since income minus expenditure equals profit. There are, however, two problems to be faced in the development of maximum profit theories of industrial location.

First, such locations are difficult to find. Profitability is not absolute, and a basic distinction must be made between long-term and short-term profitability, since decisions emphasising one or other of these considerations may require different locations. Even if this problem is solved, the number of variables involved, affecting both costs and revenues, makes the practical development of such theories very difficult.

Secondly, the whole assumption that actual decisions are made on a profit-maximising basis has been called into question. This is because governments are playing an increasingly important role in location decision-making, subordinating profits to other social goals such as full employment, and also because of the growing awareness that individuals have goals other than that of making money.

Finding the Optimum Location

Because of the practical problems involved in developing maximum profit theories, two principal approaches to location have been developed which examine the questions of costs and revenues separately. In the first, or **least cost theories**, revenues are taken as being equal at all locations, and variations in costs from place to place are examined to find the location where costs are least. This is then the optimum location. In the second, or **maximum revenue theories**, costs are taken as being equal at all locations, and variations in demand are examined to find the location giving the maximum revenue. This is then the optimum location. This is not to say that the least cost school has totally ignored revenues, nor that the maximum revenue school has ignored costs, but rather that there has been a distinct emphasis on one aspect or the other.

Least Cost Theory

There are two general classes of costs that are usually considered in manufacturing: **transport costs**, involved in the collection of raw materials and the distribution of finished products; and **processing costs**, such as labour, power, capital and services. The least cost school assumes that the manufacturer would best locate where the sum total of these costs is least.

To find the least cost location it is necessary to examine spatial variations in these costs, and also to examine the cost structures of different industries, since a location with low labour costs will not be very attractive to an industry with a small labour cost component such as oil refining, while an area with high labour costs and cheap power will not attract industries with a high labour, low power component such as textiles.

The most important attempt to develop a theory based on costs came from A. Weber in 1909. To reduce the complexity of reality, Weber, in common with all other theorists, had to simplify. His theory assumed that there was a uniform demand for a product at all locations, resulting in a uniform price, and therefore the plant located at the point of least costs would get the highest profits.

To find this point, Weber first sought the **least transport cost** location, which he considered the most important influence, using a 'locational triangle' (Fig. 16.2). Reality is simplified to two raw materials, M_1 and M_2, and one consumption point, C. The least transport cost point, P, is the point at which the total cost of moving raw materials and finished products is least. These transport costs are calculated by multiplying the weight of material or product by the distance carried, resulting in a 'pull' being exerted on the production point by each of the corners of the triangle. In Fig. 16.2a, two tonnes of

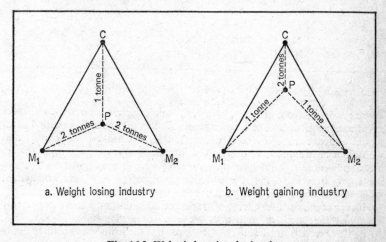

Fig. 16.2. Weber's locational triangle.

material M_1 and two tonnes of material M_2 are needed to produce one tonne of finished product. In a weight-losing manufacturing process such as iron smelting, the least transport cost location is near to the sources of the raw material, but in Fig. 16.2b, one tonne of material M_1 and one tonne of material M_2 are needed to produce two tonnes of finished product, and in a weight-gaining industry such as baking, a market-orientated location is attractive. It must be noted that only materials that are localised will have a locational effect and that materials found everywhere will be of little significance.

Weber next examined the effects of **labour costs** on location since he considered that industries would be located away from the point of least transport costs to the point of least labour costs if savings in labour costs were greater than any additional transport costs involved in such a move.

In Fig. 16.3, P is the least transport cost point, and around this point have been drawn a series of isodapanes (cost contours), or lines of equal transport cost per unit of production from P. There is cheap labour at L_1 and L_2 which would reduce costs by 15p per unit of production, and the question is whether or not it would be worthwhile for a manufacturer to relocate from P in order to take advantage of it. Clearly, any location within the 15p transport iso-

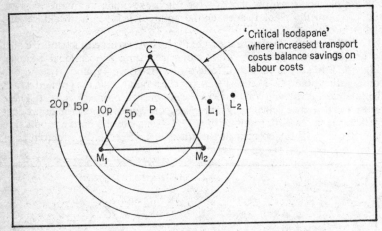

Fig. 16.3. The effect of labour and transport costs on location.

dapane would save more on labour than would be spent on extra transport and therefore L_1 would be a more profitable location than P. Locating at L_2 would increase transport costs more than any saving in labour costs and would not be attempted. Weber saw labour costs increasing in importance in location because technological developments were increasing the efficiency of transport, thus increasing the distance between the transport isodapanes, while labour costs were rising relative to other costs.

Having combined the effects of transport and labour costs, Weber thirdly examined the effect of industry's tendency to **agglomerate**. In Fig. 16.4, A, B, C, D and E are least cost locations, but the firms located there could cut their production costs by £1 per unit of production if at least three of them operated in the same location. However, they must not incur increased transport costs of over £1 per unit of production. In Fig. 16.4, the critical isodapane of £1 has been drawn round each producer and it is clear that firms C, D and E could reduce their total costs by locating in the shaded area.

Weber's attempt to find the least transport cost location and then to examine how this would be modified by other considerations has obvious limitations, and has been criticised for being too abstract. His assumptions about transport rates and the effects of agglomeration have been questioned, but the theory is important because of its pioneering nature and its effects on later writers. The real test of a theory is that it should accord with reality, and empirical studies such as W. Isard's work on the US steel industry and W. Smith's work on weight-losing industries in Britain have shown the validity of many of Weber's conclusions.

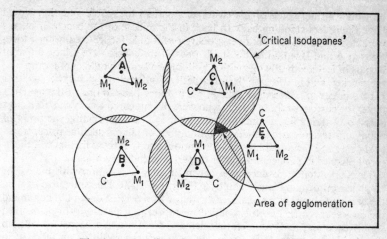

Fig. 16.4. The effect of agglomeration on location.

Maximum Revenue Theory

The most important criticism of Weber's theory is its emphasis upon supply, analysing the effect of different costs while holding demand constant at a point, thus preventing it from playing a role in plant location. To remedy this deficiency and to study the influence of demand upon location, a second school of thought has developed, searching for the location that will give the largest revenues.

Most producers of goods are likely to be competing for markets with other producers, and their locational decisions will affect, and will be affected by, the decisions of other producers. This **locational interdependence** of firms has been examined by H. Hotelling, who tried to find the location that would give the maximum sales to two ice-cream sellers on a mile of beach (Fig. 16.5).

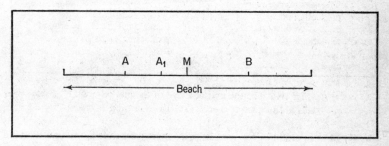

Fig. 16.5. Locational interdependence: the ice-cream sellers' problem.

If the sellers were selling the same brand of ice-cream at the same price, and the buyers, who were evenly distributed on the beach, went to the nearest seller to avoid walking further than necessary, then the best location would be at the quartiles A and B, giving each seller half of the beach as his market area. But supposing seller A moved nearer to the middle of the beach to A_1:

he would attract some of B's customers, and so the stable situation would have the sellers standing back to back in the middle of the beach. If buyers were not prepared to walk over a quarter of a mile for ice-cream, then locations at A and B would be the stable ones. If the sellers were selling different brands of ice-cream, the one with a well-known brand would capture more of the market, and in this case the seller with an unfamiliar product could either cut his prices to increase his sales at M, or move back to one of the quartiles to get the custom of those buyers who were not prepared to pay the 'transport costs' of walking far. From this analogy it is clear that finding the point of maximum revenue is dependent on a number of factors such as price, transport costs and the possibility of substitution, and that these factors will therefore influence the concentration or dispersal of industry.

The first attempt to develop a general theory of location with the major emphasis on demand was made by A. Lösch in 1940. This sought to explain the size and shape of **market areas** within which a location would command the largest revenue. Lösch simplified the world to a flat uniform plain, held supply constant, and assumed that demand for a product decreased with an increase in the price. If this price increase was the result of an increase in transport costs, then demand would decrease with distance from a production centre.

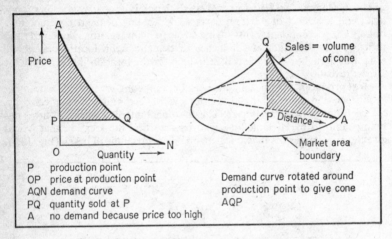

P   production point
OP   price at production point
AQN   demand curve
PQ   quantity sold at P
A   no demand because price too high

Demand curve rotated around production point to give cone AQP

Fig. 16.6. The theoretical shape of the market area.

(from A. Lösch, *The Economics of Location*, Yale University Press)

In Fig. 16.6, demand decreases as price increases, thus forming a demand curve AQN. Assuming that the price increase is the result of transport costs, by rotating the demand curve around the production point P, the shape of the market area is seen to be circular, and the size of the market area is the volume of the cone AQP.

As competition increases as other producers develop on the plain, the market areas become hexagonal to avoid overlap and the exclusion of some areas. They also become smaller as large profits are competed away (Fig.

16.7). Each product will have a different market area depending upon the relative importance of transport costs in its price, and different patterns of market areas will emerge. If these patterns are rotated around a common production centre, some of these patterns will coincide, forming points of maximum demand which should develop as concentrations of industry.

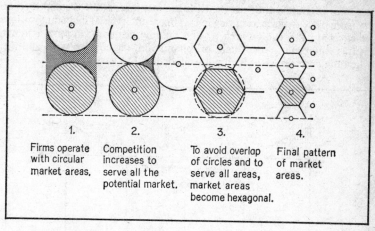

1. Firms operate with circular market areas.

2. Competition increases to serve all the potential market.

3. To avoid overlap of circles and to serve all areas, market areas become hexagonal.

4. Final pattern of market areas.

Fig. 16.7. Market areas become hexagons.
(from A. Lösch, *The Economics of Location*, Yale University Press)

Lösch's theory has been criticised for its abstract nature and its failure to take into account the problems arising from the locational interdependence of plants. Just as Weber was criticised for overemphasising supply, so Lösch was criticised for overemphasising demand, but subsequent attempts to integrate these two aspects by writers such as M. Greenhut and W. Isard have not been totally successful and there is still no generally accepted theory of location.

In recent years the search for maximum profit locations has been subordinated to the development of theories which accord more with the irregularities of the real world. Emphasis is now being placed on the fact that location decisions are taken by people, and the study of locational behaviour is increasing in importance.

Location and Behaviour

The location theories so far discussed have been based on the assumption that the location decisions were being taken by **economic man**, totally rational and in possession of perfect knowledge, and seeking the location that would give the maximum profit. Such a creature does not exist, of course, and location decisions are taken by men with limited ability and less than perfect knowledge. Nevertheless, it is still necessary for such men to choose locations where total costs are lower than total revenues, so that some profit can be made. Locations where some profit can be made are much more extensive than points of maximum profit and the search is now to find the **margins**, or limits, within which profitable activity can take place and then to explain deviations from the optimum location.

Spatial Margins to Profitability

A theoretical model of these margins has been developed by D. M. Smith which considers the interaction between costs and revenues in space in a simple form. The basis of the model is the fact that total costs and revenues vary from place to place, resulting in varying profit levels at different locations. The effects of this can be seen by first holding demand constant, assuming that this will result in a constant price, and allowing costs to vary, and then by holding costs constant, and allowing demand to vary.

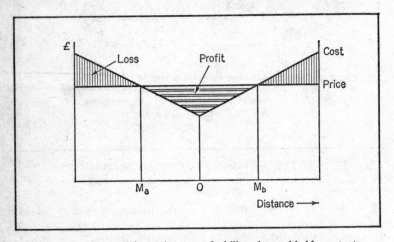

Fig. 16.8. The spatial margins to profitability: demand held constant
(after D. M. Smith).

In Figs. 16.8–16.10, cost and price are plotted on the vertical axis, and distance along the horizontal axis. In Fig. 16.8, demand is held constant so that the price obtained is equal at all points, but costs per unit of production increase with distance from point O, resulting in the V-shaped space-cost curve. In this case, O is the least cost location giving maximum profits, and M_a–M_b are the margins to profitability.

In Fig. 16.9, costs are held constant, but demand, and therefore the price that the producer can get, varies, declining with distance from point O. This results in the Λ-shaped space-revenue curve. In this case, O is the maximum revenue location giving maximum profits, and M_a–M_b are the margins to profitability.

In reality, both costs and demand vary from place to place and the effects of this are seen in Fig. 16.10, in which costs increase from point A and revenues decrease from point B. In this case the maximum profit location is at A, despite the fact that it is not the point of highest revenues. It can also be seen that different space cost and revenue curves might result in another optimum location. What this figure illustrates is that although there may be

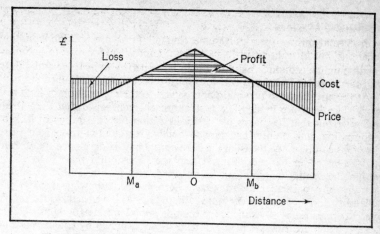

Fig. 16.9. The spatial margins to profitability: cost held constant
(after D. M. Smith).

a point of maximum profit, a profitable location may be made anywhere
within the margins M_a–M_b. The extent of these margins is affected by the
steepness of the curves, reflecting spatial differences in costs and revenues, and
these decide whether an industry can be dispersed over a wide area or whether

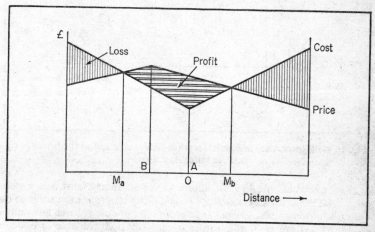

Fig. 16.10. The maximum profit location (after D. M. Smith).

it must be concentrated. Nevertheless, in theory, only one firm can be located
at the point of maximum profit and all other firms must therefore have sub-
optimal locations. In reality, many firms are operating successfully, making
profits in sub-optimal locations, and as a result, attention has turned in
recent years to an examination of how and why firms choose such locations.

Sub-optimal Locations

Profit-maximising theories assume that all firms are seeking optimum locations, but in reality it is difficult, if not impossible, for man to optimise, because unlike economic man, real man lacks perfect knowledge and ability and therefore his locational decisions must reflect these constraints.

At present there are two main approaches to the explanation of how real world locations are made. The first approach emphasises that man is an **optimiser** but that he makes his decisions within the constraints of lack of information, uncertainty, and limited ability. An attempt to explain these decisions can be made by using the behavioural matrix developed by A. Pred and discussed in Chapter Four. Using the behavioural matrix, locations within the spatial margins can be analysed, and in Fig. 16.11 the spatial margins of a particular industry have been mapped, showing two optimal locations, and the location decisions of industrialists have been plotted on the matrix. Industrialist 1 has made the right decision by using good information wisely, but Industrialist 2 is in a similar location purely by chance since he

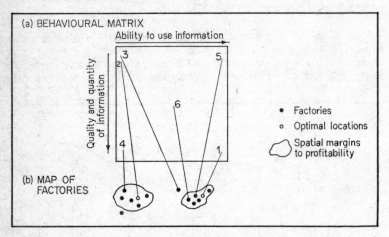

Fig. 16.11. Hypothetical industrial location decisions linked to the behavioural matrix (after A. Pred).

has poor information and little ability to use it. Industrialist 3 is like Industrialist 2 but less lucky, and since he is making no profit must soon go out of business. Industrialist 4 is making a profit but not doing as well as he might because he has not been able to use the information available to him. Industrialist 5 is in a similar location but for different reasons; he is very able but lacks good information. Industrialist 6 is making a steady profit to the best of his ability and information.

However, it is by no means certain that man is an optimiser, and a second explanation of sub-optimal locations suggests that he is a **satisficer**, prepared to accept locations with which he is satisfied rather than those which give maximum profits.

Satisficer theory can be supported, first, by the fact that it is very difficult, if not impossible, to say in monetary terms what the maximum profit from any location will be, much less what it will be in five years' time. Most firms would be satisfied, if not delighted, with profits that are higher than those of their competitors. Profitability might therefore be seen as relative, rather than the absolute that is central in the location theories. This, of course, could give a wide range of locations within the spatial margins to profitability.

Secondly, most men do not have profit maximisation as their sole aim in life. The actual choice of location within these margins would depend upon many considerations, since the men taking the decisions would have personal preferences for certain locations, especially those that they found congenial. Most men work for rewards in addition to money, such as pleasant living and working conditions, and it has been argued that these could be quantified as a **psychic income** and used as a non-cost when discussing location theory. The climatic attractions of the south-western USA have been cited as an important factor affecting the growth of new industry there since 1945, and on the negative side, the unattractiveness, real or imagined, of northern England has been offered as a factor in the reluctance of firms to locate there, despite financial inducements from the government.

However, it might be argued that the theory that men are satisficers does not sufficiently take into account the fact that psychic income might simply be another form of profit and that man does optimise, although for other rewards as well as money. Thus, in reality, satisficers might be **imperfect optimisers with a variety of goals.**

This debate is interesting but it must not be forgotten that locational decisions are increasingly being taken by firms or government departments rather than by individuals, and that the decision-making process is likely to be a corporate rather than an individual one. Thus, as firms increase in size corporate decisions may result in locations which relate to the overall pattern of the firm rather than the optimum location for the single plant. Similarly, the increasing role of governments in industrial location decision-making can produce sub-optimal locations for social, political, or strategic reasons (Chapter Twenty-three). Defence considerations have resulted in the relocation of aircraft plant in the USA, and attempts to reduce local unemployment in the UK have resulted in the exercise of some controls over location choice. In countries with planned economies, maximum profit location choices often run counter to stated ideologies, although it has been suggested that in Eastern Europe since 1956, economic considerations have been of increasing importance in location decision-making. In countries with mixed economies such as the UK, recent interest in cost–benefit analysis, which attempts to assess the social advantages and disadvantages of location decisions rather than financial considerations alone, should lead to an increase in the number of factors to be evaluated when location theory is considered in the future.

Conclusion

The real world is complex, but there would seem to be some order in this complexity, and one of the fundamental tasks of the geographer is to try to simplify this reality to allow the order to be demonstrated. Industrial location theories have been developed to explain why industry is located as it is, but the emphasis on finding the optimum location, however valuable this may be as a concept, has meant that many of the theories have not been applicable when tested against reality. Recently, there has been a change of emphasis, with more attention being given to finding the margins within which profitable locations can be made and explaining deviations from the optimum, especially by examining decision-making behaviour.

Suggested Further Reading

Chorley, R. J., and Haggett, P., *Socio-Economic Models in Geography*, Methuen, London, 1968.
McCarty, H. H., and Lindberg, J. B., *A Preface to Economic Geography*, Prentice-Hall, Englewood Cliffs, New Jersey, 1966.
Smith, D. M., *Industrial Location: An Economic Geographic Analysis*, Wiley, New York, 1971.
Thoman, R. S., Conkling, E. C., and Yeates, M. H., *A Geography of Economic Activity* (2nd edn), McGraw-Hill, New York, 1968.

PART FOUR: SETTLEMENT GEOGRAPHY

CHAPTER SEVENTEEN

URBANISATION

Urban geography constitutes a diverse and rapidly developing field of geographical study. Although settlement studies have long formed a traditional branch of human geography, a great deal of progress has been made in recent years in refining and extending many of the earlier concepts. This growing interest in the geography of towns and cities is probably a reflection of the fact that the majority of the population in the Western World lives in an urban environment, while those who do not are increasingly affected by the decisions, ideas and influences emanating from the main urban centres.

Urban geography is concerned with the **spatial** aspects of cities—their location, growth, and relationships both one with another and with their surrounding regions. It also embraces the internal patterns of cities in terms of land use, functional areas, and social and cultural patterns. Another approach to the study of towns is what may be termed the **ecological** approach, which involves consideration of the relationships between the patterns and structure of urban society and the man-made city environment with its various neighbourhoods and districts.

A basic aim is the search for recurrent patterns and the formulation of laws and theories. In this respect urban geography has a long tradition of model building, typified by E. W. Burgess's work on the internal structure of cities which dates back to the early 1920s and W. Christaller's work on the location and spacing of settlements which was produced as early as 1933.

What is a Town?

Before examining some of the main fields of study in urban geography, we must pose the seemingly naïve question: what is a town? In fact the town defies simple definition. 'Is it a physical conglomeration of streets and houses, or is it a centre of exchange and commerce? Or is it a kind of society, or even a frame of mind? Has it a certain size, a specific density? The difficulties in definition are countless, and there is very little unanimity: it seems to be all things to all men.' (E. Jones)

A variety of criteria is employed to define towns and cities for census purposes. Some countries simply adopt a certain minimum **population size** for settlement agglomerations, but the figure employed is 250 in Denmark, 2,000 in France, 2,500 in the USA, 20,000 in the Netherlands and 30,000 in Japan. It will thus be evident that published statistics for the ratio of urban to rural population in various countries have very little value for international comparison. In any case, absolute numbers mean very little. Small settlements may have urban characteristics, while in the developing world, settlements of considerable size may house largely agricultural populations. We typically think of cities as being densely populated, but only a very small

211

number of countries take into account **population density** in their definition. For example, in India a town is officially defined as having a population of over 5,000 and a density of over 386 persons per square kilometre, as well as having over 75 per cent of its adult population engaged in non-agricultural work. The latter point introduces what is probably the most important criterion; namely, the **function** of the settlement. It is generally agreed that one of the distinguishing features of towns is that they are not primarily concerned with agriculture and food production. Despite this, few countries include in their definition any reference to function other than **administration**. Some countries, such as the UK, in fact use this as the sole criterion, defining towns as those settlements having a particular type of government or administration, such as the former municipal boroughs and urban districts. This is rather like saying that a town is what the state is prepared to call a town.

It has been suggested that a more realistic definition of a town may be obtained by looking beyond these quantitative measures, and that a town or city is better defined by less tangible characteristics. It is implied that there are **sociological differences** between town and country. For example, the sociologist Louis Wirth has defined a city as 'a relatively large, dense, and permanent settlement of socially heterogeneous individuals'. According to Wirth, towns and cities have a social framework characterised by anonymity and lack of personal contact, within which there is a weakening of kinship and family ties, and their replacement by allegiance to diverse groups which, by their multiplicity, encourage mobility and social instability.

One problem with the sociological approach which defines urbanism as 'a way of life' is that it fails to take into account the physical features of the town—its buildings and streets, and their density and arrangement. Emphasis is on the city-dwellers rather than the city itself.

In the face of a bewildering array of definitions and systems of classification, the United Nations has suggested that no attempt should be made to distinguish between rural and urban populations, and that population agglomerations should be simply classified according to a series of size categories. Indeed, it is increasingly felt that the words rural and urban imply a false distinction, and that there exists a continuum of settlement forms and landscapes from the overcrowded inner districts of the largest cities to the smallest hamlets of the remote country districts. Some writers have even suggested that once large cities come into being, the term rural becomes virtually obsolete, for, with modern communications and the administrative controls exercised by the city, its influence extends to the most remote rural areas in any country.

The City in History: Origins and Dispersals

The Origin of the First Cities

The motivation and processes involved in the establishment of the very first towns are largely a matter of speculation. A necessary precondition must have been the existence of a prosperous, settled agricultural economy to enable the production of a large surplus of storable food to support a non-agricultural urban population. Freed from the work of food production, certain members of the population could thus engage in non-agricultural, specialist trades.

The earliest examples of true urban development are thought to have originated on the alluvial plains of the Tigris and Euphrates Valleys in Mesopotamia between 5,000 and 3,000 B.C. Various technological advances such as the invention of the wheeled cart, ox-drawn plough, sailing boat, systems of canal irrigation, and the development of the arts of metallurgy, all encouraged and made possible various changes in economic and social organisation. Agricultural production increased, improved transport allowed a food surplus to be assembled in towns, and new institutions were founded to deal with the storage, exchange and redistribution of food and other goods. Increasing specialisation of occupations took place in the towns and long-distance trade expanded. At its peak, Babylon, the largest of these early dynastic cities, may have reached a population of 80,000. Most were much smaller. Although evidence is scanty, the urban way of life is thought to have spread from Mesopotamia to Egypt, the eastern Mediterranean, the Indus Valley, China and South-East Asia.

Urban Origins in Europe

Between 3,000 and 2,000 B.C. urban settlement forms appeared for the first time in eastern Europe. Various specialist crafts developed in these small urban centres, and trade flourished in the eastern Mediterranean region. During the eighth and seventh centuries B.C. the Greek city states which had evolved on the Greek mainland extended their trading activities into the western Mediterranean and founded a number of colonial settlements, notably at Cumae, Syracuse and Massilia (Marseilles). By 500 B.C. urban settlements were to be found from the Atlantic coast of Spain to the Ganges Valley in India. At about this time further technical advances took place, including improved ships, implements and weapons and the introduction of coinage to facilitate trading. These developments indirectly influenced the rise of the Greek Empire, which in turn acted as a further stimulus to urban development. Existing trading centres flourished within the Empire, and new towns were founded to meet military, administrative and commercial needs.

Similarly, the rise of the Roman Empire, with its even wider military and economic horizons, was responsible for the introduction of urban life to large parts of north-west Europe. By the second century A.D., Rome itself had an estimated population of 200,000, while elsewhere in Europe a well-defined hierarchy of towns linked by new or improved routeways was established in areas under Roman rule. Their subsequent fate has been varied; some have decayed completely, others have lapsed into relative obscurity, but many, including Bordeaux, Cologne, London, Lyons and Paris, have survived to become the major cities of modern Europe.

It has long been held that the fall of the Roman Empire in the fifth century A.D. led to a decline in urban life and that for a time, trading and industry virtually disappeared. The Dark Ages in Europe have been described as a period of 'an economy without markets' (H. Pirenne). According to this view, many towns were abandoned, while in others urban life survived in very debased circumstances, but it is now held that the catastrophic impact of the fall of the Roman Empire has been overstressed.

The Medieval Revival

Nevertheless, the revival of urban life in Europe took place only very slowly. Not until the eleventh century was there a significant expansion in trade and industry. This was accompanied by rebuilding on the sites of many of the old Roman towns as well as the founding of certain new towns, often around the stronghold of a bishop of feudal lord which offered protection to traders and craftsmen.

By about 1400 the lands of western, southern and central Europe which were favourable for settlement supported a large number of small urban settlements. An increase in the number of towns rather than a growth in individual town sizes was the distinguishing feature of urban development in the Medieval period. With very few exceptions, towns remained small, generally containing no more than a few thousand inhabitants. The growth of Medieval towns was restricted by problems of disease, sanitation, water supply and fire-risk, but above all by the limits placed on the movement of food into the town from the surrounding area by means of simple and often inadequate forms of transport. It was not until the sixteenth century that a number of cities began to expand significantly in size. Most were settlements occupying key locations for communications, trade and administration, and tended to develop as capital cities or regional centres in the newly emerging nation states. By the late seventeenth century the populations of Amsterdam, Antwerp, Lisbon, Rome and Seville all exceeded 100,000, Paris had 180,000 inhabitants, Naples 240,000 and London 250,000. In the eighteenth century these towns were joined by Berlin, Copenhagen, Moscow, Palermo, St. Petersburg, Vienna and Warsaw, all with populations over 100,000.

Mention must also be made of the transfer of the European urban form to the New World following voyages of exploration which extended the limits of the known world. During the sixteenth and seventeenth centuries many small towns, often closely modelled on their counterparts in Europe, were founded in the colonial territories belonging to Spain, Portugal, France and Britain.

The Impact of the Industrial Revolution

The technical and economic changes which began with the Industrial Revolution have proved to be the most potent force affecting the development of the whole history of urbanisation. The invention of steam-powered machines was followed by the large-scale exploitation of coalfields and the creation of industrial towns on an unprecedented scale. At the same time the improvements taking place in agriculture created an increased food surplus to support the growing urban population, and, later in the nineteenth century, mechanisation also made many agricultural workers redundant and encouraged them to seek work in the new industrial centres. Improvements in transport—better roads, new canals and the development of the railways—encouraged this mobility of population, and also facilitated the movement of foodstuffs and industrial raw materials into the cities and allowed their products to be distributed to larger and more distant markets.

Thus, industrialisation and urbanisation proceeded hand in hand throughout the nineteenth century. In Britain, industry was grafted on to long-established towns, but on the coalfields new industrial towns grew up with factories and workshops adjacent to endless streets of identical working-class housing built to the minimum standards of late nineteenth-century bye-laws. 'In an age of rapid technical progress the city as a social unit lay outside of the circle of invention. Except for utilities such as gas mains, water pipes and sanitary equipment, often belatedly introduced, often slipshod and inadequate, the industrial city could claim no improvement over the seventeenth-century town. Until 1838 neither Manchester nor Birmingham functioned politically as incorporated boroughs. They were man-heaps, machine warrens, not organs of human association.' (L. Mumford)

By about 1860 just over 50 per cent of the population of England and Wales was classified as urban, a figure which had risen to 77 per cent by the end of the century. Similar changes took place in France, Germany and the USA, but several decades later than in the UK. In Scandinavia, and to a lesser extent in Mediterranean Europe, the large-scale urban consequences of industrialisation were not felt until well into the present century, while in many countries of eastern Europe the proportion of town-dwellers is still only about 30 per cent of the total population.

Another outcome of technological change has been to increase the limits placed upon the size of individual towns. Improvements in internal transport by suburban and underground railway systems, by the introduction of tram and bus services and later by the widespread use of the private motorcar, have enabled people to live at progressively greater distances from their place of work. Thus, during the late nineteenth century and early decades of the twentieth century the outward expansion of most western cities proceeded more rapidly than ever before, so that the traditional distinction between the compact built-up area of the city and the open space of the surrounding countryside was destroyed by the building of vast areas of low-density suburban housing, often lacking in any focus, plan or cohesion. By 1929 D. H. Lawrence was able to describe English towns as 'a great scrabble of ugly pettiness over the face of the land'. 'The English,' he asserted, 'are town-birds through and through, yet don't know how to build a city, how to think of one, or how to live in one. They are all suburban, pseudo-cottage, and not one of them knows how to be truly urban.'

Modern Accelerated Urbanisation

In recent decades the growth of urban settlements has continued at a very high rate in many parts of the world. New towns are being created, and large cities are becoming gigantic. In 1900 only 9·2 per cent of the world's population lived in towns of over 20,000. This proportion had risen to 20·9 per cent by 1950 and almost 30 per cent by 1970. The distribution of this urban population is spread very unevenly over the earth's surface, as shown in Fig. 17.1. Urban growth is, in fact, now taking place at a faster rate in the Tropics than in either Western Europe or North America. Despite this, the level of **urbanisation**, or proportion of urban dwellers to total population, is still much lower than in the Western World, for the rural population in tropical regions is also continuing to expand. Nevertheless, the growth in the absolute number of urban dwellers in tropical regions since about 1950 has been remarkable.

An interesting measure of recent urbanisation is the increase in the number of '**million' cities**, or cities with populations exceeding one million. In 1800 there was no city in the world with a population exceeding that figure, although

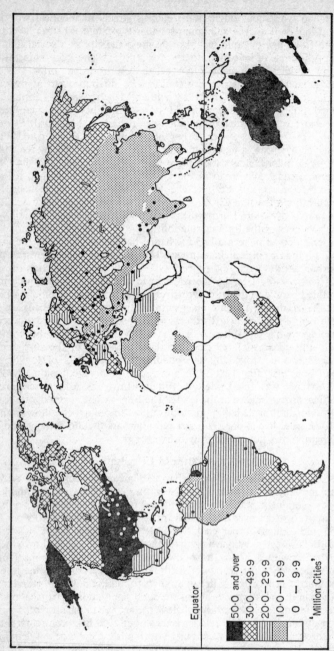

50·0 and over

30·0 — 49·9

20·0 — 29·9

10·0 — 19·9

0 — 9·9

'Million Cities'

Fig. 17.1. Distribution of population living in towns of over 20,000 inhabitants by countries, and the distribution of 'million cities'.

London, with 959,310 inhabitants, came close. By 1850 two existed (London and Paris), and by 1900 there were eleven cities with more than one million inhabitants (London, Paris, Berlin, Vienna, Moscow, St. Petersburg, New York, Chicago, Philadelphia, Tokyo and Calcutta). It will be noticed that only the last two lay outside Europe and North America.

During the present century the number of 'million' cities rose to 20 by 1920, 51 by 1940, 80 by 1960 and 129 by 1970. These totals relate to urban agglomerations, which include the population of suburban fringes and contiguous built-up areas. Their distribution in 1970 is shown on Fig. 17.1. Although the majority are still found in Europe and North America, it is interesting to note that they are increasing most rapidly in the Tropical World. In 1940 only four tropical cities had more than one million inhabitants (Bombay, Calcutta, Mexico City and São Paulo). By 1970 the number had risen to 26.

Another effect of accelerated urban growth has been to cause cities to coalesce with neighbouring towns to form a vast, amorphous urban sprawl to which the terms **conurbation** and **metropolitan city** have been applied in Britain and the USA respectively. The 'million' city is small by comparison with these gigantic urban forms, some of which exceed 10 million inhabitants. The results of this type of agglomeration can be seen around capital cities such as London, Tokyo and New York, as well as in industrial areas such as the metropolitan counties of Greater Manchester, West Yorkshire, Tyne and Wear, and West Midlands in the UK, or the Ruhr district of West Germany.

It has been suggested that by the continued operation of the same processes which create conurbations, there may occur a coalescing of these vast built-up areas to form entirely urbanised regions. It has been suggested by J. Gottmann that the whole of the north-eastern seaboard of the USA from New Hampshire to Maryland can be regarded as a single urban complex of staggering dimensions which he termed **Megalopolis**. Thus defined, Megalopolis contains about 35 million people, dwarfing even the largest cities by comparison.

The growth of cities to excessive size creates many social and economic problems, including expensive and often inadequate housing, overcrowded roads, overburdened public transport systems and pollution by smoke, fumes and noise. These conditions in turn cause stress and tension among city dwellers, and appear to be related to high levels of vandalism, delinquency and crime. Some even argue that the functioning of many large cities is in danger of breaking down, and that the city as we know it today is disintegrating. Since the mid-nineteenth century there have been various reactions to the problems of excessive urban growth, notably the development of planned urban forms. These are examined in Chapter Twenty-two.

The Pre-Industrial City

The Western city has been the subject of intensive study and investigation. Because its growth has been largely related to the impact of industrialisation it is frequently referred to as the **industrial city**. By contrast, the study of towns and cities in Africa, Asia and Latin America has been largely neglected. One notable exception is the work of G. Sjoberg who, in his book *The Pre-Industrial City*, examined the structure of urban settlements both in Europe and elsewhere in the world prior to the impact of large-scale industrialisation.

According to Sjoberg, society develops in three stages, from the self-sufficient, pre-literate, folk society having no urban settlement forms to the traditional agrarian society with limited technology and pre-industrial urban forms, and finally to the industrial, highly urbanised form of society. The **pre-industrial city** thus represents a stage in the evolution of the Western city.

The pre-industrial city is a permanent settlement generally characterised by a very compact, high-density arrangement of buildings which lacks any order or plan. Houses, workplaces, shops and other land uses are intermixed in an almost random manner. There is a general uniformity in the height and size of buildings which is broken only very occasionally by large institutional buildings such as a palace or religious centre. An enclosing wall or ditch may serve the needs of defence. The main function of such settlements is the trading and exchange of goods, which is conducted from a market place near the town centre. Manufacturing is limited to craft industries scattered throughout the town.

Examples of settlements displaying these features include the indigenous towns of Nigeria, several of which have populations in excess of 50,000, and those towns of India and China which have been little changed by Western influences. Such towns have more in common with the European medieval city than the modern industrial city. However, in many instances Western influences are making themselves felt, and in many parts of the developing world the pre-industrial city is in a process of rapid change. Business sectors with offices and shops are being added to the traditional urban fabric and modern roads are being developed to accommodate the newly introduced motorcar. In extreme cases, such as Delhi, Lahore and Ibadan, a Western-style city has been grafted on to a pre-industrial city, and two distinct urban cultures exist side by side.

Another product of the accelerating urbanisation process in the developing world is the **shanty town**. This is a district of temporary, squatter dwellings fashioned out of scrap materials, generally overcrowded, lacking in amenities and characterised by a high incidence of disease, extreme poverty and exceptionally high mortality rates. The shanty town is a familiar and depressing feature of many cities in Latin America, south-east Asia and southern Africa. Whereas in the Western city, slums are generally the product of age and decay, in the pre-industrial city the shanty town is of recent origin and is the result of too rapid growth and a failure to provide adequate accommodation for those migrating to the growing urban centres.

The Classification of Towns and Cities

It will be evident that towns and cities vary enormously in terms of age, size, lay-out, function and population characteristics. It is not surprising, therefore, that geographers have tried to clarify and seek order in such a variety of urban types by attempting to classify towns and cities. Although various criteria have been employed for classification, ranging from simple population size to types of geographical site, most systems of classification have been concerned with **occupation structure**. In other words, systems of **functional classification** have attracted most attention.

Groups of towns with similar functional characteristics may be identified by the analysis of employment or occupation statistics. Specialisation is said to exist when employment in a particular category exceeds some 'normal' level. In a crude way we are going through this process when we describe Sheffield as a 'steel town', Cambridge as a 'university town', and Blackpool as a 'resort town'. Indeed, early systems of urban classification consisted simply of applying these descriptive labels in a very subjective and arbitrary manner.

For a more precise classification it is necessary to define what is meant by the 'normal' level of employment in a given industry or group of activities. An early quantitative approach was devised by C. D. Harris in 1943 in an attempt to classify the towns and cities of the USA on the basis of employment statistics from the US census of 1930. For example, he suggested that a town could be classified as a 'manufacturing centre' if a minimum of 60 per cent of its total employment in the manufacturing–retailing–wholesaling group was in manufacturing. Using such values, which were based on the occupation statistics for a number of towns that fell into well-defined types, Harris distinguished mining, manufacturing, transport, wholesaling, retailing, university and resort/retirement cities, as well as what he termed 'diversified cities' which had high scores for a number of functions but no single dominant function. The fact that 80 per cent of the largest cities in the USA emerged as 'diversified cities' indicates the problems involved in classification, for this group included most of the chief manufacturing, wholesaling and retailing centres of the nation.

A number of later studies have used as the value for comparison a figure for the average employment in a particular industry based on data for all towns. Working in this way, a town is regarded as specialising in a particular activity when its employment exceeds the national average. This approach has been extended by the use of standard deviation, whereby different classes of specialisation are identified according to the degree of deviation above the mean. At the same time there are certain objections to this method of classification. It has been shown, for example, that the percentage of the total labour force in particular activities varies significantly with city size. The use of national averages embracing cities of all sizes may, therefore, be of doubtful value. As an alternative it has been suggested that the average occupation structure should be established for towns and cities of different size categories, and comparisons then made between the employment structure of individual towns and the mean values for their particular size group. A more fundamental objection against the use of average values, whether for all towns or groups of towns of similar size, is that they inevitably split up groups of virtually identical towns which happen to fall on either side of the critical value.

As a result of such problems, sophisticated techniques have been devised in order to distinguish towns with the greatest overall similarity rather than simply identifying the dominant function. An analysis of British towns by C. A. Moser and W. Scott is typical of this type of approach. A total of 57 attributes covering demographic, social and economic features was extracted from the census for each of the 157 towns in England and Wales with populations exceeding 50,000. A technique of 'principal components analysis' was applied to the data whereby the 57 variables were simplified into four components. By using these components the various urban centres were grouped statistically so that the towns in each group were more similar to each other than those in any other group. In this way, 14 groups were identified based on demographic and socio-economic characteristics rather than simply on the functions performed. The groups included resorts, administrative and commercial centres, industrial towns, and suburbs and residential centres.

Conclusion

The development of urban settlement forms requires a complex 'support-system' of transportation and external food supply. These conditions were first met in the Middle East, which may be regarded as the birthplace of urban civilisation. The urban way of life spread from there to other parts of the world, but nowhere was it more widely adopted than in Europe. The Industrial Revolution extended the foundations for urban growth and initiated a period of dramatic urbanisation in the Western World. As a consequence many cities have grown to excessive size, creating persistent social and economic problems. During the present century solutions to these problems have been sought in new planned urban forms. In the developing world the pre-industrial cities have also entered a phase of rapid growth and change. Classification of the wide variety of towns and cities which now exists presents many problems. Most systems of classification involve consideration of urban function, but none is entirely satisfactory.

Suggested Further Reading

Carter, H., *The Study of Urban Geography*, Arnold, London, 1971.

Dickinson, R. E., *The West European City* (2nd edn), Routledge & Kegan Paul, London, 1961.

Dwyer, D. J., *The City in the Third World*, Macmillan, London, 1974.

Gottmann, J., *Megalopolis: The Urbanized North-eastern Seaboard of the United States*, M.I.T. Press, Cambridge, Mass., 1961.

Hall, P., *World Cities*, Weidenfeld & Nicolson, London, 1966.

Johnson, J. H., *Urban Geography. An Introductory Analysis* (2nd edn), Pergamon, Oxford, 1972.

Jones, E., *Towns and Cities*, Oxford University Press, London, 1966.

Moser, C. A., and Scott, W., *British Towns: A Statistical Study of Their Social and Economic Differences* (Centre for Urban Studies Report No. 2), Oliver & Boyd, London, 1961.

Mumford, L., *The Culture of Cities*, Secker & Warburg, New York, 1944.

Mumford, L., *The City in History. Its Origins, Its Transformations and Its Prospects*, Penguin, Harmondsworth, 1966.

Sjoberg, G., *The Pre-Industrial City, Past and Present*, The Free Press, New York, 1960.

CHAPTER EIGHTEEN

THE SIZE AND SPACING OF CITIES

A great deal of interest has been shown by geographers in the relationships between towns and cities of different sizes and their spacing in the landscape. Implicit in such studies is the assumption that there is some sort of order or logic underlying the size relationships and spatial distribution of towns. It is assumed that settlements do not grow up in a haphazard or random manner and that a measurable degree of order is to be found in their size and spacing.

The Rank-Size Rule

It is obvious that in any large region there are many small towns, a smaller number of medium-sized towns and relatively few large cities. This is true for all regions of the world irrespective of the stage reached in economic development or the degree of urbanisation achieved. This regularity is clearly demonstrated when relationships between city rank and city population size are examined.

The cities in any region may be ranked from largest to smallest according to their population size. Thus, the largest city is ranked No. 1, the second largest No. 2, continuing in this way down to the lower ranking towns. It was first noticed by F. Auerbach in 1913 that when these rank numbers are plotted against their respective populations a regular relationship generally emerges. The **rank-size rule**, proposed by G. K. Zipf in 1949, attempts to express this relationship in more precise mathematical terms and states that 'if all the urban settlements in an area are ranked in descending order of population, the population of the nth town will be $\frac{1}{n}$th that of the largest town'. In other words, the population of urban settlements in a region can be arranged in the series $1, \frac{1}{2}, \frac{1}{3}, \frac{1}{4}, \ldots \frac{1}{n}$. This regularity can also be expressed by the formula

$$P_n = \frac{P_1}{n}$$

where P_n is the population of the town of rank n in the descending order and P_1 is the population of the largest city. Thus, if the largest city has a population of 2 millions, the tenth ranking town should, according to the rule, have a population of 200,000 inhabitants.

Fig. 18.1 shows in graph form the theoretical result for the rank-size rule together with the actual relationships between rank and population size for the cities of England and Wales. The use of logarithmic scales on both axes converts a concave curve into a linear or almost linear result. It can be seen that the population of London is greater than the rank-size rule suggests it should be, but that the trend of the lower-order towns accords roughly with the rule. The same situation has been observed in Northern Ireland, where the population of Belfast seems to be disproportionately large according to the rank-size rule. In this case it is also significant that the populations of the next largest towns are far smaller than might be expected. It would appear,

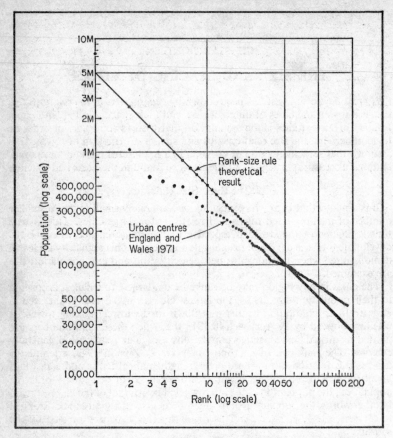

Fig. 18.1. Rank-size graphs. Theoretical result together with the result for England and Wales, 1971.

therefore, that Belfast's growth has been achieved in part by 'pirating' certain of the regional functions of the lower-order towns. It has been suggested that an effective policy of regional development should rectify this type of anomaly, and that the rank-size rule can be used as a diagnostic tool in regional planning.

The Law of the Primate City

Relationships between the largest city in a region, often referred to as the **primate city**, and the next largest city have been examined by a number of geographers. According to the rank-size rule the primate city should be twice the size of the second city. However, this is frequently not the case. The ratio between the first and second city, theoretically 2:1, varies from 1·1:1 for Canada (Montreal and Toronto) to 16·6:1 for Uruguay (Montevideo and Paysandu).

In 1939, in a study entitled 'The Law of the Primate City', M. Jefferson examined the size relationship between the primate city and the next largest cities in a selection of 51 countries. He noted that in 28 countries the primate city was more than twice the size of the second city, and that in 18 instances more than three times the next largest. Jefferson suggested that there are many reasons why one particular city might exceed its neighbours in size at an early stage in their growth, but once it had become dominant in size 'this fact gives it an impetus to grow that cannot affect any other city and it draws away from them all in character as well as in size to become the primate city. . . . The finest wares are always to be found there, the rarest articles, the greatest talents, the most skilled workers in every science and art. Thither flows an unending stream of the young and ambitious in search of fame and fortune.' (M. Jefferson)

Recently A. Linsky attempted to define in more precise terms the factors likely to generate a high **degree of primacy** or strong domination by the primate city. He demonstrated that countries with a high degree of primacy tend to display the following characteristics: small territorial extent, relatively high population density, low per capita incomes, a high degree of dependence upon agricultural exports, high rates of population growth, and, in many cases, a former colonial status. Many of these attributes are, of course, typical of developing countries.

The situation with respect to wealthier, more economically self-sufficient countries with no recent colonial history, non-agricultural economies and a slower rate of population growth is less clear. Approximately half display a high degree of primacy and half have low levels of primacy. Nevertheless, it would appear that modernisation and industrialisation encourage the development of important lower-order towns, a situation more closely in accord with the rank-size rule.

Urban Hierarchies

So far attention has been concentrated upon the primate city and other high-order centres of population. However, the size distribution of the lower-order towns is also of considerable interest. Much discussion has centred around the question of whether there is a gradual and continuous decrease of urban population size with descending rank, or whether there are groups of towns of decreasing but approximately equal size and importance. The former situation is referred to as a **continuum** of urban sizes, the latter as an urban **hierarchy**.

At this point it is appropriate to extend the range of discussion from a simple consideration of urban population sizes to include reference to the functions carried out by these settlements. The term **central place** is used to describe a settlement providing one or more services for the population living outside it. Such services may be rudimentary but essential, such as a general store, or sophisticated and specialised, such as a university. These examples may be referred to as low-order and high-order services respectively. Between these extremes is a wide range or hierarchy of intermediate functions. When a high-order function occurs in a town it is normal to find most lower-order functions also present.

It will be apparent that the population required to support different functions tends to increase as one goes higher up the hierarchy. A small general store may be able to conduct a profitable business with a mere two or three hundred regular users, whereas a university may need to draw upon a population of several hundred thousand in order to attract sufficient students of appropriate age and qualifications. The minimum number of people required to support a function or service is called the **threshold population**. If the population falls below that number or if changing taste and habits result in the existing population making less use of a service then it will cease to operate. The closure of many local cinemas in Britain in recent years is an example of this process at work. Conversely, if the population increases to approximately twice the threshold size a second competitive unit offering the same service may be established.

If the total population of an area and the threshold sizes for various functions are both known, it is possible to calculate the number of units supplying each service that may be established in the area concerned. A highly simplified example is shown in Fig. 18.2. Five services are shown with their relevant threshold sizes. Service A requires only ten people to support it, whereas service E needs 160 people (Fig. 18.2a). Assuming a population of 160 people, it can be seen that there will be only one establishment providing service E, but 16 providing service A (Fig. 18.2b). If it is further assumed, as was suggested earlier, that a high-order place will supply all lower-order services, then the number of settlements and their functional importance can be calculated. In this example there will be a total of 16 places. The largest will provide all five services, three will supply services A, B and C, four will

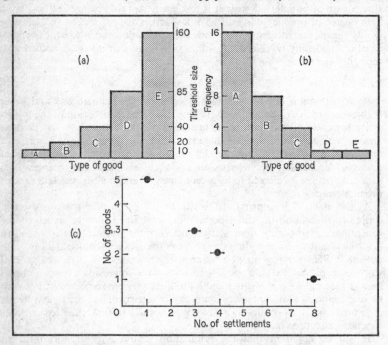

Fig. 18.2. Graphs showing threshold sizes, frequency of services and number of settlements (after B. J. Garner).

provide services A and B, and eight places will supply service A only (Fig. 18.2c).

Various studies have been made of the relationships between the number of services in towns and their population size. From what has been stated earlier it is to be expected that high-order centres with a wide range of services will have large populations. This is generally the case, although attention has been drawn to certain deviant situations. Some towns provide fewer services or functions than their population size might lead one to expect. For example, 'dormitory' towns close to a large city often lack a full range of functions. Conversely, tourist centres, drawing upon a large transient population, provide more services than their resident populations might warrant. These relationships are shown in Fig. 18.3.

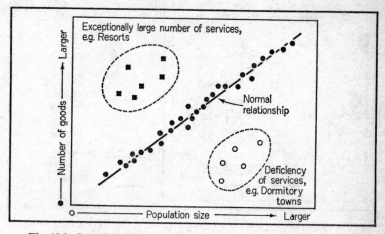

Fig. 18.3. Graph showing the relationship between population size and functional importance (after B. J. Garner).

Empirical studies along these lines have produced conflicting results. In some areas a continuous relationship between population size and functional size of settlements appears to exist, while elsewhere there is evidence of a stepped or hierarchical arrangement. Despite the inconclusive nature of such results, it is still important to appreciate the principles under consideration for they are implicit in many of the ideas underlying central place theory, which is considered next.

Central Place Theory

Central place theory is concerned with the discovery of order in the spacing of population clusters and settlements in the landscape. It is assumed that since, as we have already seen, there is a degree of order in the relationship between size and ranking of settlements in any region, there may also be some logic in the distribution or spacing of settlements of different sizes and functional importance. One of the earliest attempts to seek an understanding of the order underlying settlement spacing was that of W. Christaller in an important and influential study first published in 1933.

Christaller's Central Place Theory

Christaller's theory derived very largely from a study of central places in southern Germany. He proposed that settlements with the lowest order of specialisation would be equally spaced and surrounded by hexagonal-shaped service areas or hinterlands. For every six of these lowest-order settlements he suggested that there would be a larger and more specialised settlement which in turn would be situated at an equal distance from other settlements of the same order and also surrounded by a hexagonal service area. Progressively more specialised towns with even larger hexagonal-shaped hinterlands would be similarly located at an equal distance from each other.

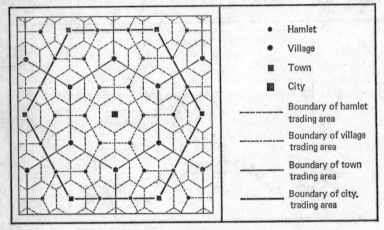

- • Hamlet
- • Village
- ▣ Town
- ▤ City
- --------- Boundary of hamlet trading area
- ─ · ─ · ─ Boundary of village trading area
- ───────── Boundary of town trading area
- ━━━━━━ Boundary of city. trading area

Fig. 18.4. Central place theory. Christaller's $k = 3$ network.

According to Christaller the smallest centres would lie approximately 7 km apart. Centres of the next order were thought to serve three times the area and three times the population. Thus, they would be located ($\sqrt{3} \times 7$) km or 12 km apart. Similarly, the next series of hinterlands would be three times larger than those of the preceding order. Such an arrangement would appear to be substantiated by Christaller's figures showing details of settlements and their service areas in south-west Germany (Table 18.1).

Table 18.1. The Urban Hierarchy in South-West Germany

Settlement form	Distance apart (km)	Population	Service area (km²)	Population
Market hamlet	7	800	45	2,700
Township centre	12	1,500	135	8,100
County seat	21	3,500	400	24,000
District city	36	9,000	1,200	75,000
Small state capital	62	27,000	3,600	225,000
Provincial head capital	108	90,000	10,800	675,000
Regional capital city	186	300,000	32,400	2,025,000

Source: After W. Christaller, from E. L. Ullman, *American Journal of Sociology*, 46, 1941.

The kind of arrangement illustrated in Fig. 18.4 and described above has been referred to as a $k = 3$ hierarchy in which the number of settlements at progressively less specialised levels follows the geometric progression 1, 3, 9, 27, . . . The $k = 3$ hierarchy is based upon what has been termed the marketing principle. Christaller also envisaged other types of hierarchies developing under special circumstances. These alternative arrangements are described on page 228.

The Theoretical Basis of Christaller's Central Place Network

A useful approach to the understanding of Christaller's ideas is to consider the evolution of settlements and their spacing in an idealised landscape. This idealised region should be thought of as being completely uniform in respect of its terrain, climate and soils and presenting equal ease and opportunities of movement in all directions—that is to say, possessing an **isotropic surface**.

It may be assumed that the first population to settle in the region would be predominantly agricultural. Families would tend to settle in groups, and small, largely self-sufficient hamlets would be established in the landscape. Since the terrain is flat and of uniform quality these hamlets would tend to be evenly distributed, say 4 km apart, each located at the apex of an equilateral triangle in order to minimise travel distances between each other (Fig. 18.5a). In reality the distance between hamlets would be determined by soil quality and the amount of land required to support a given population.

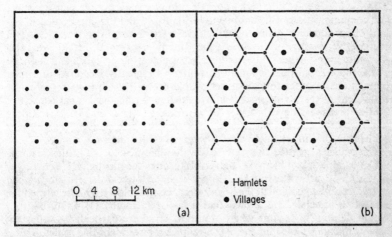

Fig. 18.5. Basic hamlet grid and the development of hexagonal service areas: (a) hamlets spaced 4 km apart on an equilateral triangle grid; (b) pattern of hamlet and village service areas governed by a $k = 3$ hierarchy.

If we next assume the development of a road network and certain technological advances whereby some specialisation of production takes place in the region, it seems likely that the population of certain hamlets will start to engage in the buying, selling and exchange of goods. If 4 km in each direction is the maximum distance that members of the surrounding communities are willing to travel to the trading hamlets (villages), it can be seen that such trading centres will attract custom from six surrounding hamlets as well as their own population. Once the first enterprises have demonstrated the profits to be derived from trading it might be expected that other trading centres will develop in response to the example of the early innovators. Assuming the original 4 km spacing of the hamlets, it can be calculated that these villages will be located at a distance of 7 km from each other.

If the threshold population for the business activities of the villages is equivalent to the population of three hamlets, it can be seen that a series of regular hexagonal trading areas will develop (Fig. 18.5b). Each of the six hamlets around a trading centre will divide their allegiance between three villages. Conversely, each village will draw upon one third of the population of six hamlets, which, together with its own population, gives a total population equivalent to that of three hamlets.

It should be noted at this point that a circular trading area would be the most efficient in terms of accessibility to the centre and size of area enclosed in relation to a given perimeter length. However, circles will not 'pack', and the superimposition of a series of circular trading areas over a region can only be achieved by creating areas of overlap or zones of vacuum. Of the various regular polygons that will 'pack' or form a regular lattice network the hexagon comes closest to retaining the properties of the circle. The principles involved are the same as those discussed in connection with the theoretical pattern of market areas around industrial centres (Chapter Sixteen).

In the idealised region under consideration we may assume that transport and communications will continue to be improved and that further specialisation of economic activities will take place. The lower-order settlements will become even less self-sufficient. At the same time several centres (towns) will specialise even further and offer a range of higher-order goods and services. These more sophisticated functions will require greatly increased threshold populations in order to yield a reasonable profit. If each town requires the equivalent of three village service areas then a further hexagonal pattern of trading areas will develop around the towns, as shown in Fig. 18.4. In the same way we can envisage the development of progressively higher-order settlements and increasingly large hexagonal trading areas.

Christaller suggested that once a k value had developed, in this instance a $k = 3$ value, it would apply at all levels through the hierarchy. He envisaged that a $k = 3$ network would develop where the lower-order settlements had to be as near as possible to the higher-order central places. This he termed the **marketing principle**. He argued that a $k = 4$ hierarchy $(1, 4, 16, 64, \ldots)$ would develop in regions where transport costs are particularly important since it maximises the number of central places on straight-line routes. This is the **traffic principle**. Christaller further suggested that in regions with a highly developed system of central administration a $k = 7$ hierarchy $(1, 7, 49, 343, \ldots)$ would tend to develop since the resultant arrangement maximises the number of settlements dependent on any one central place and eliminates the shared allegiances of other k value systems. This is the **administrative principle**. Fig. 18.6 illustrates the $k = 4$ and $k = 7$ hierarchies developed to the third order of settlement.

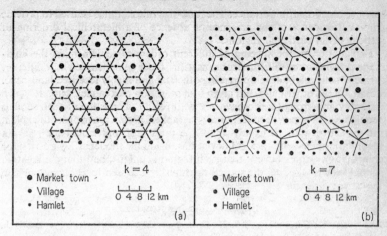

Fig. 18.6. (a) Hamlets, villages and towns in a fixed $k = 4$ hierarchy (Christaller's traffic principle). (b) Hamlets, villages and towns in a fixed $k = 7$ hierarchy (Christaller's administrative principle).

A Modification of Christaller's Model

While there can be no question of denying the fundamental importance of Christaller's work, certain limitations inherent in his model have been pointed out. For example, the assumption of the isotropic surface is never fulfilled, and therefore the theoretical arrangement of settlements in any area will inevitably be modified by local conditions. Secondly, the model is concerned with the size and spacing of settlements supplying goods and services or providing an administrative function. It is particularly appropriate, therefore, to regions emerging from a subsistence economy in which there is a clear distinction between town and country, but in economically advanced regions, it is distorted by factors such as the presence of industrial concentrations and government policies for regional development. Criticism has been levelled in particular at the fixed k value of Christaller's model, which, it is argued, shows a very poor approximation with reality.

In 1954 the economist A. Lösch presented an important modification of Christaller's model. Like Christaller, he again used hexagonal service areas, but allowed various hexagonal systems to co-exist. In Lösch's model the various hexagonal systems, $k = 3$, $k = 4$, $k = 7$ and others, operate at different levels and are superimposed on each other. The application of a variable k value produces a continuum of settlement sizes more closely in line with the theoretical result of the rank-size rule.

Conclusion

The ideas discussed in this chapter are closely inter-related. The concept of threshold populations for various services and functions aids our understanding of the ways in which functional hierarchies of settlements may evolve in a region. Although the rank-size rule is concerned solely with population size, a relationship has also been shown to exist between population size and functional importance. The rank-size rule can thus be used to provide empirical evidence of the presence or absence of a hierarchical ordering of settlements in particular regions.

Explanation of the spacing of different orders of settlement in the landscape presents more difficult problems. Christaller demonstrated how different arrangements might develop in a hypothetical and highly idealised landscape. Lösch, on the other hand, has given us a more complex model, but one which probably approximates more closely with reality. The value of such models should be kept in perspective. Some geographers argue that in order to explain the settlement pattern in any area, one must first understand the relevant theory and then examine local deviations, using the model as a yardstick for comparison. Others believe that each region is unique, and that explanation should seek to discover the special relationship between local conditions and settlement ordering.

Suggested Further Reading

Berry, B. J. L., *Geography of Market Centres and Retail Distribution*, Prentice-Hall, Englewood Cliffs, New Jersey, 1967.

Bunge, W., *Theoretical Geography* (especially Chapter 6), Gleerup, Lund, 1966.

Christaller, W., *Central Places in Southern Germany* (especially Part IB), translated by C. W. Baskin, Prentice-Hall, Englewood Cliffs, New Jersey, 1966.

Everson, J. A., and Fitzgerald, B. P., *Settlement Patterns*, Longman, London, 1969.

Garner, B. J., 'Models of Urban Geography and Settlement Location', Chapter 9 in *Socio-economic Models in Geography*, R. J. Chorley and P. Haggett (Eds.), Methuen, London, 1967.

Haggett, P., *Locational Analysis in Human Geography* (especially Chapter 5), Arnold, London, 1965.

Lösch, A., *The Economics of Location*, Yale University Press, New Haven, Conn., 1954.

CHAPTER NINETEEN

THE INTERNAL STRUCTURE OF TOWNS AND CITIES

So far attention has been directed to the origins and spread of urban settlements, their size relationships and spacing in the landscape. Another important branch of urban geography is devoted to the study of the internal structure, or morphology, of towns and cities. The term **urban morphology** refers to the physical arrangement or structure of a town; its pattern of streets, building blocks, individual buildings, their different functions, densities and lay-out.

A basic approach in studies of urban morphology involves the mapping and description of patterns of internal land use as a preliminary stage in the analysis of the processes operating to produce particular patterns of urban structure. As in other fields of geography, an essential aim is the search for generalisations and principles with a high degree of application to all towns and cities. Models of urban structure are of two kinds: partial and comprehensive. **Partial models** are concerned with the location of one set of activities, such as residential or industrial land use, while **comprehensive models** deal with all activities in the urban area and their inter-relationships.

Patterns of urban land use result from a multitude of choices and decisions about location. These are made by individuals, planners, architects, companies and by both local and central government. These decisions are influenced predominantly by economic motives. Competition in the urban land market for the use of available sites tends to result in the occupation of each site by the land use which is able to derive the greatest utility or profit from that site and is able to pay most for it.

Fig. 19.1 shows the offer prices for three types of potential land use at different distances from a city centre (O). Bid prices are based on their ability to derive advantage from central location in the city. Thus, at O, retail use, which is most dependent on accessibility, can outbid other potential users. However, the offer price curve for retail land use declines more steeply than that of offices or residences, and between distances A and B from the city centre offices can bid for sites most successfully, while beyond B, towards the urban margin, the offer price of residential land use is greater than that of either retail or office use. Thus, by a process of adjustment similar to that proposed by von Thünen for agricultural land use (Chapter Twelve), there develops an orderly pattern of urban land use which is closely related to rents, which in turn are influenced by land values.

The Land Value Surface

Since land values play a key part in determining patterns of urban land use it is useful to consider the chief influences on land values in any town. The land value surface, as the overall pattern of values is termed, is essentially a reflection of accessibility within the urban area. Accessibility is greatest at the city centre; it is also greater along radial and circumferential routes, and especially at their intersections, than it is away from them. Since some parts

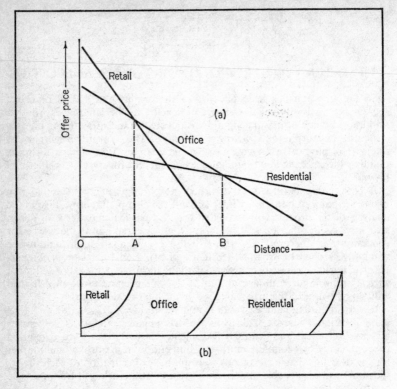

Fig. 19.1. Offer prices of retail, office and residential uses with distance from the city centre: (a) section across the urban value surface; (b) plan of the urban value surface.

of an urban area are better served by transport than others the land value surface declines more steeply from the centre in some directions than others.

The characteristics of a typical urban land value surface may be summarised as follows: land values reach a grand peak at the city centre and decline by varying amounts in different directions from the centre. Secondary peaks of high value occur at major traffic intersections. High values occur along major traffic arteries compared with values in the areas between such routes.

Although accessibility is the dominant influence, local site characteristics and other factors inevitably complicate this simple pattern. For example, in a study of Chicago, M. Yeates identified six factors which influenced the land value surface: these were distance from the central business district, distance from the nearest regional shopping centre, distance from Lake Michigan, proximity to an elevated-subway line, proportion of non-white population and population density. Nevertheless, the general concept of the land value surface provides a useful background for the study of the various land use zones of the city.

The Central Business District

The central business district, which is variously referred to as the CBD, downtown district, urban core, central area or city centre, is that part of the city which contains the principal commercial streets and main public buildings. It is essentially the core of the city's business and civic life. Its characteristics have been described as follows: 'It lies central, at least in terms of its accessibility. It has a greater concentration of tall buildings than any other region of the city, since it normally includes most of the city's offices and largest retail stores. It is the area where vehicular and pedestrian traffic are likely to be most concentrated. It averages higher assessed land values and taxes paid than any other part of the city, and it draws its business from the whole urban area and from all ethnic groups and classes of people.' (R. E. Murphy.) It has also been said that for out-of-town people the CBD is synonymous with the city itself.

In earlier times the CBD was a district of varied land use, containing residential, commercial, administrative and even industrial premises. However, over the years the rising value of CBD land and property has forced out most residential and industrial users leaving a district dominated by retail business premises, offices and institutional buildings.

Delimitation of the CBD

It will be appreciated that many of the essential CBD characteristics described above—such as building heights, accessibility, traffic and pedestrian flows, patterns of residential population, land and property values, and residents' perception of the CBD—can be readily measured and mapped. It might be supposed, therefore, that it is a relatively simple matter to delimit the CBD on the basis of these elements. Unfortunately, none of these measures is entirely satisfactory and in practice there is a high concentration of these elements at the heart of the CBD and a gradual diminution of these essential characteristics outwards towards an indefinite boundary. Indeed, the edge of the CBD is best thought of as a zone rather than a boundary. Typically the CBD merges into a 'blighted' zone of obsolete and deteriorated property which lies between the CBD itself and the surrounding residential districts of the inner city.

In a pioneer CBD study, two American geographers, R. E. Murphy and J. E. Vance Jr., suggested that land valuation data could provide the most objective and widely applicable method of CBD delimitation. Based on a study of the pattern of decline of land values outwards from the core of the CBD in nine American cities, they demonstrated that a land valuation of 5 per cent of the peak land value corresponded very closely with the extent of the CBD based upon land use patterns. Application of this technique to the delimitation of the CBD in non-American towns has shown that the decline in land values from the **peak land value intersection** to the edge of the CBD is frequently less steep than that of US cities and that a higher percentage value provides a more realistic boundary. Another serious practical problem is that many local authorities are unwilling to make valuation data available for study purposes. The best means of delimitation is probably based on a combination of land valuation data, if available, and land use mapping, whereby the transition from CBD functions to other functional areas of the city can be identified.

Whatever means of delimitation is employed it should be appreciated that the CBD is by no means a static element in the urban landscape. Despite the high investments in land and buildings, its boundaries are subject to gradual shifts in response to changing economic conditions. Murphy and Vance have referred to a zone of assimilation and a zone of discard to describe the advanc-

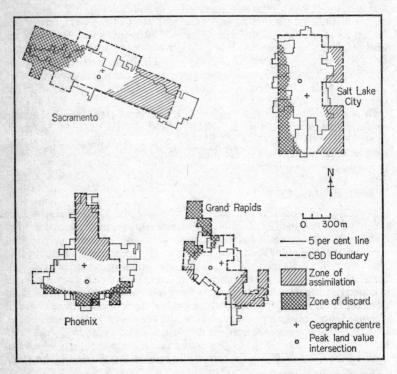

Fig. 19.2. The CBD of four American cities (Sacramento, Salt Lake City, Phoenix and Grand Rapids) showing CBD boundaries, the 5 per cent line, peak land value intersection, geographic centre and zones of discard and assimilation (after R. E. Murphy *et al.*).

ing and retreating fronts of the CBD. The **zone of assimilation** is the CBD of the future and is characterised by extensive redevelopment and the spread of shops, offices and hotels into former residential areas, whereas the **zone of discard** is the CBD of the past, lacking in prestige and characterised by low-grade retail stores, warehouses and wholesale trading premises and a high proportion of vacant property. It has further been suggested that the peak land value intersection also shifts in the same direction as the zone of assimilation as the shape and balance of the CBD become modified.

Internal Structure of the CBD

Land use in the CBD shows a tendency towards an ordered arrangement which is determined by the pattern of land values. Reference was made earlier to the peak land value intersection and the fact that land values decline around this point towards the edge of the CBD. Because of the high land values and property rentals around the peak land value intersection, only companies with a large turnover and high profits can afford to conduct their business on these prestige sites at the heart of the CBD. Thus, at the core of the CBD there are department stores, major chain stores, supermarkets and head-quarters offices, while the small trader, with only modest profits, is forced out towards the edge of the central area.

A technique of CBD land use analysis was devised by Murphy and Vance in the 1950s and has subsequently been applied with various modifications to numerous towns and cities. The original study method consisted of drawing up four concentric zones, each 100 yards in width, around the peak land value intersection and then calculating the percentages of the built-up area in each zone devoted to specific types of land use, both at street level and upper floor levels. The various establishments were divided up into three main groups as shown in Table 19.1.

Working in this way it has been shown that the hypothesis outlined above is broadly correct; namely, that CBD land use patterns tend to show an ordered adjustment to land values and distance from the peak land value intersection.

Table 19.1.   Categories of CBD Land Use

Retail business uses	Service–finance–office uses	Non-CBD uses
Food	Financial	Residential
Clothing	Service trades	Industrial
Household goods	Headquarters office	Wholesale
Car sales and service	Government and legal	Vacant
General store	Transient residence	Cultural
Miscellaneous		Educational[1]
Entertainment		Ecclesiastical

Source: Murphy, R. E., *The Central Business District. A Study in Urban Geography*, Longman, London 1972.

If this hypothesis was completely true, land use in the CBD would consist of a series of concentric zones, each with a distinct land use. This is clearly not so. Other processes operate to disturb such a simple arrangement. For example, establishments which are dependent upon each other for their everyday working tend to cluster together. Thus, a financial–legal district can often be identified with premises such as banks, estate agents, legal offices and insurance company offices. Major rail or bus termini at the edge of the CBD can create a district of distinctive land use in the outermost zone with hotels, boarding houses, restaurants and shops catering for a large transient population. In some instances small retail stores survive near the heart of the CBD adjacent to large department stores by utilising the drawing power of their larger neighbour or by selling high-grade specialist goods.

These then are some of the main processes at work in the CBD, and many more probably still await identification. It is clear that the detailed internal adjustments taking place in the CBD in response to changing economic and social conditions are so complex as to be almost impossible to unravel.

Residential Areas

One of the notable characteristics of the CBD is the relatively small size of its residential population. During the present century most large Western cities have seen an outward migration of population from their inner districts to the suburban zones around their margins. This process of residential decentralisation can be measured and expressed in more precise terms by means of an urban density gradient.

Urban Density Gradients

In 1951, based on a study of 36 cities, the economist C. Clark proposed the following formula to describe the pattern of population density in any city

$$d_x = d_o e^{-bx}$$

where d_x represents population density (d) at distance x from the city centre, d_o the central density, e an exponent of distance and b the density gradient or rate of diminution of population density with distance from the centre, a negative exponential decline. According to Clark this formula 'appears to be true for all times and all places studied, from 1801 to the present day, and from Los Angeles to Budapest'. This formula was subsequently tested by a number of studies of urban population density so that by the early 1960s almost 100 cases were available with examples drawn from most parts of the world, and for the past 150 years, yet no evidence was presented to counter Clark's assertion of the universal applicability of the equation.

As an explanation of the decline in population density between city centres and their suburbs it has been suggested that 'the poor live near the city centre on expensive land, consuming little of it, and the rich at the periphery consuming much of it. Since the land consumed by each household increases with distance from the city centre, population densities must drop.' (B. J. L. Berry, J. W. Simmonds and R. J. Tennant.) The urban density gradient may be seen, therefore, as a logical extension of urban land use theory.

It has been shown that in Western cities the density gradient diminishes as the population of the city increases. In other words, small cities are more compact than large cities. The point is well illustrated in Fig. 19.3, which shows the decline of the density gradient for London between 1801 and 1941. It will be noted that over this period there was first an increase in central density and then later a decrease. On the other hand, in Asian cities, it appears that growth in population size is accompanied by an increase in central density while the density gradient remains constant. That is to say, there is a tendency towards increased overcrowding with the maintenance of a constant degree of compactness. Such a pattern of development is typical of most non-Western cities.

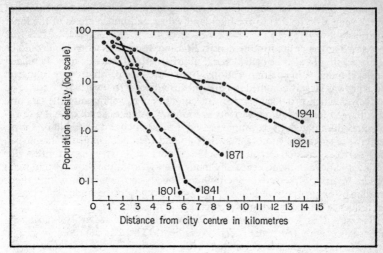

Fig. 19.3. Density–distance gradients for London, 1801–1941 (after C. Clark).

Residential Land Use Patterns

The residential function generally accounts for the largest single land use area in any city, approximately 45 per cent of the total area in towns over 10,000 in the UK. Certain general comments, related to the observations on the urban density gradient, may be made about the typical arrangement of residential land use in the Western city.

First, a few dwelling units, often of prestige status, may be found in the CBD, especially at higher floor levels. However, as mentioned earlier, the CBD is chiefly characterised by an absence of residential population. Secondly, just beyond, and often forming part of the 'blighted' or slum zone surrounding the CBD, is a residential belt of considerable density. This typically comprises large houses built in the nineteenth century, many now converted into multi-family residences, together with tenement buildings and terraces of small artisan dwellings, often in poor structural condition. Beyond this belt of inner city housing there may be wedges or sectors of housing of varying age stretching out towards the zone of suburban residences.

Large-scale suburban growth is essentially the product of the twentieth century. The development of the urban fringe, which is predominantly residential in character, may be attributed to many factors. Clearly, it must be related to the twentieth-century increase in urban population described in Chapter Seventeen. The impact of this population growth has also been augmented by social changes, notably the tendency for family and household units to become smaller, so that, even without population growth, more dwellings are required to house the same number of people. The pattern of suburban growth has also been interpreted as a reaction against nineteenth-century urban life and the poor housing conditions endured by many of those living in the inner city. In Britain this attitude was typified by the Garden City movement of the early twentieth century. Thus, a detached or semi-detached house with garden and adjacent to open space has become the ultimate goal for a large number of people; for others it is the only means of purchasing a home due to the high land values and house prices of the inner districts.

As well as the desire for low-density housing, the means whereby it could be achieved should also be considered. Suburban growth may be directly related to developments in communications. In the late nineteenth century suburban housing was largely confined to narrow belts adjacent to the newly constructed railways, which provided services for commuters travelling into the city and encouraged longer journeys to work. In many instances small outlying towns became dominated by commuters and transformed into **dormitory towns**. Later, the spread of motorcar ownership and the establishment of suburban bus services created greater travel flexibility and new opportunities for residential development, especially in areas away from the railways and main roads. In Britain the role of the building society movement in making funds available for prospective house purchasers should not be underestimated as an influence on the rapid outward spread of housing.

The suburban zone comprises extensive areas of low-density housing (in accordance with the urban density gradient). There is a predominance of single-family residences compared with the multi-family dwellings of the inner city. There is also a higher proportion of public open space as well as garden space around the individual house units. The details of house style and housing arrangements are influenced by the speculative builder and municipal housing authorities operating within the constraints of cost economies, public taste, land availability and so on. There is generally a high degree of segregation of residential areas from other land uses, and a tendency for large areas to be occupied by residents of a single income group and social class. This uniformity of social class and housing style over extensive areas of the suburbs is the product of various factors. Increased flexibility of movement has allowed a 'sorting-out' of social groups; planning rules about land use zoning and housing densities have accentuated the trend towards uniformity, while the estates of both the speculative builder and the local housing authority have rarely been characterised by variety.

Like other urban land uses the residential districts of the city are subject to constant adjustment in response to changing socio-economic conditions. In any large city it is possible to see the processes of rebuilding, renewal or rehabilitation whereby depressed areas are upgraded and made fashionable by an influx of upper-middle-class residents. This is sometimes referred to as **gentrification**. Elsewhere there may be a reverse process of **filtering down**, whereby dwellings are subdivided and pass to successively lower income and social groups. In addition there is the constant outward expansion of suburban housing. Apart from the small enclaves of wealthy residents in the inner city, the social class of residents tends to arrange itself into a general increase outwards towards the urban fringe, culminating in the so-called 'stockbroker belt'.

Secondary Shopping Centres

The large-scale suburban growth of the twentieth century has inevitably had considerable impact on patterns of retail trade within the city. Although the CBD continues to maintain its dominant status in city trading, a notable change has been in the vigorous growth of secondary shopping centres in many suburban districts. It appears that as any city grows in size its residents become less willing to travel long distances to the city centre for their day-to-day requirements. Consequently, lower-order shopping centres tend to emerge, drawing upon relatively small population catchments, and providing the cheaper, convenience goods required for everyday needs. In large cities it is possible to identify a hierarchy of retail business districts. In a study of shopping centres in Greater London, for example, A. E. Smailes and G. Hartley recognised regional, major suburban, minor suburban and neighbourhood shopping centres, while D. Thorpe and T. C. Rhodes in a study of shopping centres in the Tyneside region noted a similar arrangement of what they termed major, suburban, small suburban and neighbourhood shopping centres.

Such hierarchical arrangements are due to the differing threshold populations required to support different types of commercial function, and also to the fact that consumers spend differing proportions of their income on different goods and services, and purchase them with varying degrees of frequency. This point is well illustrated by the results of a study of shopping activity in the city of Zürich (Fig. 19.4). The diagram shows the percentage of shopping

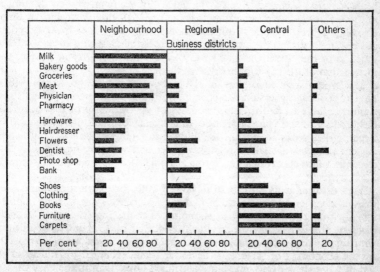

Fig. 19.4. Shopping trips by the residents of the Zürich suburb of Schwamendingen, percentage of trips to various shopping centres for goods or services.

(from H. Carol, Shopping Trips made by Residents of a Zurich Suburb, in *I.G.U. Symposium in Urban Geography*, 1962)

trips made by residents of the district of Schwamendingen to their local neighbourhood shopping centre, regional shopping centre and the CBD of Zürich for particular goods and services. The distinction between the low threshold, high-frequency services of the neighbourhood centre and the high threshold, low-frequency services of the CBD is implicit in these results.

The actual distribution of suburban shopping centres is greatly influenced by accessibility and, as a consequence, the pattern of urban land values. However, this simple relationship is complicated by variations in population density and income levels within the city. For example, A. Getis, in a study of supermarkets in South Tacoma, Washington, found no apparent regularity in their distribution. He then divided the city area into regular grid squares, calculated the income potentially available for food shopping in each square, and then distorted the simple grid pattern by redrawing the squares proportional in size to their income level, and finally plotted the distribution of stores on this new base. By transforming normal or geographic space into 'income space' in this way, he found that the supermarkets were then much more regularly distributed and showed a close correlation with the pattern of income levels in the city.

Hypermarkets

A recent development in many countries has been the opening of carefully planned, out-of-town, shopping centres in which a wide range of goods and services is available in a single gigantic complex serving populations of 250,000 or more. Such regional shopping centres or hypermarkets, as they are often termed, are well established in the USA and Canada as well as certain European countries such as Sweden and France, but are relatively few in number in the UK. One interesting example is the regional shopping centre at Brent Cross in North London. Although not strictly an out-of-town shopping centre, it illustrates the importance of accessibility, being located at the junction of the North Circular Road (A406) with the A41 and close to the intersection of the M1 Motorway with the A5.

The hypermarket concept assumes a mobile and affluent population with a high level of car ownership. Shoppers must be able to drive to an out-of-town centre, be able to afford bulk purchases of goods, and probably possess a deep-freezer to store large quantities of convenience foodstuffs at home. The hypermarket seeks to change traditional shopping patterns by attracting customers who will make a relatively infrequent visit, say monthly, to purchase in bulk items which are normally bought locally on a weekly or even more frequent basis.

Various arguments have been advanced both for and against the hypermarket idea. Its supporters claim that the new centres relieve congestion in already overcrowded suburban shopping districts, that shopping is made pleasant and easy where all services are located in a single planned centre with adjacent car parking facilities, and that large discounts are made possible by the economies of scale and the lower rentals charged to traders in an out-of-town site where land values are much lower than in the city. On the other hand, there are those who argue that it is inconvenient to have to travel to an out-of-town centre, that such centres are of no use to the poor and elderly who lack the means and ability to make bulk purchases and travel long distances, that the discounts are theoretical rather than real, and are, in any case, offset by travel costs, that out-of-town centres with parking for several thousand cars consume excessive amounts of valuable land (up to 100 ha) and also destroy neighbourhood shopping allegiances and community spirit and cause a decline in the shopping facilities of the inner city.

Industry in the City

As described in Chapter Seventeen, the importance of industrial activity varies enormously from one city to another. In some instances industrial activity may be the very reason for a city's existence, while elsewhere other functions dominate and industry is scarcely represented. Much depends on the regional and economic setting of the city concerned. It is possible, therefore, to do no more than make certain broad generalisations about the location and morphology of industrial districts within the city.

It should be appreciated that the major influences on industrial location have been examined in Chapter Fifteen and that in the present context emphasis is placed on the various secondary factors which influence the detailed location of industry within the city itself.

Industry Close to the Central Area

In many cities it is easy to underestimate the amount of industry located close to the city centre due to the fact that it generally consists of small units consuming relatively little power and often interspersed with other land uses, although occasionally it may be concentrated to form a distinctive industrial quarter.

Industry occupying a central location may need access to skilled labour drawn from the whole urban area, or draw heavily upon the specialised services found in the CBD, or distribute its products either to retailers in the CBD or to customers over the whole urban area. In some instances these industrial premises of the inner city may be relic features facing severe competition from suburban manufacturers and occupying low-grade sites in derelict areas, but for many other manufacturers, centrality is still essential and no other site would offer the same basic advantage. Although production is varied, typical industries include precision engineering (instruments, tools, office equipment, etc.), the manufacture of fashion clothing, printing and newspaper industries. Skill in design and production is often more important than investment in large premises and elaborate equipment.

Industry Close to Waterways and Railways

Industries consuming large amounts of bulky raw materials are generally located adjacent to harbour installations, navigable rivers or canals, or railways. Many industries of this type, such as grain-milling, sugar-refining and saw-milling, are concerned with the processing of imported raw materials. Others, such as motor manufacturing and oil refining, require in addition very extensive sites which are only available at the edge of the urban area. A further group of industries in this category are those which create a nuisance because of noise or noxious fumes or dust; for example, metal smelting, paint and varnish production, pulp and paper manufacturing and cement production. Such industries also tend to be located adjacent to bulk transport facilities but away from residential areas.

The location of public utilities, such as gas and power stations, is influenced by similar considerations. Power stations, for example, consume large amounts of fuel which is most economically brought by water and which requires extensive sites for storage. They also require water for cooling processes, create noxious steam and gases, produce large amounts of waste material which must be disposed of, and yet at the same time function most economically close to the urban area that they serve. Areas of estuarine marshland downstream of a port provide good sites for these and similar types of industry.

A closely related group of industries includes those which do not necessarily need a waterfront location, but nevertheless benefit from close association with the industries described above, and in many cases use the products of the first group for further processing. Examples include the manufacturing of certain foodstuffs, cigarettes, chemicals and engineering products.

Industry in the Suburbs

The rise of manufacturing industry in the suburbs is the result of a number of twentieth-century influences on industrial location in the city. With the growth of road transport for the movement of certain raw materials and products, there has been a strong incentive for many industries to move away from rail and water terminals and from the congested districts of the inner city to suburban locations. This greater flexibility in choice of site has been aided by the growing use of electrical power in industry. Cheaper sites and the presence of a large labour force in the suburbs have also acted as strong incentives in this process of industrial decentralisation.

Suburban industry typically shows a greater degree of order and planning than that of the inner city, often being housed in single-storey, purpose-built factories with an ordered layout of machinery and space for storage of materials, parts and products. It is generally located close to main roads, either radial routes leading out of the city or 'circular' by-pass routes. In some instances a whole district of factories, workshops and supporting services may be developed to create an **industrial estate** such as the Park Royal industrial estate in west London or the Team Valley trading estate, 5 km south of Newcastle-upon-Tyne.

The products of suburban industry are extremely varied, but show a marked emphasis on light consumer goods aimed at the local urban market; for example, foodstuffs, furniture, clothing and electrical goods.

Theories of Urban Structure

Although each city is unique in respect of the detailed pattern of its internal land use, there is nevertheless a considerable degree of repetition in the broad geographical arrangement of the various categories of urban land use from one city to another. As a result a number of theories have been formulated which attempt to describe and explain the patterns involved.

The Concentric Theory

The **concentric or zonal theory** of urban land use was first proposed in 1923 by E. W. Burgess, an urban sociologist, in an attempt to explain the pattern of social areas within the city of Chicago, but was later seen to have more universal application. Burgess's model is based on the idea that the growth of a city takes place outwards from its central area to form a series of concentric zones (Fig. 19.5).

At the centre of the city is the CBD (Zone I), the focus of commercial, social and civic life. This is surrounded by an area of transitional land use (Zone II) containing industrial premises, obsolete housing and slum property occupied by lower social groups and a high proportion of immigrants. This

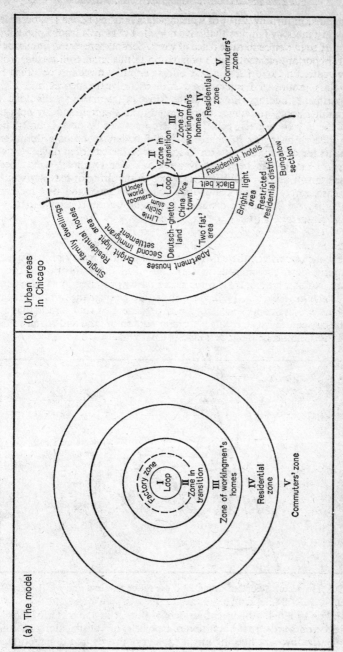

(a) The model

(b) Urban areas in Chicago

Fig. 19.5. The concentric theory of urban structure: (a) the model; (b) urban areas in Chicago (after E. W. Burgess).

is surrounded in turn by a belt of working-class housing (Zone III) occupied in many instances by families that have migrated outwards from Zone II but still require to live close to their place of work. Second-generation immigrants form an important element of the population in this zone. Still further from the city centre, in Zone IV, is a belt of single-family dwellings occupied by middle-class groups and interspersed with exclusive residences and high-class apartment buildings. Finally, at the fringe of the urban area is Zone V, the commuter zone, which may be separated from the continuously built-up area of the city by a green belt. Here there may still be open country and former villages changing in character and function to become dormitory settlements for commuters who travel to work in the city each day.

Burgess's model has been widely criticised. For example, it has been suggested that it makes insufficient reference to the siting of industry which, in any case, rarely forms a continuous concentric zone, and that the concentric zones are inevitably distorted by major transport axes and topographical features.

The Sector Theory

Discrepancies between the concentric model and the reality of urban land use patterns have encouraged the formulation of other theories of urban structure. Notable among these is the **sector theory** proposed by H. Hoyt and M. R. Davie in 1939 (Fig. 19.6). According to the sector theory, patterns of urban land use are conditioned by the arrangement of routes radiating out from the city centre which create a sectoral pattern of land and rental values which in turn influence the urban land use pattern.

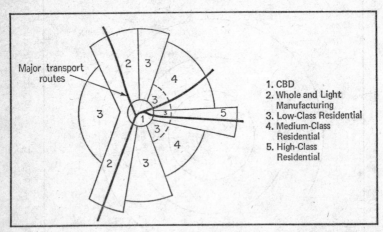

Fig. 19.6. The sector theory of urban land use (after H. Hoyt and M. R. Davie).

According to Hoyt, a high-rent residential district in one sector of the city will migrate outwards by the addition of new belts of housing along its outer arc. Similarly, low-rent housing might expand outwards in a different direction. In other words, once contrasts in land use have developed near the city centre, these differences will be perpetuated as the city expands. This idea of a wedge-like expansion is an improvement on the earlier concentric model in that it takes into account both the distance and direction of expansion, and acknowledges the importance of transport routes on the growth of the city.

An interesting attempt to combine elements of both the concentric and sector theories has been presented by P. Mann. His model, illustrating the structure of a hypothetical British city, includes four sectors (A–D) within which concentric growth zones (1–4) are allowed to co-exist (Fig. 19.7).

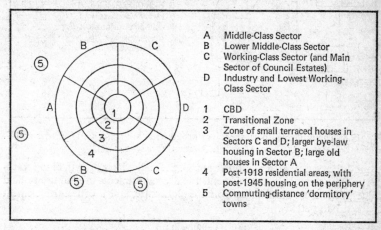

A Middle-Class Sector
B Lower Middle-Class Sector
C Working-Class Sector (and Main Sector of Council Estates)
D Industry and Lowest Working-Class Sector

1 CBD
2 Transitional Zone
3 Zone of small terraced houses in Sectors C and D; larger bye-law housing in Sector B; large old houses in Sector A
4 Post-1918 residential areas, with post-1945 housing on the periphery
5 Commuting-distance 'dormitory' towns

Fig. 19.7. The structure of a hypothetical British city. This diagram combines elements of both the concentric and sector theories. The diagram assumes a prevailing wind from the west (after P. Mann).

The Multiple Nuclei Theory

The concentric and sector theories have the advantage of an essential simplicity, but actual patterns of urban land use are generally far more complex and varied than either model would suggest. Consequently, in 1945 a less rigid model capable of application to a variety of urban patterns was proposed by C. D. Harris and E. L. Ullman. This was termed the **multiple nuclei theory**. It was suggested that land use patterns in most large cities develop around a number of discrete centres or nuclei rather than a single centre as described in the concentric and sector models. The clustering of related land uses around these nuclei in the city creates a cellular structure, the pattern of which will be largely determined by the unique factors of site and history of any particular city. The multiple nuclei theory does not produce a simple model of urban structure appropriate to each and every city, but rather suggests a number of general principles which are relevant to the land use pattern of most cities (Fig. 19.8).

At the present time there is a strong tendency to reject the idea of a simple model or theory to explain patterns of urban land use. It is now widely acknowledged that all three theoretical elements—concentric, sector and multiple nuclei—may be found in any large city, and that they are not mutually exclusive. Alternatively, it has been suggested that different processes operate at different periods in the city's growth. First, early growth may be

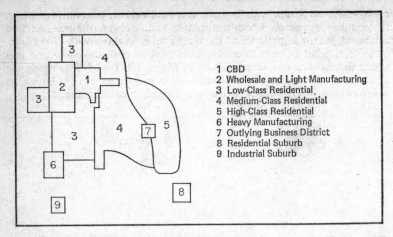

1 CBD
2 Wholesale and Light Manufacturing
3 Low-Class Residential
4 Medium-Class Residential
5 High-Class Residential
6 Heavy Manufacturing
7 Outlying Business District
8 Residential Suburb
9 Industrial Suburb

Fig. 19.8. The multiple nuclei theory of urban structure (after C. D. Harris and E. L. Ullman).

around the central area and other nuclei. Secondly, later growth along transport routes creates a sector element. Finally, adjustments of land use to land values, dependent on distance from the city centre, add a concentric element to the urban pattern.

Conclusion

In this chapter attention has been drawn to the underlying importance of the urban land value surface, which itself is the product of competition among different land users for the most accessible sites in the city. The importance of accessibility is typified by the geography of the CBD which presents many rewarding themes for study: notably the relationships between land values and land use, and the shifts and adjustments around its margin in response to changing social and economic conditions in the city. Residential land use accounts for a large part of the built-up area of any city, and varying patterns of housing and population density may be related to the factor of distance from the city centre. In large cities a hierarchical arrangement of secondary shopping centres has developed in response to the recent growth of suburban housing. Patterns of industrial location vary enormously from one city to another, although a recurrence of certain types of site preferences can be discerned.

Several attempts have been made to formulate comprehensive models of urban structure. Although they aid our understanding of the processes at work in the evolution of urban land use patterns, none is entirely satisfactory. Each city is, in a sense, unique, its particular structure determined in large part by the configuration of its site and the special historical processes to which it has been subjected.

Suggested Further Reading

Bartholomew, H., and Wood, J., *Land Uses in American Cities*, Harvard University Press, Cambridge, Mass., 1955.
Everson, J. A., and Fitzgerald, B. P., *Inside The City*, Longman, London, 1972.

Gottmann, J., and Harper, R. A. (Eds.), *Metropolis on the Move: Geographers Look at Urban Sprawl*, Wiley, New York, 1967.

Johnson, J. H. (Ed.), *Suburban Growth. Geographical Processes at the Edge of the Western City*, Wiley, London, 1974.

Martin, J. E., *Greater London. An Industrial Geography*, Bell, London, 1966.

Murphy, R. E., *The American City. An Urban Geography*, McGraw-Hill, New York, 1966.

Murphy, R. E., *The Central Business District. A Study in Urban Geography*, Longman, London, 1972.

Robson, B. T., *Urban Analysis: A Study of City Structure*, Cambridge University Press, Cambridge, 1969.

Scott, P., *Geography of Retailing*, Hutchinson, London, 1970.

Yeates, M. H., and Garner, B., *The North American City*, Harper & Row, New York, 1971.

CHAPTER TWENTY

CITY AND REGION

From preceding chapters it will be clear that any city is inextricably bound up with its surrounding area to operate as a unified **functional region**. Relationships between towns and their surrounding areas are implicit in the hexagonal service areas of central place theory. Even the origin and emergence of urban settlement forms depended on the provision of a food surplus from the surrounding countryside. Much later, the effects of the Agricultural Revolution were equally vital in allowing towns and cities to grow to unprecedented sizes during the Industrial Revolution.

The modern city is just as closely tied to its surrounding region as earlier cities, perhaps even more so. Improved transport and communications have allowed towns to extend their services further into the surrounding rural area, and have also permitted urban workers to live far beyond the city limits and travel to work each day. It has been said that 'to a degree quite unknown in the past the inhabitants of the areas between urban centres look to the towns and are drawn within their spheres of influence' (A. E. Smailes). Thus, town and countryside are still economically and socially interdependent. The exact nature of the economic dependence of any town upon its surrounding region is next considered more closely.

The Urban Economic Base

A town cannot exist simply by servicing its own population, and in order to flourish and expand, a proportion of its goods and services must be sold beyond its own limits. It follows from this that a proportion of any urban labour force is directly concerned with the production of goods and services for 'export'. These are termed **basic** or **city-forming workers**, since their efforts bring money into the town, thus enabling the purchase of raw materials, foodstuffs and other goods which the town cannot supply for itself. The remaining workers are referred to as **non-basic** or **city-serving workers**, since their role is to service the needs of the urban population itself. Although essential to the functioning of the town, the non-basic workers depend upon the revenue brought into the town by those in the basic sector. This interpretation of urban occupation structure is known as the **basic/non-basic concept**. It provides some insight into the way in which an urban population supports itself, and further illustrates the fact that any town is economically dependent on the extra-urban population.

The ratio of basic to non-basic workers is difficult to calculate. One method involves the collection of data from individual firms about the size of their work-force and percentage sales in local and out-of-town markets. The firm's labour force is then divided proportionally into basic and non-basic sectors. Thus, a company with 100 workers and selling 60 per cent of its production in non-local markets is scored with 60 basic and 40 non-basic workers. Scores for all firms in the city can then be totalled. Results of this type of study suggest that the basic to non-basic ratio is directly related to city size. The larger the city, the greater the proportion of non-basic workers. This is not because the amount of out-of-town trade decreases, but rather because the amount of business conducted between firms and individuals within the city itself increases as the city grows larger.

Another approach concerns the sources of income of the urban population. Incomes derived from local and out-of-town sources can be estimated for a town by means of a questionnaire survey among a sample of residents. The proportion of income from the two sources can then be used to provide a basic to non-basic ratio.

A further technique is known as the **minimum requirements method**. This was used in a study of the occupational structure of cities in the USA. Settlements with populations over 10,000 were divided into size groups and the percentage labour force in various occupational categories extracted from the census for each city. The lowest recorded percentage for each occupation in any size group was taken to be the minimum necessary for a city of that size to function. This minimum requirement was regarded as the non-basic population, and workers in excess of this minimum value were assumed to be basic workers. In this way a basic to non-basic ratio was established.

The choice of definition and delimitation of a town will influence its ratio. For example, should dormitory towns be regarded as forming part of the urban or extra-urban population? Another problem is that non-basic industries may extend their marketing area, and in so doing acquire basic characteristics. Thus, the ratio has no stable value through time. Also, many workers undertake both basic and non-basic activities. For example, power workers provide a service for both the urban and out-of-town populations. The basic to non-basic ratio is, therefore, conceptually weak, and provides only a very approximate measure of the functioning of any town and its economic relationships with the surrounding region.

Delimitation of the Urban Field

Various terms have been used to describe the area linked economically and socially to an urban settlement. The word '*umland*' has been widely used by German and Scandinavian geographers; 'hinterland' is frequently applied to the area served by a port. Other terms include 'sphere of influence', 'zone of influence', 'catchment area', 'tributary area' and '**urban field**'. The latter is now probably the most widely used descriptive term. The term '**city region**' is generally reserved to describe a similar situation on a much larger scale.

Urban geographers have devoted considerable attention to the problems of delimiting urban fields. The task is by no means an easy one, and presents many practical difficulties. A number of indices are normally selected which are appropriate to the level of specialisation of the town in question and which reflect its various functions as a centre of employment, marketing, retailing, entertainment and social activities, administration and so forth. Not only must the chosen indices reflect these functions, but the data must also be capable of being expressed in cartographic form. The aim is to construct a series of boundaries marking the extent of the area over which the town exerts its various influences.

Considerable ingenuity has been displayed in the selection of indices for this purpose. Measures which have been widely used include the catchment areas of secondary schools and general hospitals, the delivery area of major stores, the place of residence of employees in large industrial firms and offices, and newspaper circulation areas, among many others. Fig. 20.1 shows the zones of influence around four towns in West Cornwall using a number of such indices. Another method of delimiting the urban field of small urban settlements involves the use of local bus timetables. The frequency of buses tends to diminish away from town centres until a point is reached where buses run more frequently to a neighbouring centre. On this basis the urban field of a town has been defined as the area within which it is the most accessible centre by bus. Unfortunately, the recent reduction in bus services in many rural areas, together with the increased mobility of the rural population resulting from increased car ownership, has largely invalidated this simple notion.

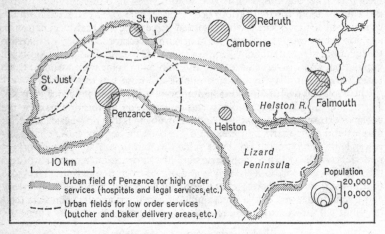

Fig. 20.1. Urban fields in West Cornwall.

Apart from the use of bus timetables, the methods of delimitation described above use information gathered in the town itself, and, in a sense, look outwards from the town towards the surrounding rural areas. This approach may be reversed by directing attention to the rural inhabitants themselves and analysing their patterns of movement and choices of towns for different goods and services. Such information can, of course, only be derived by questionnaire survey, and, like the urban-centred techniques, involves a very considerable amount of fieldwork to produce a meaningful result. Fig. 20.2 illustrates the urban fields of two small towns in Somerset defined by the frequency with which the surrounding rural population visits each centre for selected goods and services.

Margins of the Urban Field

Whatever indices are chosen to measure the extent of a town's urban field, the various boundaries recorded will inevitably show a lack of correspondence. The basic problem is that the various criteria represent different levels of specialisation. Some services, such as a local secondary school, will have a catchment area which covers only the town and its immediate surroundings, while others, such as a bakery, dairy or local newspaper, may serve the popula-

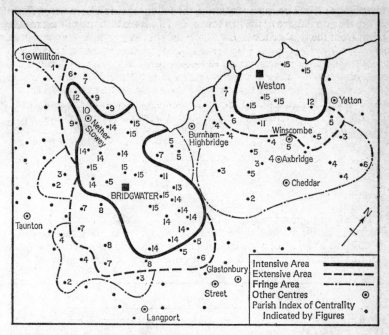

Fig. 20.2. Urban fields in part of Somerset. The map shows the intensive, extensive and fringe areas of the urban fields of Weston-super-Mare and Bridgwater.

(from H. E Bracey, Intensive, Extensive and Fringe Areas of Weston-super-Mare and Bridgwater, *Trans. Inst. Brit. Geogs.*, 19, 1953)

tion over a much wider area. Even at a given level of specialisation there are serious problems. The delivery area of one retail store may differ from that of another store selling a similar range of goods, for the size of the market area depends very much on the initiative, enterprise and efficiency of the management. Even with the most careful selection of indices, all that can be achieved is a series of boundaries which indicate the approximate extent of the area served by the town, but not its precise limits. In some studies a median boundary is drawn around the town based on the limits produced by the various independent measures, but more usually the varying limits produced by different criteria are presented individually and the map-user is left to draw his own conclusions. In view of these problems attempts have been made to delimit urban fields on a theoretical basis.

Breaking Point Theory

The theoretical position of the margin of an urban field can be calculated by using a technique known as breaking point theory. This is a simple variation on the standard gravity model described in Chapter Six. The **breaking point** between two towns divides the people who will travel to one town from those who will travel to another town for similar services. If enough breaking points can be established around a town, its theoretical urban field can be delimited in that way. The position of the breaking point (x) between two towns (i and j) can be calculated using the following formula, in which P_i and P_j are the populations of the two towns, and d_{jx} is the distance of the breaking point from the smaller town, j.

$$d_{jx} = \frac{d_{ij}}{1 + \sqrt{\dfrac{P_i}{P_j}}}$$

Thus, if two towns with populations of 40,000 and 5,000 respectively are located 18 km apart, the breaking point will lie at a distance of 4·9 km from the smaller town (Fig. 20.3a).

$$d_{jx} = \frac{18}{1 + \sqrt{\dfrac{40,000}{5,000}}}$$

$$= 4·9 \text{ km}$$

The use of population size as the force of attraction on either side of the breaking point is obviously open to criticism. However, the technique can be modified in a variety of ways by using other indicators such as the size of the working population rather than total population, or the number of retail

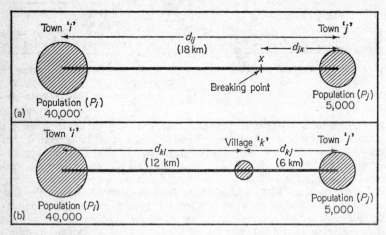

Fig. 20.3. (a) Location of the breaking point between two towns according to the breaking point theory. (b) Diagram to illustrate the law of retail trade gravitation.

service outlets in each town. Another modification of the basic formula involves expressing the distance between the two urban centres in terms of time. In this way the breaking point can be established as lying at a certain travel time from each town.

The Law Of Retail Trade Gravitation

Yet another modification of the basic gravity model has been used to predict the proportion of retail trade that two towns will derive from a settlement (k) lying between them. Again, this is relevant to the whole question of the theoretical delimitation of urban fields. The law of retail trade gravitation may be expressed by the following formula

$$\frac{M_{ki}}{M_{kj}} = \frac{P_i}{P_j} \times \left(\frac{d_{kj}}{d_{ki}}\right)^2$$

where M_{ki} is the volume of k's trade in town i; M_{kj} is the volume of k's trade in town j; P_i and P_j are the population totals of i and j respectively; d_{kj} is the distance between k and j; and d_{ki} is the distance between k and i. Substitution of the population figures and distances shown in the hypothetical situation illustrated in Fig. 20.3b gives the following result

$$\frac{M_{ki}}{M_{kj}} = \frac{40,000}{5,000} \times \left(\frac{6}{12}\right)^2$$
$$= 2 \cdot 0$$

On the basis of these figures it can be predicted that the population of village k will patronise the services of town i twice as much as those of town j. A breaking point can be found from the law of retail trade gravitation by a process of trial and error. This involves estimating the position of the breaking point, testing it against the formula and then shifting its position until a one-to-one relationship has been found.

These theoretical approaches to the problem of delimiting urban fields are based on the assumption that the population residing in the areas between the towns will organise their shopping expeditions in a rational, logical manner, selecting those towns which lie closest in terms of either time or distance, or which offer the most complete or most economic range of services. This may not necessarily be the case. People may be quite satisfied to accept alternatives to the most economic way of organising their visits to the city, and do not always behave in a manner which gives the optimum economic return. Furthermore, as described in Chapter Two, man's actions are influenced by what he thinks exists, rather than by what actually exists.

In the context of retailing activity, the rural population may have incomplete information about the urban services available, or may evaluate travel distances in a distorted manner. For example, in a study of retailing patterns in the San Francisco Bay area it was shown that customers frequently overestimated the distance to what they regarded as unattractive shops, such as discount or cut-price stores, and underestimated the distances to prestige department stores. It was concluded that 'neat, often circular, market areas drawn on a map, therefore, may be very poor representations of geographic purchasing patterns dependent on the operation of highly variable elements of human behaviour'. In other words, the various theoretical techniques for delimiting urban fields provide no more than an indication of the likely position of breaking points between settlements and the probable extent of a town's influence over its surrounding area.

The Size and Shape of Urban Fields

The size of an urban field depends essentially on the degree of development of the town as a central place. Thus, the urban field of an industrial town which has not grown up specifically to service the surrounding population will tend to be more restricted than that of a market town of equivalent size. Moreover, out-of-town shoppers will probably find the industrial town less attractive to visit than the market town, and this will further restrict the size of its urban field.

The spacing of neighbouring towns will also have an important effect on the size of an urban field. A service centre of moderate importance may have a relatively large urban field if there are no competing centres located nearby.

Good roads and good public transport can extend the range of a town's influence in a particular direction while, conversely, physical barriers such as a river or estuary can isolate areas relatively near an urban centre. For example, the population of the Lizard Peninsula falls firmly within the urban field of Helston, while Falmouth, a much larger centre, is relatively little used, due to the circuitous journey round the estuary of the Helford River (Fig. 20.1). Thus, urban fields rarely form symmetrical rings, but rather assume irregular figures, the outermost points of which are found along main roads.

It should also be made clear that urban fields are subject to constant change in response to social and economic developments. Adjustments may be caused by the opening of a new bridge, the building of a section of motorway, the opening of a new shopping centre, a reduction in the frequency of buses along a particular route, or even simply a change in shopping preferences.

Relationships Between Urban Fields

Just as there is a grading of towns by size and function, so there is a grading of urban fields. The urban fields of the most important central places encompass the restricted urban fields of the lower-order towns. The inhabitants of the smaller towns and their surrounding districts look to these secondary centres for low-order services, but also visit the major centres at less frequent intervals for high-order goods and services. Reference to Fig. 20.1 will illustrate the point. The urban field of Penzance extends over the whole of the western extremity of Cornwall, the nearest rival centre of comparable importance being the urban complex formed by the adjacent towns of Camborne and Redruth. The smaller urban fields of St. Just, St. Ives and Helston are 'nested' within the larger urban field of Penzance and supply their surrounding populations with relatively low-order services.

When the fields of influence of a number of major centres are put together on a single map, it will be seen that there are **zones of overlap** of the various urban fields. In Fig. 20.1 the urban field of Camborne/Redruth has not been mapped, but there can be no doubt that it overlaps with that of Penzance to the west. This is, in fact, a normal state of affairs, especially in highly urbanised countries where towns are located relatively close together. Residents in a zone of overlap will divide their trading allegiance between two or more towns. The reverse situation, a **zone of vacuum**, where the urban fields of two towns fail to meet and leave a zone with no urban allegiance, is quite rare. In the UK, for example, it has been estimated that less than 5 per cent of the total population lives more than 8 km from a town, and only 10 per cent lives more than one hour's travel by public transport from a city centre. The zone of vacuum is most typical of developing countries where the process of urbanisation is little advanced and towns are still widely spaced.

In view of the problems of delimitation and the complications produced by zones of overlap between urban fields, numerous studies have emphasised the fact that urban fields should be thought of as a series of zones rather than a single area delimited by a linear boundary. Such an approach is typified by the example in Fig. 20.2 in which the urban fields of Weston-super-Mare and Bridgwater are each divided into intensive, extensive and fringe areas of influence. In a similar manner, A. E. Smailes has suggested that any urban field can be divided into three zones: a **core area** which largely corresponds with the contiguous built-up area of the town and in which the majority of the population look to the town for shopping, entertainment and employment; an **outer area** in which the town is used for high-order services and local centres for low-order, day-to-day services; and a **fringe area** in which the town is the place of work for only a small proportion of the employed population but is still utilised for high-order functions such as higher education and specialised professional services.

Urban Fields and Local Government Boundaries

In the UK the pattern of local government boundaries drawn up in the 1890s, when the distribution of population and conditions of transport and population mobility were quite different from those of today, remained virtually unchanged until 1974. The old local government structure consisted of administrative counties and county boroughs, with the former containing well over a thousand municipal boroughs, urban districts and rural districts. The whole system was based on an artificial and arbitrary division between town and country which has been shown to be unrealistic.

Attention has been drawn to the fact that an increasing number of people live in the country but work, shop and are educated in towns. Solutions to urban housing problems are increasingly being sought in new towns and overspill projects in the surrounding countryside. In the following chapter it will also be shown how town dwellers are increasingly turning to the countryside for leisure and recreation. Thus, many towns are extending the range of their urban field, and the old distinctions between town and country are rapidly being broken down. It has been said that 'the gradual rise of areas of metropolitan dominance in the nineteenth and twentieth centuries has stamped a new geographical pattern on many countries and is now a force to be taken into account in the regional geography of some countries. Because large cities tend to organise the areas around them, both socially and economically, they can be said to form nodal or functional regions.' (J. H. Johnson)

By the mid-twentieth century the old local government boundaries in the UK showed little accordance with the pattern of urban fields and city regions which had evolved since they were drawn up some 60 years earlier, and bore no relationship to the contemporary pattern of life and work. The creation of the Greater London Council in 1965, with a greatly enlarged administrative area for London, represents the first attempt to adjust these outdated boundaries. A Royal Commission was subsequently set up to consider how best local government boundaries in the rest of the country could be brought into line with modern social and economic conditions, and its recommendations, contained in the Redcliffe–Maud Report, were published in 1969. The findings of the Commission were not fully accepted by the government, but major changes in local government boundaries were carried out in Northern Ireland in 1973, in England and Wales in 1974 and in Scotland in 1975. The new pattern in England and Wales comprises 53 counties, including six metropolitan counties and Greater London, which are subdivided into 369 district authorities. The metropolitan counties cover six major conurbations, but only correspond with their built-up areas, and, contrary to the recommendation of the Redcliffe–Maud Report, exclude the adjacent commuting areas with which they are closely tied. Apart from the new county of Avon, centred on Bristol, the boundary changes scarcely take into account the concept of the city region.

Conclusion

Towns and their surrounding regions are mutually interdependent. Some indication of a town's economic dependence on extra-urban areas can be deduced from its occupation structure as expressed by the basic/non-basic ratio. A number of techniques, mostly variations on the basic gravity model, have been developed to locate the theoretical extent of the urban field, or area over which a town extends its influence. In practical terms a variety of indicators can be used to demonstrate the approximate limits. Precise delimitation is impossible and the urban field is probably best thought of as a series of zones of declining urban influence, the outer zones generally overlapping with those of adjacent urban fields. As shown by the example of the UK, local government boundaries often fail to correspond with the social and economic realities of urban fields and city regions.

Suggested Further Reading

Ash, M., *Regions of Tomorrow*, Evelyn, Adams & Mackay, London, 1969.

Dickinson, R. E., *City and Region: A Geographical Interpretation*, Routledge & Kegan Paul, London, 1964.

Dickinson, R. E., *The City Region in Western Europe*, Routledge & Kegan Paul, London, 1967. (This is an abridged version of *City and Region*, by the same author.)

Duncan, O. D., *et al.*, *Metropolis and Region*, Oxford University Press, London, 1960.

Smailes, A. E., *The Geography of Towns*, Hutchinson, London, 1953.

CHAPTER TWENTY-ONE

RURAL SETTLEMENT AND SOCIETY

Unlike many other fields of geographical investigation, the study of rural settlement has, with few exceptions, received relatively little attention in recent years. Indeed, this point is true of many aspects of rural geography. It was recently noted that 'from being at the core of studies in human geography prior to the Second World War, the countryside, as a field of geographical investigation, has been relegated to an inferior position. Such a decline of interest contrasts with the rapid and sophisticated growth of research and expertise in aspects of urban geography and, of course, reflects the impact of the worldwide process of urbanisation.' (H. D. Clout)

Rural geography includes the study of social, economic, land use and settlement patterns in areas which may be recognised by their landscape characteristics as 'countryside'. Several aspects of rural geography, such as rural land use and rural depopulation, have been considered earlier, and this chapter is chiefly concerned with settlements in the countryside such as farmsteads, hamlets, villages and even small towns. These are examined from various points of view, including their physical structure, economic function and social and demographic characteristics.

Geographers have approached the study of rural settlements in many ways. For example, in the 1930s the French geographer, Jean Brunhes, concentrated on such detailed aspects as regional variations in house design, building methods and materials, and the influence of the physical environment on these features. Others have attempted to clarify the historical development of rural settlement patterns by a study of place names and a variety of documentary evidence. Obviously, such an approach is closely allied to the field of historical geography, and, as such, lies outside the scope of this study. At the present time it is probably true to say that the changing social and demographic structure of village settlements is attracting most attention.

Aspects of Village Settlement Study

Three main aspects of rural settlement study may be identified: site, form and distribution. Site is concerned with the relationship between a dwelling or group of dwellings and the immediate physical environment. Village form involves consideration of the relationships between one dwelling and another and the patterns formed by various arrangements of houses and buildings. Analysis of distribution extends the study over a wider area, and takes into account the spacing and density of villages and hamlets in a regional setting. In many instances the three elements are inter-related, although not inevitably so. Village form may be dictated by the configuration of site, and the availability of suitable sites with, for example, abundant water supply, may influence the resultant distribution pattern. However, this is not always the case. Particular settlement forms may develop quite independently of local site conditions. Similarly, in a region with an abundance of potential village sites or with uniform terrain, the range of site choices will be very great and the pattern of settlements may bear no relationship to the distribution of suitable sites.

The Siting of Villages

Consideration of site factors forms a useful starting point in the study of rural settlements. It is assumed that the early settlers in any area made more or less rational judgements in their choice of sites for dwellings, although chance may have played some part. Thus, the obvious advantages of certain sites in an area may explain their occupation from an early date. For example, knolls, islands and other slightly elevated 'dry-point' sites in areas of marsh or poor natural drainage such as the Fens, Dutch polders or coastal marshes of north Germany have long held an obvious attraction for settlement. Similarly, well-drained gravel terraces overlooking alluvial valley floors, but without the flood risk of the latter, provide attractive sites in many lowland areas. Conversely, in areas with limited available supplies of water, dwellings tend to cluster around 'wet points' such as springs, ponds and wells. In the UK this point is well illustrated by the spring-line villages found at the foot of chalk and limestone cuestas. Elsewhere, the need for an easily defended site may have been important in early times. Hilltop villages and settlements sited on the neck of land within a river loop fall in this category.

Many local studies have emphasised the importance of aspect in the siting of villages. In many deeply-cut, east–west orientated Alpine valleys, for example, almost all the farmsteads and villages are found on the south-facing slopes which enjoy longer hours of sunlight than their north-facing counterparts. Availability of building materials and fuel, and the opportunities for agriculture in an area must also have been important considerations in the original selection of village sites.

Village Form

In analysing the various forms of rural settlement a basic distinction can be drawn between nucleated and dispersed settlement. A grouped or **nucleated settlement** is one in which the houses, farms and outbuildings are clustered together in close juxtaposition, and there is a clear contrast between the settlement agglomeration and the surrounding farmland. In areas of **dispersed settlement**, isolated farms and dwellings are scattered irregularly throughout the countryside. It has been suggested that dispersion indicates a close relationship between the dwelling and the place of work, each house being located in the group of fields worked by its owner.

Much discussion has centred around the problem of determining which, if either, of these settlement forms precedes the other. Does dispersion result from a decline of nucleated villages and an outward spread of population from the old centres, or does nucleation result from the concentration of former dispersed settlement, or do the two forms develop separately and independently with different influences operating at different times? One hypothesis is that long periods of stability with freedom from invasion favoured an outward spread of homesteads from nucleated centres, while troubled times with threats of attack led to a concentration and clustering of dwellings for common security. Another suggestion is that nucleated forms tend to develop in lowland areas with rich soils where farmers can live within easy reach of their fields and yet still enjoy the social amenities of village life. By contrast, it is argued, difficult, rugged, upland terrain favours dispersed settlement. However, the answers to these questions are still by no means resolved. In any case the distinction between the two settlement forms is not always clear. There are many different degrees of dispersion and many different forms of nucleation.

In order to advance the analysis of rural settlement forms beyond the simple descriptive terms 'nucleated' or 'dispersed', various statistical methods have been devised to express the degree of dispersion or nucleation of rural population. For example, if the population of the chief village in a parish, commune or other small rural unit is known, together with the total population of the unit, then it is possible to calculate the following **coefficient of dispersion** (C)

$$C = \frac{p \times n}{P}$$

where P is the total population of the rural unit, p is the population living outside the main village and n is the number of settlements.

Extreme forms of nucleation have been developed by societies engaged in hunting and pastoralism in many different parts of the world. Examples include the longhouses of the Boro in Amazonia which provide communal dwellings for groups of extended families, the kraals of the Masai in East Africa which house a number of families in a tight circle of huts around a central enclosure for livestock, and the peublos of the Hopi Indians in Arizona.

In Europe various forms of nucleated settlement have been identified. A widespread type is the **green village**, with houses and church clustered around a small village green or common. A linear form, sometimes referred to as a shoestring or **street village**, is often found along routeways or where conditions have impeded a lateral development of the settlement, as along the river dykes of the Fens or Dutch polders. The term **cruciform village** is applied to villages which have developed at an intersection of routes. Cruciform villages show considerable variety according to the angle formed by the roads and the degree of infilling between the roads. There are, of course, many combinations and variations on these basic forms, and many formless village settlements which consist of apparently random arrangements of streets and houses.

Some geographers have extended the analysis of village form almost into the field of ethnography by studying such features as building plans, architectural features, construction techniques and building materials.

In the New World early settlers attempted to re-create features of their homelands. Thus, the appearance and lay-out of the large nucleated villages in New England owes much to the West European rural traditions, while in many parts of the Mid-West there are villages founded by Scandinavian communities which reflect North European building styles and construction techniques for houses, churches, barns and even boundary fences. Later settlement in the USA was strongly influenced by the federal government. Lands beyond the Ohio River were accurately surveyed and divided into a regular grid pattern of townships, sections and quarter-sections before being allocated to settlers. In the western states, therefore, the rural population tends to be dispersed, with occasional small townships, monotonously alike, and laid out on a strict grid plan.

The latter point serves to remind us that not all villages have evolved gradually, and that planned rural settlements exist in many parts of the world. Recent examples include the Israeli *kibbutzim* and the *ujamaa* villages of Tanzania.

The Distribution of Villages

Christaller's central place theory includes reference to the spacing of hamlets, villages and other low-order centres in the settlement hierarchy. He argued that small clusters of dwellings or hamlets would be more or less self-sufficient at the time of their establishment and would require a certain area of land to support their population. This would tend to produce an even distribution of hamlets, each one about 4 km from its neighbour. Similarly, village settlements would tend to assume an even distribution at a distance of about 7 km from each other (see Chapter Eighteen). However, since the isotropic conditions necessary for this regularity of spacing are rarely, if ever, fulfilled, the theoretical approach provides no more than a starting point in the analysis of rural settlement patterns.

A useful technique for comparing actual distribution patterns is known as **nearest-neighbour analysis**. This may be applied to single dwellings and farmsteads as well as to hamlets and villages. In the latter case, distances are measured between each village and the neighbouring village which lies closest to it. It is then possible to calculate the nearest-neighbour index (R_n) by means of the formula

$$R_n = 2\bar{d}\sqrt{\frac{n}{A}}$$

where A is the size of the area concerned, $\bar{d}$ is the mean distance between villages and n is the number of villages. In theory, values for R_n can range from zero, when all villages would occupy the same location, to 2·15, when the villages would have the maximum spacing and would be regularly distributed according to central place theory. If the settlements are distributed purely at random then the value for R_n is 1·0. Values above and below 1·0 indicate a tendency towards even spacing and clustering respectively.

In reality the distribution of villages and hamlets in any area is the outcome of a complex interaction of many factors, including relief, soils, water supply, defensive needs and special historical considerations. For example, many villages in Europe grew up around the sites of Roman villas, Saxon manors or Medieval monasteries. As with most cultural features of the landscape, cause-and-effect relationships in rural settlements are complex, and simple explanations in terms of a single factor are always suspect. The physical environment rarely imposes absolute limits on rural settlement patterns. It has been pointed out, for example, that 'a study of settlement maps over the last 150 years will show that in Wales the limit crept upward during the expansion of the rural population in the first half of the nineteenth century, then crept down, leaving many a field to go back to mountain pasture and many a derelict stead.' (E. Jones). In other words, one can only talk about limits of settlement at a specific time.

The antiquity of village patterns should be borne in mind. Most arose under conditions totally different from those of today, so that explanations in terms of contemporary influences are rarely satisfactory. With the exception of the planned villages mentioned earlier, patterns of village form and distribution in most parts of the world have evolved slowly and over many centuries, gradually adapting to changing social and economic circumstances. In recent decades the product of this slow evolution has been severely disrupted. Traditional settlement forms and patterns in many areas have been radically changed by economic developments and new pressures and demands on the countryside. These contemporary influences on rural settlement and society are considered next.

Rural Depopulation

In Chapter Six reference was made to the decline of rural settlements in many parts of the Western World as a result of rural depopulation. It is appropriate to examine this process in greater detail at this point.

A reduction in the number of rural residents in any area can come about in two ways. First, the number of deaths may be consistently higher than the number of births. In such a situation biological depopulation will occur, provided that the natural decrease is not compensated for by a positive net migration balance. Secondly, and more usually, there is a small but fluctuating excess of births over deaths, but the resultant natural increase is counteracted by a strong negative migration balance. In other words, the chief cause of rural depopulation is the outward migration of large numbers of the rural residents. Biological depopulation tends to occur only after an area has suffered population losses by migration for many years.

The causes of this movement from the country are both economic and social. A great deal has been written about the reduced demand for agricultural labour due to the mechanisation of farming and its effects on rural districts. In England and Wales, for example, a peak of 1·9 million farmworkers was reached in 1861. This number fell to just under one million by 1901, and, apart from a slight increase during the Second World War, has fallen steadily during the present century. By 1971 there were less than 200,000 full-time farmworkers in England and Wales.

The discarding of workers by agriculture has been matched by a similar process in many other rural trades and occupations. Craftsmen such as blacksmiths, wheelwrights, saddle-makers, thatchers and others have all experienced a sharp decline in the demand for their services in recent decades. Indeed, most have now disappeared completely from village life. Corn-grinding has moved from small village mills to larger, more efficient mills in the urban centres. Similarly, small-scale rural manufacturing units have also found themselves unable to compete with large-scale industry in the towns. During the last hundred years in the UK, for example, furniture workshops have virtually disappeared from the villages of the Chiltern Hills, papermills from the valleys of Devon and textile mills from East Anglia.

As well as a decline in employment opportunities during the present century, poor living conditions in many rural districts have also contributed to the process of depopulation. Even today housing conditions in many rural areas lag far behind those of the towns in respect of such facilities as piped water supply, gas, electricity and mains drainage. Overcrowding is common in many homes, with several generations of a farming family often occupying a small tied cottage or single house. Nor are improvements in living standards easily made in a job which has long paid lower wages than those of workers in manufacturing industry.

For many young adults, the city is seen as the only means of escape from an environment which offers few opportunities and little prospect for personal advancement. Numerous surveys carried out among rural migrants in a variety of countries have emphasised 'better employment opportunities' as the dominant motive for the move from village to town. There is a strong belief among rural migrants that their material aspirations can only be fulfilled in the city. Secondary attractions revealed by such studies include better shopping facilities, improved housing conditions, greater opportunities for educational advancement and the wider range of entertainment and recreational facilities of large urban centres.

Of course, many of these attractions may be imagined rather than real. Thus, the question of environmental perception arises again. How much information does the prospective migrant have about wage levels, job vacancies, house prices and life generally in the city? How accurate and complete is this information? By what processes is this information diffused from the urban centres? How does each individual evaluate this information, complete or otherwise? It has been suggested that each potential migrant has a subjective concept of 'place utility' based on personal aspirations, personal experience, and information derived from family, friends and the mass media. The decision to migrate involves assessment of the varying merits of town and country. On this basis a decision may be made to move to the city, or the decision may be postponed, or there may be a change in aspirations and readaptation to the rural environment.

From these remarks it might be assumed that rural depopulation would be greatest in areas offering the fewest employment opportunities, having the least adequate housing and social facilities and imposing the greatest hardships upon everyday life. Generally speaking this is true. In most European countries the level of outward migration is highest in the isolated and peripheral districts and in areas of extreme physical hardship. However, correlations between social and physical environment and rates of depopulation are by no means exact. A number of studies have emphasised the importance of various intangible qualities such as local pride, sense of community, social integration, and local leadership and initiative, in 'holding together' and maintaining the demographic stability of rural communities, even where social and economic conditions leave much to be desired

Urbanisation of Rural Settlements

Reference was made in Chapter Twenty to the ways in which large urban centres progressively extend their social and economic influence into the surrounding urban field to create what have been described as 'mentally urbanised, but physically rural parts of the country'. So far this process has been considered largely from the point of view of the city itself. However, it is appropriate at this point to examine the specific nature of this urbanisation process on the rural settlements themselves, and to study the ways in which a social transformation of traditional rural settlement and society may be brought about.

Commuter Villages

In Chapter Nineteen it was described how improvements in transportation during the present century have enabled city workers to live far from their place of work and undertake long journeys to and from the city each day. New motorways have increased the distance that workers are able and willing to travel, so that commuting hinterlands are becoming wider year by year. In this way the old social distinction between town and country is becoming increasingly blurred.

The newcomers to the villages include some elderly couples moving to the country for retirement, but by far the largest group consists of relatively wealthy, upper- or middle-class families still retaining strong links with the city. This movement of middle-class executives and professional workers from the city is evident in most parts of the Western World. Thus, most villages and small towns within a 50 km radius of a large city have shown a steady increase in their population in recent years. However, this overall growth conceals the decline in the number of long-term village residents and agricultural workers described earlier. In particular, the children of long-established village families tend to move away on completion of their education, at marriage or simply in search of employment. Thus, by a combination of migration flow and counterflow the age, class and social structure of many villages has changed radically in recent decades.

In these commuter villages, society has now become sharply segregated into working-class and middle-class groups, a situation similar to that found in urban centres. The distinction is emphasised by differences in the behaviour patterns of the two groups. The long-term residents are strongly village-orientated. They depend on the village area not only for their employment, but also for most of their social contacts and associations. Their action-space is much more restricted than that of the recently arrived, middle-class families. By contrast, the newcomers very rarely depend on the locality for their livelihood, have a much higher level of car ownership, enjoy greater mobility and retain strong contacts with the city, not only for work, but also for shopping, entertainment and social activities. Many observers have suggested that this polarisation of rural society into a two-class structure has destroyed the essential character and community spirit of many villages. 'They are no longer the sorts of place where a country person can feel at home. The talk in the bar tends to be about production figures instead of harvest yields.' (*The Times*)

Second Homes

In many of the more affluent countries of the world there has been a marked increase since about 1950 in the number of households owning a second rural home for weekend and vacation use. This process, which has been described as 'seasonal or temporary suburbanisation', takes many forms. The residential units themselves vary from caravans and houseboats to converted cottages and farms and even architect-designed, purpose-built villas and chalets. They may form an integral part of a village settlement or be arranged in the form of estates by property developers. Their usage varies from a regular two or three days per week, to very infrequent vacation visits.

In 1967 it was estimated that only about 1 per cent of households in the UK possessed a second home, but there can be little doubt that the number is increasing rapidly. The proportion is already much higher in a number of countries. In the USA about 5 per cent of the total housing stock consists of second homes, and vacation dwellings account for approximately 10 per cent of the new residences being built. In Sweden and France as many as 20 per cent of the urban households enjoy the use of a second home.

The proportion of families owning second homes in any country is basically related to living standards as expressed through such factors as car ownership, length of paid holidays and simply the availability of personal finances for the purchase of a home for occasional use only. The distance of these second homes from the permanent or first residence is largely determined by travel times. In Europe many weekend homes are found in villages quite close to the major cities, whereas in North America, where faster travel speeds are possible on a superior system of motorways and freeways, a drive of 300 km to a weekend retreat is not considered unreasonable.

The distribution of second homes is also clearly related to the town dweller's perception of what constitutes an attractive rural environment. Strong preferences are shown for upland areas with varied landscapes, areas adjacent to woodland, heathland and water features such as rivers, lakes, reservoirs and coasts. Many urbanites also seek 'unspoilt' rustic communities for their country retreats, but by their very presence may eventually destroy the qualities which they value so highly. The development and use of second homes is essentially a leisure activity of the relatively affluent, and, as such, the locations considered desirable are greatly affected by the changing whims of fashion. An important influence, therefore, is the diffusion of information about different areas between actual and potential second home purchasers.

Wide differences of opinion are held about the social and economic consequences of the growing movement towards second home ownership. There are those who see the development of second homes as a rational use of the countryside in remote and backward rural areas. They draw attention to the opportunities which it creates for local owners to sell land and property at prices which would not be paid by local residents, the increased patronage of local shops, cafés and public houses, and the employment provided for local builders, gardeners and housekeepers. On the other hand, there are many who oppose the trend, claiming that it creates excessive traffic on rural roads and increased demand on rural services, such as water supply and mains drainage, which are largely financed by the permanent population.

It is also argued that second homes contribute to a break-down of rural society by depriving local residents of homes which stand empty for much of the year. 'For the rustic couple recently married in the church of the village of their birth the housing outlook is indeed bleak. When they enter the estate agent's office they are likely to meet the man with a house and job in London who has just offered over £2,000 more than they can afford for a primitive house which could be home to them, but which he intends to occupy for no more than two months in every year.' (*The Times*)

A further problem is that of the visual intrusion created by concentrations of 'home-made' huts and chalets in areas of scenic beauty. In Norway, for example, where large unplanned communities of huts and cottages have grown up in many mountain and lakeside areas, attempts have been made to plan and coordinate this type of development in order to prevent the creation of rural slums. With the continuing rise of second home ownership in many countries this type of control will become even more essential in the future.

Leisure Activities in the Countryside

The countryside has long attracted the more affluent town-dwellers for leisure and recreational activities. The main change in recent years has been the massive growth of numbers involved in such pursuits. Tourism now represents the most rapidly growing form of urban encroachment on the countryside. This increased scale of activity is the result of many influences, including rising living standards, longer paid holidays, reductions in the length of the working week and increased mobility of the population. Interest in the countryside has been further stimulated by education and the mass media, and by the growth of organisations such as the Ramblers Association, Caravan Club and Youth Hostels Association which have a policy of introducing the pleasures of the countryside to town-dwellers. Specialist outdoor activities such as rock-climbing and caving have also grown, while the rise of the travel industry has brought cheap organised holidays within the means of almost all families.

The seasonal or periodic invasion of rural areas by large numbers of visitors gives rise to important social and economic changes, especially in the most popular tourist areas, where the pressures on recreational resources are extremely great. Hotels and boarding houses enjoy a busy trade, farmers and other villagers supplement their regular income by taking in guests, part-time work is available in hotels and catering establishments or in the production and sale of souvenir articles, farmers and market gardeners can dispose of milk, eggs, fruit and vegetables to local hotels, while village shops, garages and other services receive increased patronage from visitors.

On the other hand, there are a number of adverse effects associated with this influx of urban population, notably traffic congestion on narrow country roads, litter and pollution in the vicinity of picnic areas and beauty spots, conflict between farmers and tourists, the visual impact of camping and caravan sites on the landscape and the intrusion of urban-style filling stations, cafés and other buildings in both villages and the countryside. Some writers have even suggested tourism also contributes to the breakdown of traditional village society. It is argued that the attitudes and aspirations of villagers become changed by contact with townsfolk, that tourism introduces an element of rivalry and competition among those offering services, and that friction develops between those who have improved their income and standard of living and those who have derived no benefits. In these ways, it is suggested, the cohesiveness of village life is undermined by outside influences.

Conclusion

The traditional approach to the study of rural settlement involved consideration of village site, form and distribution. In recent years geographers have shown greater interest in the rapid and far-reaching changes experienced by most rural settlements in the Western World. In remote isolated areas, and areas of physical difficulty, most villages have experienced a steady loss of population by outward migration during the present century. Closer to the large urban centres this loss of population has been counteracted by an influx of new residents from the cities. The growth of second home ownership and the increasing use of the countryside for leisure activities represent other forms of this urbanisation process. In these ways the traditional social structure of many villages has been radically changed. Social and economic change in rural areas is inevitable. The countryside cannot be preserved as some sort of monument to the past, but the scale of recent changes means that the conflicting demands now being placed upon it will require very careful planning and integrated management schemes in order to achieve the fullest benefits for the greatest number of people.

Suggested Further Reading

Ashton, J., and Harwood Long, W. (Eds.), *The Remoter Rural Areas of Britain*, Oliver & Boyd, Edinburgh, 1972.

Beresford, J. T., *et al.*, *Land and People*, Leonard Hill, Leighton Buzzard, 1967.

Bracey, H. E., *Industry In The Countryside*, Faber, London, 1963.

Bracey, H. E., *People And The Countryside*, Routledge & Kegan Paul, London, 1970.

Bracey, H. E., *English Rural Life*, Routledge & Kegan Paul, London, 1970.

Chisholm, M., *Rural Settlement And Land Use* (2nd edn), Hutchinson, London, 1968.

Clout, H. D., *Rural Geography: An Introductory Survey*, Pergamon, Oxford, 1972.

Hoskins, W. G., *The Making Of The English Landscape*, Hodder & Stoughton, London, 1960.

Pahl, R. E., *Urbs in Rure*, London School of Economics, Geographical Papers, No. 2, 1965.

Patmore, J. A., *Land And Leisure*, David & Charles, Newton Abbot, 1970.

Savile, J., *Rural Depopulation in England and Wales. 1851–1951*, Routledge & Kegan Paul, London, 1957.

CHAPTER TWENTY-TWO

URBAN AND RURAL PLANNING

The geographer is not only concerned with past and present distributions and interactions, but also with the future. Because of the resource problems arising from population growth, and the complexity of modern urbanised and industrialised societies, it is becoming increasingly necessary to plan. Planning has been described as 'an ordered sequence of operations, designed to lead to the achievement of either a single goal, or to a balance between several goals' (P. Hall), and the goals of geographical planning are both economic and social. Economic goals might be the identification of 'best locations' for services, or the prevention of damaging spatial imbalances in the distribution of industry. Social goals might be the development of improved urban environments or the reduction of socially divisive spatial differences in levels of income.

To this end, there are two main types of geographical planning. First, there is **physical planning**, which is concerned with physical developments such as urban renewal, new town building or rural land-use planning. Secondly, there is **economic planning**, which is concerned with the spatial aspects of economic development, and with resource planning. These two types are very closely linked in practice, but they are given different emphasis at different levels of planning. In this final section of the book, planning problems will be examined at local, regional, national and international levels.

Urban Planning

Many early settlements may be described as planned towns in the sense that they were built to a pre-conceived, and often highly formal, ground plan. In Europe the most impressive results of such formal town planning were achieved in the so-called Baroque Era of the seventeenth and eighteenth centuries. Masterpieces of urban design from this period include the reconstruction of Rome in the late sixteenth and early seventeenth centuries, the building of the Palace of Versailles with its adjacent planned settlement, and the laying out of the German town of Karlsruhe. In Britain the best example of town planning from this period is provided by the eighteenth-century development of the spa town of Bath. However, town planning in the modern sense, involving economics, sociology, politics and many other disciplines, rather than simply large-scale architectural design, is much more recent. In fact, the development of modern urban planning may be interpreted as a response to various economic and social problems that had their origins in the events of the Industrial Revolution, which initiated a period of rapid and largely uncontrolled urban growth (Chapter Seventeen).

The aims of twentieth-century town planning are to solve these problems, and more modestly, to prevent their duplication. Town planners have not always succeeded in these objectives, and many writers have argued persuasively against the planning process. Nevertheless, the essential aim is to improve the quality of urban life and to 'provide for a spatial structure of activities or of land uses which is in some way better than the existing pattern without planning' (P. Hall). The methods employed to attain these objectives provide a broad twofold division of urban planning activity. First, there are various techniques designed to limit the outward spread of the largest cities and to encourage decentralisation of their population and industry. Secondly, a variety of planning methods is used to improve environmental conditions in the cities themselves and to provide a more rational and efficient arrangement of urban land use.

Urban Decentralisation

Various reactions to rapid and excessive urban growth may be noted. First, there have been attempts to limit the formless spread of suburban housing by the creation of an encircling **green belt**. For example, a green belt around London, some 15 km wide, was delimited on the Greater London Plan of 1944, and eventually approved by the government between 1954 and 1958. The amount of new building in London's green belt has subsequently been restricted, although by no means completely prevented, and there is some evidence that it has encouraged more compact forms of urban development around the margins of the built-up area. On the other hand, certain planners believe that a series of green 'wedges' bringing open space further into the city would be preferable to the straitjacket of the present green belt.

A more positive planning device is the attempt to decentralise industry and population from the largest cities and to break the pattern of long-distance commuting into their centres by the creation of new towns. The new town concept is not new. In Britain it has certain antecedents in the building of a number of **model townships** in the second half of the nineteenth century such as Saltaire (1852), Bourneville (1879), Port Sunlight (1886) and Creswell (1895), all financed by philanthropic, paternalistic factory or mine owners. These early planned factory towns had counterparts in other industrialised countries. Planned townships to house factory workers were built at Noisel-sur-Seine, France (1874), Pullman, Illinois (1881), and Agenta Park in the Netherlands (1883).

Aspects of the new town movement may also be traced back to the planning and building of a number of **garden suburbs** in the late nineteenth and early twentieth centuries, such as Bedford Park, Acton (1875), and Hampstead Garden Suburb (1907). The latter was influenced by the publication in 1898 of Ebenezer Howard's ideas on **garden cities**, which may be seen as a reaction to the Victorian industrial city. Howard's vision of the garden city became reality in 1903 when work started on the building of Letchworth, followed in 1919 by the founding of Welwyn Garden City. His 'garden planning' ideas also influenced housing developments elsewhere, as in the now famous suburban housing development built at Radburn, New Jersey, during the 1930s.

The new town concept was revived in 1944 with the publication of Sir Patrick Abercrombie's Greater London Plan in which it was suggested that a number of **new towns** should be built beyond the limit of London's proposed green belt. These were envisaged as towns of moderate size intended to function as economically viable units with a full range of manufacturing and service industries and modern shopping facilities. It was hoped that they would attract population and industry from the overcrowded inner districts of London.

Following the New Towns Act of 1946, work started on the planning and building of the first group of newly designated new towns. Their distribution is shown in Fig. 22.1. Common to them all was a strict zonation and segregation of industry, housing and other land uses. Housing was built at low density in the suburban tradition (about 5 houses per ha) but, following ideas first proposed by the American planner, Clarence Perry, arranged to form a series of **neighbourhoods** with shops, schools and other amenities planned for a population of about 5,000. Many lessons were learned from the building of the first generation of new towns, and those designated and planned between 1956 and 1965 show certain changes. For example, the neighbourhood principle was less strictly applied, and, in order to reduce the distance of journeys to work, industry was less rigidly zoned and segregated from housing. Housing densities were increased, and, with the steep rise in car ownership during the 1950s and 60s, much greater attention was given to the problems of traffic in towns. New towns, such as Cumbernauld, which incorporate these changes are sometimes referred to as second generation new towns. The third, and most recently designated, group of new towns is characterised by a wide variety of plans, and again represent a questioning of earlier concepts and a search for new urban forms. Many, such as Milton Keynes, with a planned population of 250,000, are much larger than those built earlier.

Fig. 22.1 shows the 33 British new towns designated up to 1974. All are in varying stages of completion. Nevertheless, more than 1·5 million people were living in new towns in that year. The building of new towns has been described as a unique contribution by the UK to the theory and practice of town planning and architecture. The concept has also been adopted in many other countries, and, as well as such well-known examples as Brasilia and New Delhi, a number of highly sophisticated new towns are now to be found in Sweden, Finland, France and the USA.

Mention should also be made of the **expanded towns** shown in Fig. 22.1. These are towns which have agreed to take 'overspill' population from London and other major centres in order to stimulate their own economic development and to help solve the problems of overcrowding and congestion in the major conurbations.

Planning Within the City

The formulation of plans for new towns provides an opportunity for a complete assessment of urban planning objectives, and represents the most spectacular results of the planner's work. However, most planning activity is concerned with the improvement of existing towns. Such work must be carried out within the constraints of an outdated urban structure, and must attempt to reconcile the conflicting interests of a large existing population. Furthermore, the legal complexities stemming from a multiplicity of ownership and the financial burden of compensation mean that redevelopment and renewal is a slow and piecemeal process. In one sense, therefore, urban renewal poses even more complex problems than new town building.

Underlying all modern planning within cities is the concept of **land use zoning** or long-term segregation of conflicting land uses. In the UK, following

Fig. 22.1. Garden cities, new towns and expanded towns in the UK. Welwyn Garden City was founded in 1919 as the second of the garden cities and was later incorporated into one of the first generation of new towns. The expanded towns shown on the map are those in which 1,000 new houses had been built in 1971 according to the terms of the Town Development Act of 1952.

the 1947 Town and Country Planning Act and the creation of local planning authorities, each authority was required to produce a development plan showing existing land use, and proposals for its reorganisation over a 20-year period into distinct zones for industry, housing, recreation and so forth. The 1947 Act meant that any landowner wishing to develop a site had to apply for planning permission; the authority could refuse permission if the development was not in accord with its plan. The Act also enabled authorities to acquire properties and sites for redevelopment, and established a system of compensation to owners for lost rights.

Housing conditions in most large cities are a matter of serious concern. As well as a frequent shortage of dwelling units, much of the housing stock of the blighted inner city districts has been allowed to deteriorate, is overcrowded, in poor structural condition, lacking in amenities and badly located, often adjacent to main roads, railways and factories.

Compared with many other European countries the renewal of urban housing in the UK has proceeded only slowly during the post-war period. It has been estimated that **slum clearance** at an average rate of 75,000 dwellings per year since 1950 has, in fact, proceeded less slowly than the rate at which houses are becoming obsolete. The level of achievement varies from one planning authority to another. In some cities only small-scale, piecemeal renewal has been attempted, while in others very ambitious and imaginative projects have been completed. Some of these have involved rebuilding on the original site— for example, in the Barbican project of London, the Park Hill–Hyde Park scheme in Sheffield and the Gorbals redevelopment in Glasgow—while others have involved the transfer of population to new housing developments at the edge of the city. Well-documented examples of the latter process include the building of the Roehampton Estate in south London and the Gleadless Valley Estate in Sheffield. As in the new towns, the neighbourhood unit scheme is an essential feature of the most successful of such post-war housing estates.

In recent years much discussion has centred on the relative merits of urban **rehabilitation** and comprehensive **redevelopment**. Rehabilitation involves installing modern amenities in old houses which are structurally sound, carrying out essential repairs and in many cases dividing large properties into smaller dwelling units. Supporters of rehabilitation argue that redevelopment is wasteful of resources, destroys community life, creates urban deserts during the demolition and rebuilding stage, produces new building on an inhuman scale and that change is not necessarily for the better. Conversely, the proponents of redevelopment argue that it is the only way of solving the inherited problems of poor design and lay-out, that human scale and diversity can be achieved in new building, that rehabilitation is simply a postponement of inevitable redevelopment, and is in effect planning for the present rather than the future. In reality the arguments tend to be economic rather than social. In this connection much depends on the age, structural condition and type of buildings concerned. In some areas rehabilitation has been shown to be more economic, while elsewhere demolition and rebuilding has proved to be less so.

Another serious problem which has influenced the structural plans for both new towns and the redevelopment of existing cities is that of **urban transportation**. Of particular concern is the rapidly growing number of private motorcars, so that functionally, economically and visually the motorcar now threatens both large cities and small towns alike. Physical danger, noise, pollution and travel delays on congested roads are now an everyday experience for the city-dweller. What is also unfortunate is that countries with the highest levels of private car ownership have tended to neglect and allow a deterioration of their public transport systems so that there is little incentive for commuters and others to use crowded, unreliable and costly public transport rather than private cars. Until recently planning devices to improve the flow of urban traffic were small-scale and largely ineffective, including little more than the creation of one-way traffic systems and controls on parking. In 1963 *Traffic in Towns*, a report prepared by a team headed by Sir Colin Buchanan, demonstrated a more positive approach; namely, the idea of **traffic segregation**. This involves the subdivision of towns into environmental units in which vehicles have only limited access and the pedestrian is dominant. These environmental areas are connected to the rest of the town by a network of improved roads which carry the bulk of the traffic. This concept has been applied with varying degrees of success in a number of towns. However, it is true to say that the problems of urban traffic are still far from being resolved, and arguments still rage between those in favour of banning cars from city centres, and those who advocate the construction of urban motorways and multi-level interchanges similar to those found in many American cities.

The conflict between motor vehicles and pedestrians is nowhere more acute than in city centres. In most large cities the pattern of streets and buildings grew up in a random manner or was laid out long before the advent of motor traffic. It was a district designed to serve a population many times smaller than at present. In their original form, most city centres are totally inadequate for modern requirements. Consequently, much post-war urban planning has been concerned with **city centre redevelopment.** This has generally involved the elimination of land uses making no contribution to the function of the CBD, and the segregation of vehicular and pedestrian traffic. Notable examples include the Lijnbaan in Rotterdam, Hötorget Centre in Stockholm and the central area of Coventry.

The City of the Future

Reference was made in Chapter Seventeen to the rapid growth of urban population in most parts of the world. One of the basic planning issues of the twentieth century has therefore been a search for the most appropriate forms of settlement in which to house this growing number of city-dwellers. Stemming from the early work of Ebenezer Howard, the solution adopted in Britain has been to restrict the continued outward expansion of the largest centres and to establish new growth points in the form of new and expanded towns. This raises further questions: should the number of new towns be allowed to increase, and, if so, where should they be located, how large should they be and what form should they take?

One approach, typified by the new towns around London, has been to establish a series of **satellite towns** around an existing centre. Such satellite towns are planned as self-contained, discrete units, theoretically independent of the central city. An alternative form is the **radial or finger plan**, in which new towns or new suburbs are developed along the radial routes, either urban motorways or suburban railways, leading out from the city centre. In this case commuting and other links between the new towns and the central city are acknowledged and accepted, but made as efficient as possible. A radically different approach is that of the **linear city**, first proposed by the Spanish architect, Arturo Soria y Mata. In this case growth is envisaged along a single axis of high-speed, high-intensity transportation. Industrial development is allowed along one side and offices and shops on the other, with housing just beyond. Such a plan gives residents easy access to open space, and allows for virtually unlimited expansion. Soria y Mata succeeded in building only a few kilometres of his linear city (El Cuidad Lineal) on the outskirts of Madrid, and this has been largely swallowed up in the amorphous growth of the modern city. However, the linear concept underlies the 1965 plan for Paris and Lower Seine. In this, new town developments are proposed along two roughly parallel motorway routes north and south of the Seine between Paris and Rouen. The linear concept also reappears in modified form in the ideas for a **ring city**. The dominant transport route becomes a ring with a number of towns along its length and open space in its centre. Urban growth in the so-called Greenheart Metropolis of Randstad Holland is tending to assume this form.

Finally, reference should be made to the highly individual ideas of the American architect-planner, Frank Lloyd Wright, and the Swiss-born architect, Le Corbusier, both of whom designed buildings which are masterpieces of modern architecture, as well as producing blueprints for cities of the future. Wright argued that widespread car ownership had ended the need for activities to be concentrated in city centres, and proposed the idea of a carefully planned, low density, **dispersed city**. In his so-called Broadacre City, single-family homes were each surrounded by open space; housing districts were interspersed with shops and factories, and a vast 'rururban' environment lacking any nucleus was linked together by a network of super-highways. Although differing in many respects from Wright's description of the dispersed city of the future, the post-war growth of many American cities has produced a low-density structure which is not dissimilar from his basic concept. In Los Angeles, for example, over 70 per cent of the dwellings are detached houses and over 60 per cent of the 'downtown' area consists of urban motorways and other roads. In contrast to Wright's low-density urban structure, Le Corbusier aimed at achieving very high overall densities while leaving up to 95 per cent of the ground unbuilt upon. The urban landscape advocated by Le Corbusier in his book, *The Radiant City* (*La Ville Radieuse*), consisted of massive, skyscraper blocks widely separated in finely landscaped open space. He also aimed at a complete flattening out of the urban density gradient, the elimination of high concentrations of buildings in the CBD and the substitution of virtually equal densities all over the city. Although Le Corbusier's principles have nowhere been applied in their extreme form, his ideas nevertheless had a strong influence on post-war planning in many countries. 'All over Britain the remarkable change in the urban landscape during the late 1950s and the 1960s, as slum clearance produced a sudden unprecedented crop of skyscrapers, is a mute tribute to Corbusier's influence.' (P. Hall)

Rural Planning

In the past, most attention has been given to urban planning in Britain, reflecting the fact that 77 per cent of the population live in towns. However, 90 per cent of the land area of Britain is rural, and this must also be carefully planned, especially since the countryside is now changing rapidly under the influence of three main factors. First, urban influences are increasing. The townsman's desire to live and play in the countryside, in commuter villages, second homes and recreation areas, is adding to an already heavy demand for food, water supplies and land for housing and industry. The urban impact is so strong in many regions that it is now very difficult to see town and country as separate entities. Secondly, economic and technological factors are changing the structure and methods of farming, with significant landscape consequences. Thirdly, rural depopulation is having an increasing influence on settlement patterns and the provision of services, especially in remote rural areas. In the face of these three factors there is considerable pressure for economic, social and land-use changes, and a basic planning problem in Britain is whether the countryside should be protected or developed.

The first real attempt to formulate rural planning came during the Second World War with the reports of the Barlow Commission in 1940 on the distribution of population and industry, the Uthwatt Committee in 1942, which advocated machinery for land-use planning, and the Scott Committee in 1942, whose basic approach was to protect the countryside for agriculture. These three major reports had a considerable influence on post-war planning, and the Scott Committee report in particular affected rural planning proposals in the Agriculture Act of 1947 and the Town and Country Planning Act of the same year. The emphasis in this legislation was to control development for the benefit of the farmer, although the interests of other users of the countryside were recognised in the National Parks and Access to the Countryside Act of 1949.

As a result, there has been a strong protectionist element in rural planning since 1947. This is necessary in many respects, because to the farmer the countryside is a workplace which must be protected, but it also reflects a strong romantic preservationist attitude, based on the myth of an unchanged and unchanging countryside. However, the countryside is continuously changing, because of internal pressures such as depopulation and agricultural development, and because of external pressures from the town. As a result, there must be planning policies aimed at reconciling conflicting interests and producing positive, beneficial changes, rather than simply maintaining the status quo. This will not be easy, for while the countryside is a national heritage which must be conserved, it is also a vital economic unit and cannot be preserved as a rural museum. R. J. Green has written that the period since 1947 has been one of 'wasted opportunity for positive rural planning', but to accommodate the inevitable changes taking place in the countryside, there is now an increasing emphasis on policies concerned with both development and conservation, and a more integrated approach is being advocated. This integrated planning will be discussed after some aspects of life, work and leisure in the British countryside have been examined.

Settlements and Services

The settlement structures and provision of services in the country have developed under quite different conditions from those operating today, and to meet present needs, settlements and services must be rationalised, especially in remote rural areas.

Unfortunately, it is not easy to decide how settlements should be rationalised. An important policy in Britain has been the designation of **key villages**, which should be large enough and sufficiently well equipped to provide a range of services for their rural hinterlands. In these villages, expansion would be encouraged, while withdrawal would be planned and aided from smaller, declining settlements. However, although policies identifying key villages have been followed successfully in counties such as Norfolk, Lincoln and Devon, little has been done to run down small settlements. There has been some limited closure of mining hamlets in Durham, but the political and social problems of implementing this policy are formidable.

There is also a need for the rationalisation of services, because as depopulation takes place the demand for services decreases, and the provision of shops, health and educational facilities, piped water and drainage becomes uneconomic. On the other hand, such services are essential to the remaining population. This conflict between social desirability and economic viability is well seen in the problems created by the contraction of public transport facilities in rural areas since the mid-1950s. Rail and bus services have contracted because declining population, increasing car ownership and changing social habits have led to a decrease in demand at a time when costs are rising, and most rural services are now no longer viable. Unfortunately, the loss of public transport hits vulnerable groups such as the poorly paid, the elderly and the young, who cannot afford cars. A crucial task facing the rural planner is to provide viable public transport to keep such groups mobile, whether it be through car pools, community minibuses, school buses or postbuses. One solution would be to concentrate immobile people in key villages, but such direction would be politically unacceptable.

At a more local level, there is also the need for effective planning within villages. The general practice has been to infill vacant plots and allow small extensions in the form of council or private housing estates, but such development has been criticised because it often destroys the character of the village. Many people feel that hammerhead culs-de-sac in low-density estates simply reflect the worst type of suburban development and are totally inappropriate in the country. It has been suggested that where population is growing rapidly, it might be better to build **new villages** rather than spoil existing ones, and planning authorities at Bar Hill in Cambridge, Studlands Park in Suffolk and New Ash Green in Kent have allowed privately developed new villages to be established.

Agricultural Change and the Landscape

Since 1945, there has been considerable change in the structure and methods of farming, as economic necessity and technological developments have stressed the need for efficiency. The major trends in Britain have been the enlarging of farms, because the shortage of agricultural labour has led to the need for much greater mechanisation, and the modernisation of farm buildings. The impact of these trends has been so marked that it has been suggested that the landscape is changing as rapidly now as during the period of parliamentary enclosure in the eighteenth century. The major change has involved the removal of hedgerows, which, it is claimed, waste land, interfere with machinery and harbour vermin, and it has been estimated that the 800,000 km of hedgerow in England and Wales was disappearing at a rate of 8,000 km a year in the period 1946–63, especially in the arable areas of eastern England.

The feared ecological consequences of hedgerow removal are not yet apparent, but there is already concern about its effect on the landscape. Since 'the satisfaction of the aesthetic and intellectual demands of society is one of the roles of landscape' (Countryside Commission), there is clearly a need to conserve it, but it must also be remembered that the agricultural landscape is essentially functional. There must therefore be planning to ensure that current changes provide landscapes as interesting as the ones that are replaced, because many people feel that while huge featureless fields and stark functional buildings are efficient, they are inappropriate in an English landscape that must be carefully conserved.

Visitors in the Countryside

One of the major changes in recent years has been the increasing number of townspeople in the countryside, many as residents, either permanent in commuter villages, or on a short-term regular basis in second homes. The problems created by these urban villagers or seasonal suburbanites were discussed in Chapter Twenty-one. On a much larger scale are the increasing numbers of people visiting the countryside for recreational purposes on an irregular short-term basis, particularly at weekends and public holidays. On one hand, they bring considerable benefits, especially by providing employment, but on the other, they create heavy pressure at popular centres, particularly where there is easy access by car. There must be planning to cater for these recreational demands, and there is currently a range of designated areas where visitors can go. In fact, 9 per cent of England and Wales is covered by National Parks, and a further 6 per cent by Areas of Outstanding Natural Beauty, both established under the 1949 Act (Fig. 22.2). More recent legislation in the Countryside Act of 1969 established country parks and picnic sites, the first long-distance route (the Pennine Way) was opened in 1965, and there are currently seven forest parks and over 120 nature reserves open to the public.

Unfortunately, the recreational use of the countryside is not yet well coordinated and many conflicts still have to be resolved. Even in the National Parks, recreation has to compete with agriculture, water supply and forestry, and in some parks with the military, mineral workings and even a nuclear power station. There is also a financial problem, because the local authorities who administer the parks find it difficult to raise money for car parks, picnic sites and information centres, and despite being called National Parks, there is no central control. As a result, in 1970–1, the 10 National Parks as a whole spent less than a quarter of what the Greater London Council alone spent on its parks and open spaces.

Recreational planning must be part of an integrated approach to land-use planning, and the establishment of the Countryside Commission under the 1968 Act was a step in the right direction, since its policy is to emphasise use and conservation rather than preservation. Integrated planning can be focused on particular resources or particular areas, and these two approaches are briefly examined.

Forestry and Integrated Planning

Not only have there been considerable changes in agriculture, but also in forestry, where the amount of woodland increased from 1·4 million ha in 1947

Fig. 22.2. Major urban areas, National Parks, Areas Of outstanding Natural Beauty and long-distance footpaths in England and Wales.

(6 per cent of the land area of Britain) to 1·9 million ha in 1973 (8 per cent). Despite this increase, native forests supply only 10 per cent of Britain's timber needs, and it has been suggested that marginal agricultural land, especially in upland areas, should be afforested at a rate of 25,000 ha a year. This would have a considerable effect on the landscape, and the suggestion has not met with universal approval, but the development of forest resources is one area where different aspects of rural planning could be integrated to develop and conserve the countryside.

Forestry touches rural planning at a number of points which are often at issue, such as the provision of employment, industrial development, agriculture, water supply and amenity. Forestry gives direct employment and provides the raw material for associated industries such as pulp and paper. It can generate new roads and services and many declining settlements could be reinvigorated by an influx of forest workers who are needed at a ratio of about 1 : 40–50 ha of forest. It can be successfully integrated with agriculture since forests provide shelter for stock and grazing land, and evidence from Scotland and mid-Wales shows that agricultural productivity from sheep and cattle can be substantially increased. Forests are also valuable in water resource management because the trees slow the rate of run-off, and more recently it has been realised that they have tremendous recreational potential. If coniferous forests are planted with regard to visual considerations and ruler-straight lines are avoided, they can add much to the landscape and provide excellent cover for car parks and picnic sites. The Forestry Commission, which owns more than half of Britain's forests, is increasingly allowing the use of forests for recreation. This is not new because the first forest park was opened at Loch Lomond in 1936, and there are now six others, but as demand has increased, more areas are being opened for camping, pony-trekking, hunting and other activities. In some areas, forests might even be considered primarily for their recreational rather than their economic value.

It is clear that forestry can be integrated with other forms of land use and Forestry Development Areas have been proposed, covering areas of at least 12,000 ha, where economic and social requirements can be met. However, even small forests can be used for purposes other than simply producing timber. The Quantocks Forest in Somerset covers only 900 ha but it provides timber, direct and indirect employment, wild life and water supply, and as an area of great natural beauty it attracts over 14,000 visitors a year.

The Regional Approach to Integrated Rural Planning

Because settlement, agriculture, forestry, industry, water resources and recreation do not exist as separate entities but are closely integrated, economic, social and land-use planning must take this into account. There is a clear need for such multi-purpose planning at local, regional and national level to co-ordinate development and conservation. If agriculture is declining in an area, for example, the agricultural potential of the land can be assessed, farms reorganised on the best land, and the remaining land can be allocated to industry, water storage, forestry or recreation. Settlement can be rationalised to suit new needs, and services can be provided for resident and visitor. Integrated planning has been undertaken in France, but there has been little progress in Britain. To some extent, the Highlands and Islands Development Board, which was established in 1965 and covers half of Scotland, has such a planning function, but other proposals, such as those in the 1967 Agriculture Act for the establishment of rural development boards for Mid Wales and the Northern Pennines, have not been implemented.

Conclusion

Modern urban planning is concerned both with a search for solutions to economic and social problems inherited from earlier periods of uncontrolled urban growth, and with the direction of contemporary urban growth into acceptable and efficient forms. It involves decentralisation of population from centres of excessive size into various forms of carefully planned new towns. It also involves a reordering of the structure of existing towns by techniques such as land use zoning, housing redevelopment and rehabilitation, traffic management and central area redevelopment. At present large-scale and rapid changes are also taking place in the countryside, and these too must be carefully planned. Rural planning has two aspects: planning to conserve what is of value in the countryside, and the formulation of positive changes for the future benefit of those who live in, and those who visit, the countryside.

Suggested Further Reading

Bell, C., and Bell, R., *City Fathers: The Early History of Town Planning in Britain*, Penguin, Harmondsworth, 1972.

Bracey, H. E., *People in the Countryside*, Routledge, London, 1970.

Buchanan, C., *Traffic in Towns*, Penguin, Harmondsworth, 1964.

Clout, H. D., *Rural Geography*, Pergamon, Oxford, 1972.

Fairbrother, N., *New Lives, New Landscapes*, Penguin, Harmondsworth, 1972.

Green, R. J., *Country Planning*, Manchester University Press, Manchester, 1971.

Howard, E., *Garden Cities of Tomorrow*, Faber, London, 1965.

Jacobs, J., *The Death and Life of Great American Cities. The Failure of Urban Planning*, Penguin, Harmondsworth, 1965.

Merlin, P., *New Towns. Regional Planning and Development*, Methuen, London, 1971.

Osborn, F. J., and Whittick, A., *The New Towns. The Answer to Megalopolis*, Hill, London, 1963.

Patmore, J. A., *Land and Leisure*, David & Charles, Newton Abbot, 1970.

Schaffer, F., *The New Town Story*, MacGibbon and Kee, London, 1970.

Tetlow, J., and Goss, A., *Homes, Towns and Traffic*, Faber, London, 1965.

Thomas, D., *London's Green Belt*, Faber, London, 1965.

Westmacott, R., and Worthington, T., *New Agricultural Landscapes*, Countryside Commission, 1974.

CHAPTER TWENTY-THREE

PROBLEMS OF ECONOMIC DEVELOPMENT: DIFFERENCES BETWEEN REGIONS

Despite the fact that a major trend in the study of economic and social geography is the identification of similarities between places and phenomena over the earth's surface to produce a body of theory, the fact remains that the real world is very diverse. This diversity is produced by major environmental contrasts, the uneven distribution of natural resources, and regional differences in the history of human development.

In the past, geographers have been largely content to describe these differences, but the current concern is to analyse the problems arising from this diversity, and to offer solutions in the form of planning proposals. One major area where this new problem-approach in geography has been focused, concerns the differing levels of economic development that are found between countries, and between regions within countries. This chapter is concerned with differences between regions within countries, especially with the nature and causes of the various forms of the 'regional problem' and with attempts to solve the problem, particularly in Britain. The following chapter is concerned with differences between countries, especially with the problems of 'underdevelopment' and the gulf that exists between the rich and poor countries of the world.

Regional Inequalities

Economic development is not evenly spread within countries, because environmental factors and the operation of economic and social processes described earlier in the book produce spatial concentration and specialisation. As a result, for example, 70 per cent of manufacturing output in the USA takes place on 7 per cent of the land area in the North-East Manufacturing Belt.

In consequence, there are usually widely differing levels of economic and social well-being within any country. Because of the social and political problems they present, such differences have long been studied on a class basis, but increasing attention is now being given to their geographical aspects.

Measuring Regional Inequalities

Unfortunately, economic and social well-being is difficult to define and thus to measure, because so many factors are involved and because no one index of regional prosperity gives quite the same results as another. Nevertheless, there are two main indicators of economic health which are generally used.

The first of these is employment opportunity, and in Britain at least, **unemployment** has been a major yardstick of regional inequality since the 1920s, providing a strong impetus to successive governments' attempts to develop an effective regional policy. Despite this policy, there are still marked spatial differences in levels of unemployment (Fig. 23.1) and the average

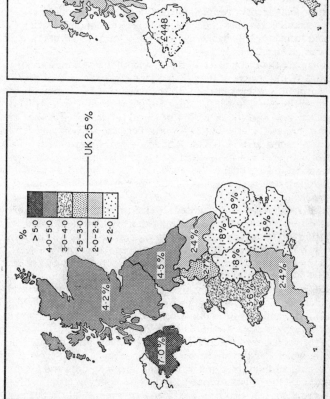

Fig. 23.2. Per capita income in the UK, 1971–2, by regions.

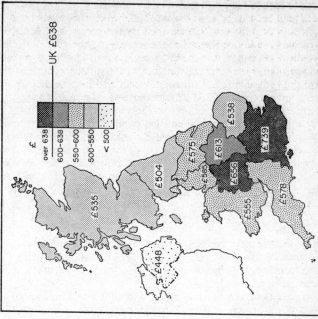

Fig. 23.1. Average unemployment rates in the UK, 1963–73, by regions.

annual rate of unemployment in the period 1963–73 showed a steady increase from the south-east to the north and west of the UK.

A similar gradient can be seen in Fig. 23.2, which uses the second main indicator, wealth or affluence, as measured by the **per capita income**. Here, only two regions are above the national average, but the general decline in affluence to the north and west of the UK is maintained. The per capita income of a region is probably the best single indicator of its affluence, but wealth and poverty are not only dependent on employment and income, but also on a wide range of other economic and social indicators. The type of industry in a region, its rate of growth, the out-migration of population, the number of young people in further education, housing quality, social service provision, and the general quality of the environment must also be taken into account when assessing standards of living. Unfortunately, such features are difficult to quantify, but despite this a multiple index based on a combination of different indicators is probably the most accurate way of defining regional inequalities. An attempt has been made by P. Lloyd and P. Dicken to construct such an index but there is, as yet, no universally accepted measure.

Types of Regional Problem

The nature and extent of regional inequalities vary from country to country and are constantly changing under the influence of economic, social, demographic and technological change. Nevertheless, four main types of regional problem can be identified.

First, there are those countries with **undeveloped** regions, most clearly seen in the Third World, where economic development is, at best, of small scale and concentrated in a few centres, with the result that large areas are totally lacking in development. In Nigeria, for example, there are marked differences in personal wealth and the provision of social services such as health and education between the large but backward Northern Region, and the more prosperous Western and Mid-West Regions, especially around the Federal Territory of Lagos. Even in developed countries large undeveloped regions can exist, such as the northlands of Canada, but undeveloped, or more usually underdeveloped, regions in developed countries can be considered as a second type of problem.

Depressed rural areas characterised by below average incomes, limited industrialisation, agriculture as a declining source of livelihood, and serious out-migration are found in all the developed countries. The Mezzogiorno of southern Italy is a classic case of an underdeveloped region within a developed country, agriculturally based, and with average incomes only 68 per cent of the national average. Despite having 38 per cent of the population and 40 per cent of the land area, the Mezzogiorno contributes only 25 per cent of the national income, with the rest coming from the industrialised north. The US South is similar, and was in 1938 a kind of colony of the US, economically distressed, socially backward, and out of the mainstream of national economic growth. Progress has been made in the South but there are still states such as Mississippi, which has the lowest per capita income and the second highest rate of out-migration in the country, forming large areas of rural distress. In both these cases the causes of inequality involve complex historical factors, but rural problems can also be more clearly environmental. In Scandinavia the problem regions are in the north, where a harsh climate and unbalanced employment structure result in low incomes and unemployment in primary industries, encouraging out-migration to the south.

Declining industrial areas present a third type of problem and are found in parts of Britain, Belgium, France, the Netherlands and in New England and West Virginia. Such areas are usually associated with early industrialisation, and slow-growing or declining industries such as coal or textiles dominate the industrial structure. Low earnings, an ageing economic and social infrastructure, vulnerability to economic recession, and serious out-migration are characteristic, and such regions have suffered from competition from new industrial countries, new industries and new sources of power. A process of industrial adjustment is needed to renovate these regions, but although this is taking place in regions such as New England, it is necessarily long and difficult.

The fourth type of problem region represents what might be considered the positive side of inequality: the **concentration** of wealth, opportunity and population in urban and industrial areas. However, the attractive power that such concentrations have in drawing resources from other regions and the pressure on physical and manpower resources resulting from growth make for problems just as serious as those of declining or underdeveloped regions. In the Third World the concentration of economic and social investment in cities such as Lagos produces overwhelming differences in opportunity between town and country, encouraging migration and overstraining the capacity of towns to cope with rapid growth and the problems of congestion. In the developed countries this excessive concentration in cities is very marked. Paris has 20 per cent of the population of France on 2 per cent of the land area, while 35 per cent of the Danish population live in Copenhagen. As a result, the problems of congestion, both economic and social, are increasing rapidly, and in the USA in particular, within these areas of concentration, new depressed areas are being created in the inner cities as employment opportunity moves to the suburbs. Concentration is not confined to cities in the developed world, however, since whole regions can be affected. The population of California increased by 27 per cent in the period 1960–70, while in Europe, concentration in regions such as South-East England and the western Netherlands has encouraged governments to adopt policies of dispersal.

Policies to solve this and other regional problems are increasingly being developed by governments, and since the regional problems of different countries are varied and complex, a wide range of policy is necessary. However, to be effective, these policies must be based on an understanding of why spatial inequalities are produced in the process of economic development.

Regional Analysis

Inequalities are produced over a long period of time as complex economic, social and political factors operate within a physical environment characterised by diversity and an uneven distribution of resources. The process of economic development under these conditions is consequently very complex, and attempts have been made by economists and geographers to understand this process through the formulation of models of economic development, although no one model has yet been universally accepted.

Few models have been concerned with the spatial aspects of development.

This lack of concern with spatial differences in economic development has its basis in classical economic theory which assumes that uniform costs, perfect competition and the perfect mobility of capital and labour produce equilibrating forces to maintain inter-regional equality. Thus, unemployment in a declining region will lead on the one hand to out-migration to more prosperous regions, but on the other hand to a reduction in labour costs, thereby attracting new industry. However, in reality, inter-regional equilibrium based on perfect mobility is never reached, because labour and capital are not perfectly mobile, nor are resources and markets uniformly distributed, and as a result regional inequalities are universal.

The best known non-spatial model was formulated by W. Rostow in 1955 and identifies five stages of economic development (Fig. 23.3), with take-off into self-sustaining growth coming about as one sector of the economy develops rapidly and encourages the growth of other sectors. Thus, the Industrial Revolution in Britain was led by the cotton industry, which in turn encouraged the textile machinery industry, transport improvements, service industries in the expanding towns and so on. However, if economic development affects the structure of the economy by producing leading sectors, then

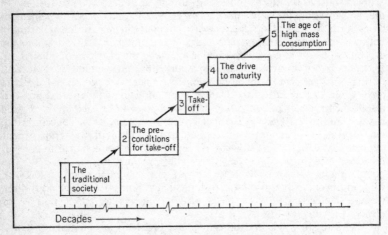

Fig. 23.3. The Rostow model of economic development.
(from R. J. Chorley and P. Haggett, *Models in Geography*, Methuen)

it may be inferred from the Rostow model that the distribution of economic activity will be similarly affected, with the emergence of leading regions. In nineteenth-century Britain, the leading sectors of the economy such as cotton and iron were certainly characterised by regional specialisation and concentration, and many economists now consider that economic development encourages regional inequalities. As a result, models have been formulated which more directly explain spatial differences in development.

Cumulative Causation and Spatial Interaction

The most important model attempting to explain spatial variations in economic prosperity was developed by G. Myrdal in 1956, in which it was argued that, contrary to classical theory, economic market forces increase regional differences rather than decrease them. Myrdal identified two associated processes which cause unequal growth.

First, economic development takes place in a region initially because of the natural advantages that it offers, such as the presence of power and raw materials. Then, once such a region moves ahead of the others, a process of **cumulative causation** takes place as acquired advantages (Chapter Fifteen) are developed to reinforce the status of the region and ensure that it continues to grow and stay ahead of the others. In Fig. 23.4 the way in which one development produces another is illustrated in the form of a flow diagram.

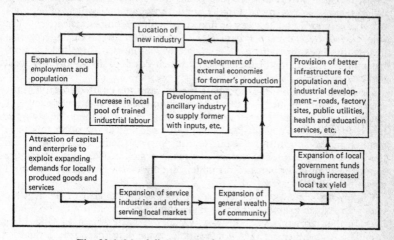

Fig. 23.4. Myrdal's process of cumulative causation.

(from R. J. Chorley and P. Haggett, *Models in Geography*, Methuen)

Secondly, and closely associated with the first, a process of **spatial interaction** takes place as labour, capital and commodities move into the growing region. Such growth produces a **backwash effect** in that other regions lose skilled labour and capital to the growth region and their markets are flooded with goods, preventing local development. As a result, growing and stagnating regions are produced. On the other hand, as the national economy expands, the benefits of growth begin to affect all regions and the **spread effect** of an expanding economy may encourage the process of cumulative causation to occur and self-sustaining growth to take place in other regions.

There are thus three stages of regional differentiation through which a country passes on its way to development in the Myrdal model. A pre-industrial stage when there are few regional inequalities; a second stage when great inequalities are produced by cumulative causation and its backwash effect as the economy 'takes off' and expands rapidly; and a third stage as the spread effect of growth operates to reduce regional differences. It has been suggested that the spread effect of growth needs to be supplemented by government action in the form of a vigorous regional policy, but in Britain at least, regional inequality is a persistent feature despite years of government intervention—which supports the view that the forces producing regional inequalities are much more powerful than the spread effects operating to reduce them.

Export Bases and Regional Multipliers

The basic principles of the Myrdal model are generally accepted, especially when applied to present-day developing economies, but other models have been advanced to explain regional inequalities in more developed economies. The most important of these is the model which emphasises the key role played by a region's **export base** in determining its rate of economic growth. Thus, a region which can produce goods and services and export them to other regions grows more rapidly than those regions which either lack exportable goods and services or find it difficult to compete effectively. The role played by the export base is also important in producing regional inequalities because it creates the income which, in turn, supports the non-basic or service sector of the economy which develops to supply the local market.

Despite its limitations, export base theory can thus be used to explain the rise of dominant regions, but of course, economic bases are not permanent or unchanging. The export base of old coalmining areas in Britain, for example, has been eclipsed by a decline in demand as technical developments have resulted in the substitution of oil for coal in many industries. Export base theory can also be used therefore to explain regional differences in mature economies and contributes to an understanding of the regional problem of declining industrial areas.

Closely associated with export base theory is the concept of the **regional multiplier**, which examines the way that economic growth in a region stimulates further growth. As industries within the basic sector expand, they stimulate each other, so that, for example, expanding machinery industries require more steel, and increases in steel manufacture require more machinery. Furthermore, as export earnings flow into a region, the service industries expand to supply the increased demand from workers in the basic industries. This interaction operates as a multiplier process in which growth stimulates further growth in a complex rising spiral of production.

To measure the regional multiplier effect, **input–output analysis** can be applied, when an increase in inputs into an industry can be measured against the resulting outputs of associated industries, and the effects of growth in one sector can be seen on the whole system.

The Concentration of Economic Activity

The process of economic growth therefore produces marked differences between regions, but even within prosperous regions, development is never evenly spread. Earlier discussions of industrial location theory (Chapter Sixteen), central place theory (Chapter Twenty), and so on, should help explain how the friction of distance is a major factor producing the concentration of economic activity. Some places, by virtue of their favoured location relative to sources of materials, markets, labour and so on are economically more attractive and thus form natural **growth poles** and expand faster than other areas. These growth poles are usually urban–industrial complexes and offer economies of agglomeration. They are found in all advanced economies and such concentrations can interact with their surrounding regions, spreading prosperity from the core to the periphery. Because of this, the growth pole concept has been used by governments in their regional economic planning as a method of stimulating growth, but because spread effects operate slowly, peripheral locations are still the least prosperous. Thus, economic prosperity in Britain declines to the north and west from London, and in the EEC, Scotland and the Mezzogiorno are among the poorest regions.

The concentration of economic prosperity and opportunity would therefore appear to be a natural outcome of the process of development, but the presence of such concentrations and the fact that their export bases might be eroded creates many economic, social and political problems. As a result, governments are playing an increasing role in the location of economic activity and the formulation of regional policies has been undertaken to tackle these problems.

Regional Policy: Why Governments Intervene

Faced with spatial differences in levels of economic development and social welfare, governments have first to decide whether or not to intervene to reduce them. Since some regional differences are inevitable, this decision will largely depend on the level at which it is considered that they become a problem, and will thus vary from country to country. Secondly, and this is examined in the next section, having decided to intervene, governments must determine what types of intervention would be the most effective in reducing these differences.

Most people would agree that a government has a duty to intervene in the economic and social welfare of the state, although there may be some disagreement over its extent. Intervention is desirable, first, to allocate resources to agreed purposes, and secondly, to decide on the location of new investment, particularly on the issue of whether to take capital to labour, or labour to capital.

Despite this, there is no universal agreement that governments should intervene directly to reduce regional inequalities, and opponents of regional policy point out that, apart from its political implications, such policy ignores the fact that specialisation and change are essential features of the space-economy. Location theory suggests that spatial specialisation is the most efficient use of immobile resources and that as change takes place, new locations are necessary. It is argued that planning freezes the geography of production and inhibits the operation of equilibrating forces, thus maintaining inefficient patterns of production which can only be sustained by massive amounts of regional aid.

However, classical location theory assumes that decisions are optimal, while in reality industrialists are at best imperfect optimisers (Chapter Sixteen), making their decisions with reference to the costs of the firm and ignoring other elements in the costs of location such as the provision of local services or the inefficiency of congested roads. It also assumes that equilibrating forces are fully operational, but the mobility of labour, for example, is constrained by family ties, council house waiting lists, imperfect knowledge of opportunities and so on.

Also, governments are playing an increasingly important role in affecting location decisions indirectly. Labour laws in the USA affected the relocation of the cotton textile industry in the South (Chapter Fifteen), and energy policy in the Netherlands, by emphasising natural gas, has led to the run-down of coalmining in Limburg and the need therefore to attract new industry into that area. As a result, non-interventionist arguments are difficult to sustain and governments are developing regional policies to intervene directly in the space-economy for five main groups of reasons.

First, **social** reasons encourage governments to combat unemployment, reduce income differentials and curb out-migration, since marked regional differences in these fields produce social unrest. Social welfare is an important consideration in planned and mixed economies, but even in the USA some limited intervention has been necessary to alleviate distress in depressed areas such as West Virginia and the textile towns of New England. Social welfare was usually the original aim of regional policy but the importance of a healthy social environment as a factor aiding the recovery of distressed industrial areas is currently being stressed.

Secondly, although social reasons remain important, regional policy is increasingly being implemented for **economic** reasons. The desire of governments to utilise fully the resources of the state, to reduce transport costs and to overcome the problems of congestion in growth areas have been important in many countries. In addition, the wastage of labour resources through unemployment in depressed areas and the problem of wage inflation in growth areas suffering a labour shortage have provided more immediate concerns.

Thirdly, **political** reasons have played an important role since development aid must be distributed in such a way as to avoid grievances. This is especially true in federal states such as Canada or Nigeria which have strong linguistic and cultural differences between regions, but even in the UK, nationalist interests must be considered. However, a more common political incentive to reduce unemployment in the Western democracies is that the unemployed are likely to vote for the opposition at election time.

Fourthly, **strategic** reasons have also played a role. The need to maintain a strong productive capacity for times of war helps maintain basic industries, while relocation in safe areas affects the development of strategic industries. Disputed border regions such as the Ussuri and Amur valleys between the USSR and China are also being developed to establish claims of occupance.

Finally, **the need to coordinate** sectoral planning in housing, industry, education and so on provides a strong practical reason for regional policy. In this way, conflicts over land use between industry, agriculture, housing and recreation can be resolved through closely integrated regional and physical planning.

The relative importance of these reasons in affecting regional policy differs from time to time and from country to country. In the UK, social reasons were dominant in the 1930s but were replaced by strategic reasons in the 1940s, while these were in turn replaced by economic reasons in the 1960s. Nevertheless, whatever the reasons affecting it, regional policy is now a very important influence on the location of manufacturing and service industry and has become one of the major factors affecting the geography of economic and social welfare in many countries.

Regional Policy: How Governments Intervene

There is no single regional policy that can be applied to all countries, but there are many national policies which have been developed under three main influences. The first of these concerns **the nature of the regional problem**, which varies greatly from country to country, with the result that what may be an appropriate policy in the UK is unlikely to be right in Brazil. Secondly, the **economic-political system** influences what type of policy is possible, depending on whether the economy is planned as in the USSR, mixed as in the UK, or *laissez-faire* as in the USA. In the USSR, economic activity takes place within an overall plan, but in mixed or *laissez-faire* economies, policy might be designed to tackle specific problems such as unemployment, or a group of problems relating to specific depressed areas. Thirdly, **the structure of government** influences policy. In countries with a centralised system such as France, the problem is to arouse local interest in implementing planning proposals coming from Paris. In federal countries such as West Germany, the problem is that the individual Länder have power and revenue, and the task of the federal government in redistributing resources to needy areas is very difficult. In countries with strong local government units holding responsibility for physical planning, as in the UK, there are often conflicts when local interests have to be subordinated to national plans.

Despite these difficulties and differences, the aims of regional policy have common elements in all countries. The need is to encourage development or adjustment in underdeveloped or depressed areas, or to control growth in favoured areas without actually stopping it, and thus to reduce regional inequalities to acceptable levels. This is not easy because many basic conflicts may have to be reconciled. Economic development might require the movement of population to areas of growth potential, but social welfare might require drastic changes in the economic structure of depressed regions. Present welfare versus future development might also be an issue if the policy of favouring depressed areas leads to a decline in prosperity in favoured areas, thus affecting national economic prosperity. Nevertheless, action to reduce large regional inequalities is required, and one of the first tasks of regional policy makers is to define areas of need.

Defining Areas of Need

Unfortunately, this is not easily done, because, as with the problem of measuring regional inequalities discussed earlier, no single index can be used, although unemployment levels have been a favourite in the past. However, low incomes, poor housing, unbalanced industrial structures and restricted educational opportunities are only some of the many other important considerations.

Even if criteria of need can be isolated, there is still the problem of defining the regions in which they exist since the boundaries are unlikely to be clear-cut lines (Chapter Three). Any new programming region might cut across existing functional regions, while areas just beyond the aided region might become comparatively less attractive and develop into 'grey areas' requiring assistance themselves. Nevertheless, decisions have to be made and problem areas have been designated as development areas in which a wide variety of policy measures have been tried (see Figs. 23.5 to 23.10).

Regional Policy Measures

Having identified those areas which need aid, there are basically three ways in which industry, for example, can be moved into them: by compulsion, by bribery, or by making development areas so attractive that industrialists move spontaneously. The mixture varies from country to country depending on the economic–political system, but before action is taken, a decision has to be made whether to assist all areas of need or whether to concentrate only on those with growth potential. Similarly, it must be decided whether or not to give indiscriminate aid to those regions chosen or whether to concentrate on points of maximum potential (growth poles). A basic problem is that it is not clear how regional economies work and therefore the costs and benefits of alternate policies are difficult to assess. As a result, regional policy formulation is not a precise science and accurate predictive models are difficult to develop. In such circumstances a wide range of policy measures has been tried, which can be grouped in three categories.

The first consists of two types of **public sector investment.** First, there are infrastructure developments, ranging from the building of new cities such as Brasilia or new towns in Britain, to road improvement schemes or derelict land clearance in development areas. Secondly, there are training, education and welfare measures designed to increase occupational and geographical mobility. The latter involves **intervention in the location of private industry;** either positively, by offering inducements in the form of tax concessions or grants to firms willing to locate in development areas; or negatively, by applying direct controls over expansion, or by increasing taxes, in attractive areas. The third involves **offering inducements to individuals** in the form of cash or land grants; either to enable them to leave poor areas such as parts of Ireland and Sweden by giving compensation to farmers for their land, or to encourage development in new areas such as the dry zone of Sri Lanka by granting land to new settlers.

Regional Policy and Regional Planning

Much regional policy in the past has simply been depressed area policy aimed at alleviating the hardships produced by low incomes and unemployment. However, increasing attention is being given to regional development policies which include all regions, both weak and strong, and which are essentially national policies with a strong regional component aimed at overall social and economic growth.

Within such a regional policy there is a need for **regional planning,** for regional policy is basically central government policy-making for the regions, whereas regional planning concerns policy-making at the regional level. Thus, although growth-pole policy might not be acceptable at national level because it neglects depressed regions, it could be applied within regions to concentrate aid at points of maximum potential rather than spread it indiscriminately. Regional plans can be drawn up within the framework of a national plan to achieve coordination between economic and physical planning, but this is very difficult. In Britain, for example, the Economic Planning Regions established in 1964 simply overlie a very complex system of overlapping and uncoordinated functional and administrative regions, and this leads to many conflicts. However, the establishment of a comprehensive regional policy within an overall national plan is a very difficult task, as can be seen from an examination of nearly fifty years of regional policy in Britain.

Regional Policy in Britain

In many respects, Britain can still be considered as 'two nations' with a less prosperous north and west dominated by a nineteenth-century industrial structure, and producing lower incomes and higher unemployment, and a prosperous south-east with an industrial economy largely developed in the twentieth century and diversified by the growth of tertiary and quaternary employment (see Figs. 23.1 and 23.2).

The regional problem in Britain reflects this division and has two basic elements. First, there is the problem of high unemployment resulting from the economic structure of the depressed areas and the environmental deficiencies historically associated with early industrialisation. Secondly, there is the problem of the concentration of population and economic opportunity in the South-East and Midlands, which not only produces congestion within the region, but adversely affects less favoured areas by attracting investment and labour.

For a variety of reasons, economic, social, political and environmental, successive governments have tried since the late 1920s to bring the two nations together by developing policies to solve the regional problem. Unfortunately, policy has not always been coordinated and it is only recently that the two aspects of the regional problem have been seen as part of a single, national problem.

Regional Policy Measures

Because Britain is a 'mixed economy' of state and private enterprise, the power of the government to intervene in industrial location has its limits, and as a result a 'carrot and stick' technique has been used in regional policy. The carrot to attract industrialists to depressed areas has taken the form of a variety of inducements, while the stick has taken the form of controls over development in areas where the government wishes to restrict growth.

Three main types of policy measure have been used to attract industry to depressed areas. First, there have been infrastructure investments and improvements. Investments include the building of new factories, trading estates and roads, and although the new towns were originally built to solve some of London's problems, they have more recently been incorporated into regional and national planning. Infrastructure improvements have been largely concerned with derelict land clearance, beginning in 1945 and re-emphasised in 1970, and also with urban redevelopment in the older conurbations. Secondly, there have been measures to train manpower and make it more mobile. In fact, grants and loans for training and migration formed the first attempt at regional policy in 1928, and although a migration policy was not successful then, a number of subsequent measures have helped key workers migrate between regions. Training continues to be important, and grants are given to firms to train their workers or else this can be done at Government Retraining Centres. Thirdly, direct aid has been given to firms in the form of grants, loans or tax concessions. Currently, emphasis is being placed on grants and these are given mainly as investment grants, building grants, and as a Regional Employment Premium (REP) to reduce labour costs in manufacturing in the depressed areas.

To restrict growth outside the assisted areas, the government began to use Industrial Development Certificates (IDC) in 1947 and Office Development Permits (ODP) in 1965. Following the 1972 Industry Act, any industrial development over 1,394 m² in the non-assisted areas (and over 929 m² in the South-East) needs an IDC, and office developments over 278 m² in the South-East need an ODP. Thus, by refusing certificates and permits in congested areas and granting them in depressed areas, location can be controlled.

This mixture of compulsion and persuasion has characterised the development of British regional policy, which is summarised in Table 23.1 and Figs. 23.5 to 23.10, and discussed in the following section.

The Development of British Regional Policy

British regional policy has been developed over a period of almost 50 years, and five main periods can be identified.

Regional policy began in 1928 and **until 1939** was concerned with only one aspect of the regional problem, unemployment, which was running at very high levels during the economic recession of the late 1920s and early 1930s.

Table 23.1.   Major Developments in British Regional Policy—
Areas Receiving Government Assistance

Year	Event	Area	Refer to
1928	Industrial Transference Board		
1934	Special Areas (Development and Improvement) Act	Special Areas	Fig. 23.5
1937	Special Areas Amendment Act		
1940	Report of the Royal Commission on the Distribution of the Industrial Population (Barlow Report)		
1945	Distribution of Industry Act	Development Areas	Fig. 23.6
1946	New Towns Act		
1947	Town and Country Planning Act		
1950	Distribution of Industries Act		
1960	Local Employment Act	Development Districts	Fig. 23.7
1964	Department of Economic Affairs	Economic Planning Regions	Fig. 23.8
1964	Industrial Training Act		
1965	Control of Office and Industrial Development Act		
1966	Industrial Development Act	Development Areas	Fig. 23.9
1967	Special Development Areas designated	Special Development Areas	Fig. 23.9
1969	The Intermediate Areas (Hunt Committee Report)		
1970	Local Employment Act	Intermediate Areas	Fig. 23.10
1972	Industry Act		

This was particularly marked in parts of northern England (75 per cent at Jarrow in 1933), central Scotland and south Wales. The first attempt to reduce these levels came in 1928 when money was provided to retrain labour and encourage it to migrate to more prosperous areas, but this policy was neither economically successful nor socially popular and, as a result, subsequent policy has been more concerned with moving capital to labour. The change began in 1934, when the Special Areas Act made the first attempt to redevelop the depressed areas by encouraging firms to move into the areas shown in Fig. 23.5. However, pre-war policy was not very successful, despite the Special Areas Amendment Act of 1937, because the legislation was not very effective and it was realised that only when the national economy is growing do firms wish to expand and thus make it possible for government to intervene in location decision-making. As a result, the economic structure of the depressed areas remained unchanged, leaving them vulnerable to any future recession.

During the period **1939–45**, the regional problem was reduced because the economy boomed under the war effort and the government relocated many factories for strategic reasons in the depressed areas. However, much more important in the long term was the Report of the Barlow Commission, which examined both aspects of the regional problem together for the first time. Reporting an unsatisfactory distribution of industry and population, it recommended that the government should play an active role in achieving a satisfactory balance of industry between the regions and that the congested areas should be decentralised, especially by the dispersal of industry from London.

During the period **1945–60**, policy was influenced by the Barlow Report and under the 1945 Distribution of Industry Act, the Special Areas were replaced by more extensive Development Areas in which much industry was relocated in the immediate post-war period (Fig. 23.6). At the same time, dispersal from London was encouraged by the New Towns Act of 1946 and by the use of IDCs under the Town and Country Planning Act of 1947, and during the post-war economic boom, the industrial structure of the Development Areas was diversified to some extent. On the other hand, there was still little effort to coordinate the physical planning provisions of the 1946 and 1947 Acts with the development of a true regional policy, and this led to many conflicts. Thus, the new towns were built in South-East England where IDCs were difficult to obtain. However, in the 1950s, the general economic downturn preoccupied the government and Development Area policy was not fully pursued after 1951, with the result that by 1958, unemployment was again a serious matter in the depressed areas. The basic cause was that the old economic structure had not been changed and that the declining, traditional, heavy industries needed to be supplemented with new expanding industries.

The problems of the late 1950s led to a new policy in the period **1960–66**, based on the Local Employment Act of 1960, which changed the emphasis from a Development Area policy to a Development District policy aimed at eradicating pockets of high (over 4·5 per cent) unemployment (Fig. 23.7). However, this social emphasis was soon modified because it was clear that granting aid solely on the basis of unemployment levels created problems, and that wider economic criteria must also be considered. In 1964 the Department of Economic Affairs was established and the country was divided into ten Economic Planning Regions (Fig. 23.8). This was an important step, because

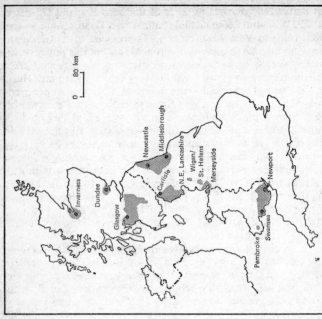

Fig. 23.6. The Development Areas, 1945–60.

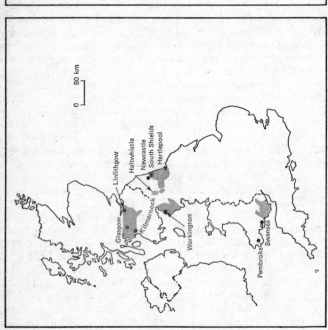

Fig. 23.5. The Special Areas, 1934–9.

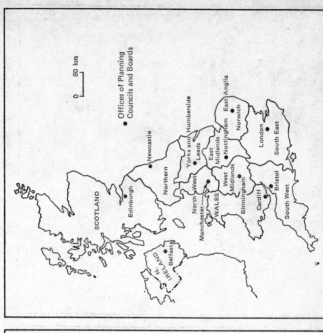

Fig. 23.8. The Economic Planning Regions, 1964.

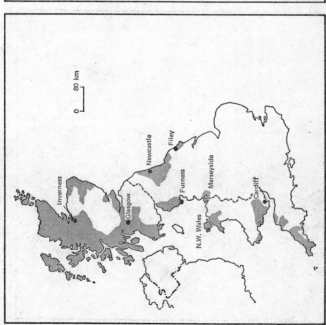

Fig. 23.7. The Development Districts, 1960.

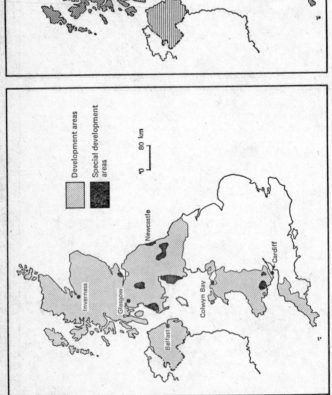

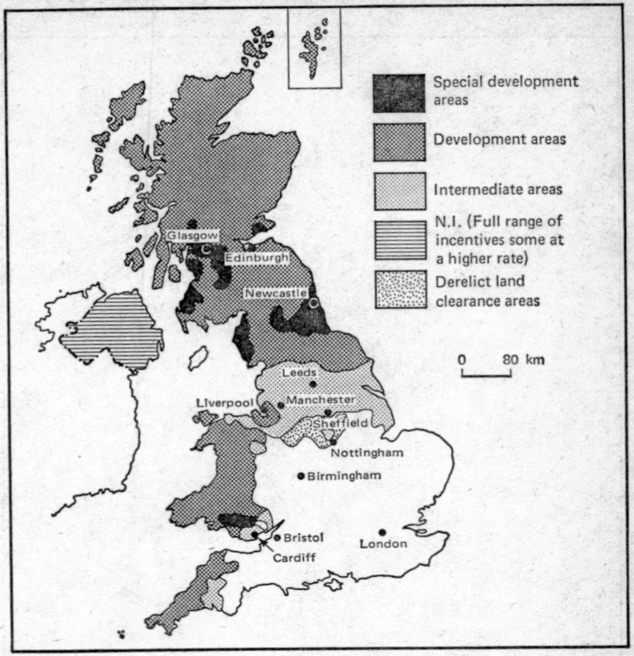

Fig. 23.10. The assisted areas, 1975.

Special development areas

Development areas

Intermediate areas

N.I. (Full range of incentives some at a higher rate)

Derelict land clearance areas

0   80 km

Glasgow
Edinburgh
Newcastle
Leeds
Liverpool
Manchester
Sheffield
Nottingham
Birmingham
Bristol
Cardiff
London

Development areas

Special development areas

0   80 km

Inverness
Glasgow
Newcastle
Belfast
Colwyn Bay
Cardiff

Fig. 23.9. The Development and Special Development Areas, 1967.

although its practical impact was small, it recognised the links between national and local government and between physical and economic planning. Attention was also turned to non-industrial employment when restrictions were placed on office development in Greater London in 1965 and over the Midlands and South-East in 1966.

The change back to a Development Area policy came with the Industrial Development Act of 1966, and **since 1966** it has been possible for manufacturers to locate in assisted areas at places where the potential is greatest, and not just where unemployment is high. Such locations have been assisted by investment and building grants and the labour-subsidy benefits of the REP. The Development Areas have been modified to some extent by the designation of Special Development Areas in 1967 when colliery closures were leading to high levels of unemployment in some areas (Fig. 23.9), but the principle has remained. In addition, the Intermediate Areas were designated by the Local Employment Act of 1970, following the Hunt Report of 1969, and offer somewhat lower levels of assistance (Fig. 23.10). As a result of these changes, increasing attention was being given in the late 1960s to the development of a regional policy concerned with regional economic growth rather than a simple Development District policy aimed at reducing unemployment. More money was being spent and a wider range of measures was being used, and this was further developed in the Industry Act of 1972 which aimed to encourage national economic growth while giving additional incentives in the form of grants for development in the assisted areas.

However, despite almost 50 years of regional policy and the expenditure of large sums of money, there are still marked regional spatial inequalities in Britain. The assisted areas still suffer from higher unemployment, lower incomes, out-migration, a very slow rise in total employment and so on. Nevertheless, it can be claimed that these inequalities would have been much greater if there had been no policy. Industry has been encouraged to move in and environmental improvement schemes have been undertaken, but as discussed earlier, the backwash effects of economic development are much stronger than the spread effects, and therefore uniform development is not possible. The task of government is to establish permissible levels of inequality, and then to adopt policies which will contain inequality while at the same time allow national economic growth.

Conclusion

Regional inequalities are an inevitable consequence of economic development, but because of the economic, social and political problems which they create, governments try to keep such inequalities to a minimum. At one time, regional policy was mainly concerned to solve specific problems such as high levels of unemployment, but it has been increasingly realised that the regional problem is part of an overall national problem, and that regional policies must be formulated within policies for national economic development. However, national economic development is not easily achieved, as will be seen in the following chapter.

Suggested Further Reading

Alden, J., and Morgan, R., *Regional Planning: A Comprehensive View*, Leonard Hill, Leighton Buzzard, 1974.

Coates, B. E., and Rawstron, E. M., *Regional Variations in Britain*, Batsford, London, 1971.

Hall, P., *Urban and Regional Planning*, Penguin, Harmondsworth, 1974.

Keeble, D. E., 'Models of Economic Development', in R. J. Chorley and P. Haggett (Eds.), *Socio-Economic Models in Geography*, Methuen, London, 1967.

Lloyd, P. E., and Dicken, P., *Location in Space: A Theoretical Approach to Economic Geography*, Harper and Row, New York, 1972.

McCrone, G., *Regional Policy in Britain*, Allen and Unwin, London, 1969.

Manners, G., Keeble, D., Rodgers, B., and Warren, K., *Regional Development in Britain*, Wiley, London, 1972.

Morrill, R. L., and Wohlenberg, E. H., *The Geography of Poverty in the United States*, McGraw-Hill, New York, 1971.

OECD, *The Regional Factor in Economic Development*, OECD, Paris, 1970.

Open University, Course D342, *Regional Analysis and Development*, Open University Press, Milton Keynes, 1974.

Problem Regions of Europe (series), Series editor: D. I. Scargill, Oxford University Press, London, 1973– .

Sant, M., *Regional Disparities*, Macmillan, London, 1974.

CHAPTER TWENTY-FOUR

PROBLEMS OF ECONOMIC DEVELOPMENT: DIFFERENCES BETWEEN COUNTRIES

Differences between regions within countries are only one form of spatial inequality. Perhaps even more important are differences between countries. International differences are obviously inevitable in view of the diversity of the earth's surface, but they have been intensified by the process of economic development. As a result, there are now wide differences in levels of economic and social welfare, and in levels of technical ability between countries. These differences create many problems.

This chapter is concerned with examining the nature of underdevelopment and the problems which the underdeveloped countries face. Attention is also given to possible solutions to these problems and the importance of development planning in raising standards.

Differences Between Countries

Because of the interplay of a considerable number of factors, widely different levels of development can be found between countries. Many attempts have been made to classify world economic systems and a simple classification has been suggested by D. W. Fryer (Fig. 24.1). This conceals wide differences within each group, but serves to emphasise the gap which exists between a few rich, highly developed countries, principally in the middle latitudes, and a large number of poor, semi- or underdeveloped countries which make up the 'Third World' in lower latitudes. Considerable variations in standards of living exist, although they are difficult to define because it is not easy to measure the differences between the rich and the poor. The United Nations has suggested that the best measure would be a multiple index including such elements as income, health, education, housing and so on, but information in these fields is not easy to obtain and standardise.

The differences might be difficult to define, but they are easy to see, and an increasing concern with the problem of world poverty led the United Nations to designate the decade 1960–70 as the UN Development Decade with the object of reducing differences in wealth between countries by using aid from the developed countries to increase economic development in the semi- and underdeveloped countries. Two main factors prompted this concern. The first was a moral conviction that poverty, hunger and disease were denying millions of people their basic rights. Secondly, there were many practical considerations, such as the vast potential market which increased standards in poor countries could provide for the trading nations of the developed world, and on the negative side, the threat of a pandemic if disease in the Third World were not controlled. However, despite the efforts of the United Nations the gap between rich and poor is widening and a major concern now is to prevent the poor from becoming absolutely rather than just relatively poorer.

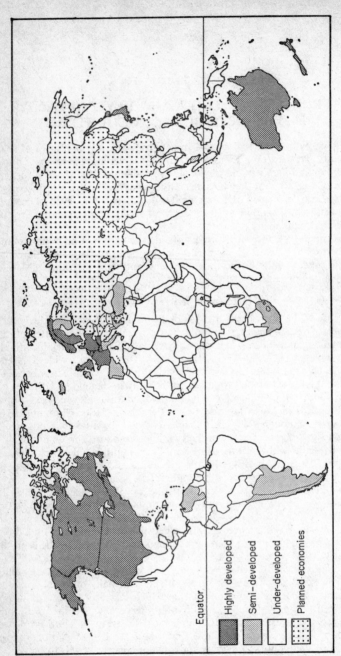

Equator

Highly developed

Semi-developed

Under-developed

Planned economies

Fig. 24.1. World economic systems (after D. W. Fryer).

Developing the Underdeveloped Countries

Because of their increasing importance, more and more attention is being given to the problems of the Third World in the hope that once the nature and causes of the problem are understood, effective economic development can take place to improve the quality of life for over two thirds of the world's population.

The Nature of Underdevelopment

The distinguishing feature of the underdeveloped countries is poverty, but there is no rigid division between the rich and poor countries of the world, rather a continuum ranging from absolute poverty to considerable wealth. It is therefore possible to talk of semi-developed countries occupying an intermediate position on the continuum, and even in the planned economies a range of development exists.

Among the underdeveloped countries themselves there is much diversity, and the problems faced by such countries as Brazil or Chad are markedly different, as are their prospects for development. As a consequence, there can be no single solution to the problem of underdevelopment and each country will need to take its own course.

Nevertheless, despite this fact, the underdeveloped countries share a number of characteristics which, although difficult to measure, are distinctive. First, and most important, they are poor. In 1970 the per capita income of the underdeveloped countries averaged $210 per annum compared with $2,690 for the developed countries, and although the use of the per capita income as a measure of wealth has its drawbacks, it is probably the best available. The degree of poverty varies from country to country within the Third World (Fig. 24.2), but when compared with the per capita income figure of $4,289 for the USA, Ethiopia's $71 can only represent abject poverty. Such striking differences in wealth are aggravated by the fact that wealth is also badly distributed among the population within countries. In the USA, although 10 per cent of the population have 27 per cent of the national wealth, in Colombia 2·6 per cent have 40 per cent, and in Gabon 1 per cent have 56 per cent. Secondly, the occupational structure of the Third World is overwhelmingly agricultural, with little manufacturing or service employment. In the USA agriculture provides under 5 per cent of employment, but in Africa and south Asia the figure is between 70 and 90 per cent. The type of agriculture is essentially subsistence and is associated with unemployment or underemployment, which runs at over 20 per cent in rural India. Thirdly, as a consequence, the geographical distribution of the population is essentially rural, and despite recent rapid urban growth, urban populations represent less than 20 per cent of the total compared with 77 per cent in Britain. Fourthly, under the influence of a high birth rate and a high (although declining) death rate, the structure of the population contains a high proportion of non-productive people under the age of fifteen (Chapter Seven). Fifthly, as a consequence of poverty, there are serious problems of nutrition. Undernourishment is produced by deficiencies in the quantity of food, with the population of many countries averaging less than the critical limit of 2,200 calories per head per day, and malnutrition is produced by deficiencies in the quality of food, especially by diets containing little protein (Fig. 24.3). As a result,

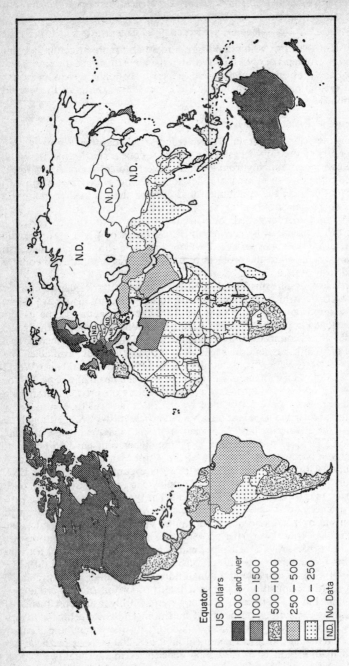

Equator

US Dollars

1000 and over
1000 — 1500
500 — 1000
250 — 500
0 — 250
N.D. No Data

Fig. 24.2. Per capita incomes, 1963–8.

(from M. Chisholm and B. Rodgers, *Studies in Human Geography*, Heinemann)

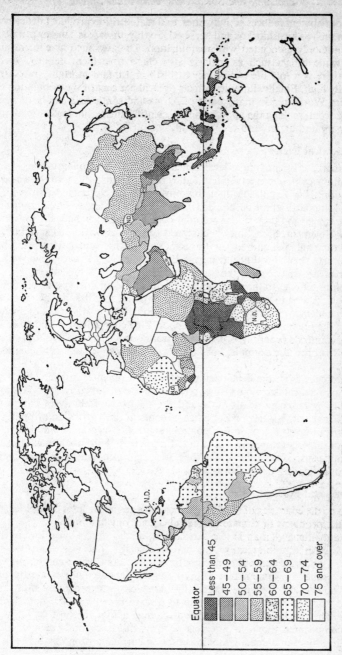

Fig. 24.3. Daily supply of total protein (grammes).

(from M. Chisholm and B. Rodgers, *Studies in Human Geography*, Heinemann)

Equator

Less than 45
45—49
50—54
55—59
60—64
65—69
70—74
75 and over

undernourishment reduces activity rates, and malnutrition produces deficiency diseases such as kwashiorkor and beri-beri. Sixthly, disease is a major problem and is not only associated with malnutrition. Diseases such as cholera are killers while others such as malaria also cause permanent debility. As a result, there is a low life expectancy at birth and infant mortality rates are especially high. Finally, illiteracy affects over 50 per cent of the population of the Third World and in many parts of Africa and south Asia can be as high as 80 per cent, making the application of scientific and technological methods to industry and agriculture very difficult.

The Historical Factor

The characteristics of underdevelopment described above operate to produce 'a commonwealth of poverty' inhabited by more than two thirds of the world's population. It is regrettable that this poverty is closely related to the high material standards of the developed world, but most underdeveloped countries have at some time been under colonial control which has had a strong exploitative element. Sometimes it has been direct exploitation as exemplified by the removal of hundreds of thousands of slaves from Africa, while at others it has been aimed at integrating the colonies into an economic system which has largely benefited the 'mother country'.

Opinions differ as to the merits and demerits of the colonial system but there is a strong feeling in many parts of the Third World that despite the granting of independence to former colonies, neo-colonialism is still a major factor keeping the underdeveloped countries poor. Neo-colonialism is said to exist when a country's economy is controlled from outside, by the world price of cocoa or rubber, for example, but this is a situation which will be difficult to remedy.

Interference from the developed countries also operates less directly. The spread of medical technology has created many of the current population problems by reducing death rates, and the political instability of countries such as Pakistan, Nigeria or Zaire has its roots in the imposition of political boundaries during the period of colonial control. However, there are other causes of underdevelopment operating at present, and although they operate in a complex process of interaction, they can be grouped under three headings: environmental, economic and social.

Environmental Problems

Most of the countries of the Third World face environmental difficulties, of which the problems of climate and resources are outstanding.

Climate influences man in two ways. First, it has a direct effect on human activity, both physiologically and psychologically, and was expressed in Chapter One in the concept of a 'climatic comfort' zone where conditions are most tolerable for human life. Many underdeveloped countries are on the fringes or outside this zone, especially in regions where activity rates are reduced and the body is more prone to disease because of the hot, damp climate. The precise effects of climate on human activity are not yet known, being complicated by such things as poverty, disease, ignorance and poor diet, but, although climate is not an absolute barrier to progress, it is still a limiting influence.

Secondly, climate has an indirect effect through its influence on agriculture, transport and other economic activities. Conditions in the Tropics present considerable difficulties for the farmer since the soils are heavily leached by high rainfall, or parched by frequent drought, or liable to flooding or erosion. In addition, there is a wide range of plant and animal pests and diseases to be overcome. Extreme climatic conditions also affect transport facilities, especially roads, which are easily washed out or baked into solid furrows, while heat, dust and water badly affect transport machinery such as lorries or railway locomotives.

Natural resources can be very important in the process of development, providing a base for industrial growth or earning foreign currency from their export. However, the distribution of the world's energy resources, especially coal and oil (Chapter Fourteen), highlights the fact that many of the underdeveloped countries lack the raw material base on which the developed countries have grown to wealth and power, and this is likely to prove a severe handicap to development in a world where minerals are becoming increasingly scarce. On the other hand, the potential for hydro-electric or solar-generated energy is quite considerable in many parts of the Third World, and Africa possesses 40 per cent of the world's hydro-electric power potential. The difficulty will be to realise this potential.

Despite their importance, resource problems are not the basic cause of underdevelopment, since countries such as Denmark, Switzerland and Japan have achieved high levels of development on a very limited resource base. Resources are neutral (Chapter Twenty-five) and only become useful if technology and the will to use it are available. Many of the problems arising from climatic difficulties can also be overcome by the use of medical drugs, pesticides, scientific farming practices and so on. The causes of underdevelopment cannot be found in environmental determinism, despite the constraints which undoubtedly exist. Those countries with an abundance of natural resources undoubtedly have much better prospects for development than those which do not, but the physical environment is only one part of the total human environment, where economic and social influences are very powerful.

Economic Problems

The problem of underdevelopment has been described by H. W. Singer as being made up of 'vicious circles within vicious circles, and of interlocking vicious circles', and two of these are illustrated in Fig. 24.4. The need is to discover how to break out of the circle of poverty into self-sustaining growth, but before this breakthrough is possible, a number of economic problems will have to be overcome.

First, there is a serious shortage of capital in the Third World to finance the establishment of industry, agricultural improvement, transport systems and so on. It has been suggested that an underdeveloped country needs to invest 12–15 per cent of its net national income in order to diversify and advance its economy, because this is the sort of figure which will give rates of return which are larger than the rate of population increase. The surplus can then be reinvested to give further returns and the economy can then, in the words of W. Rostow, 'take off' into cumulative self-sustaining growth, and the vicious circle will be broken. Not all writers agree that developing countries need to invest at least 10 per cent of their national income, but only 5–6 per cent on average is currently being invested, compared with 20 per cent in the USA, and any return on levels as low as this is needed simply to sustain the growth in population. This inability to produce capital is made more intense by the inability of many countries to attract capital, especially private capital, because of the risk of poor or uncertain returns. Rich investors prefer to invest in stable developed countries. Because capital is therefore scarce, its price in terms of interest rates is very high, and although much capital investment has

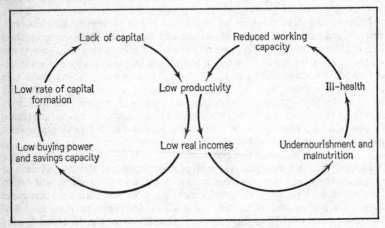

Fig. 24.4. Circles of poverty and ill-health.

been in the form of government aid from the developed countries, much has been in the form of loans on which interest has to be paid. The servicing of such loans has been a major drain on the developing countries and it has been estimated that between 12 and 15 per cent of their foreign exchange earnings go back to the developed countries as interest. To overcome this problem, much aid has been given since 1970 in the form of low-interest loans or outright grants, but the problem of capital scarcity remains.

Secondly, the size of the domestic market in the Third World is often not large enough to sustain industrial development because the purchasing power of the consumer is too low. This is part of the circle of poverty and the problem is compounded by the fact that it is extremely difficult for a developing country to break into international markets where they have to compete with the advanced industrial producers of the developed world.

Thirdly, the infrastructure of most countries of the Third World is poorly developed. Power supplies, transport networks, industrial and commercial services, education facilities—all the things which form the framework within which economic activity takes place—need to be developed. Unfortunately, such facilities are very expensive to establish and give only small returns in the short term. In the developed countries they have been created over a long period but they must be provided quickly in the Third World to enable economic progress to be made.

Fourthly, the economies of most underdeveloped countries are unbalanced and there is much inefficiency. Despite the fact that at least 50 per cent and up to 90 per cent of employment is in agriculture, countries such as India,

Pakistan, Egypt and Indonesia have to import basic foodstuffs. Even where commercial agriculture is practised, problems arise because exports are usually dependent on a small range of commodities, with monoculture the typical agricultural system. Ghanaian cocoa, Malaysian rubber and Gambian groundnuts represent over 60 per cent of commercial crops in these countries, while other countries such as Chile or Bolivia are dependent on a small range of minerals such as copper or tin. This makes them very vulnerable to changes in world prices or technological advances such as the development of synthetic substitutes, when markets can fall disastrously. On the other hand, manufactured products are imported in increasing quantities, and the price of these items has been increasing more rapidly than the price of most primary products, especially agricultural commodities. The blame for this situation must rest largely with the trading policies of the developed countries, which tend to maintain the colonial system of exchanging manufactured goods for primary commodities. Attempts are being made by the countries of the Third World to establish a world commodity stabilisation programme, but there has been considerable opposition to this from the developed countries who dislike interference in the free mechanisms of commodity trade.

On the other hand, some primary commodities, such as oil or scarce minerals, have been increasing rapidly in price, but for countries which do not possess such commodities these increases create serious problems. Minerals such as copper, tin and zinc, and fuels such as oil have become very expensive and the developing countries will not easily be able to compete with the developed countries in buying them. It might be argued that there is a vast hydro-electric power potential in the Tropics which will help solve these problems, but such installations are very expensive to establish and economic problems start to reinforce each other when scarce capital resources are sought to develop them.

These economic problems are not insuperable, certainly not for well endowed countries such as Brazil, but they present massive problems for the poorest countries. However, these problems do not operate in isolation, but within a social framework which itself plays a major role in economic development.

Social Problems

Economic development cannot be explained simply by economic factors, but there is some debate about the role that social and cultural factors play. Most writers agree that they are important, and A. Mountjoy claims that 'perhaps more than anything else it is the human factor that is most underdeveloped, and it is upon improvement in the quality and condition of the human factor that in the first instance other material development depends', but other writers such as C. Kindleberger claim that 'sociocultural determinism' alone cannot explain economic development. Nevertheless, whatever its precise role may be, the social framework is very important because economic factors can only bring improvement where social attitudes and institutions are responsive to change. For development to take place, there must be a desire for change and a willingness to sacrifice for the future, but many societies in the Third World are extremely complex and conservative, and custom, law and belief make any change difficult. This gives the human factor a special significance because capital for infrastructure investment can at least be borrowed, but social change must come from within and its effects can be quite painful.

The human problems of the countries of the Third World fall into two main groups, the first concerned with the quantity and quality of the population, and the second concerned with social institutions and attitudes.

The Third World is currently undergoing a rapid demographic revolution which took over a hundred years to develop in Europe and which was accompanied by a great economic expansion capable of sustaining it. The obvious consequence of the current revolution is a vast increase in population without the corresponding economic expansion. Annual rates of population growth are over 2 per cent in the Third World with countries such as Mexico and the Philippines over 3·4 per cent. This can be compared with an increase of only 0·6 per cent per annum in Britain in the period 1963–73 (Fig. 24.5). The prime cause of this increase has been a fall in the death rate since about 1920 when death control spread from the advanced economies in the form of improved medicine and the control of disease, but in many countries there has also been a rise in the birth rate as well.

It is estimated that by the year 2000 the population of the Third World alone will be 4,900 millions compared with a world total of 4,000 millions in 1975, and this increase is likely to occur for a number of reasons. First, the death rate, although falling, is still higher than in the developed countries and can therefore fall further. Secondly, the birth rate remains high and family planning campaigns will have to overcome considerable ignorance, superstition and political resistance. Thirdly, the age of marriage in the underdeveloped countries is low, giving a woman a long child-bearing period. In India only about 6 per cent of women over the age of 15 are unmarried compared with about 25 per cent in Britain. Fourthly, with over 40 per cent of the population under the age of 15, the potential fertility is enormous.

This rapidly growing population creates serious problems because people have to be fed, housed, clothed and provided with jobs from capital resources which are in short supply or which would be better invested for future growth. In too many countries population increase is greater than economic growth and standards of living are inevitably falling. Population growth not only retards economic development, but it has been suggested that it is an actual cause of underdevelopment. Unfortunately, one of the first consequences of development is a fall in the death rate and thus the problem reinforces itself.

It is not only the quantity of the population that creates problems, because the quality of the population in terms of ill-health and illiteracy also causes concern. It has already been seen that ill-health affects vast numbers of people in the Third World and that this is a key element in the circle of poverty. Unfortunately, any attempt to alleviate this problem is likely to reduce the death rate and thus aggravate already serious problems of population growth. Nevertheless, standards of health must be improved if development is to take place.

Illiteracy is also a major handicap, presenting difficulties in the diffusion of new techniques, machinery and ideas. Television and radio can help, but the written word is a vital medium of communication. Most important of all, illiteracy limits horizons and reinforces traditional practices, however inefficient or harmful, and literacy could be a major tool in making the necessary changes in attitudes and institutions without which development cannot take place.

Most writers agree that changes in social attitudes and institutions are vital

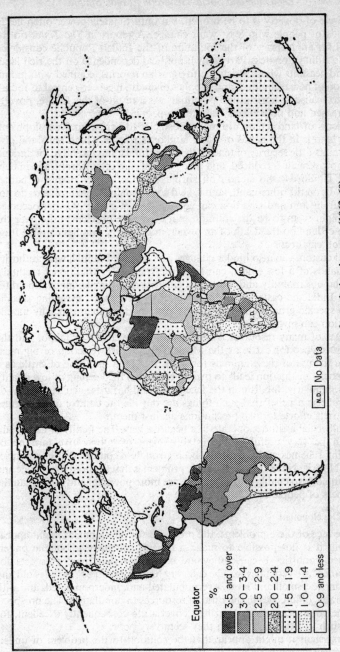

Equator

%
3·5 and over
3·0–3·4
2·5–2·9
2·0–2·4
1·5–1·9
1·0–1·4
0·9 and less

N.D. No Data

Fig. 24.5. Average annual rate of population increase (1963–68).
(from M. Chisholm and B. Rodgers, *Studies in Human Geography*, Heinemann)

if the circle of poverty is to be broken, but unfortunately power often lies in the hands of people who least want change. A report in *The Times* on the twenty-fifth anniversary of the founding of the Indian Republic considered that 'the ruling Congress Party's own political dependence on the rich landlords and peasants whose resistance to agrarian reforms, coupled with monopolisation of new techniques and supplies of credit, has been central to India's failure to realise its agricultural potential'. As a result of this failure, poverty has increased and now affects 300 million people.

Problems of land tenure are major obstacles to agricultural development. If most land is in the hands of a few landlords who levy high rents and give their tenants little security of tenure, the opportunity and incentive for agricultural improvement is reduced, and many tenants are often chronically in debt to their landlords who siphon off surplus production as interest (Chapter Eleven). If, on the other hand, land is held communally, these problems do not arise, but custom and tradition can equally restrict change. Owner-occupied farms might seem to be the solution, but even here problems arise over the division of land on the death of an owner, and in large families extreme fragmentation can occur.

Social custom can also hinder change. The extended family, with authority in the hands of a few elders, can lead to a respect for traditional methods, restrict labour mobility and individual enterprise, and make innovation difficult. In India the caste system has similar consequences, assigning specific roles to specific groups and restricting the advantages that a socially mobile population can give.

The use of many resources is hampered by convention or taboo, and the Hindu reverence for cattle or the Moslem and Jewish rejection of pig meat prevents the use of these animals for food. In Africa the value of cattle as a sign of social distinction leads to overstocking and the keeping of low quality animals. Similarly, fatalism in the face of natural hazards such as drought or floods reflects a belief that such things are outside the control of the farmer and restricts efforts to take precautions against them.

Not all social attitudes operate in a negative way. The family or clan tradition can be very useful in the establishment of cooperative farming or marketing schemes and these have been strongly recommended in countries such as Nigeria. Nevertheless, the basic problem is that the need for change and the technology to enable it to take place are more powerful and rapid than the willingness of people to accept it.

Future Development

In the face of these problems, the prospects for development might appear poor, but it is not possible to make a general statement about the underdeveloped countries because they are so diverse that their prospects for development are very uneven. The category 'underdeveloped' includes old and new countries, small and large, overpopulated and underpopulated, and with considerable differences in the ratio of resources to population. The prospects for some countries such as Brazil or Nigeria are consequently excellent, for others such as Ethiopia or Mali they seem very poor.

At first sight it might appear that the solution to the problem of underdevelopment is industrialisation, since the rich countries of the world are industrialised. However, despite the attractions of industrialisation, it is only one form of development. Industry can raise the per capita income, provide jobs, help solve balance of payments problems and save foreign exchange, but it will not in itself feed the population or restrict its growth. It has been said that the underdeveloped world cannot simply import the Industrial Revolution from abroad, uncrate it like a piece of machinery, and set it in motion. On the other hand, the introduction of industry need not necessarily be large-scale and capital-intensive. So-called '**intermediate technology**' industries can be developed as they have been in China, where they are carried out and maintained by local craftsmen using little more than tools and skills already possessed, are labour intensive, and serve local needs. Where capital is short, it might be much more effective to spread it thinly among a large number of small industries than to concentrate on a few major projects, whatever their prestige value. However, for development to take place there must be changes other than industrialisation, which many writers consider more important.

First, one of the things that became clear as the Development Decade progressed is that agricultural improvement is essential. This improvement is needed to provide food to increase standards of living and remove the need for expensive imports and the consequent loss of foreign exchange; to provide a supply of raw materials such as cotton or rubber for home-based industries or for export; to release labour in the underpopulated countries to work in secondary and tertiary activities; and to raise the level of the domestic market so that effective demand grows to consume the products of industry.

Agricultural improvement can be brought about, first, by changes in agrarian organisation, especially by changes in land tenure to free peasant farmers from exploitation by a landowning ruling class, as in Egypt where cooperative schemes have been developed to replace the services such as credit or marketing previously provided by the landlord. Agriculture can also be diversified to relieve the problems of monoculture such as soil erosion or overdependence on world commodity prices. Secondly, improvement can come from increases in agricultural productivity. This can be brought about in many countries by increasing the cultivated area with land settlement schemes such as those associated with the Aswan Dam in Egypt, government-sponsored settlement in the dry zone of Sri Lanka, or the stimulus to settlement given by the building of Brasilia away from the coast in Brazil. It can also be brought about by intensifying production in existing agriculture by promoting improved types and methods of farming and the use of fertilisers and pesticides. The application of intermediate technology can also be important in agriculture where new methods and tools 'intermediate between the tractor and the hoe' can be brought within the reach of farmers without large-scale, capital-intensive schemes such as dam building. The spread of innovation is difficult, but it has been suggested that the establishment of model farms spread widely through the countryside to encourage change could be very effective.

A second major area in which change is necessary is in the provision of an infrastructure. A sound framework is not only necessary for industry. For agriculture to operate efficiently there must be good transport services to market produce, power supplies for rural electrification schemes, sound agricultural advisory services and technical facilities, and provision for at least elementary education. Since investment in such schemes is expensive, and gives only low returns in the short term, the role of government in the process of development is critical, and it is clear that there must be careful planning.

Planning Development

In order to plan for the future, governments must first decide what it is they want. Some governments, in countries such as Haiti, are not interested in development, but for most countries, economic and social objectives must be established which in general terms should seek to raise material standards and provide a full life for all citizens. Defining 'a full life' presents problems and social objectives are likely to be difficult to establish, often involving the reconciliation of conflicting political ideologies, but the establishment of economic objectives, such as increasing the food supply and providing employment, will be less difficult. Even here, however, problems arise, because short-term objectives such as reducing unemployment might conflict with long-term objectives such as increasing productivity which might best be achieved with machines.

Secondly, methods of achieving these objectives must also be decided. Planning is essential, but can planning by consent in a democratic system be effective when there is so much vested interest to be overcome? On the other hand, if planning is imposed by centralised government agencies, then bureaucracy and totalitarian control might result. The road to progress will differ from country to country, but does India or China provide the best model?

Whatever the political considerations, the basic need is to remove hunger, poverty and disease, and various attempts have been made to understand how development occurs, so that economic strategies can be applied to future development. The most influential of these has been a model of economic growth developed by W. Rostow who identified five stages through which countries pass on their way to development (Fig. 23.3). This has proved a very attractive model but it has lost much support because many economists say that it lacks a mechanism linking the different stages, and that the pattern of investment cited by Rostow cannot be found when tested against the economic history of the developed countries. It must also be asked whether the Western example can be applied in the very different conditions of the Third World. Since the history of past processes of development cannot readily provide a model, economists have suggested different and often conflicting strategies to encourage economic advance, and two main types can be distinguished.

Balanced growth, in which agriculture and industry advance side by side, has been advocated by some economists as the best way of achieving economic growth. Industry and agriculture are seen as being interdependent, with improvements in agricultural productivity supplying food, creating an enlarged rural market for manufactured goods and releasing labour to work in industry, which in turn provides machinery, fertilisers and a market for agricultural products. In this situation, a spiral of growth can be developed and economic progress takes place as advances are made across a broad front. Unfortunately, the build-up of momentum is likely to take a long time even if an initial stimulus is provided, and a considerable degree of coordination would be necessary between the industrial and agricultural sectors of the economy.

However, not all economists believe that balanced growth is the right path to development and there are many who advocate **unbalanced growth**. On the one hand, some argue that increased agricultural production is the first priority for development, since this provides the base on which future industrialisation will take place. On the other hand, some argue that only rapid industrialisation can help a country break out of the circle of poverty. In industry, the advocates of unbalanced growth have suggested that industries which are characterised by interdependence, such as mechanical engineering, can be established as pace-setters to lead industrial development and pull the rest of the economy along. Such industries would be located at points of maximum potential development and would form growth poles to which new industries would be attracted (Chapter Twenty-three). However, growth poles are practically and politically difficult to locate and establish, and the intermediate technology group has suggested a totally different approach to development. The group advocates small-scale industrialisation using technologies within the reach of the poor, and it seems likely that projects of this type will play an increasingly important role in development planning.

Which of these views will produce economic development most effectively is not clear, and will in any case differ from country to country, but ultimately the economy must 'walk on two legs' and the distinction between industry and agriculture as alternative forms of development must not be made too strongly. Overemphasis on one or the other ignores the complexity of the process of development and also the role that service industries play in it.

Conclusion

The natural diversity of the world inevitably means that there are many differences between countries, but the scale and nature of the differences between the rich and poor countries create serious problems for the world community. In the underdeveloped countries, poverty, hunger and disease affect hundreds of millions of people and there must be a concentrated effort by national governments and international agencies to overcome them.

It is possible to be optimistic or pessimistic about the prospects for solving these problems, but because of the wide range of countries involved, it is difficult to generalise. In some countries the potential for growth and progress is enormous, while in others the obstacles to be overcome are truly formidable, but whatever the problems, the solution has two main elements. First, there must be economic development to increase agricultural and industrial production and to provide an infrastructure for growth. This need not be capital-intensive, high-technology development because intermediate technology might be more effective initially, but development is needed to overcome poverty, hunger and disease. Secondly, there must be control over the rise in population to enable the benefits of development to be effective. Not all countries are overpopulated but economic progress in many countries is simply engulfed by the growth in population and if this growth is greater than the ability to support it, poverty must inevitably increase.

Identifying solutions is not the same as carrying them out, but attempts must be made, and economic planning by governments is essential because of the size and complexity of the development process. For the same reason, there will have to be large-scale aid from the developed countries in the form of capital investment and technical assistance, and more controversially, changes in trading policies so that the gap between the price of manufactured goods and the price of commodities is not constantly widening.

The best form of economic planning is difficult to identify and will differ from country to country, but the planning of changes in social structures and attitudes is likely to be even more difficult. The rate of population growth must be cut to manageable levels, but the barriers of ignorance, superstition and suspicion are considerable. Many social structures, especially class divisions between landlord and tenant, also provide barriers to change, and some writers consider that vested interest can only be overcome by revolution. Whatever happens, economic development will require change, and the values of Western urbanised society are not unquestionably superior to those it is suggested they should replace. Economic development will bring considerable material benefits to those countries which experience it, but much of value in terms of social stability will be lost.

Suggested Further Reading

Bernstein, H., *Underdevelopment and Development*, Penguin, Harmondsworth, 1973.

Bhagwati, J., *The Economics Of Underdeveloped Countries*, Weidenfeld and Nicolson, London, 1966.

Chisholm, M., and Rodgers, B., *Studies in Human Geography*, Heinemann, London, 1973.

Chorley, R. J., and Haggett, P., *Socio-economic Models in Geography* (Chapter 8), Methuen, London, 1968.

Hodder, B. W., *Economic Development in the Tropics* (2nd edn), Methuen, London, 1973.

Hoyle, B. S., *Spatial Aspects of Development*, John Wiley, London, 1974.

Mountjoy, A. B., *Industrialisation and Underdeveloped Countries* (2nd edn), Hutchinson, London, 1966.

Mountjoy, A. B., *Developing the Underdeveloped Countries*, Macmillan, London, 1971.

Myrdal, G., *Economic Theory and Underdeveloped Regions*, Methuen, London, 1963.

Scientific American, *Technology and Economic Development*, Penguin, Harmondsworth, 1965.

CHAPTER TWENTY-FIVE

THE PROBLEM OF RESOURCES

In order to live, man must use the earth, and the demand for basic **needs** such as water and food is increasing rapidly as populations increase at exponential rates. However, the demand for materials to satisfy man's **wants** is increasing even more rapidly as these wants grow in size and complexity as standards of living rise in the process of economic development.

All those elements of the earth which are useful or necessary to man can be considered as **resources**, and a **resource process** takes place when they are extracted and used by man and returned as wastes. This resource process is a basic and central theme in geography for three reasons. First, the extraction, use and disposal of resources constitute a major component of the ecological system in which man interacts with the physical environment. Second, since resources are not evenly distributed over the earth's surface, their movement constitutes a major component of the spatial system in which man interacts with man. Third, and most important, the resource process draws both these systems together into a single system of human activity over the earth's surface.

The nature and intensity of this activity is dependent upon the cultural and technical levels of different societies, but human activity is having an increasing impact on the four basic components of the **ecosphere**. These are the biosphere of plants and animals, the lithosphere of soils and minerals, the hydrosphere of rivers and oceans, and the atmosphere of weather and climate, and each has been modified in some degree by man. To ensure the best use of resources and to avoid disastrous interference in natural ecosystems, there is a pressing need for **ecosystem management and planning** by the establishment of control systems in which feedbacks can be manipulated to promote beneficial changes and to restrict adverse ones.

The basic problem underlying any planning of the earth's resources is the fact that the earth's supply is ultimately finite, while demand is continuously growing in size and nature. However, this simple equation is complicated by the fact that although any single resource is in fixed supply, the definition of what is is a resource, particularly in relation to those elements which are useful rather than necessary to man, varies greatly from time to time and from place to place, depending on the cultural and technical level of the society using it.

The Nature of Resources

In the thirteenth century, Marco Polo reported that petroleum 'is good as a salve for men and camels affected with itch or scab', but, although petroleum was also used for burning, its value as a source of industrial and domestic fuel, a source of motive power, a lubricant, and a raw material for the petrochemical industry has only been fully realised in the twentieth century. Other resources have been valued for an even shorter period, and the use of uranium in the production of nuclear fuels is a very recent development. On the other hand, the development of coal-fuelled iron smelting greatly reduced the value of charcoal as a basic resource. Resources are therefore **cultural appraisals** rather than absolute assets, and are produced as the elements of the objective environment are filtered through the processes of perception and evaluated as necessary or useful.

However, elements do not become resources simply by being perceived as such, because there are many different factors operating to constrain the use of potential resources. First, there is the technological factor, and although it is known that a vast amount of energy is available from the process of nuclear fusion, man is at present unable to harness it. Secondly, there is the cultural factor, and many religious and cultural taboos operate to restrict the use of certain animals as a source of food or the use of excrement as fertiliser. Thirdly, there is the political factor, which can restrict the exploitation and exchange of strategic minerals, or limit the extent of contentious methods of mineral extraction such as strip-mining. Fourthly, and operating as the most important single influence, there is the economic factor. Resources are greatly affected by price and will only be used if the costs are not too high. If the price of a particular resource rises, then previously uneconomic sources can be used, or substitutes will be sought. Thus, the recent rise in the price of oil has made the North Sea, despite the high costs involved, an attractive source, even on economic grounds, while plastics have been increasingly substituted in many industries previously using metals. However, economic costs are not always easy to work out, because many commodities have social or strategic values which are difficult to quantify, while the use of resources often creates costs, such as the cost of waste disposal, which are borne by the community as a whole.

Types of Resources

Despite the fact that resources are relative in that the same elements vary in importance from society to society, they can nevertheless be classified into two major groups.

The first group consists of **natural resources**, which can be further divided into two subgroups: **renewable resources**, including the biotic resources exploited in farming, fishing and forestry, and the income-energy coming from the sun, which is used directly in charging modern solar batteries or, more extensively, indirectly through older methods of harnessing the power of wind and water; and **non-renewable resources**, largely made up of the energy-capital of the earth in the form of fossil fuels, but also including many minerals, such as the lead content of petrol, which are similarly lost once they have been used. Many non-renewable resources such as metals are currently lost because they are simply dumped after use, but as metals such as copper and lead become increasingly scarce and valuable, such a policy is increasingly seen to be foolish.

The second group consists of **non-utilitarian resources** whose value is social rather than practical. As Western society has increased its standard of living, elements such as clean air and water, or access to unspoiled recreation areas have become more valued. However, the demand for these two types of resource can lead to conflicts, since the exploitation of natural resources destroys non-utilitarian ones. Thus, wilderness is replaced by farm or mine, while a basic conflict arises between the freedom to enjoy the non-utilitarian resources which is given by the use of the motorcar, and the often disastrous effects the car has on these resources through its role as an air, noise and visual pollutant.

Assessing Resources

There is therefore a basic problem. On the one hand, it is clear that many resources currently being used are non-renewable, and that the use of some resources destroys others. On the other hand, many elements which are currently considered as resources might be appraised differently in the future as new resources are developed.

As a result, there are many different ways of assessing resource prospects. One extreme is the **Malthusian view** which sees the stock of resources as a finite supply rapidly being depleted by large and increasing demands resulting from uncontrolled population growth and increasing aspirations. The consequence of this will be the exhaustion of resources and the impoverishment or even destruction of man. At the other extreme is the **technological view** which concedes that although the stock of resources is ultimately finite, the bounds of possibility within these limits are so extensive that the exhaustion of resources is not a practical problem. Technology may deplete some resources, but it also has a capacity for creating others, and as a result all problems can be solved if technical progress is maintained and economic and social constraints can be overcome.

Between these two extremes, ways have to be found of producing a practical assessment of the earth's supply of resources and of the demand likely to be placed on them so that a coordinated resource policy can be developed to balance them sensibly. Such a policy must also include consideration of the problems of waste and pollution arising from the resource process.

The Problem of Supply and Demand

The uneven distribution of the earth's resources and the economic, social and political constraints affecting their exploitation and circulation make any overall assessment of supply and demand very difficult, but the resources problem is a global one which ultimately affects all men.

The Supply of Resources

A major task for the planner is to decide which resources are vital and then to discover the size of the available stock. This stocktaking has been considerably aided by the development of techniques for the **remote sensing of the environment** such as aerial and satellite photography. Resource evaluation from satellites is particularly valuable as infra-red photography, radar scanning and other technical developments have supplied new tools to increase our knowledge of the earth and its potentials. The launching of the Earth Resources Technology Satellite ERTS-1 from the USA in 1972 was a major step forward since it was specifically designed to record and transmit resources information back to earth, but there is still a great deal of work to be done before knowledge of the stock of resources is complete. A more difficult task is the assessment of future technological innovations and the forecasting of the economic conditions under which they, and known but currently uneconomic resources, may be profitably used. However, a brief examination of food, mineral and energy supplies will illustrate some resource problems.

At present, enough food is being produced to feed the world population (4,000 millions in 1975), although there are serious problems arising from its maldistribution. It is also possible to increase food supplies as population increases because, of the 25 per cent of the earth's surface which is potentially arable, and the 25 per cent which is potentially pastoral, only about half of each is currently being used. It is also possible to use much of the present agricultural area more intensively. However, this is much more a technical than an economic potential. About one third of the potential arable, for example, lies within the tropics, where leaching and the creation of hard-pan soils will necessitate vast inputs of fertilisers and drainage schemes, thus imposing heavy demands on energy and mineral supplies, in order to produce uncertain returns. Nor is the more intensive use of the oceans likely to lead to a vast increase in food supplies. Although fish is a valuable source of protein, it seems unlikely that production will increase to more than $2\frac{1}{2}$ times the present production of 65 million tonnes per annum, and there is already concern about cod stocks around Iceland and herring stocks in the North Sea. Thus, although increases in production are possible, it has been estimated that food supplies are unlikely to increase by more than eightfold under foreseen conditions, and this will put the limit of population growth at about 30,000 millions, with the vast majority at starvation levels. At present rates of increase this figure will be reached in the year 2075.

Mineral ores are localised and exhaustible and are therefore a potential source of friction, but on the whole there are plentiful supplies of minerals. However, the question of whether or not they could become **ores**, capable of being worked at a profit, is dependent on technology and economics, and as a result estimates of reserves are very unreliable. There are already shortages of mercury, tin, tungsten, gold and copper, and alternative sources or substitutes are being sought. The search is very wide ranging but it seems that, as with food supplies, the oceans are unlikely to be a very fruitful source, especially from the rocks beyond the continental shelves, although sediments on the sea-bed are potentially valuable. Even in shallower waters, economics and technology place constraints on development and it must be recognised that ore deposits are in finite supply under present economic and technical conditions, and that the exhaustion of some deposits is imminent.

Despite the fact that vast amounts of energy reach the earth every day from the sun, there has been a great deal of concern over the possibility that energy supplies may soon be exhausted. It has been estimated that there is only about 50 years' supply of oil and gas, and 200–300 years' supply of coal at present rates of extraction, and some experts believe that these might be better used as raw materials rather than being burned to provide energy. However, the problem is that the vast amount of low-intensity energy coming from the sun is difficult to concentrate, and its conversion into electricity will not be economic until at least the year 2000 in the UK. Similarly, although wind, water and tidal power have long been available to man, their large-scale exploitation raises many technical problems, and only hydro-electric power is developed to any great extent. The same is true of attempts to tap geothermal energy. Although geothermal energy is used to produce electricity in volcanic areas, the need to drill to depths of at least 3,600 m elsewhere raises considerable engineering problems. In fact, current economic and technical conditions make the replacement of fossil fuels as the principal sources of energy very difficult, despite their threatened exhaustion and the pollution problems created by the release of hydrocarbons into the atmosphere as they are burned.

The Demand for Resources

Problems also arise when attempts are made to measure the size and nature of future demand. One thing is certain, the demand for resources will continue to rise, but the two main causes of this rise are difficult to forecast.

The first cause of increased demand is population growth, but how far will, or can, population grow? The problem of forecasting population growth is discussed in Chapter Eight, but many experts agree that only zero growth will provide the long-term solution. One projection suggests that world population must level off below 10,000 millions by the year 2050 to enable reasonable standards to be achieved, but although rates of increase are slackening in some developed countries, there is little sign of an overall abatement of human fertility. As a result, this increase in numbers puts great pressure on resources because more and more people have to be fed, clothed and sheltered, even though this may only be at subsistence levels.

However, when this increase in numbers is combined with rising aspirations and the development of technology capable of sustaining high standards of living, a second cause of increased demand is created. The revolution of rising expectations, especially marked since 1945, has led to the establishment of a consumer society, based on cheap energy, for which demand was increasing at a rate of 12 per cent per annum until the oil crisis of 1973. Unfortunately, the consumer society has been based on a robber economy in which large amounts of resources have been used, and the benefits of which have been denied to the vast majority of mankind. In 1972, each person consumed an average energy equivalent to 2130 kg of coal, but this varied from 204 kg a head in India to 10,928 kg in the USA. The differences between the high-consumption/low-population economies with great technical abilities to consume and yet create resources, and the low-consumption/high-population economies with limited technical abilities create great instability and are a potential source of friction. Unfortunately, the greater the level of economic development, the greater the demand for resources, and any attempt to raise living standards in the Third World will increase the imbalance between man and resources. At present, many Third World countries are committed to Western-style development based on urbanisation and industrialisation involving high consumption of decreasingly available energy, but even in the West, increasing concern for the 'quality of life' suggests that this may not be the surest path to happiness.

The remarkable developments in science and technology made during the last 200 years have made it possible for many environments to support much greater populations than formerly; however, if population growth and increasing aspirations cause demand for resources to outstrip supply, then overpopulation will be the result.

The Problem of Waste and Pollution

Faced with the danger that demand will outstrip supply, the twin problems of waste and pollution are increasingly important. Unfortunately, the creation of waste and pollution arises during the exploitation, use and dispersal of resources for both economic and technical reasons, and the problems associated with these three stages of the resource process are frequently intensified when accidents occur. Some of these problems are examined in the following sections.

Exploiting Resources

As man's numbers and technology have increased, he has exploited the earth's resources more intensively, but this activity is producing increasing amounts of waste and pollution. The exploitation of minerals has sterilised large areas as pits are dug to remove iron, copper, clay and so on, and as waste from the underground mining of coal or gold is tipped. There were over 100,000 ha of derelict land in Britain in 1967 and despite attempts to reclaim such land, it is increasing at a rate of over 1,400 ha per annum as coal, clay, gravel and sand are worked. On a world scale, much larger acreages have been affected by attempts to extend and intensify agriculture, and overcropping and overgrazing have led to the progressive breakdown of soil structure and its erosion by wind and water in many regions. In the USA alone, 5 per cent of land suitable for agriculture or forestry has been completely ruined, 15 per cent has lost three quarters of its topsoil, and 41 per cent is subject to moderate erosion.

Attempts to increase agricultural production have also produced pollution. First, the use of artificial fertilisers is an essential part of high productivity, but as the chemicals are gradually washed from the land by the normal processes of the weather, the resulting concentration of nutrients in rivers and lakes creates problems. This process of nutrient enrichment, especially by nitrogen and phosphorus, is known as **eutrophication**, and its effects on the flora and fauna of lakes such as Lakes Erie and Ontario have been so dramatic that such lakes are thought to be in danger of 'dying'. The use of agricultural chemicals has also created a second form of pollution. Herbicides, fungicides and especially insecticides are being used in increasing amounts to maintain and increase production by providing protection against diseases and insect pests. Unfortunately, many insecticides such as DDT or Dieldrin do not break down very quickly and as a result they can build up in animal tissue. This has serious implications for humans, who are at the top of a food chain, and many Americans are already legally unfit for human consumption because of the high levels of DDT in their bodies. The problem is so serious that countries such as Sweden, Denmark and the USA have banned the use of DDT, but its cheapness and efficacy mean that it is still used in large amounts in many parts of the Third World where priority is necessarily given to increasing food production.

Using Resources

Many resources are used wastefully, especially energy. There are often sound technical reasons for this, for while power stations with 55–60 per cent efficiency are planned, the best UK stations are only 36 per cent efficient at present. Moreover, some UK power stations are only 20 per cent efficient, and as a result, overall UK efficiency was only 29 per cent in 1973–4. The magnitude of the problem of resource waste can be illustrated by the fact that if overall efficiency could be increased from 29 to 32 per cent, there would be a saving of 10 million tonnes of coal per annum. However, the problem is not only technical but is also associated with Britain's policy of locating larger and larger power stations away from concentrations of population, and a further 10 per cent is lost in transmission. In Sweden, thermal power stations are much smaller and are more market-orientated, and this has the added advantage that instead of wasting heat in massive cooling towers, the steam can be used for home heating over distances of up to 25 km.

The use of resources in industry also creates pollution, and this comes about in two ways. First, there is the discharge of pollutant side-effects in manufacture, storage and distribution. Thus, it is estimated that industry in the UK discharges 2 million tonnes of smoke, 1·5 million tonnes of ash and 5 million tonnes of sulphur and gases into the atmosphere every year, adding considerably to the problem of air pollution. This could often be greatly reduced, but the cost would have to be borne by the manufacturer who is thus reluctant to take action, despite the fact that some industrial discharges are highly toxic.

Secondly, the product itself might be a pollutant. The motorcar is an outstanding culprit as it pours out nitrous oxides into the atmosphere, creating petrochemical smog in sunny, motor-dominated areas such as Los Angeles, which in turn does serious damage to people, crops and trees. More recently, there has been concern that the fluorocarbons used as propellant gases in aerosols may be attacking the ozone concentrations in the stratosphere, thus removing the earth's protective barrier against dangerous ultraviolet radiation.

Disposing of Resources

The disposal of resources once they have been used is accompanied by massive waste. This waste is essentially an economic problem because it is usually cheaper, measured simply in direct production costs, for the manufacturer to use new materials than to collect and reuse old ones. However, the economics of the 'throw-away society' are being increasingly questioned because the real costs of dumping are enormous and have to be borne by the community as a whole It is inevitable that there should be some waste within the resource process, but at present recoverable quantities of limited resources are simply being squandered as 'rubbish' is buried or burned.

Nevertheless, under present economic conditions, large amounts of waste have to be disposed of, and this creates problems which have to be overcome. Social change over the last 40 years has meant that domestic waste has become much bulkier, for while ash and dust have fallen from 55 to 19 per cent of the total weight, paper has increased from 15 to 34 per cent. As a result, much larger holes have to be found by local authorities in which to bury it, and these are becoming scarce and expensive. Other solid wastes create even more difficult problems, and nuclear wastes, which can remain radioactive for up to 250,000 years, have at present to be stored under very secure conditions to prevent leakage.

On top of the problem of knowing what to do with large amounts of waste material from resource use, there is also the increasing problem of pollution, especially from the liquid wastes of domestic, industrial and agricultural sewage. At present, vast amounts of liquid wastes are simply poured into rivers, lakes and oceans without any form of treatment, with the consequent loss of valuable sources of fertilisers, minerals and so on. Unfortunately, this also contaminates water supplies and heightens the risk of diseases such as cholera, dysentery and typhoid. Different sorts of risk arise from industrial pollution, and after the River Cuyohoga had become so heavily polluted with inflammable materials that it ignited and burnt down two bridges in Cleveland in 1969, it had to be declared an official fire-risk. More serious, the discharge of mercury waste from a plant near Minamata in Japan led to serious neural damage among many local inhabitants after they had eaten fish and shellfish contaminated with mercury, but despite such warnings the discharge of toxic wastes continues on a world scale, endangering life and polluting other resources.

Accidents

In fact, accidents occur at all three stages of the resource process, and provide spectacular, but usually short-lived, examples of waste and pollution. The most spectacular accidents usually involve oil, due to the fact that of an annual production of over 2,500 million tonnes more than 60 per cent is transported by sea in ships of ever-increasing size. Thus, when the *Torrey Canyon* was wrecked in 1967, 120,000 tonnes of oil was lost, and much of it ended up on the holiday beaches of Cornwall and Brittany. Unfortunately, the problem did not end there because 10,000 tonnes of detergent was used to clean up the polluted beaches which were a threat to the tourist industry on which thousands of people depended for their livelihood. The detergents had even greater biological effects than the oil, by killing mollusca such as limpets in vast numbers. Since 25 per cent of total oil production passes through the English Channel, and this is the world's busiest shipping lane, many experts agree that it is only a matter of time before another disaster of *Torrey Canyon* proportions occurs. However, even simple accidents can have major consequences, and when drums containing only 100 kg of the insecticide Endosulfan rolled off a barge into the River Rhine in the summer of 1969, thousands of fish were killed.

Planning Resource Use

In recent years there has been increasing concern that the relationship between man and nature is becoming unbalanced, and that even though man can be considered apart from nature in many ways, he is basically dependent upon it. This recognition of the need for environmental management and planning is not the same as its implementation, but it is an important step in the right direction.

The Need for Planning

Resource planning is necessary for two main reasons. First, to avoid the possibility of the exhaustion of resources, and second, to avoid disastrous human interference in natural ecosystems.

In view of man's ability to create resources, it seems unlikely that the earth's resources will become exhausted, but on the other hand certain resources are already in short supply, and many others have a very limited availability. There is, therefore, an urgent need for a dynamic equilibrium to be reached in which supply and demand are sensibly balanced. Since demand is very difficult to control, the first priority must be given to increasing supply, and this can be done in a number of ways. First, a full exploration of the earth's supply of resources must be undertaken so that total stocks can be assessed and their useful life calculated. A start has been made with the development of more sophisticated remote sensing techniques, but the stocktaking is far from complete. Secondly, once it is known which stocks are seriously depleted, technology must develop alternative resources before such stocks are totally exhausted. Thirdly, resources must be conserved by the reduction of waste. This will create difficulties because it will require a revolution in attitudes, but if cost–benefit analysis is applied to issues such as the disposal of used resources, it will become clear that much current practice is not only wasteful but is also uneconomic when all costs are accounted. When many resources are in finite supply, **recycling** is essential.

The possibility of an ecocatastrophe in which man's activities create so much pollution that the earth's natural systems begin to disintegrate is the second cause for concern. It is not possible simply to ban pollution because this would mean the end of cars, aircraft, fertilisers, detergents and many other conveniences and aids, but on the other hand it is clear that pollution must be controlled. There is a need to discover which pollutants are harmful and which are simply unpleasant, and then to discover the limits within which man can safely operate and beyond which irreversible damage will take place. There has been some progress, and an international conference in 1972 agreed that there must be a reduction in the dumping of certain wastes into the oceans, but much more international cooperation is necessary. Unfortunately, this is very difficult to achieve, and there are serious obstacles to the planning of resource use on a world scale.

Planning Problems

The obstacles to the effective planning of resources can be examined in two categories. First, there is the problem of controlling demand, and secondly, there is the problem of resource allocation.

The demand for resources is rising because for many groups of people the quality of life is improving, and this must be seen as a positive objective of the whole resource process. Unfortunately, demand is also rising simply to maintain an increase in the quantity of life, but unless this is controlled the resource process will eventually be swamped. Population growth must be controlled, because even at the desperately low rate of resource use achieved by the vast majority of the world's population, its sheer size will lead to the eventual exhaustion of resources without any necessary improvement in living standards. Similarly, although ecosystems have a remarkable ability to absorb high levels of pollution, many are in danger from the enormous volume of wastes with which they have to cope. However, despite the fact that population growth brings few benefits and considerable problems, the control of human fertility is beset with social and political constraints. It seems likely that unless rapid world-wide economic growth produces demographic conditions such as those in the developed countries, where voluntary restraint is allowing population to grow slowly, there will almost certainly be involuntary controls on growth such as famine, disease and war.

Because resources are not in unlimited supply and are unevenly distributed, their allocation depends on a number of problematical criteria which are difficult to plan. Even within countries, resource allocation is a difficult problem and conflicts arise over, for example, whether land should be used for farming or housing, or whether forests should be used for timber or amenity. When the question of planning resources on a world scale arises, economic and political divisions raise almost insuperable problems. Until relatively recently resources have been plentiful and when shortages occurred they were overcome by territorial or commercial expansion. However, as the supply of resources diminishes and competition for them increases, there is an urgent need for planning and cooperation to avoid conflict, since there is now little room for expansion. It would be Utopian to expect that there could be resource planning on a world scale, but the problems are world-wide nonetheless, and must be confronted.

Conclusion

The study of the resource process is of fundamental importance in geography because the production, collection, processing, distribution, consumption and disposal of resources are a basic influence on the nature and distribution of population, settlement, transport, agriculture and industry. The resource process also integrates the ecological and spatial systems, within which man interacts, into a single system of human activity over the earth's surface.

Because resources are cultural appraisals, they are difficult to assess, but it is clear that many currently vital resources are likely to remain so for the foreseeable future. Unfortunately, these resources are in limited supply and under increasing demand. Resource management is therefore essential, but resources are not evenly distributed over the earth's surface, and as a result the planning of resource use is beset with economic, social and political problems because these human systems are themselves characterised by division. However, supply must be increased and more equitably distributed, and demand must be substantially reduced, because a workable method of allocating the earth's resources is vital if global stability is to be achieved.

Suggested Further Reading

Arvill, R., *Man and Environment*, Penguin, Harmondsworth, 1967.
Chisholm, M. (ed.), *Resources for Britain's Future*, Penguin, Harmondsworth, 1972.
Cloud, P. (ed.), *Resources and Man*, Freeman, San Francisco, 1969.
Commoner, B., *The Closing Circle: The Environmental Crisis and its Cure*, Cape, London, 1972.
Detwyler, T. R. (ed.), *Man's Impact on Environment*, McGraw-Hill, New York, 1971.
Ehrlich, P. R., and Ehrlich, A. H., *Population, Resources, Environment: Issues in Human Ecology*, Freeman, San Francisco, 1972.
Goldsmith, E. R. D. (ed.), *A Blueprint for Survival*, Penguin, Harmondsworth, 1972.
Maddox, J., *Domesday Syndrome: An Assault on Pessimism*, Macmillan, London, 1972.
Meadows, D. H. (ed.), *The Limits to Growth*, Earth Island, London, 1972.
National Academy of Sciences: Committee on Resources and Man, *Resources and Man*, Freeman, San Francisco, 1969.
Nicholson, M., *The Environmental Revolution*, Penguin, Harmondsworth, 1972.
Scientific American, *Energy and Power*, Freeman, San Francisco, 1971.
Simmons, I. G., *The Ecology of Natural Resources*, Arnold, London, 1974.
Smith, P. J. (ed.), *The Politics of Physical Resources*, Penguin, Harmondsworth, 1975.

INDEX

INDEX